Indians, Missionaries, and Merchants

Indians, Missionaries, and Merchants

The Legacy of Colonial Encounters on the California Frontiers

KENT G. LIGHTFOOT

University of California Press

BERKELEY   LOS ANGELES   LONDON

Maps 1–11 adapted from cartography by Landis Bennett.

University of California Press
Berkeley and Los Angeles, California

University of California Press, Ltd.
London, England

First paperback printing 2006
© 2005 by The Regents of the University of California

Library of Congress Cataloging-in-Publication Data

Lightfoot, Kent G., 1953.
    Indians, missionaries, and merchants : the legacy of colonial
encounters on the California frontiers / by Kent Gronoway Lightfoot.
        p.   cm.
    Includes bibliographical references and index.
    ISBN 978-0-520-24998-1 (pbk. : alk. paper)
    1. Indians of North America—First contact with Europeans—
California.   2. Indians of North America—Missions—California—
History.   3. Indians of North America—Commerce—California—
History.   4. Franciscans—Missions—California—History.
5. Federally recognized Indian tribes—California.   6. Federal aid
to Indians—California.   7. United States—Politics and government.
8. United States—Social policy.   9. United States—Race relations.
I. Title.
E78.C15L47   2005
979.4′02—dc22   2004008784

Manufactured in the United States of America

14   13   12   11   10   09   08
11   10   9   8   7   6   5   4   3

The paper used in this publication is both acid-free and totally chlorine-
free (TCF). It meets the minimum requirements of ANSI/NISO Z39.48–
1992 (R 1997) (Permanence of Paper).♾

For Peg and Vern
with much love for showing me the beauty
and enchantment of California

Contents

Illustrations

TABLES

Preface

Why are some California Indian tribes recognized by the U.S. government, although others remain unacknowledged? This question is not a trivial one. Federal recognition brings with it many economic and political benefits, including ownership of lucrative Indian gaming facilities, access to the health care, housing, and job programs provided by the Bureau of Indian Affairs, and participation in multimillion-dollar cultural resource management programs. In contrast, Indian peoples not recognized by the United States government receive no such privileges. Treated as poor cousins, members of these unacknowledged groups continually confront skepticism about their identity as "real" Indians not only from the federal government but also from the general public, local government agencies, and some scholars.[1] Much of this skepticism stems from a perceived disconnection with the past, a break that severely ruptured the transmission of native languages, crafts, food ways, and ceremonies—what many consider the essences of Indian identity—to subsequent generations.

I began asking the above question more than a decade ago, when I initiated the archaeological study of culture contact between native peoples and European colonists in the greater San Francisco Bay Area. Commencing my research at Colony Ross, a mercantile enterprise founded by a Russian company on the magnificent but rugged coast of what is now Sonoma County in northern California, I had the privilege to collaborate with members of the Kashaya Pomo tribe. Russian merchants settled in the heart of Kashaya territory, and this Indian group endured the brunt of their colonial campaign from 1812 to 1841. Yet, despite their close interactions with foreigners, the Kashaya were able to maintain a strong Indian identity by cultivating a close connection to their ancestral past. Seventy-three years after the Russian colony closed, the U.S. government purchased property for the

Kashaya, establishing a small reservation in 1914. Today, as a federally recognized tribe, the Kashaya celebrate a seasonal schedule of dances, feasts, and ceremonies, and elders still speak the Kashaya language. Prominent in much of their ritual and social life is the consumption of native foods and the teaching of Kashaya values and world views. Although many of the younger men and women leave the Kashaya reservation to find jobs in nearby cities, they return home for tribal celebrations and family gatherings.

A very different picture of Indian life materializes scarcely more than one hundred kilometers to the south. Along the eastern shore and on the peninsula of San Francisco Bay, I have worked with members of the Ohlone Indian community who trace their genetic and cultural heritage back to mission Indians. Their ancestors, incorporated into Spanish missions founded by Franciscan padres in the late 1700s and early 1800s, survived many decades of missionary fervor. Today, the Ohlone Indian descendants are visible members of the San Francisco Bay Area community, voicing concerns over the continued development of former tribal lands, leading public workshops on native crafts and life ways, and working on historical and archaeological projects that highlight their tribal heritage. But as members of "unacknowledged" Ohlone tribal groups, they are treated very much as second-class citizens. Their Indian identities are continually contested as they actively seek federal recognition and legal status in the state of California.

Who, then, is a "real" California Indian? I have heard on more than one occasion members of unacknowledged tribes referred to as "Mexicans" who simply see opportunities for claiming California Indian ancestry. Others believe that the Hispanic colonial program was so brutal, divisive, and ultimately successful that few genuine Indian practices persisted or exist today.

In working with the Kashaya Pomo, Ohlone, and other native groups, I began to contemplate the role that culture contact has played in structuring our perception of native communities today. How much of the current distribution of federally recognized tribes can be explained by specific colonial histories? What about the distribution of "unacknowledged" Indian groups? And what are the long-term implications of native peoples tangling with Franciscan padres or Russian merchants?

In writing this book, I have sought to compare native experiences in the Spanish (and later Mexican) missions and in the Russian mercantile settlements, on the central and southern coasts of California respectively, and to evaluate how these colonial outcomes contributed to the development of new kinds of native identities, social forms, and tribal relationships. My thesis is simple: we shall not understand the current status of Indian tribes in California without a detailed investigation of their colonial histories and their subsequent encounters with anthropologists and government agents.

The holistic approach of historical anthropology provides firm grounding for consideration of how missionary and mercantile colonies may have contributed to divergent outcomes that still reverberate in California Indian communities. In drawing on sources from ethnohistory, ethnography, native texts, and archaeology, I construct multiple histories from the perspectives of the diverse peoples who populated the multiethnic colonies. In rethinking how we write colonial histories through the systematic inclusion of archaeology, native narratives, and historical documents, I not only question and evaluate traditional historical scenarios, but bring out new insights about colonial California.

In the following chapters, I show that tremendous cultural transformations took place among all the coastal hunter-gatherer peoples who engaged with the Hispanic and Russian frontiers. My findings indicate that many local communities did not become culturally extinct, but maintained a strong sense of their Indian heritage and world views. In the process of reproducing themselves in new social settings they created innovative kinds of Indian identities, social forms, and tribal relationships. As they entered the late nineteenth and early twentieth centuries, however, only some of these native peoples were recognized as "real" Indians by federal Indian agents, by other government officials, and by anthropologists. These gatekeeping authorities excluded from the process of federal recognition those other native groups whose Indian beliefs and practices deviated too far from the norms of early anthropological conceptions of California tribal peoples.

Acknowledgments

The genesis of this book took place when William Simmons and I began co-teaching anthropology courses on colonial California at the University of California at Berkeley a little more than a decade ago. Bill directed a significant ethnographical and ethnohistorical project on Native Californian history in northern California, while I participated in archaeological and ethnohistorical research on the Russian mercantile outpost of Colony Ross. The courses we taught (California Frontiers, California Historical Anthropology) experimented with a comparative approach for examining California Indians' encounters with Spanish, Mexican, Russian, and early American colonial programs, using multiple lines of evidence drawn from ethnohistory, ethnography, native narratives, and archaeology. Although we intended to coauthor a book for use in the classroom, Bill turned the project over to me after it became clear that professional obligations associated with his new administrative post at Brown University precluded his continued participation. I am deeply indebted to Bill for his mentoring and professional guidance over the years.

The majority of the research and much of the initial writing of the book was completed during my sabbatical year (1999–2000), supported by funding from the President's Research Fellowship in the Humanities, University of California, and the Humanities Research Fellowship, University of California at Berkeley. My wife Roberta and I were blessed to spend that year at the School of American Research in Santa Fe, New Mexico, where I served as the Weatherhead Resident Fellow. The School of American Research's excellent facilities and professional staff provided a unique opportunity for me to think, write, and discuss my book project with fellow resident scholars in seminars and lectures, at dinners, and over drinks. I am especially thankful to Doug Schwartz and Nancy Owen Lewis, who helped in every way possible; to the library staff, Lucie Olson and Bradley Pearce, who could find any published paper, no matter how obscure, on colonial California; and to my fellow resident scholars who worked closely with me in developing some of my ideas—Chris Boehm, Patricia Greenfield, Miles Miller, Paul Nadasdy and Little Cat, Estevan Rael y Galvez, Susan Ramirez, and John "Big Man" Ware.

This book would not have been possible without the help and support of many people involved in archaeological and ethnohistorical research at the Fort Ross State Historic Park. The Fort Ross Archaeological Project has been generously supported by the California State Parks, by grants from the National Science Foundation (BNS-8918960, SBR-9304297, SBR-9806901), by funding from the Committee on Research and the Stahl Endowment of the Archaeological Research Facility, University of California at Berkeley, and by corporate assistance from the American Home Shield Corporation, a subsidiary of ServiceMaster Consumer Services L.P., and Bob Schiff's McDonald's Restaurant in North Berkeley. I am most grateful for the expertise, support, and friendship of the many fine persons who work for California State Parks, and my special thanks go to Breck Parkman, Glenn Farris, Dan Murley, and Bill Walton, who have made the research at Fort Ross possible. The fieldwork has been a collaborative project with the Kashaya Pomo tribe, and I appreciate greatly the advice, knowledge, and insights of our project's co-director, Otis Parrish, and of Violet Parrish Chappell, Vivian Wilder, and Warren Parrish. The field and laboratory work would never have happened without the organizational genius and generosity of Ann Schiff, the many years of leadership and teaching provided by Roberta Jewett, and the critical support provided by the Pedotti clan (Alex, Dave, Renie, Lucas, and Ty) when meat or drink ran low. I am indebted to the Fort Ross Interpretive Association, which has served as a strong advocate for the study and interpretation of Colony Ross, and especially to Lyn Kalani, who has assisted me whenever possible over more than a decade. Finally, I wish to thank all the wonderful undergraduate and graduate students from the University of California at Berkeley who have participated in the summer field schools at Fort Ross and made them such a success. Although space does not allow me to mention all concerned by name, I do want to recognize the efforts that Professor Meg Conkey, Sherry Parrish, Tanya Smith, and Dennis Ogburn of the Archaeological Research Facility; Sharon Lilly, Vicky Garcia, and Sandy Jones of the Anthropology Department; and Gary Penders of Summer Sessions have played over the years in administering and running this field school program.

Early drafts of this book were read and commented on by Patrick Kirch,

William Simmons, Roberta Jewett, and Jim Clark. A revised manuscript was then critically reviewed for the University of California Press by Robert Hoover, Glenn Farris, David Hurst Thomas, and an anonymous reviewer from the Press's editorial board; I appreciate greatly the excellent and constructive comments from each person in making this a better book. I discussed specific ideas and issues incorporated in the book with a number of scholars, including James Allan, Aron Crowell, Michael Dietler, Glenn Farris, Lynne Goldstein, Richard Hitchcock, Robert Hoover, Kathleen Hull, Ira Jacknis, Roberta Jewett, John Johnson, Patrick Kirch, Antoinette Martinez, Peter Mills, Sannie Osborn, Breck Parkman, Otis Parrish, Dan Rogers, Stephen Silliman, William Simmons, Gil Stein, Barb Voss, and Thomas Wake. I also received excellent feedback and many constructive comments on an earlier draft from my spring 2003 graduate seminar (Archaeology of Colonialism), which included Esteban Gomez, Sara Gonzalez, Shanti Morell-Hart, Sven Ouzman, and Lee Panich.

My sincere thanks to Blake Edgar, Jim Clark, and Jenny Wapner for all their help and assistance in shepherding this project through the University of California Press. I am deeply appreciative of the tremendous effort that Paula Friedman and Suzanne Knott contributed in copyediting the manuscript and making it a more readable book. Landis Bennett deserves credit for creating the basis for the maps for the book as well as for reproducing the historical images. My gratitude for the excellent service provided, in searching for manuscripts and historical images of colonial California, by the Bancroft Library, specifically by Peter Hanff, Jack Von Euw, and Susan Snyder. I appreciate the assistance of the Bancroft Library, the California Historical Society, and the Oakland Museum in providing the historical images reproduced in the book.

Finally, I must pay tribute to my extended clan, who have both supported and put up with me for the last few years while I worked on this volume— Vern and Peg, Inky and Patty, Dan and Meta, David and Marsha, Jill and Dave, Mark and Leslie, Mary and Neal, Gordy and Terry, and my fourteen fabulous nieces and nephews. And this book would never have seen the light of day without the encouragement, assistance, intellect, and companionship of my dear Roberta.

1 Dimensions and Consequences of Colonial Encounters

Voices of the past become muted over time. Such is the case with the telling of California's colonial history. We accentuate Spanish recollections that indelibly mark the contemporary landscape with Mission Revival buildings, reconstructed missions and presidios, place names, and even Taco Bell restaurants. But the full diversity and significance of the state's colonial past have been lost in the hustle and bustle of our twenty-first-century world. An eerie silence pervades the memories of thousands of native peoples and Russian colonists who, like the Spanish, participated in the creation of the California frontiers. We tend to forget that this state was forged at the crossroads of the world, for it was here that the extensive colonial domains of Imperial Spain and Tsarist Russia first touched on the Pacific coast. The roots of our modern ethnic diversity can be traced back to this colonial encounter among Indians, Spaniards, Mexicans, Russians, Native Alaskans, and many other peoples.

As the site of one of the last major colonial expansions of the Spanish Crown in the late 1700s, California became the northernmost province of a vast empire that stretched across much of southern North America, Central America, and South America. By 1812, California was also the southernmost frontier of an extensive Russian mercantile enterprise centered in the North Pacific (see map 1). With the coming of the Russians, the fertile coastal shores of central California were transformed into the borderlands of two distinctive colonial domains. A chain of Franciscan missions and presidios, extending from San Diego to the greater San Francisco Bay, emerged as the cornerstone of the Spanish colonial enterprise in what became known as Alta California. But just beyond the northern reaches of the Presidio of San Francisco, Russian workers felled redwoods to build the impressive palisade walls and stout log structures of Ross—the administrative center of

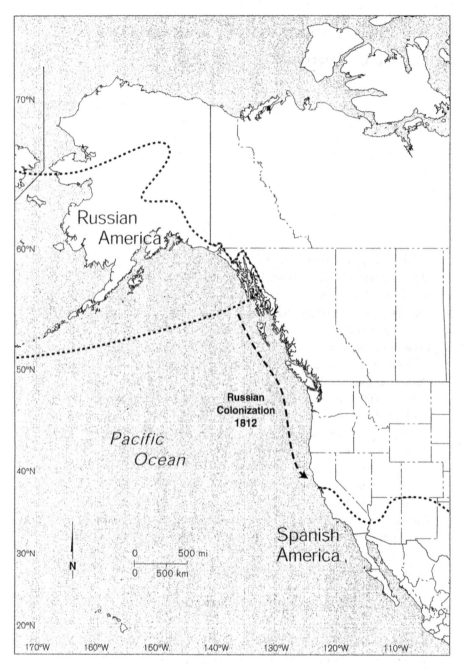

Map 1.   Pacific Coast of North America, showing the colonial domains of Imperial Spain and Tsarist Russia, and the path of Russian colonization in 1812. The northern boundary of Spanish America and eastern delimitation of Russian America are approximate; they portray the edges of a broad swath around Spanish colonies and Russian settlements and trade outposts.

the first mercantile colony in California. In transforming the region into a unique contact zone in North America, Spanish and Russian colonists populated the coastal landscape with their own distinctive adobe and Siberian-style wooden houses, churches, and forts and laid the foundations for two very different colonial programs.

Caught within and between the Spanish and Russian colonies were thousands of native peoples residing in a plethora of small communities that dotted the coastal zone of southern and central California. As hunter-gatherer peoples, they made their living from both the sea and land by hunting marine mammals and terrestrial game, fishing for coastal and freshwater fishes, gathering edible plant foods, and collecting shellfish. These native communities varied greatly in language, tribal affiliation, population, and settlement pattern, yet they had much in common in their material cultures, broader world views (religious practices, dances, ceremonies), trade networks, and subsistence pursuits. Most coastal groups were organized into small polities, which have been traditionally defined by anthropologists as "tribelets," "village communities," or "tiny nations." Anthropologists have grouped those individual polities in which the members spoke similar languages into broader ethnolinguistic units. The Spanish and later the Mexican colonial system incorporated native peoples from eight major language groups of coastal California: Miwok, Ohlone (Costanoan), Esselen, Salinan, Chumash, Gabrielino, Luiseño, and Diegueño. The Russian managers of Colony Ross interacted primarily with native peoples who spoke Coast Miwok, Kashaya Pomo, and Southern Pomo languages.

MISSIONARY AND MERCANTILE COLONIES

The hunter-gatherer communities of the central and southern coasts of California were initially incorporated into one or the other of two kinds of colonial institutions—missionary and mercantile colonies.[1]

Franciscan Missions

Spain relied on the Franciscan Order to manage the Indian population of its northernmost frontier, where the padres implemented a plan to transform the coastal hunter-gatherer peoples into a peasant class of neophyte Catholics. The Spanish, and later Mexican, colonial system consisted of twenty-one Franciscan missions, four military presidios, and three civilian pueblos along the coastal zone of southern and central California (map 2). The first mission and presidio were constructed in San Diego in 1769. The last Franciscan mission,

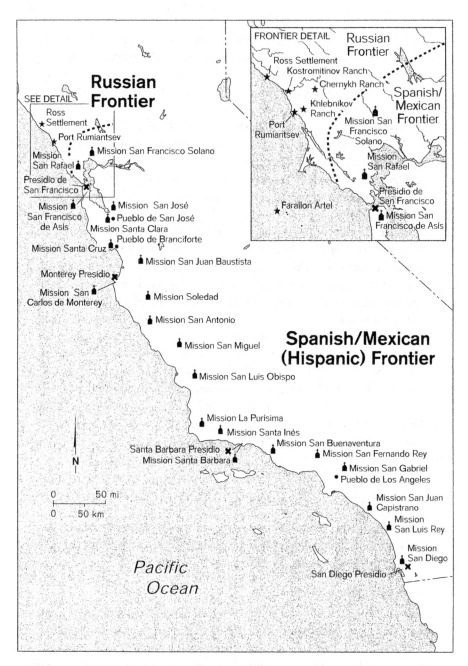

Map 2. The California frontiers of Spanish/Mexican and Russian colonization. By 1823 the entire chain of Hispanic missions, presidios, and pueblos had been founded, along with the Russian settlements of Ross, Port Rumiantsev, and the Farallon Islands *artel*. The Russian ranches (Kostromitinov, Khlebnikov, Chernykh) were not founded until the 1830s.

San Francisco Solano, was erected in Sonoma in 1823, after an independent Mexico had assumed political control of Alta California. The Franciscan missions were designed from the outset to be the focal node of native and Hispanic interactions in colonial California. The missions typically housed two padres (the majority from Spain), a mission guard of six soldiers (most of whom were mestizos or mulattos of Spanish, African, and/or native ancestry from northern Mexico), and a thousand or more baptized Indians or neophytes recruited from nearby coastal villages and, in later years, from more distant communities in the interior (e.g., the Great Central Valley). Situated within or near the central mission quadrangle was the adobe church, *convento* or residence for the priests, dormitories and houses for neophytes, residential quarters for the mission soldiers, storerooms, work areas for the preparation and cooking of communal meals, and rooms for craft production. Developed as agricultural centers, the outlying mission lands incorporated hundreds of hectares of fields bursting with wheat, barley, and corn, as well as smaller walled gardens and orchards. Thousands of head of cattle and sheep, grazing on open livestock range, dotted the agrarian mission landscape.

Colony Ross

The first mercantile colony in California was founded by the Russian-American Company, a commercial monopoly representing Russia's interests in the lucrative North Pacific fur trade. In establishing the Ross settlement in 1812, on the rugged coastline 110 kilometers north of the Spanish Presidio of San Francisco, the Russians created the administrative and mercantile center of the Ross colonial district (or counter). This counter eventually included a port at Bodega Bay (Port Rumiantsev), three ranches or farms, and a hunting camp, or *artel*, on the Farallon Islands (map 2). Known collectively as Colony Ross, the district served as the California base for harvesting sea otter and fur seal pelts, for raising crops and livestock, and for producing manufactured goods—many of the latter of which were traded, both legally and illegally, to Franciscan missions in return for wheat and barley. The Russian-American Company assembled an international, multiethnic workforce for its California colony that included Russians, Creoles (persons of mixed Russian and native blood), and Native Alaskans. The company also recruited local Pomo and Miwok Indians as laborers. The majority of the pluralistic population resided at the Ross settlement, where the formidable redwood log stockade contained residences for the Russian managers and staff, a barracks for single men, an official quarters for visitors, kitchen facilities, administrative offices, and storehouses. Beyond the walls of the stockade ethnic neighborhoods were established where other workers resided, including lower-class Russian and Creole craftspersons and laborers, Native Alaskan sea-mammal hunters, and the Pomo and Miwok men and women who became part of the Ross community.

The Franciscan missions and Colony Ross exemplify two ways that European colonial powers integrated local indigenous peoples into colonial infrastructures. At the vanguard of colonial expansion across the Americas, missions and fur trade outposts constituted the social settings where many North American Indians experienced their first sustained interactions with colonial agents. The arrival of missionaries and merchants in native territory often preceded, by many years, the waves of settlers that poured across much of North America in search of land to establish private homesteads, ranches, and farms. Because the settlement of California took place late in Spain's and Russia's colonial expansion in the Americas, both countries had many decades of experience in managing and overseeing native peoples in other regions, as well as in observing the colonial practices of other European nations.

Missionary colonies in North America were founded by various Christian sects that sponsored evangelization among native peoples. A steady stream of missionaries representing many Protestant denominations, Roman Catholic orders (e.g., Franciscan, Jesuit, Dominican), and the Russian Orthodox Church descended upon Native American communities, commencing in the late 1500s and 1600s, flowing rapidly across the Eastern Seaboard, the American Southwest, the American Southeast, and the North Pacific. Missionary colonies soon became established in most of the North American colonial territories of Spain, France, Russia, and, to a lesser extent, Britain. Even if somewhat suspicious of overzealous evangelists, European governments supported and even advocated missions in North America, because the missions offered a relatively inexpensive way to transform "wild" native peoples into a laboring class (see, e.g., Beaver 1988:435–439; Brown 1992:26; Jackson and Castillo 1995:31–39; Wagner 1998:443; and Weber 1992:242). Many missionary settlements were designed to be self-sufficient, with natives serving as a communal work force for constructing the mission infrastructure (e.g., churches, residential buildings, agricultural features), for raising their own food (through agriculture, gardening, and ranching), and for manufacturing their own household objects, clothing, and craft goods.[2]

Significant theological differences permeated the policies and practices of the missionary orders.[3] But, in stepping back from this evangelical diversity, we see that what differentiated the missionary settlements from other colonial institutions in North America was a focus on the two "c's"—conversion and civilization. Missionaries launched explicit enculturation programs designed to teach native peoples the Gospels, Christian worship, language skills, and the central importance of European and Euro-American world views, life ways, and economic practices. Most missionaries not only strove to make their colonies self-sufficient but also introduced European menus, dress, and crafts to indigenous populations.

Mercantile outposts, such as Colony Ross, were typically founded by commercial companies that had in common an agenda of exploiting available resources (land, animal, mineral, and people) for great profits.[4] The lucrative fur trade propelled many merchants to participate in the intensive harvesting of both terrestrial and marine mammals. Following the first European explorations of the Atlantic Coast and New Mexico in the late 1500s and early 1600s, the fur trade shifted to the tributaries of the Upper Missouri, the Rocky Mountains, and the Pacific Slope, as other areas became overhunted.[5] By the late 1700s and early 1800s, the fur trade was dominated by British companies (Hudson's Bay Company, North West Company) and American enterprises (American Fur Company, Pacific Fur Company) in the United States and Canada, and by the Russian-American Company in the North Pacific. These companies hunted or trapped diverse land mammals for furs and skins, but the primary economic engine of the terrestrial fur trade was the beaver, the fur-wool of which was used in the manufacture of hats for European and American gentlemen, from the 1500s through the early 1800s. The maritime fur trade focused on the hunting of sea mammals, primarily sea otters and fur seals, along the Pacific coast from Alaska to Baja California.

Like the missionaries, the merchants also focused on Indians. They depended on native peoples for economic success, using them to procure and process furs and exploiting them as porters and manual laborers.[6] But in contrast to the administrators of mission colonies, the businessmen who managed mercantile companies put little emphasis on directing the path of culture change among native groups. The primary reason that mercantile companies interacted with natives was not to transform their values and cultures; it was to exploit them as cheap labor. Thus, although missions measured success as a colonial endeavor by the number of native conversions and by the inroads made in modifying "pagan" life ways, mercantile colonies measured success by the economic bottom line—profits generated for owners and stockholders.[7]

COLONIAL CONSEQUENCES

Since missionary and mercantile colonies were founded on fundamentally different principles, the two types of colonial programs instituted differing policies and practices for the treatment and administration of native peoples; native entanglements with the missionaries and merchants appear to have produced divergent trajectories of culture change. The central questions I pose are twofold: How did native negotiations within the Franciscan missions and Colony Ross transform the natives' tribal organizations, cultural practices, and Indian identities? And how did these cultural transformations ultimately influence which native groups would become federally recognized in the late nineteenth and early twentieth centuries?

At first glance, the answers to these questions may seem pretty straightforward. The Franciscans have been portrayed in the academic literature as highly destructive to traditional native cultures, in contrast to the more benevolent Russian merchants. The Franciscan missionary program has been viewed and depicted as either white or black, seldom with shades of gray. Written descriptions of the California missions have focused on variations of the "white legend" or the "black legend," either ennobling the missionaries for their personal sacrifices or vilifying them as brutal and heartless in their treatment of Indian neophytes. When I attended grade school in the late 1950s and early 1960s in northern California, I learned about the kindly Franciscan fathers who dedicated their lives to helping the California Indians (see Thomas 1991 for the historical genesis of this perspective). Then, in the late 1960s and 1970s, with the rise of the "Brown Power Movement" in California universities (Monroy 1990:xiv), a very different story of the Franciscans' participation in California history emerged. With the vitriolic confrontation that greeted the proposed canonization by the Catholic church of Father Serra, the first president of the California missions (see, e.g., Costo and Costo 1987), the general public became aware of how destructive the Franciscan colonial program was to traditional Native California life ways and cultures.

Yet this point had been made in the anthropological literature for more than a century. Scholars had declared, until quite recently, that most mission Indians and their cultures had become extinct by the late 1800s and early 1900s. Stephen Powers made this observation in one of the first systematic ethnographic studies of California Indians in 1871 and 1872. "There will be found in these pages no account of the quasi-Christianized Indians of the missions. Their aboriginal customs have so faded out, their tribal organizations and languages have become so hopelessly intermingled and confused, that they can no longer be classified" (Powers 1976:16–17). The eminent historian Hubert Howe Bancroft added to the perception that the mission Indians had ceased to exist (see Haas 1995:173–174). But the most significant pronouncement was made by Alfred Kroeber, a professor at the

University of California at Berkeley who helped establish its Anthropology Department and University Museum (now known as the Phoebe Hearst Museum of Anthropology) in 1901. Kroeber's perspective proved extremely influential since he (and his Berkeley colleagues) laid the foundations for California anthropology and the academic study of Native Californians. Kroeber (1925:275, 544, 550–551, 621) observed that most of the hunter-gatherers who once resided along the coastal zone of central and southern California had either become extinct or had "melted away" to a handful of survivors.

As noted, scholars have characterized Russian and native encounters in California as much more benign than those engendered by the Franciscan mission system. There is a general perception that local Indians were well treated by the Russians. For example, Heizer and Almquist (1971:11–12, 65–66) noted that the commercial agenda of the Russian-American Company encouraged colonial administrators to cooperate with local Indians and to treat them kindly and fairly. Spencer-Hancock and Pritchard (1980/1981: 311) were even more laudatory in praising the Russians for their humane treatment of the Kashaya Pomo and contrasted this relationship to the "often harsh colonization policies of the Spanish."

These one-dimensional views of colonial interactions suggest that what happened to coastal hunter-gatherers in southern and central California depended largely upon whether they became entangled with the cruel Spaniards or with the more humane, good-natured Russians. But the outcomes of colonial encounters are never quite so simple. An analysis of the current roster of federally recognized Indian tribes in California brings this point home. In 2002 the Bureau of Indian Affairs recognized 108 tribal groups as "official" Native American corporate entities.[8] The spatial distribution of these tribes is remarkable.

At first glance, there appear to be few federally recognized tribes in the coastal zone of central and southern California. This was the picture I got when Roberta (my wife) and I first visited the impressive visitor center at Indian Grinding Rock State Historic Park in the northern Sierra Nevada foothills, one of the few parks in California devoted to Indian history. While viewing the prominent wall map displaying past and present Indian lands, I was struck that, with the exception of a small dot representing the Santa Ynez Band near Santa Barbara, a vast coastal strip was devoid totally of acknowledged tribes and Indian reservations. In fact, there was so much empty space on the map that the exhibition designers had inserted a prominent caption, "Indian Lands Today," to cover up the extensive blank area once home to hundreds of coastal Indian communities.

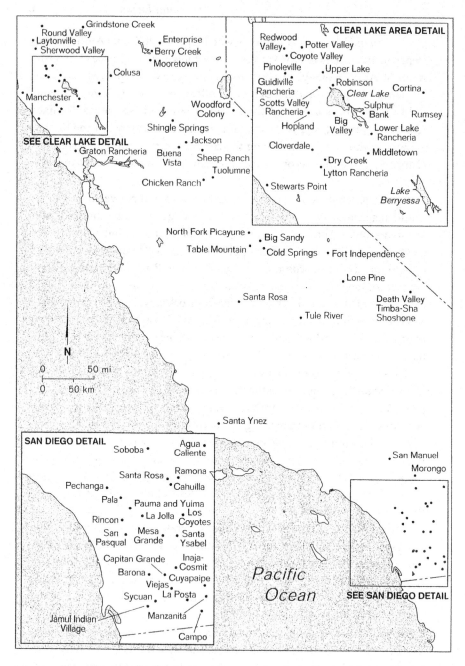

Map 3. Federally recognized Indian lands in central and southern California. The location of Indian reservations is current as of 2002. Of the reservations affiliated with the mission Indians in southern California (see table 1), all but four are shown; Augustine, Cabazon, Torres-Martinez, Twenty-Nine Palms are located beyond the eastern edge of the map. (Adapted from Kammeyer et al. 2002:55–161; Tiller 1996:228.)

Yet a closer look at this spatial distribution presents a more complex picture, as illustrated in map 3. North of San Francisco Bay, in the area of the historic Russia frontier, are the Kashaya Pomo, who have maintained their Stewarts Point reservation since 1914, and the Coast Miwok/Pomo peoples of the Federated Indians of Graton Rancheria, who were granted federal recognition in the closing days of the Clinton Administration. A gap of 540 kilometers exists between the northern area of San Francisco Bay and Los Angeles, in which only a single federally recognized group is found—the Santa Ynez Band of Chumash Mission Indians (in Santa Barbara County). But a plethora of federally recognized tribes materialize in the southernmost portion of the state—well within the colonial frontier of the Franciscan missions. Of the more than thirty tribal groups who can trace cultural and genetic affiliations back to the mission Indians, almost all were associated with the two southernmost Franciscan missions (Missions San Diego and San Luis Rey) (table 1). These groups include Cahuilla and Cupeño peoples, who were recruited into the missions from the interior, and Luiseño and Diegueño peoples from the coastal zone, who today reside on a number of small and medium-sized reservations in the upland valleys of San Diego and southern Riverside Counties (Carrico and Shipek 1996; Shipek 1978; Stewart and Heizer 1978).

It is clear from this closer inspection of current tribal distribution that in comparing the long-term implications of missionary and mercantile colonies we must rise above the one-dimensional stereotypes that have characterized past depictions of native and colonial relationships. In the aftermath of European colonialism, the descendants of most mission Indians have been portrayed as having become extinct, but this is not the case. Today every major language grouping incorporated into the Franciscan missions is represented by descendant Indian communities. Tribal organizations that trace genetic and cultural affiliations to the Coast Miwok, Ohlone, Esselen, Salinan, Chumash, Gabrielino, Luiseño and Diegueño linguistic territories are political players in contemporary California. But the majority of these groups are not acknowledged by the Bureau of Indian Affairs, and they continue to seek federal recognition and legal status as Indians.[9] In considering the long-term implications of tangling with padres and merchants, I think the real issue to address is why some native groups who were engaged with the Franciscan missions and Colony Ross became federally recognized tribes, but other mission Indians to this day remain unacknowledged, stuck in a cultural limbo with their Indian identities continually contested.

To evaluate critically these questions—what happened to native peoples in missionary and mercantile colonies, and why some tribal groups ulti-

TABLE 1. Federally Recognized Tribes of California with Mission
Indian Descendants

Tribal Affiliation	Mission Descendants
Cahuilla	Agua Caliente Reservation—Agua Caliente Band of Cahuilla Indians
	Augustine Reservation—Augustine Band of Cahuilla Mission Indians
	Cabazon Reservation—Cabazon Band of Cahuilla Mission Indians
	Cahuilla Reservation—Cahuilla Band of Mission Indians
	Los Coyotes Reservation—Los Coyotes Band of Cahuilla Mission Indians (Cahuilla, Cupeño)
	Morongo Reservation—Morongo Band of Cahuilla Mission Indians (Cahuilla, Serrano)
	Ramona Reservation—Ramona Band or Village of Cahuilla Mission Indians
	Santa Rosa Reservation—Santa Rosa Band of Cahuilla Mission Indians
	Torres-Martinez Reservation—Torres-Martinez Band of Cahuilla Mission Indians (Desert Cahuilla)
Diegueño	Barona Reservation—Barona Group of the Capitan Grande Band of Mission Indians
	Campo Indian Reservation—Campo Band of Diegueño Mission Indians (Kumeyaay)
	Capitan Grande Reservation—Capitan Grande Band of Diegueño Mission Indians
	Cuyapaipe Reservation—Cuyapaipe Community of Diegueño Mission Indians (Kumeyaay)
	Inaja-Cosmit Reservation—Inaja Band of Diegueño Mission Indians
	Jamul Indian Village (Diegueño/Kumeyaay)
	La Posta Indian Reservation—La Posta Band of Diegueño Mission Indians
	Manzanita Reservation—Manzanita Band of Diegueño Mission Indians (Kumeyaay)
	Mesa Grande Reservation—Mesa Grande Band of Diegueño Mission Indians
	San Pasqual Reservation—San Pasqual Band of Diegueño Mission Indians
	Santa Ysabel Reservation—Santa Ysabel Band of Diegueño Mission Indians
	Sycuan Reservation—Sycuan Band of Diegueño Mission Indians (Diegueño/Kumeyaay)
	Viejas Reservation—Viejas (Baron Long) Group of Capitan Grande Band of Mission Indians (Diegueño/Kumeyaay)

Tribal Affiliation	*Mission Descendants*
Luiseño	La Jolla Reservation—La Jolla Band of Luiseño Mission Indians
	Pala Reservation—Pala Band of Luiseño Mission Indians (Luiseño, Cupeño)
	Pauma and Yuima Reservation—Pauma Band of Luiseño Mission Indians
	Pechanga Reservation—Pechanga Band of Luiseño Mission Indians
	Rincon Reservation—Rincon Band of Luiseño Mission Indians
	Soboba Reservation—Soboba Band of Luiseño Mission Indians
	Twenty-Nine Palms Reservation—Twenty-Nine Palms Band of Mission Indians (Luiseño, Chemehuevi)
Chumash	Santa Ynez Reservation—Santa Ynez Band of Chumash Mission Indians
Serrano	San Manuel Reservation—San Manuel Band of Serrano Mission Indians

SOURCES: Compiled from Bureau of Indian Affairs (2002:46328–46331) and Kammeyer et al. (2002:55–161).

mately became federally recognized and others did not—I have undertaken a detailed cross-cultural comparison of the Franciscan missions and Colony Ross. The research methodology for undertaking this comparative analysis is holistic, multidimensional, and diachronic. The approach is holistic because its emphasis on historical anthropology draws on sources from ethnohistory, ethnography, native texts, and archaeology to construct a fairly balanced and multivoiced perspective on the past. The approach is multidimensional because my analysis of mission and mercantile colonial programs is structured around seven dimensions of colonial encounters (enculturation programs, native relocation programs, social mobility, labor practices, interethnic unions, demographic parameters, and chronology of colonial encounters) potentially important in the divergent outcomes of Indian survivors in the Hispanic and Russian frontiers. The analysis is diachronic because it considers not only colonial encounters among Indians, missionaries, and merchants but what happened to tribal groups in the colonial aftermath, specifically in the late nineteenth and early twentieth centuries, when they confronted anthropologists and agents of the U.S. government.

HISTORICAL ANTHROPOLOGY

Archaeology, in concert with other data sources of historical anthropology, anchors my study of colonial encounters along the Hispanic and Russian frontiers. I have thought long and hard about the critical role that archaeology should play in the construction of colonial histories, since my own encounter with an inquisitive visitor during an excavation at the Fort Ross State Historic Park in 1991. That encounter began with a flash of white light that nearly blinded me. Standing in an excavation unit directly south of the reconstructed Ross stockade, I acknowledged the man in topsiders (no socks), pure white linen pants, and white turtleneck sweater, with a bulky flash camera hanging from his neck. It was a spectacular day: the sun was just breaking through the morning fog, revealing the nearby wooded mountains, grass-encrusted marine terrace, and choppy grey Pacific Ocean. "Found any gold yet?" called the white-clothed man. He grinned, taking a snapshot of me and of several University of California, Berkeley, students earnestly troweling sediments around abalone shells, fire-cracked rock, and glass and ceramic artifacts freshly unearthed in the historic Native Alaskan Village site. I looked quickly at his gold-embroidered captain's cap. A yachtsman, probably from one of the affluent coastal communities in southern California.

"No gold," I replied, "just another chest full of these damn Russian kopec coins from the 1820s. You know, with the fall of the Soviet Union, they are worthless today." The razor sharp sea dog looked skeptical: "You're kidding aren't you—then what are you finding?" I immediately commenced with a well-rehearsed routine on the discovery of an important midden deposit associated with the interethnic household of an Alutiiq man and Kashaya Pomo woman. With my minilecture only half-finished, he stopped me with a sarcastic "midden deposit—that is a code word for garbage, right? Spending your time excavating rubbish seems like a waste of time." The man continued with a sharp question, "Why excavate trash from a historic-age site when you can read written records on what happened here?" As I stood silent, thinking how to respond, he walked briskly away, noting in a loud voice to his wife that he could not understand why we didn't do "real" archaeology, such as working on temple sites in Mexico, finding lost cities in South American jungles, or recording Paleolithic cave art paintings in France.

I recall that after the man left, I turned to face a number of skeptical undergraduate students who wanted to know why we were point-plotting each artifact from midden deposits. They asked two excellent questions: Was it really worthwhile to spend all summer digging garbage? And what kind of information would this work provide that we could not already glean from the archives of the Russian-American Company and the journals of the Russian workers stationed here? My first response was to make a note to ask Ranger Bill Walton to keep any well-dressed yachtsmen out of the park during the remainder of our excavation. But in retrospect the incident forced me to think carefully about how archaeology should be integrated into the construction of colonial histories.

Archaeology, archival documents, ethnographic observations, and native narratives together comprise the holistic study of historical anthropology, the most powerful approach for investigating the past, outside of a time machine. The integration of multiple lines of evidence from documentary, oral, and archaeological sources produces a broader and more inclusive view of history. Most important, the sources contribute distinctive historical perspectives from the vantage of peoples from varied cultural backgrounds and homelands. In the investigation of missionary and mercantile colonies characterized by pluralistic populations from around the globe, the multiple perspectives provided by historical anthropology take on added significance. They allow us to hear the muted voices of the colonial past.

I recognize, however, that using documentary, oral, and archaeological sources to study the past is anything but simple and straightforward. Each is characterized by its own analytical constraints, biases, and interpretive problems.

The primary sources for writing most histories of North American missionary and mercantile colonies are texts penned in most cases by affluent or educated European and Anglo-American men. For the California colonies, these sources include the baptismal, marriage, and burial books of the Franciscan churches, letters and journals of the padres, written correspondence of the Russian-American Company, and journals of company employees (see, for example, Kostromitinov 1974; Khlebnikov 1990; Palóu 1966; Geiger 1976; and Serra 1955b). Letters and journals of erudite European men who visited the colonies, often as part of military, trading, or scientific expeditions to the Pacific coast of North America, are another important source.[10]

Although these documentary sources remain the backbone of most historical analyses today, there is a move afoot by some scholars of colonial California to de-emphasize European accounts because of their biased view of lower-class laborers, specifically Native Californian men, women, and children (see discussion in Phillips 1993:10–11). It is true that many European observations of local native peoples were spotty and filtered through the puritanical eyes of Franciscan padres or the less than empathetic attitude of Hispanic soldiers, Russian merchants, and other foreign visitors. They often portrayed Indians as pitiful creatures who were only a minor backdrop in the construction of a European history of the California colonies (see Rawls 1984).

But as Sahlins (1992:4–14) emphasizes in his own research in the Pacific, most European writings in colonial contexts are not so much biased representations of history as culturally constructed texts that present eyewitness accounts from the vantage point of elite, literate, Western males. Firsthand observations of the Hispanic and Russian frontiers are invaluable sources, as they present a necessary European perspective on events and encounters that unfolded in each colony. These sources are particularly helpful in constructing the policies and practices that Franciscan missionaries and Russian merchants devised for colonizing and subjugating local native peoples—what I refer to as colonial structures. Such written accounts are often quite explicit about how the writers intended to incorporate native peoples into the California colonies. I employ these sources to reconstruct the "intended" colonial structures of the Franciscan missions and Colony Ross.

Native narratives offer a much-needed indigenous perspective on colonial history. The recent use of these texts has led to significant breakthroughs in our understanding of colonial California.[11] But, like European accounts, native narratives are characterized by analytical problems. Writings of natives who participated in colonial encounters are rare in California (see Castillo 1989a:117). Most native narratives are either oral histories or oral traditions. Oral histories are accounts told by individuals of events that happened in their lifetimes, often many years after they happened; most reminiscences about the Franciscan missions were collected in the late nineteenth century by historians interviewing elderly ex-mission Indians, primarily through Herbert Bancroft's history project, or by early twentieth-century anthropologists, such as John P. Harrington (Castillo 1989a, b; Librado 1979). Narratives that have been transmitted by word of mouth from one generation to another are defined as oral traditions (see Vansina 1985:11–13, 27–30). Many Native Californian groups maintain rich oral traditions of their colonial encounters. We are fortunate that Robert Oswalt, a linguistic anthropologist, transcribed in the late 1950s a number of stories detailing the experiences of Kashaya Pomo men and women with Russians and Native Alaskans at Colony Ross in the early 1800s (Oswalt 1966).

An extensive scholarship exists on the use of oral histories and traditions in anthropology, folklore, and history. The many challenges of using oral narratives (especially oral traditions) to broaden our understanding of the past are outlined in detail elsewhere.[12] My point here is that these sources can provide a unique perspective on history by providing an insider's view on the past, a window for contemplating the world views, myths, ideological constructs, and social relationships of past peoples (see, for example, Dundes 1980; Echo-Hawk 2000; Erdoes and Ortiz 1984; Finnegan 1996; Lummis 1992; and Mason 2000). Such sources are particularly useful in the study of missionary and mercantile colonies because they present indigenous perspectives on European colonial structures, and hint at how the policies and practices of colonization were perceived, mediated, and even transformed by the actions of native peoples.

Archaeology presents yet another window for viewing the life ways and interactions of Europeans and natives in colonial contexts. Although native populations may be largely invisible in some European accounts, or presented in a biased and unrealistic manner, the material remains left behind by poorly documented people can often be recovered and interpreted by archaeologists. In "democratizing" the past, archaeologists advance new perspectives on minority populations and on their entanglements with the dominant colonial culture (see Deagan 1991; Deetz 1991). Archaeology is especially relevant for studying the day-to-day practices of native peoples in colonial contexts; how people conducted their daily lives—their organization of space and the built environment, their performance of mundane tasks, their use of material culture—can tell much about their identities, world views, and social relationships.[13] A "practice-based" approach in archaeology that dwells on everyday activities and routine interactions can provide new insights on how native people in pluralistic colonial settings both organized and made sense of their lives during their encounters with "others."[14]

It is the little routines that people performed day in and day out that produced much of the patterned material remains recovered in the archaeological record. Here is where the study of midden or garbage deposits can play such a critical role in the construction of colonial histories. Through the careful recovery of material remains from such deposits, we can examine the social actions of natives in missionary and mercantile colonies. We can see how they processed and cooked foods, what they ate, what kinds of craft goods they produced, and how they incorporated European objects into their daily lives, and we can even glimpse the social gatherings and ceremonies in which they participated. By considering the spatial organization of these deposits and identifying those associated with "public" and "private" spaces, we can generate interpretations about how native peoples "acted" in the public arena and what they actually did behind closed doors in their own residences. This practice-based approach offers the opportunity to examine native agency—the kinds of strategies and tactics natives employed in their encounters with European colonists. In concert with native narratives, archaeology provides a perspective for considering how Indian peoples negotiated and mediated colonial structures in the practice of daily living.

California is an ideal place to examine native agency within missionary and mercantile colonies, given the massive amount of archaeological field-work completed in recent years. Funded primarily by cultural resource man-agement (CRM) legislation at the federal and state level, archaeological re-search has now been undertaken at most of the twenty-one missions, four presidios, and three pueblos of the Hispanic frontier. Many of these projects have excavated and analyzed midden deposits from mission quadrangles, neophyte quarters, and nearby Indian villages (see, for example, the recent studies undertaken by Rebecca Allen 1998; Julia Costello 1989; Paul Farns-worth 1987, 1992; Glenn Farris 1991; Larry Felton 1987; Roberta Greenwood 1975, 1976; Robert Hoover 1985, 1989; Ruben Mendoza 2001, 2002; Russell Skowronek 1998; and Phillip Walker and John Johnson 1992, 1994). The archaeological remains of Colony Ross have also been the focus of study by scholars and tribal elders from the California Department of Parks and Recreation, the Kashaya Pomo tribe, and the University of California at Berkeley (see, for example, Farris 1986, 1989b, 1990; Lightfoot et al. 1991, 1997; Martinez 1997, 1998; Parkman 1996/1997; Parrish et al. 2000; and Wake 1995, 1997a, 1997b).

But this flurry of work has yet to make much of a dent on mainstream interpretations of colonial history in California, despite the millions of dol-lars spent on archaeology in the Golden State each year. A perusal of the history books on colonial California readily available to the public shows hardly a mention of this work. Most people would probably still agree with the skeptical yachtsman—why do archaeology when you can read about the past in historical documents? But, as we shall see, the holistic approach of historical anthropology—with a strong dose of archaeology—can provide new and powerful insights about colonial California.

INCORPORATING HISTORICAL ANTHROPOLOGY
IN COMPARATIVE ANALYSES

How are historical sources, native narratives, and archaeology employed in my comparison of the Franciscan missions and Colony Ross? My approach focuses on how native peoples negotiated the varied policies and practices of missionary and mercantile colonies in California—what I refer to as the conjuncture of colonial policies and native agency. Using documentary, oral, and archaeological sources, I trace through time what happened to native peoples who confronted different colonial structures—that is, the intended social and economic hierarchies that colonial administrators devised to keep native peoples in their "proper" places. I then consider how native peoples employed varied strategies and tactics to negotiate these structures. A critical component of this approach is reconstructing the intended colonial structures designed to subjugate and control the labor, life ways, and even souls of native peoples. Many of the structures imposed on tribal groups were experiments in social engineering calculated to dominate the action of natives and colonists alike (Stoler and Cooper 1997:4–5). This kind of social engineering often involved formal enculturation programs, massive relocations of native peoples, the perpetuation of colonial status hierarchies, and the employment of highly stratified systems of labor that were explicit attempts to regulate and exploit the social, political, and economic relations of the laboring underclass.

Native actions in these oppressive social environments were never unrestrained or unfettered. Colonial administrators attempted to control peoples' movements and actions by force, surveillance, corporal punishment, and other means (see Dietler 2000). Thus, native agency in colonial settings involved the dialectical struggle between native intentions and desires and the dominance hierarchies these confronted. As Silliman (2001a:194–195) notes, the daily practices of native peoples may best be viewed as "practical politics" in which they negotiated their social positions and identities within the social and political hierarchies of colonial frontiers that were only partially their own construction. Any perspective that attempts to understand the diverse outcomes of colonial encounters must take into account not only the native viewpoint—the natives' cultural values, practices, families, tribal organization, and histories—but also the nature of the dominance hierarchies and colonial contexts that engaged them.

A top-down perspective is best for understanding the specific set of colonial structures imposed on native peoples in any colonial setting (see Silliman 2001b:382). Written accounts by Europeans involved directly with the planning and implementation of the colonization program provide the best sources for reconstructing the intended colonial structures. In contrast, the study of native agency is best undertaken through a bottom-up perspective— what actually happened when individual people confronted colonial hierarchies in the practice of day-to-day living (Silliman 2001b:382). Native narratives and archaeological sources are ideally suited for examining native experiences in colonial contexts, specifically how native persons negotiated and moderated colonial structures in the process of conducting day-to-day social actions.

DIMENSIONS OF COLONIAL ENCOUNTERS

Seven dimensions of colonial encounters serve as common variables in my comparative analysis of the Hispanic and Russian frontiers. These dimensions structure my examination of the interface between the intended colonial structures and native agency—that is, of how the dominance structures of missionaries and merchants were mediated in practice by native peoples. Using these variables, I examine how the different principles that guided missionary and merchant interactions with native peoples were played out in day-to-day practices. My ultimate purpose is to evaluate those dimensions (or combinations of dimensions) of colonial encounters that may have been most critical in the genesis of native strategies leading to the divergent outcomes of northern mission Indian groups (such as the Ohlone), the southernmost mission peoples (Luiseño, Diegueño), and the Kashaya Pomo.

Enculturation Programs

Enculturation programs were employed to transform the social, economic, political, and religious practices of indigenous peoples. These programs varied along a continuum of "directed" culture change. As first articulated by acculturation researchers in the 1930s and 1940s, directed culture change involves encounters in which one society clearly dominates another and forces its values, life ways, and world views upon the subservient one (see Linton 1940c:502). At one end of the continuum were the directed enculturation programs of missionaries and slave plantation owners in North America, who explicitly tried to alter the basic values and ideological structures of native groups using a suite of coercive, and often brutal, methods, such as spying, corporal punishment, and curtailment of freedom, among others (Jackson and Castillo 1995:31–39; Saunders 1998; Singleton 1998:179–181; Wilkie 2000a). The purpose of these enculturation programs was to create a reliable, subservient labor class that would imitate, to some degree, the cultural practices (language, clothing, diet, work ethics) of the dominant order. Other forms of directed enculturation programs were employed by the U.S. government on Indian reservations, where explicit attempts were made to transform traditional nomadic hunter-gatherers into sedentary farmers (Elkin 1940; Harris 1940; Heizer and Almquist 1971:67–91; Phillips 1997).

At the other end of the continuum were colonial enterprises that lacked formal enculturation programs and strategies of directed culture change. Mercantile companies typically exerted little effort in directing cultural transformations among native peoples. They could employ oppressive methods to obtain furs, goods, and labor from native peoples, and they often treated their Indian hunters poorly (see, e.g., Crowell 1997:10–16; White 1991:94–141), but merchants rarely forced the natives to change their diets, dress, language, tools, or house types. In some cases, colonial administrators allowed native workers to follow their traditional life ways and ritual practices—at least as long as these did not adversely affect the profitability of the mercantile colonies.[15]

The comparison of the missionary and mercantile enculturation programs and how they were received by natives may be useful for understanding the varying historical trajectories of Indian peoples in California. To what degree were the Franciscan padres successful in their directed efforts to modify the cultural values and practices of mission Indians? And how did the consequences of such efforts compare to the less stringent enculturation program used on native peoples at Colony Ross? Can one see an association between directed and less directed enculturation programs, and the acceptance or assimilation of European material objects and cultural practices among native peoples over time? Or did the more rigid enculturation efforts result in native strategies of insubordination, open resistance, and even violence against cultural innovations forced by particular colonial regimes (see Cusick 1998:6)?

Native Relocation Programs

The founding of new European colonies often involved the removal of native peoples from their ancestral lands and their resettlement in newly created colonial places, including missions, plantations, mines, and barrios. Native relocation programs varied greatly in the manner (e.g., force, economic incentives) in which indigenous populations were "persuaded" to move, in the distances they were moved from homeland villages, and in the kinds of social and physical environments in which they were resettled. The most "directed" and disruptive native relocation programs in North America took place on Indian reservations, slave plantations, and mission colonies. The creation of federal reservations in the United States often involved uprooting native peoples from their tribal lands, transporting them even hundreds of miles to alien regions, and forcing them, in many cases, to share reservation lands with other native groups, some of whom might be traditional enemies (for examples, see papers in Linton 1940b). Slave plantations in the American South and Caribbean created oppressive social landscapes populated by peoples uprooted from distant homelands, in which white planters dictated the placement and arrangement of workers' housing and exerted considerable influence on the kinds of material culture obtained by enslaved peoples (Armstrong 1998:383; Thomas 1998; Wilkie 2000b; Wilkie and Farnsworth 1999).

Missionary orders in North America, especially the Franciscans, deployed native relocation programs to facilitate the settlement of native converts at mission complexes. Franciscan priests advocated the *reducción* (aggregation) of native peoples into mission centers to facilitate the natives' indoctrination, provide a more formidable defense against hostile natives and other antagonistic colonial agents, and enable the missionaries to maintain better surveillance of their neophyte wards. The specific practices of *reducción* programs varied in time and space. Where traditional native settlement patterns were dispersed and/or residentially mobile, such as among hunter-gatherer communities in Texas and California, missionaries commonly removed natives from settlements in the hinterland for relocation into centrally placed missions. Where native peoples were already aggregated in villages and towns, such as among some agricultural tribes in Florida, or the Pueblo Indians of New Mexico, however, missions tended to be built in existing native settlements. This latter strategy created far fewer disruptions to local populations, although some resettlement did take place among sedentary natives to maintain the size of mission towns after lethal epidemics swept through local populations.[16]

The least directed relocation programs tended to be associated with mercantile colonies, such as fur trade outposts, where colonial agents typically gave local natives a wider latitude over where they could live. However, the spatial organization of these settlements usually reflected the underlying social and status hierarchies of the colonizers, and typically involved the segregation of residential neighborhoods into class-based segments for managerial elites, non-Indian workers, and Indians (Crowell 1997a:224–227; Lightfoot 1997b:4–5). Merchants often employed economic incentives to induce some natives to live near colonial settlements and participate as local laborers; this stimulated a process of population aggregation around many trade outposts, where "post" or "Home Guard" Indians resided (Swagerty 1988:370).

The comparison of missionary and mercantile resettlement programs is important for understanding how different kinds of native identities were constructed in colonial settings. Much has been written recently about the importance of place and Indian identity (see Basso 1996; Momaday 1974). The cultural meaning of landscape is paramount to many native peoples, since their creation stories and history are often embedded in the "landmarks of memory" where both mythical ancestors and deceased relatives once lived. In his seminal book, *Cycles of Conquest,* Spicer (1962:576–577) concluded that a critical factor in the continuation of native identities in the

American Southwest was the maintenance of residence patterns within traditional tribal territories. The sacred relationship between land and ancestors appears to have been significant in symbolizing the continuity of group identities. Kicza (1997:14–15) also observed that consistency in the occupation of rural indigenous communities facilitated the maintenance of identities, political organizations, and ritual systems over time.

In considering this dimension, I examine the impact that missionary and mercantile relocation programs had on native peoples' identities in colonial California. What are the implications of the fact that some groups maintained villages in their ancestral homeland, and how might this continuity have contributed to the nourishment of a tribal identity, especially on the Russian frontier? And what are the long-term implications of the Franciscan *reducción* program, which forced natives from many alien communities to reside in centrally located missions some distance beyond their traditional tribal territories? Could this resettlement program have instigated a process of tribal fragmentation that led to the reconstitution of new social groupings among some northern mission Indians, such as the Ohlone speakers in the San Francisco Bay Area?

Social Mobility

Social mobility refers to the permeability of colonial hierarchies and the ability of native workers to advance to positions of greater responsibility and social status within the colonial system. European colonies in North America were typically organized into tightly stratified, segregated hierarchies. One's position in the colonial hierarchy largely determined one's social status, living quarters, job title, and compensation. Since the dominant culture defined the positions, one's perceived ethnicity typically played a critical role in where one was initially placed. For example, the large fur companies (Hudson's Bay Company, North West Company, Russian-American Company) recruited a pluralistic labor force to populate trade outposts. At the apex of the hierarchy were a few Europeans who managed the company's affairs at home and in the field. The next tier, divided into various ranks, consisted of a larger number of lower-class Europeans and peoples of mixed European and native blood who served as clerks, traders, artisans, and skilled or semi-skilled tradespersons. The lowest tier of the pyramid contained the contract and day laborers who performed the bulk of the manual labor. They tended to be native peoples, enlisted from local and distant tribes (see Burley 1985; Lightfoot et al. 1991; Monks 1985; Ray 1988). Stratified hierarchies also permeated most missions, which inevitably placed European missionaries at the top, lower-ranking European and mixed-blood soldiers and mission staff personnel in the middle, and Indian converts at the bottom (see, e.g., Costello and Hornbeck 1989:316–317).

The dimension of social mobility varied greatly in both mercantile and missionary colonies. Fur companies, such as the Hudson's Bay Company and North West Company, differed in degree of stratification, segregation of managers and workers, and flexibility in the ways people could advance in the colonial hierarchy (Prager 1985). Outposts situated in the distant frontier tended to be less rigidly structured than those located near company headquarters. Missions also varied in degree of social mobility, as some Protestants provided training for the native ministry (Beaver 1988:433, 436). Some Roman Catholic orders (e.g., Franciscans) developed their own hierarchy of Indian officials, who were accorded status and responsibility in mission colonies. Neophytes promoted to these positions managed Indian labor and helped maintain discipline in missionary communities (Jackson and Castillo 1995:37–38). This system of promotion produced a dual layer of traditional (chiefs, shamans) and colonial Indian officials (*alcaldes*) in many California missions.

The ability of native peoples to initiate strategies of upward mobility for perceived social, political, or economic advantages may have been an important dimension stimulating culture change and identity transformation in colonial settings. Advancement in the colonial hierarchy may have provided benefits that translated into higher-paying positions, greater access to manufactured commodities and high-status goods, expansion of the pool of potential marriage partners, consumption of a broader range of foods and medicine (which may have prolonged the survival of family units under unhealthy conditions), and occupation of colonial residential housing. Native people seeking social mobility forged close relations with colonists and/or manipulated their own identities to assimilate into higher-status colonial groupings. This usually entailed the adoption of symbols, behaviors, and ideologies associated with members of higher-ranking groups. Consequently, people choosing this strategy would have broadcast their close connections with high-status groups or constructed new colonial identities by embracing new forms of dress, foods, architecture, and ceremonial practices (Lightfoot and Martinez 1995; McGuire 1982:164). I consider here the dimension of social mobility in missionary and mercantile colonies in California, and evaluate how different strategies of native activism may have produced diverse kinds of outcomes for Indian groups.

Labor Practices

As Silliman (2000:18–28; 2001b) recently wrote, labor practices permeated and structured the experiences of most native peoples in colonial settings in North America. Since colonial regimes almost universally exploited native peoples as cheap labor, an important dimension of colonialism is its labor practices—how individuals were incorporated into labor systems, the means of recruiting them, their compensation, their selection for specific kinds of jobs (e.g., by skill, gender, social status), and their overall treatment. Labor practices involving the recruitment, organization, and compensation of workers varied considerably among individual missionary and mercantile colonies. For example, laborers were "recruited" by enslavement and force (e.g., kidnapping, war captivity), by religious conversion, by laws mandating that natives work for colonists, by military alliances that stipulated the allocation of native workers to colonial agents, and by economic incentives (Cook 1976b:300–316; Phillips 1980; Silliman 2000, 2001b).

In North America, native peoples were incorporated into forms of labor organizations ranging from enslavement to communal, peonage, convict, and day (or contract) systems. Labor systems dependent on slaves for the economic success of colonial enterprises are exemplified by the slave plantations of the American South, but other colonial programs in North America also incorporated aspects of these labor systems by enslaving or forcing natives to work against their will. In communal systems of labor, often associated with missions, each member of the community contributed labor to a common pool of agrarian and craft activities, from which each individual received support in the way of food, shelter, clothing, and other necessary goods (Cook 1976b:301–302). Peonage systems, especially prevalent on Hispanic ranchos and early Euro-American ranches in California, were based on patron/client relationships between owners and Indian workers. Native peoples furnished a wide range of laboring activities in the fields and served as domestic workers for the rancho owner, who in return provided them with a place to live, food, some manufactured goods, and security (Cook 1976b:302; Monroy 1990:100–101,150–154; Phillips 1990:37–38; Silliman 2000). Convict labor systems, commonly employed in many colonial contexts, forced Indians accused of breaking colonial laws to serve time undertaking hard manual work (Langellier and Rosen 1996:71, 75,111–112; Monroy 1990:71, 150–151).

Day or contract labor systems characterized many of the mercantile companies. Company managers hired native workers for a specified number of days, as contract laborers to complete specific tasks, or as salaried employees. The workers were compensated in a variety of ways. Some were paid in trade goods (e.g., iron and copper goods, textiles, tobacco, firearms, alcohol) or in kind (e.g., food or goods produced in the colony), others in scrip that could be exchanged for goods in company stores, or money (see, e.g., Cook

1976b:316–322; Gibson 1988:386–388; Kardulias 1990; Monks 1985; Pyszczyk 1985; Wolf 1982:175). It was not uncommon for some workers or native trappers to be paid in advance, in a credit system that could put them into debt for life (Ray 1988:340–342).

A comparison of labor practices may provide a better understanding of why native workers initiated a diverse range of responses to specific colonial regimes. Peoples' identities in colonial settings were often associated with the jobs they performed, which varied from unskilled manual laborers and domestic servants to semiskilled or skilled craftspersons, artisans, agricultural specialists, and managerial staff (clerks, accountants, administrators, and owners). A thorough examination of the colonial labor system is necessary in order to consider whether native peoples could be promoted to higher-ranking jobs and how this possibility influenced their social status and economic stature and the interactions among natives and colonists. As a significant symbol of colonial oppression, labor also rallied workers to resist the regimentation and imposition of colonial managers (Silliman 2000, 2001b). Since most native peoples' encounters with colonial regimes centered around labor practices, their treatment as laborers colored how they chose to respond and negotiate with the imposed colonial structure.

Specifically, I examine the different labor regimes in the California frontiers, and consider how the Kashaya Pomo and mission Indian groups, such as the Ohlone, initiated different strategies for coping with the labor burdens placed upon them.

Interethnic Unions

A growing body of research explores how members of interethnic unions or marriages played important roles as cultural brokers and intermediaries in pluralistic colonial contexts. Cohabitation between colonial agents and tribal members promoted political alliances (especially between colonial agents and elite native families), facilitated trade relations, produced polyglot translators and interpreters, and provided sex partners (Deagan 1995:452–453; Swagerty 1988:371; Wagner 1998:442; Whelan 1993:254–256). Colonial and native partners could also serve as conduits for introducing each other's cultural values and material objects into daily practices, in pluralistic families on colonial frontiers. More important, the offspring of interethnic unions produced mixed blood or "creole" populations, who were often at the forefront of creating innovative, synergistic cultural practices that were neither purely native nor purely colonial but something new. Some mixed-blood populations constructed their own group identities in colonial settings, through the process of ethnogenesis (Deagan 1998).

The frequency of interethnic unions varied greatly across space and time in North American colonies, tied to such factors as the population size and sex ratios of colonial and indigenous populations and the changing perceptions of mixed marriages among the colonizers and natives. Although some European governments may have attempted to prohibit interethnic fraternization on moral and racial grounds, it is not clear that such policies succeeded on the distant frontiers. Furthermore, some colonial powers, including Spain, Russia, and France, favored and even encouraged interethnic marriages in specific colonial contexts as strategies for populating faraway colonies with political allies and workers.[17] Tribal groups differed in how they perceived sexual relations with outsiders (Ronda 1984:62–63, 208, 232–233), and their views about interethnic unions often changed over time from their experiences with colonizers (see, e.g., Aginsky 1949:290). Gender politics and cultural proscriptions influenced interethnic unions, since the majority involved colonial men and native women. Several studies have noted the power and influence that non-European women wielded in colonial societies through interethnic unions (Deagan 1990:240–241; Martinez 1998; McEwan 1995:228–229).

I will examine the frequency and kinds of interethnic unions that unfolded on the Hispanic and Russian frontiers and the degree to which these relationships manipulated or transformed colonial identities. Did the creation of interethnic unions stimulate the process of ethnogenesis in certain colonial contexts? And did the process of ethnogenesis displace or modify traditional Indian cultural practices and identities, thereby contributing to the creation of new cultural constructs among some native peoples, especially women and children?

Demographic Parameters of Colonial and Native Populations

The dimension of demographic parameters has probably received the most attention, primarily because of the ongoing debate about the introduction of Euro-Asian pathogens to Native Americans, and the devastating effects that epidemics had on local populations.[18] Some scholars view native depopulation as a significant factor in the transformation of colonizer-native interactions. They argue that native population collapse resulted in the extinction of native languages; contributed to the loss of traditional knowledge, material culture, and rituals as entire cohorts of elders were eliminated; produced refugee communities in which survivors amalgamated into fewer and fewer settlements; and fostered the development of creole communities and cultures, as the frequency of interethnic and intertribal marriages increased (see Deagan 1998:28–29; Dobyns 1983:311, 328–332; Dobyns

1991:550–552; Milanich 1995:xvii; Rogers 1990:53–54, 81–84, 92; and Salisbury 1982:101–106). There is no question that early European exploration and later colonization had grave effects on the health and cultural survival of native groups; the real puzzle revolves around the specific timing and spread of epidemics, and around the magnitude of native population loss (see Baker and Kealhofer 1996; Larsen 1994; Larsen and Milner 1994; Verano and Ubelaker 1992).

In considering the outcomes of native entanglements with specific colonial regimes, it is important to examine the changing relation between native and colonizer population parameters (such as the number of people, sex ratios, and family sizes). Changing population ratios of colonizers/natives would have had important ramifications for the kinds of encounters that might take place. A context of a relatively small number of single men, rotating in and out of a colony's workforce during the initial period of colonization, has far different implications for colonizer-native interactions than has a colonial context where hordes of settler families are unleashed into an area suffering from severe native depopulation.

I will compare the different demographic histories of native peoples in the mission and mercantile colonies of California. What is the evidence for demographic decline among native peoples in the Franciscan missions and Colony Ross? And how did certain demographic histories contribute to later perceptions that some mission Indian groups had become extinct or simply melted away?

Chronology of Colonial Encounters

The temporal dimension of colonial encounters received considerable attention by early acculturation researchers and by later culture-contact scholars. The former traced the adoption, acceptance, and spread of innovations among native peoples through different stages of the acculturation process (Linton 1940a:470; Smith 1940:34). More recent investigators highlight the differences in kind of colonizer-native interactions that take place in the early and later episodes of encounters. Much attention has focused on "first contacts," including early European explorations and the establishment of new colonies, but recent papers stress the importance of examining later postcontact interactions in well-developed colonial settings, as such relationships often differ significantly from first encounters, where dominance patterns and cycles of violence have not been fully established (Hill 1998; Ruhl and Hoffman 1997). That an important dimension of the chronology of colonial encounters is the transformation of colonizer-native interactions over time becomes especially germane when comparing the encounters of first-generation colonizers and native peoples with those of second-, third-, and fourth-generation persons born and raised in the colonies. For example, Kicza (1997:13–14) suggests that it takes about three generations for creole populations to become distinct ethnic entities in colonial settlements.

I evaluate the implications of the differences in chronologies of colonial encounters represented by the Franciscan missions and by Colony Ross. Catholic padres worked with several generations of neophyte communities over seventy years or so. In contrast, Russian-American Company managers and laborers spent a total of only twenty-nine years in northern California. Did the extended chronology of the missions contribute to the disintegration of traditional tribal entities and the creation of new social forms and political organizations? Did the shorter chronology of Russian colonialism facilitate the maintenance of native cultural practices and tribal identity on the Russian frontier?

DIACHRONIC PERSPECTIVE

My comparative analysis considers not only encounters that took place between native peoples and colonists, but also what happened to tribal groups in the aftermath of European colonization in California. I evaluate how these colonial experiences contributed to the development of new kinds of native identities, social forms, and tribal relationships. I then examine how scholars and government agents reacted to these innovative tribal groupings in the late nineteenth and early twentieth centuries. These gatekeepers of Indian authenticity accepted some of the novel tribal developments as "legitimate" Indian traits but challenged the authenticity of others and so ultimately provided the basis for denying federal recognition to many native groups. An important point I make in this book is the critical role that anthropologists played in defining the cultural traits or "essences" of California Indian cultures, and how the anthropologists' models of tribal organization and Indian identity influenced the decision-making process involved in the allotment of federal lands to "homeless" Indians between 1906 and 1930.

2 Visions of Precolonial Native California

A California condor flew majestically along the Pacific coastline in the mid-1700s, looking down on the many smoke plumes rising from hundreds of villages dotting the landscape below. From this lofty vantage the bird could see a distinctive pattern—that of village clusters demarcated by large settlements surrounded by one or more diminutive hamlets. Each village contained dome-shaped thatched houses with adjacent outdoor hearths and extramural work areas where people might be busily flaking stone tools, manufacturing fishing lines, nets, and cordage, tending fires, and preparing acorn gruel for meals. The larger settlements would have been quite impressive from the air. One or two imposing semisubterranean, earth-covered buildings overshadowed the smaller thatched houses. These ceremonial structures and the central places immediately encircling them were reserved for community-wide celebrations: rituals, feasts, and dances. Communal granaries, used for storing nuts, seeds, and other foods, stood near the village centers. A short distance away, cemeteries formed the sacred areas where the community buried or cremated its recently deceased and venerated the ancient ones with recurrent commemorative ceremonies.

Open space radiated beyond each large settlement and its associated smaller hamlets. Men, women, and children would walk back and forth from the settlement clusters to nearby environs. Here they gathered shellfish in bayshore habitats, fished for species of rock cod along the rocky shoreline, traveled up fertile riparian corridors to gather sedges and other materials for making baskets, and checked on the nearby oak groves to estimate when and where acorns would be ready for harvest. The more distant hinterland contained few people, except the occasional hunters rushing home from a successful hunt with choice cuts of venison. This outlying area transitioned into an empty no-man's land, a potentially treacherous zone marking the jealously guarded boundaries for each of the small polities.

The above describes how anthropologists in the early 1900s might envision the hunter-gatherer communities along the central and southern California coasts just prior to Spanish and Russian colonization. Elsewhere I have argued that a strong grounding in prehistory is critical for evaluating the full impact that European exploration and colonization had on native societies (Lightfoot 1995); here I stress that, to understand what happened to native peoples in the aftermath of Hispanic and Russian colonialism, we need to reconstruct a vision of native prehistory as seen by early anthropologists. Anthropological models of traditional native polities and culture served as the yardstick for evaluating the degree of change that had taken place among Native Californian communities by the early twentieth century. Opinions about what constituted the essence of "pure" Indian culture became critical when the U.S. government began purchasing land for "legitimate" California Indians. Those native groups who maintained cultural practices and identities that fit these anthropological constructs stood a much better chance of gaining federal recognition than did other Indian communities.

The aim of this chapter is to flesh out how anthropologists conceptualized precolonial native societies. The chapter focuses on the work of Alfred Kroeber and his colleagues who laid the foundation of California anthropology during the period from 1901 to the late 1930s. These pioneering fieldworkers, most associated with the University of California at Berkeley, devoted their efforts to reconstructing aboriginal cultures of California as they would have looked at the time of first contact. Employing the "memory culture" methodology, anthropologists interviewed tribal elders about old Indian ways, and classified Native Californians by language, culture area, and polity. The "Kroeberian" model of California Indians presented in this chapter will be returned to later, when I compare this idealized vision of prehistory with the actual tribal organizations and Indian cultural practices that grew out of colonial encounters in the Hispanic and Russian frontiers.

RECONSTRUCTING NATIVE CALIFORNIA SOCIETIES

Alfred Kroeber joined the faculty at the University of California, Berkeley, in 1901 with the founding of the school's Anthropology Department and University Museum. A protégé of Professor Franz Boas at Columbia University, young Kroeber brought to Berkeley the latest advances in anthropological thinking and ethnographic methods. Although ethnographic observations of California Indians had been recorded in the late nineteenth century by Stephen Powers, Alphonse Pinart, Stephen Bowers, Lorenzo Yates, and others, Kroeber was the first to develop a systematic program of study (see Heizer 1978b). In creating the Ethnological and Archaeological Survey of California in 1903, his primary goal was to reconstruct aboriginal California as it would have appeared before the destructive influence of Western civilization. As Simmons (1997:51) summarizes, "Interest in the past, what Kroeber once described as 'the purely aboriginal, the uncontaminatedly native,' dominated research on Native Californians until the 1930s, when anthropologists in general turned away from 'conjectural history' to the study of how communities functioned in the present and how they fared in the course of change."

Kroeber recognized the urgency of undertaking his "salvage" program; the ravages of Western civilization had left no Indian community untouched by the early twentieth century. Rather than initiate participant observations about the daily lives and cultural practices of people residing in contemporary native communities, Berkeley ethnographers chose to employ "memory culture" methodology, designed explicitly to mine information about past native cultures. They conducted interviews with a few native elders from each tribal group, requesting them to recount memories of their youth and to recite stories of the old days, stories handed down from their grandparents' and parents' generations. The ethnographers asked about oral traditions concerning historical events, myths, legends, and religious and political practices. A concerted effort was made to record linguistic information, through word lists and even sound recordings, that could be used to classify distinctive languages and dialects.

Duncan Strong, who initiated fieldwork among several southern Californian groups in the winter of 1924–25, presented an excellent account of the challenges of reconstructing Native California memory cultures.

> Whenever, as in the present case, the ethnologist follows some time after the effacing hand of civilization has done its work, he must perforce assume the rôle of social paleontologist. Little but the bones or framework of social institutions survive when the whole social organization has ceased to function. Yet it is from these remains that he must assiduously reconstruct the image of that which formerly existed. . . . But if one can be content with reconstructing the mold within which these forces were once active much may be done, so long as members

of the groups survive who remember the old forms that once regulated
their lives. From such informants not only the *mores* of the group may
be obtained, but also adequate objective data to determine the degree
of efficacy and control which the various rules and beliefs formerly
exerted. In this manner a reasonably accurate picture of the social
machinery may be obtained, but it is a still and not a moving picture.
(Strong 1929:2–3)

The primary concern in using this method was the timing of European
contact, and, more importantly, how many years had passed since major
disruptions caused by Western civilization had taken place in California Indian societies. Kroeber (1966:89) argued that native ownership and land use
in some areas of California, such as northern California and the Sierra
Nevada foothills and mountains, "still persisted undiminished and untouched . . . as late as 1849–50." Consequently, interviews were sought with
elders born in the early-to-mid-nineteenth century (preferably before the
Gold Rush), as it was believed that many effects of European and American contact could be carefully filtered out through detailed analysis. In addition to relying on native consultants, the fieldworkers used previous
ethnographic reports (e.g., Stephen Powers's), and observations by earlier
colonists and explorers (e.g., early Anglo settlers' notes, Franciscan missionary records) to assist in reconstructing "pristine" aboriginal cultural
life ways. The Berkeley anthropologists undertook fieldwork among some
native groups who had been participants in the historic Russian and Hispanic frontiers. However, as detailed in chapter 8, they instituted significant
biases in the selection of native groups for study from central and southern California. Only a few of the descendant communities of the mission
Indians were investigated, but other native peoples, associated with the Russian colonial program, became important consultants in this study of California Indians.

A wealth of ethnographic information was collected and published, and
the publications remain key sources for anyone attempting to understand
California Indian peoples. The Berkeley ethnographers published the results
of this massive undertaking primarily in the *University of California Publications in American Archaeology and Ethnology* and in the *University of
California Anthropological Records*, as well as in the authoritative monograph *Handbook of the Indians of California* (Kroeber 1925). For all intents
and purposes, these publications comprise the basic foundation for the academic study of Native California societies.

In grappling with the great diversity of native Californian societies, early researchers created a framework for classifying Indian peoples by language, culture area, and polity. This conceptual scheme provides the primary organizational structure for defining Native Californian groups to this day.

LANGUAGE

The linguistic diversity of California fascinated early anthropologists. They reported more than one hundred languages, or about 20 percent of the languages found in all of native North America. California languages could eventually be classified into a four-level system of progressively smaller language groupings: stock, family, language, and dialect. Of the six or seven language stocks recognized in California, three—Hokan, Penutian (Utian), and Uto-Aztecan—were spoken by the majority of the native peoples caught within the historic Spanish/Mexican and Russian frontiers. My description below is based on relatively recent syntheses presented by Hinton (1994), Moratto (1984:529–574), and Simmons (1997:56), as well as on discussions of individual language families and languages by other specialists (e.g., Bean and Shipek 1978; Bean and Smith 1978; Hester 1978a, b; Levy 1978; Luomala 1978).

Hokan Stock

Linguistic anthropologists further subdivided the Hokan speakers of central and southern California into the Pomoan, Chumashan, Yuman, and Salinan families, each of which contained a number of related languages or dialects (map 4). Of the seven languages classified as Pomoan, two—Kashaya Pomo and Southern Pomo—would have been commonly spoken on the Russian frontier. The languages of the Chumashan family were dispersed across the Santa Barbara Channel region and northern Channel Islands; consequently, the Franciscan missions founded in "Chumash country" incorporated speakers of at least four Chumash languages from the islands, and at least five from the mainland. The Yuman family was represented by the Diegueño language of the very southernmost stretch of coastal California, where at least two dialects, or even separate languages—northern Diegueño (Ipai) and southern Diegueño (Tipai and Kumeyaay)—were noted. The Salinan family, speakers of which resided north of the Santa Barbara coast, may have been divided into two or three languages or dialects. In addition, the Esselen language, the affinity of which with the Hokan Stock is somewhat debatable, was situated on the central coast directly north of the Salinan speakers.

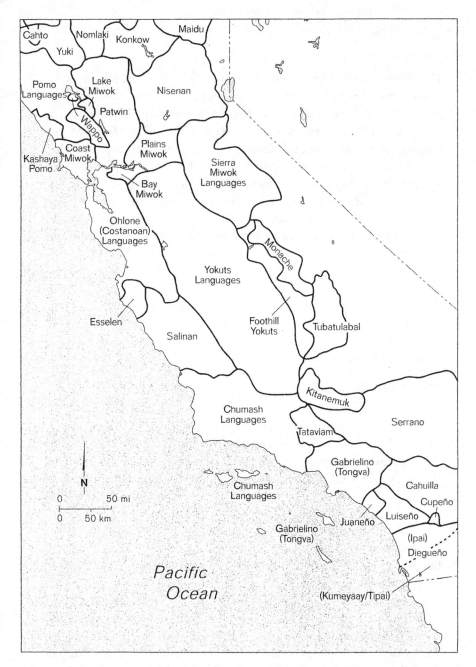

Map 4. Indian languages of central and southern California. Only languages of the central and southern California culture areas, as originally defined by Kroeber, are shown. Native peoples inhabiting the eastern section of the map, where no languages are illustrated, were classified into the Great Basin and Colorado River culture areas. (Adapted from Heizer 1978a:ix; Hinton 1994:27.)

Penutian Stock

The three major families of the Penutian stock—Miwokan, Ohlone (Costanoan), and Yokutsan—were represented in the missions of central California (map 4). Early linguists mapped the Saclan (Bay Miwok) language along Suisun Bay and the San Joaquin River delta, and the Coast Miwok language of northwestern San Francisco Bay had speakers represented in both the northern Hispanic frontier and the Russian frontier. Linguistic anthropologists divided the extensive Ohlone family into at least eight languages, distributed in a broad swath from San Francisco Bay south to Monterey Bay and Big Sur. The Yokutsan family comprised a number of languages, some of which would be spoken in the northern Franciscan missions when intensive recruitment took place in the San Joaquin Valley.

Uto-Aztecan Stock

The Takic family was well represented in some of the southernmost missions, where at least six distinctive languages were spoken. These included the Serrano, Cahuilla, Cupeño, Luiseño, Gabrielino (Tongva), and Juaneño languages (map 4).

Ethnolinguistic Units

The language groups discussed above represent a classificatory system devised by anthropologists and linguists to make sense of the linguistic diversity of California. Roland Dixon and Alfred Kroeber (1913, 1919) and others defined some of the major linguistic stocks, such as Hokan and Penutian, after only a little more than a decade of fieldwork. From the outset, some specialists challenged the creation of some of these linguistic groupings (Kroeber 1935:6). And questions continue to be raised about the utility of the Hokan and Penutian stocks classification and about the genetic relationship of various linguistic families (see Hughes 1992:325). However, with the publication of Kroeber's map of California showing "native tribes, groups, dialects, and families" in 1922 (Kroeber 1922, map 1), and the detailed discussion of these entities in his classic *Handbook of the Indians of California* in 1925, these groupings became codified into rigidly bounded ethnolinguistic units (see map 5). No introductory book on California Indians would be complete without an updated version of Kroeber's map or discussion of these ethnolinguistic units. Thus, as Simmons (1997:56) recently noted, these ethnolinguistic units tend to be equated with tribal groupings in California (see, for example, Klimek 1935:21).

But, in clarifying the nature of these groupings, I think it is fair to say

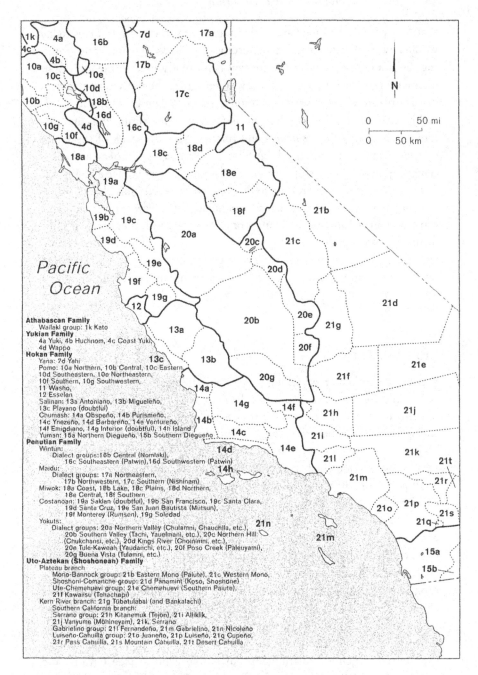

Map 5.   Ethnolinguistic units of central and southern California. These units, as originally defined by Kroeber, have taken on a life of their own. (Adapted from Kroeber 1922, map 1.)

that the spatially bounded areas illustrated so prominently in maps today would have had little meaning to precolonial peoples. The linguistic groupings do not define *tribes* as the concept is normally used in the anthropological literature: as, that is, a people who recognize themselves as members of a distinct social group with a common territory and unifying political leadership. Kroeber's ethnolinguistic units merely define similarities and differences in linguistic constructs and relationships. To speak of the Pomo people is "really to speak of a large family of languages, not of an actual social group with a leadership structure" (Simmons 1997:56; see also Kunkel 1974:9). It is critical, therefore, to distinguish between individual Californian Indian polities and broader ethnolinguistic units. Few of these language groupings ever functioned as autonomous, sociopolitical entities in California. The one notable exception may be the speakers of the Kashaya Pomo language, who, as discussed later, developed a unified tribal organization and who "are the only Pomo linguistic group with a name for themselves as a whole" (McLendon and Oswalt 1978:277).

CULTURE AREA

Kroeber embarked on a lifelong project of dividing California (later, all of North and Central America) into culture areas. These "geographical units of culture" or "ethnic provinces" (to use Kroeber's terms) were defined by the spatial distribution of diagnostic cultural traits in relation to natural physiographic regions. Although Kroeber (1939:1–3) never advocated a deterministic relationship between environment and culture, he did recognize an important relationship between the growth of cultures and the kinds of subsistence practices and surplus production that could take place under distinctive environmental conditions. He initially defined three or four culture areas in California (Kroeber 1904b, 1920), but in the mid-1930s the number increased to five major culture areas (as well as the adjacent Great Basin culture area) (Kroeber 1936:106). By this time, Kroeber had instituted a new program of culture element surveys in which native informants were asked about the presence or absence of cultural traits taken from a standardized list of one thousand to eleven hundred items. These trait lists were statistically analyzed to define better the spatial pattern of culture areas and to examine the "genetic relationship" of native groups[1] (see Gifford and Kroeber 1937; Klimek 1935; Kroeber 1936). Curiously, rather than following the boundaries of major language stocks, these culture areas crosscut Hokan, Penutian, Uto-Aztecan, and other language groupings. The upshot was that people speaking very different languages were often classified together in the same culture area and physiographic region. Two culture areas defined by Kroeber are pertinent to this book, the central and southern areas.

Central California

This extensive culture area encompasses the northern and southern Coast Ranges, the adjoining coastline, the Sacramento and San Joaquin river valleys, and the foothills and high valleys of the northern and southern Sierra Nevada mountains. Here, however, I am concerned with a much smaller area that includes the southern section of the northern Coast Ranges, the greater San Francisco Bay, and the southern Coast Ranges (map 6). This fog-shrouded landscape of spectacular coastlines, bountiful estuaries, and narrow coastal mountain valleys is largely the product of millions of years of faulting and folding along the San Andreas seismic zone. The surprisingly rugged Coast Ranges rise, in some cases, abruptly from the sea to more than fifteen hundred or eighteen hundred meters. The vegetation varies with elevation gradients, distance from the coast, and latitude, but the most distinctive types include coastal redwoods, closed-cone pines (Bishop, Monterey, and knobcone pines), evergreen oaks, Digger pines, and chaparral. In stark contrast to the Coast Ranges, the relatively flat shore of the San Francisco Bay, draining 40 percent of California through the Sacramento–San Joaquin Basin, supports the greatest expanse of contiguous tidal marshland on the Pacific Coast of North America.

The central coastal region is home to the Pomo, Coast Miwok, Bay Miwok, Ohlone (Costanoan), Esselen, and Salinan speakers. The aboriginal culture elements that made these groups distinctive, from Kroeber's perspective, are as follows. Each of these groups practiced a mixed hunter-gatherer economy that took advantage of diverse coastal resources, including shellfish, fish, and sea mammals. Local peoples built small vessels (*tule balsas*), for use on San Francisco Bay and other protected bodies of water, but there is little evidence for oceangoing boats and deep sea fishing. Berkeley ethnographers emphasized the terrestrial/riparian component of the central California subsistence practices, especially the harvesting of salmon and acorns, along with the hunting of deer, elk, and waterfowl. Family groups lived in village communities, and initiated residential movement from coastal to interior valleys in response to food supply and social factors. The villagers constructed prominent sweatlodges or roundhouses—large semisubterranean structures of wood and earth—in the center of their settlements. Domestic abodes, dispersed around the ceremonial buildings, consisted of

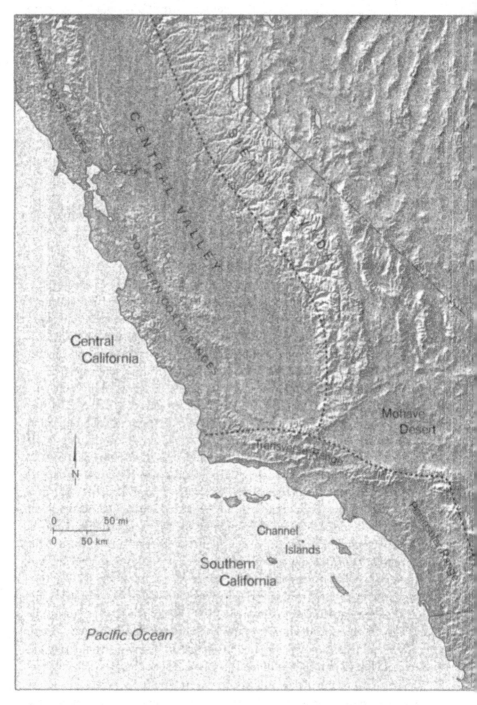

Map 6. Central and southern California showing major physiographic features.

smaller versions of the roundhouses, or of pole-and-thatch structures. In some places, village dwellers built conical houses from redwood boards and bark slabs. The central coast peoples produced a range of crafts, including spectacular feathered baskets, magnesite beads, and clamshell disk beads, the latter serving as a form of shell money. They practiced similar ceremonial cults, most notably the Kuksu cult, which played a significant role in the ritual activities of much of the central coast.

Southern California

A broad swath of islands, coastal strip, mountains, and adjoining deserts, this culture area extended south from the Santa Barbara Channel to Baja California (map 6). My focus is on the coastal peoples who lived in the shadows of the Transverse and Peninsular Ranges, the backbone of this region. The Transverse Ranges, created by a series of east-west faults, include the Santa Monica, San Gabriel, and San Bernardino Mountains, as well as the northern Channel Islands, which extend this vertical landscape out to sea. The Peninsular Ranges, forming the northern end of the long Baja California peninsula, are rugged mountains situated along the west side of the San Andreas seismic zone. Like that of the central coast, the vegetation of this area ranges greatly. It varies from the former marshy grasslands of the Los Angeles Basin to coastal sage scrub, chaparral-covered hillsides, and, at higher elevations, coniferous forests. The coastal area bounded by the Transverse and Peninsular Ranges sustains an extremely rich marine environment, the product of favorable currents and upwelling that bring bottom nutrients to the surface, where they feed a complex food chain of invertebrates, fish, and sea mammals, centered around extensive kelp forests.

Kroeber's "culture elements" of the southern coastal region, ancestral homeland of Chumash, Gabrielino, Luiseño, and Diegueño speakers, include the following.

The area boasted some of the most impressive maritime hunter-fisher societies in North America. The Chumash and Gabrielino, in particular, skillfully harvested shellfish, fish, sea mammals, and sea vegetables, using diverse sophisticated tools and harvesting strategies. Their large seagoing canoes (*tomol*) epitomized this maritime culture. Constructed from planks sewn and glued together, and propelled by double-bladed oars, these impressive water craft, measuring 3.7 to 9.1 meters in length, would shoot across the Santa Barbara Channel reaping pelagic fish and sea mammals, and transporting people and cargoes between the Channel Islands and the mainland. The coastal region supported relatively populous villages with large dome-shaped thatched houses, semisubterranean sweatlodges, fenced ceremonial enclosures, and formal cemeteries. A high degree of craft specialization developed in the region, where artisans produced magnificent stone mortars, chipped stone blades, and shell beads and ornaments, as well as steatite pots, pipes, and effigies by the thousands. The southernmost groups made excellent ceramic vessels in gray, brown, and red. As described by early Spanish accounts, the largest villages supported celebrated chiefs and a complex system of sociopolitical ranking. Southern coast peoples participated in the Chinigchinich cult, in which the ingestion of the Toloache plant (jimsonweed) induced hallucinations and visions.

POLITY

Alfred Kroeber defined the *tribelet* as the basic political unit of Native California outside the Northwest and Colorado River culture areas. Initially describing these units as "village communities" in his 1925 *Handbook of the Indians of California,* he later developed more fully the concept of the tribelet, beginning with his 1932 publication, *The Patwin and their Neighbors* (Kroeber 1932). Kroeber eventually outlined four characteristics of this native polity that made it unique among North American Indians (see, e.g., Kroeber 1966).

First, as the largest autonomous or self-governing political unit, a tribelet consisted of a village community composed of a principal village, which often served as the sociopolitical center, and a cluster of smaller outlying hamlets. This settlement cluster or village community was the largest political grouping over which local leaders had recognized authority (Kroeber 1966:94–95). Most tribelets recognized one or more chiefs or headmen, with the dominant leader residing in the principal village, and lesser chiefs or heads in nearby hamlets. Kroeber (1966:107) believed that these chiefs had "next to no true authority," and that they led more by example and skilled oration. Their duties involved presiding over feasts, sponsoring ceremonies, settling quarrels, and addressing community assemblies. Kroeber (1966:106–107) downplayed the role of economic specialists and political retainers in most tribelets, arguing that all members participated in hunting and gathering activities.

Second, the tribelet was the largest landowning group in most of Native California. Tribelet territories varied considerably in size; size depended largely on the topography and productivity of the land, but was typically less than several hundred square kilometers. People could walk from the principal village to the tribelet's boundary within one-half to one day. A major implication of having such small territories was that the larger ethnolinguistic units defined by anthropologists actually comprised many autonomous tribelets.

> In any strict usage, the word "tribe" denotes a group of people that act together, feel themselves to be a unit, and are sovereign in a defined territory. Now, in California, these traits attached to the Masut Pomo, once again to the Elem Pomo, to the Yokaia Pomo, and to the 30 other Pomo tribelets. They did not attach to the Pomo as a whole, because the Pomo as a whole did not act or govern themselves, or hold land as a unit. In other words, there was strictly no such tribal entity as "the Pomo": there were 34 miniature tribes. (Kroeber 1966:100)

Third, the tribelet was a demographically small-scale entity. Kroeber (1925) initially defined the population of most village communities as averaging only about one hundred people. In later years, however, after more memory culture interviews had been completed, he argued that the size of most tribelets ranged between one hundred and five hundred people, usually averaging about 250 individuals (Kroeber 1966:92). He estimated that about five hundred to six hundred tribelets were once distributed across Native California.

Finally, there was some speculation that unilineal descent groups, especially those defining membership along the male line, might have been a basic organizational feature of many tribelets. Kroeber, somewhat ambivalent about this possibility, noted that "California was long regarded as a region lacking clans, group totems or other exogamous social units." (Kroeber 1922:287). But he candidly admitted that "more recent information, however, due mainly to the investigations of E. W. Gifford, shows that some form of gentile organization was prevalent among nearly all groups from the Miwok south to the Yuma" (Kroeber 1922:287–288).[2] Edward Gifford (1918; 1926) and Duncan Strong (1929), in undertaking field research among Indian groups in central and southern California (e.g., Sierra Miwok, Serrano, Cahuilla, Cupeño, and Luiseño), found indications of patrilineal lineages or clans, and also the complementary existence (in some cases) of totemic moieties that played a critical role in the ceremonial and social life of local communities. Strong (1929) noted that some of the patrilineal lineages were grouped into larger clans associated with a group priest, ceremonial house, and sacred bundle. Gifford (1926) proposed, in fact, that patrilineal lineages (along with the possibility of a few matrilineal lineages) were an integral part of the body politic of Native California, and that in prehistoric times these formed widespread autonomous political units that eventually became integrated into tribelet organizations.

REVISIONISTS' PERSPECTIVES

The conceptual framework of language, culture area, and polity constructed by Kroeber and other early anthropologists still permeates most interpretations of Native Californian societies. But I hasten to add that these concepts have not gone unchallenged through the years—they have been criticized and debated. Although my purpose in discussing the Kroeberian model is to outline how early anthropologists perceived the "pure" essence of "untainted" Native California societies, I find it illuminating to consider these critiques. Keep in mind that some anthropological constructs that influenced how federal Indian agents and other government agents would evaluate and classify descendant Indian communities many decades ago have undergone modification and refinement in recent years.

A new generation of anthropologists, infused with theoretical principles from cultural ecology and cultural evolution, revised the conceptual underpinnings of California anthropology in the 1960s and 1970s. These revisionist thinkers questioned the idea that native Californians were passive hunter-gatherers who simply collected the fruits of a "wild" and "pristine" land. Instead they viewed California Indians as nurturing land managers who constructed an anthropogenic landscape through deliberate human intervention over the course of many thousands of years. The revisionists credited native peoples with creating and maintaining various kinds of productive habitats through fire management, tillage, pruning, broadcasting of seeds, weeding, and conservation practices (see, e.g., Bean and Lawton 1976; Lewis 1973; Shipek 1977).

This innovative perspective of hunter-gatherer practices went hand in hand with new ideas pertaining to the body politic of California Indians. Revisionist scholars argued that by intentionally manipulating indigenous plant communities, such as grasslands and oak woodlands, local hunter-gatherers increased the yields per hectare of wild seed and nut crops (e.g., Bean and Lawton 1976). Such "proto-agricultural" practices, it was argued, in turn supported powerful hereditary elites on a scale never acknowledged by Kroeber and his colleagues. According to this perspective, the political and religious specialists who constituted this elite class amassed surplus goods, financed lavish feasts and elaborate ceremonies, sponsored craft specialists and retainers, and participated in farflung regional exchange networks (see papers in Bean and Blackburn 1976; Bean and King 1974).

Although scholars entertained new ideas about the political organization of California Indians, Kroeber's tribelet model was not scuttled but remained a core component of revisionist thinking. Most scholars still appreciated the tribelet as a meaningful concept, so long as the definition of Native California polities was broadened to include the following three refinements.

1. The upper range of the populations and territories under the control of tribelet leaders was expanded from Kroeber's original estimates. Bean (1976:101) noted that the population of a tribelet could be well over a thousand people in productive places, and that tribelet territories could range between 130 square kilometers (50 square miles) and 15,600 square kilometers (6000 square miles) in size.

2. The hierarchical organization of some tribelets was championed. Lowell Bean and others proposed that high-ranking elite families maintained control of tribelet communities, serving as political administrators, religious leaders, and intertribelet brokers. Below the elite class came the economic specialists, such as basket makers, traders, clamshell disk bead producers—some of whom were organized into exclusive craft guilds. Commoners occupied the bottom rung of the tribelets, caught up in the day-to-day activities of hunting and gathering practices. In some cases, slaves may have been kept by tribelets. Bean (1976) argued that most hierarchical positions were ascribed at birth, and that little social mobility probably existed for most tribelet members.

3. Renewed attention was focused on the possibility that broader political organizations, including political confederacies and tribelet alliances that spanned extensive territories, might have extended beyond the level of single tribelets (Bean 1976:103; Bean and Lawton 1976:46). Anthropologists contemplated larger-scale polities that administered extensive populations under a united political organization. They now entertained the possibility that complex chiefdoms once flourished in the rich coastal environments of central and southern California, especially in the Chumash-speaking homeland.

Today, many archaeological and ethnohistorical studies are focused on the nature of "complex hunter-gatherers" in coastal California—the rise and elaboration of sophisticated coastal economies, extensive trade networks, craft specialization, and incipient political hierarchies (see Arnold 1995, 2001; Glassow 1996, 1997; Johnson 1982, 1988; Jones 1992; Lightfoot 1997a; Moss and Erlandson 1995; Raab 1996; and Raab et al. 1994). The southern coast witnessed the rise of probably the most elaborate social and political hierarchies in California. Ample evidence exists for the specialized production of microblades, shell beads, steatite ollas, bowls, and effigies that were widely traded across the islands, coastal mainland, and interior (see, e.g., Arnold 1992, 2001; Gamble 1991:432–433; Heizer and Treganza 1971). Bioarchaeological analyses of cemeteries document the rise of elite families or lineages who maintained differential access to bead wealth, plank canoes, and other key resources as a consequence of ascribed status (e.g., Gamble et al. 2001).[3]

Scholars today recognize that the ethnographic data collected by early Berkeley anthropologists represent a treasure trove of information on Native Californian societies. Yet, in appreciating the significance and monumental efforts of this fieldwork, they also recognize problems that underlie reconstructions of the past based on memory culture interviews (see Kunkel 1974; McLendon and Oswalt 1978:276–277). Kroeberian anthropology perpetuates a synchronic view of Native Californians captured forever in the "ethnographic present," with no appreciation of their deep and diverse histories. Kroeber believed he could reconstruct a baseline for aboriginal California peoples using the memory culture methodology, because he assumed that little change had taken place in these cultures over time. But this assumption is no longer tenable, given archaeological findings of histories that extend back twelve thousand years or more for some Native California peoples.[4]

Early anthropologists underestimated the full effects of early European contact on Native Californian societies (e.g., Kroeber 1923). Their memory culture interviews were based on the assumption that elders born before the Gold Rush would provide a window into aboriginal times, especially in areas beyond the Spanish/Mexican and Russian colonial frontiers. Yet significant cultural transformations associated with European contact may have taken place at a much earlier date. European exploration of California's coast began in 1542 with the Cabrillo-Ferrelo voyage, and contact between foreign sailors and coastal hunter-gatherers continued to take place over the next sixty years. These encounters may have unleashed deadly epidemics, initiated new kinds of trade relations, and fostered innovations in ceremonial practices that could have had far-reaching repercussions along California's coast and beyond.[5]

Furthermore, there are significant problems in using classic California ethnographies in diachronic research. In order to reconstruct an aboriginal baseline, Kroeber and his colleagues collapsed or conflated observations from different ethnohistorical sources and native interviews into a monolithic account, which was then projected back into prehistory. This conflation of time renders these ethnographic reconstructions notoriously difficult to use in the study of culture change. I have become frustrated on more than one occasion because it is not clear whether specific observations depicting social practices, house types, or ceremonial gatherings were about the early twentieth, late nineteenth, or mid-nineteenth centuries, or even earlier times (see, for example, Lightfoot et al. 1991:121–145). In reality, the memory culture methodology probably reveals more about the generation of Indians and anthropologists of the late nineteenth and early twentieth century than about some idealized precolonial past.

THE IMPACT OF KROEBERIAN ANTHROPOLOGY

Alfred Kroeber and other early anthropologists left an enduring legacy about California Indian societies. Even though later scholars advanced revisions to the Kroeberian model, most of its basic concepts involving language, culture area, and polity continue to be widely used. Almost any book on California Indians will include an updated reproduction of Kroeber's classic map of ethnolinguist units, and discussion of tribelet organizations (see, for example, Heizer 1978a; Heizer and Elsasser 1980; Heizer and Whipple 1971; Rawls 1984; and Rawls and Bean 1998). What makes coastal California truly unique is that this coast was one of the most densely populated regions in all of native North America (see, for example, Kroeber 1939:143), yet the majority of its settlements and polities continue to be viewed as small-scale entities. The limitedness of the territories of most tribelets has fostered a common perception that Native Californians were extremely provincial in their movements and attitudes. No one has said this better than Robert Heizer (1978d:649):

> California . . . was a region holding a large number of societies that
> had limited knowledge, understanding, experience, and tolerance of
> neighboring peoples. California Indians, while perhaps knowing indi-
> viduals in neighboring tribelets, for the most part lived out their lives
> mainly within their own limited and familiar territory. Nothing illus-
> trates more the deep-seated provincialism and attachment to the place
> of their birth of California Indians than the abundantly documented
> wish for persons who died away from home to have their bodies (or
> their ashes if the distance was too great) returned for burial at their
> natal village. Living out the span of existence from birth to death with-
> in an area bounded by a horizon lying not more than 10 or 15 miles
> from one's village and not having talked to more than 100 different
> persons in a whole life must have made one's world small, familiar,
> safe and secure.

A common perception emerged that most native people did not travel more than a few kilometers from their birthplace, that they did not interact much with "foreigners," that social networks did not extend much beyond the tribelet boundary, and that each polity was homogenous with regard to the linguistic and cultural backgrounds of its members (see Leventhal et al. 1994:300–305). Ethnographers noted that Indian elders often knew the stories behind every named rock and landmark in their territory, and could recite creation stories and myths about how their ancestors had played a part in the creation and early use of the landscape (Kroeber 1925:472–473, 656–660; Ortiz 1994; Oswalt 1966); the fact that the elders were so familiar with the cultural topography of their local lands contributed to the perception of hyper-parochialism.

Thus, Kroeber and his colleagues created a world of traditional California Indians that focused "tribal" identity at the scale of the local community. This vision of native societies was like an image of many multicolored billiard balls glued onto the landscape, their hard, almost impenetrable bodies each containing a homogenous population. The scene painted in the opening paragraphs of this chapter illustrates this concept of small, sharply bounded native polities replicated across the coastal zone. Each would have had its own ceremonial center, village cluster, and outlying territories for hunting, fishing, and gathering. Each would have had its own political and religious leaders and renowned craftspeople.

That tribal identity became fused in the early anthropological literature with a local community of less than five hundred people had significant implications for how native peoples were defined and treated in the aftermath of Spanish/Mexican and Russian colonization: "Indian" identity became associated with the specific repertoire of languages, cultural practices, food ways, and ceremonies that characterized individual village communities. As we will see, how closely native groups conformed to this anthropological model would greatly influence their chances for federal recognition and their acceptance as "true" Native Californians.

3 Franciscan Missions in Alta California

My quest to visit all twenty-one Franciscan missions in Alta California led me to La Purísima Mission State Historic Park on an unseasonably warm day in early November 2001. This magnificent park preserves the buildings and grounds of the second site of Mission La Purísima Concepción. Initially founded in 1787 in what is now Lompoc, California, this mission (the eleventh one constructed in Alta California) was moved five kilometers north to its present location after a devastating earthquake in 1812. On the day of my visit, the core of the mission complex—the remarkable church, cemetery grounds, *convento,* chapel, craft shops, and residences for soldiers and mission overseers—was full of tourists, most of us dressed in our native costume of sneakers, blue jeans, brightly printed Hawaiian shirts, and wide-brimmed straw hats. As Roberta and I ambled through the buildings, the size and extent of the adobe structures, with many of the rooms furnished with period artifacts, impressed us.[1]

What made the La Purísima experience truly memorable, however, was the hike beyond the reconstructed mission core to the local environs where neophytes once toiled at agrarian activities.[2] Following a nicely maintained interpretive trail, we viewed the foundations of the neophyte barracks, excavated by Professor James Deetz and students from the University of California, Santa Barbara, in the early 1960s. We explored the springhouse containing a filter system of sand to purify water from nearby springs and reservoirs, water that was then channeled through underground clay pipes to the central fountain of the mission. Off the beaten path, we found the rectangular foundations of the old tanning vats unearthed by Professor Deetz and his students. Our exploration also allowed us to inspect the notorious "mystery column" excavated in the late 1990s by Professor Robert Hoover and students from California Polytechnic State University.[3] But what made the most impact on me were the many hectares of agricultural fields, their old dams and water channels still in place. As I looked back at the plowed fields, agrarian structures, aqueduct system, neophyte-barrack foundations, and distant church and other buildings, the full magnitude of all these missions swept into view. It struck me, in the dying twilight of that day, how meticulously the Franciscans had designed the mission complexes to serve as massive enculturation machines—monumental agricultural and craft centers where they would attempt to transform Native Californians into Catholic peasants.

THE FOUNDING OF THE MISSIONS

California is unique in the United States in that its initial period of European exploration and contact with natives was not followed by European settlement for many years. The first coastal explorations took place when Spanish and English ships, during five separate voyages (i.e., the Cabrillo-Ferrelo, Drake, Unamuno, Cermeño, and Vizcaíno expeditions), visited the southern and central coasts (between 1542 and 1603).[4]

With the colonization of the Philippine Islands and the flowering of the Manila trade in the late 1500s, the Spanish Crown entertained the idea of establishing a port in Alta California.[5] A protected harbor with dock facilities would provide sanctuary for the lumbering 300–500-ton Manila galleons, loaded with spices, silks, velvets, gold and silver jewelry, and other valued goods, as they made their long trek across the Pacific Ocean, following the northern Japanese Current, en route to Acapulco, New Spain.

The early coastal explorers had frequent encounters with local Indians while mapping the coastline, filling water casks, collecting firewood, and taking possession of the land for the Christian monarchs. The first glimpses of the European ships and men elicited surprise and much astonishment among the Indians. But emissaries and leaders from various polities soon greeted the voyagers—typically making long welcoming speeches, then exchanging food and goods, and then issuing invitations to visit the native villages. The voyagers' accounts describe meetings with local Indian communities where men and women danced, traded foods and craft goods, and even incorporated the Europeans in native ceremonies and rites.[6]

Then for over one hundred years there was silence from the bearded strangers. The Spanish Crown, weighing financial and political factors, abandoned plans to build a permanent port in Alta California to service the Manila galleons. With the termination of official Spanish exploration, no recorded interactions took place between native peoples and Europeans in California until the late 1700s. After the spurt of early voyages, probably Native Californians would spy an occasional Manila galleon sailing south within sight of land; no doubt some ships made landfalls to repair leaks after the Pacific crossing and to take on fresh water. Shipwrecks and foundering vessels probably washed up on California shores during and after turbulent storms.[7] But we know little about these encounters.

Thus, the "second coming" of the Spanish to Alta California in 1769 must have been an impressive, but unexpected, sight for native peoples. Under the capable leadership of Gaspar de Portolá, the first overland exploration of California took place from the missions in Baja California to San Diego Bay. This was quickly followed by Portolá's famous trek to the margins of San Francisco Bay, in search of the "Port of Monterey" so glowingly described by Sebastian Vizcaíno and his chief pilot (Francisco Bolaño) in their 1602–03 voyage. Natives watching from nearby chaparral thickets and oak woodlands would have first glimpsed the Spanish scouts on horseback, scouring the countryside in search of the best routes northward and for sources of potable water, pasture, and firewood. Spanish trailblazers followed, laboring with spades, picks, crowbars, and axes to build a rough trail for the main contingent of well-armed "leather-jacket" (soldados de cuera) soldiers and officers, Christian Indians from Baja California, and a handful of Franciscan padres. The rear guard consisted of armed soldiers and sweating muleteers who drove lines of pack mules burdened with food, tools, and equipment for sustaining the expedition and for building new settlements in Alta California.

Portolá followed a colonization plan crafted by José de Gálvez, the visitador general (inspector general) for Spain's North American colonies, with the support of Marqués de Croix, Viceroy of New Spain. Gálvez had been assigned by the king of Spain, Carlos III, to implement some of his Bourbon reforms, which Gálvez began when he arrived in New Spain in 1765 (see Weber 1992:215–242). These reforms included modernizing the bureaucratic structure of the frontier government and reducing costs, as well as shoring up the defense of the northern frontiers from hostile natives and European powers. The Russians were of special concern to the Spanish Crown.[8] Disconcerting rumors had spread among the Madrid court for several years about Russian expansion into the North Pacific.

Finally, in 1767 the Spanish ambassador in Moscow sent word that the Russians had allegedly landed somewhere in North America; the size of the Russian force was reported to be sufficiently large to have sustained three hundred casualties at the hands of the Indians (Hutchinson 1969:5). News of Russia's transgression solidified Spain's decision to colonize Alta California, thereby creating a buffer zone to keep the valuable mines and economic enterprises of the northern provinces of New Spain out of harm's way from the expanding Russian frontier, as well as from the ever-restless British (Weber 1992:238–239).

The colonization of Alta California was intimately linked to existing Spanish settlements along both sides of the Gulf of California. Inching northward from central Mexico in the 1560s and 1570s, and gaining momentum in the 1600s and early 1700s, Spanish colonists established presidios, missions, and mining towns (known as *reales*) in Sinaloa and Sonora. The discovery of gold and silver unleashed a boom economy (though one with occasional busts) that attracted newcomers. Although previous attempts to settle nearby Baja California had been thwarted in the 1530s and in 1685, a Jesuit mission frontier finally took root in 1697, with missions branching ever northward by the mid-1700s.[9] The Baja missions would serve as stepping stones into Alta California, and the founding population of soldiers and settlers in the new frontier would be recruited mostly from Sinaloa, Sonora, and Baja California (Mason 1998:65–68).

The Gálvez and Croix plan called for the construction of a port facility and a small fleet of ships at San Blas (south of Sinaloa on the Pacific coast) that would service the California colonies (Stanger and Brown 1969:29–30).[10] The first duty of the ships would be to ferry reinforcements and bulk supplies (food, building equipment) to San Diego Bay, where they would rendezvous with Portolá and his land expedition, which was setting out from the northernmost Baja California missions. Portolá had been instructed to erect a presidio and mission at the "Port of San Diego" and the "Port of Monterey," as well as to build a third settlement complex halfway between the two ports, where a mission was to be founded and named San Buenaventura (Palóu 1955:54). The presidios would house soldiers and civil government officials, including the governor (who, in the early years, was typically a military official). The missions would support the ecclesiastical side of the new colonies, with the padres placed in charge of the spiritual and temporal needs of the Indians (Jackson and Castillo 1995:27).

Missions had played a pivotal role in Spanish settlement in the Americas for more than two-and-one-half centuries, with the Franciscans establishing missions in New Spain beginning in 1524 (Garr 1972:292; Hanson 1995:16). But by 1769, some Spanish administrators and at least one bishop believed missions had outlived their usefulness as colonial institutions, arguing that they were ineffectual for converting natives to Christianity and that they retarded commercial development in frontier zones (see Guest 1978:100–106; Hutchinson 1969:70–73). Gálvez and Croix faced a difficult situation—how to neutralize a heavily populated region located some distance from the Hispanic settlements of New Spain.[11] The low-cost solution was to turn once again to the missionaries, because they provided a settlement strategy both inexpensive and tailor-made for densely populated coastal areas (see, e.g., Garr 1972:292–293; Weber 1992:242).

The missionaries tapped for service in Alta California had received their training in the College of San Fernando in Mexico City, first established by the Franciscan order in 1733. Known as the *Fernandinos*, they cultivated a reputation as tough task masters in the founding of missionary colonies. Recruited primarily from Spain to attend the seminary in Mexico City, they had great spiritual zeal, political savvy, and a traditional approach to the proselytization of natives that set them apart from other Catholic missionaries of the late 1700s and early 1800s (Guest 1978; Servin 1965:130). The founding fathers of the Alta California missions, including Fathers Junípero Serra, Francisco Palóu, and Juan Crespi, received their initial missionary posts in Sierra Gorda (Querétaro, Mexico), where they cut their teeth working with native peoples. The padres then took over administration of the Jesuit missions in Baja California, after the Spanish Crown expelled the Society of Jesus from its colonial domains in 1767. The Fernandinos wasted no time pushing the envelope of the northern frontier, founding in 1768 their own mission, San Fernando de Velicatá, only 480 kilometers south of San Diego Bay (Mason 1998:18). After using the peninsular settlements as critical logistical bases in their initial establishment of missions at the Port of San Diego and Port of Monterey, the Franciscans released the Baja missions to the Dominican Order in 1772 in order to concentrate their efforts on the Alta California frontier.[12]

Under the adept direction of their first Father President, Junípero Serra, the Franciscans created a mission system in Alta California that was notable for its rapid growth. Although the initial Gálvez and Croix plan authorized the construction of only three missions, as soon as Father Serra stepped foot in California as part of the Portolá land expedition, he mounted a tireless campaign for more missions and more padres (see Palóu 1955:101–102). He envisioned a chain of missions that would settle the entire population of coastal hunter-gatherers in southern and central California into Christian communities: "If placed at proper intervals—say every twenty-five leagues, more or less, like the ones nearby—they would form from San Diego to here [Mission San Carlos], stepping stones, so that every third day one might sleep in a village. With that, peace would be assured, and passage through all the country made easy; and a postal service may be established" (letter of Father Serra to Viceroy Bucareli, August 24, 1774) (Serra 1955a:143).

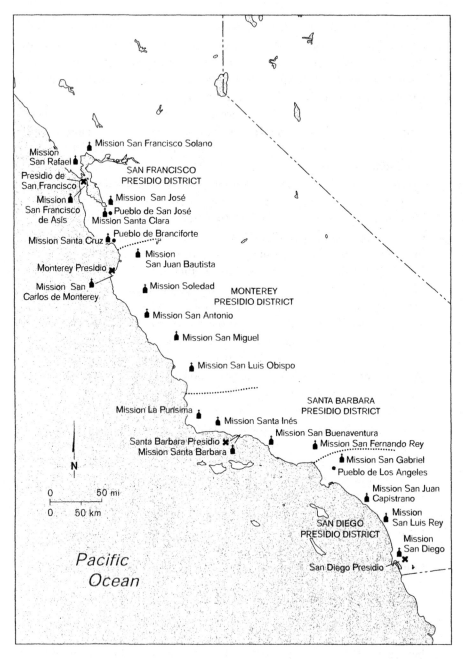

Map 7.   Presidio districts of Alta California. The twenty-one Franciscan missions were divided into four presidio districts. The boundary (dotted) lines dividing the districts are only approximate.

The construction of missions took place in growth spurts, depending upon available funding, whether padres and soldiers could be found to serve within the missions, and whether the Fernandinos could obtain permission and assistance from civil authorities in New Spain and California. Father Serra focused his efforts on maximizing the overall extent of the mission system. He laid the groundwork for the spatial structure of the entire system, which was divided into four presidio districts (San Diego, Santa Barbara, Monterey, San Francisco) oriented in a line paralleling the coastline from south to north (map 7). Within each presidio district, soldiers and padres first founded a military fort and nearby mission; in subsequent years, the Fernandinos placed additional missions on a roughly north/south line radiating out at greater distances from the initial pair of settlements.

Father Serra oversaw the founding of the first missions paired with presidios in each of the four districts, as well as some additional missions. In the southernmost San Diego Presidio District, he worked on Mission San Diego (1769), as well as Mission San Gabriel (1771) and Mission San Juan Capistrano (1776). In the Santa Barbara Presidio District, he realized his dream of establishing Mission San Buenaventura (1782) in Chumash-speaking country, in the same year that the presidio was founded. In the Monterey Presidio District, he directed the construction of Mission San Carlos de Monterey (1770), as well as Mission San Antonio (1771) and Mission San Luis Obispo (1772). In the northernmost Presidio District of San Francisco, he promoted the construction of Mission San Francisco de Asís (1776) in conjunction with the presidio, as well as nearby Mission Santa Clara (1777).

After Father Serra's death, in 1784, the second Father President, Fermín Lasuén, plugged the extant holes in the mission chain. Under his capable leadership were completed the last mission (Mission San Luis Rey 1798) in the San Diego Presidio District, all but one of the remaining missions in the Santa Barbara Presidio District (Mission Santa Barbara 1786, Mission La Purísima 1787, Mission San Fernando Rey 1797), the three remaining missions (Mission Soledad 1791, Mission San Miguel 1797, Mission San Juan Bautista 1797) in the Monterey Presidio District, and two additional missions (Mission Santa Cruz 1791, Mission San José 1797) in the San Francisco Presidio District.[13] The last three missions were founded in the 1800s: Mission Santa Inés (1804) in the Santa Barbara Presidio District, and Mission San Rafael (1817) and Mission San Francisco Solano (1823) in the San Francisco Presidio District.

Designed to be self-sufficient agrarian communities, the mission complexes supported from five hundred to twelve hundred Indian neophytes.

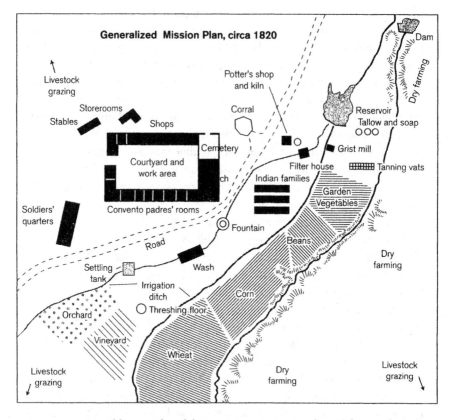

Figure 1. Spatial layout of model Franciscan mission in Alta California, about 1820. The neophyte village(s), soldiers' quarters, specialized craft shops, and diverse agricultural features were situated near the mission quadrangle. (Reproduced from Costello and Hornbeck [1989:312]. Used by permission of the Smithsonian Institution Press.)

Although each mission had its unique architectural history and distinctive characteristics, Father Serra and Father Lasuén standardized the overall spatial layout of the missions. Each mission complex, which took more than twenty or even thirty years to develop fully, resembled the following idealized description (e.g., Costello 1989a:88–91; Costello and Hornbeck 1989:310–313; Hoover 1985):[14] the central quadrangle, built around an enclosed interior courtyard, contained the church, the *convento* (or apartments for the two resident padres), visitors' quarters, kitchens, storage rooms, craft production areas, and the *monjerio* (dormitories for young girls and unmarried women). (See figure 1.) However, frequent earthquakes, which caused damage to almost all of the missions at one time or another, did facilitate modifications to this basic design. For example, after the 1812 earthquake, the second site of Mission La Purísima was rebuilt in a linear rather than a quadrangular pattern (Costello and Hornbeck 1989:312; Farris and Wheeler 1998:4).

The Franciscans usually located the neophyte village(s) for married couples and families outside the main quadrangle (figure 2). Traditional pole-and-thatch houses distinguished the architecture of these villages until adobe barracks or structures could be built. However, Farris (1991) and Farris and Wheeler (1998:13) emphasize that chronic housing shortages existed at most missions and that only a small percentage of Indian families lived, at any one time, in the adobe structures. The families resided in linear apartment blocks, usually one room wide and divided into single-room apartments. Archaeological and documentary research indicates that most apartments had a small front yard, front door, central interior hearth, back window, and back yard (Allen 1998:30–38; Farris 1991:22–27; Hoover and Costello 1985:8–20). Some exceptions to this architectural plan existed, such as at Mission La Purísima, where neophytes lived in apartment suites divided into two separate rooms (Deetz 1963:177–179; Farris and Wheeler 1998:12–13).[15] The padres also placed the residences for the *escolta*, or mission guard, usually consisting of a corporal and five soldiers, outside the quadrangle, typically on the side opposite the neophyte village (Costello and Hornbeck 1989:310).

The landscape in the near hinterland contained corrals; irrigation complexes of reservoirs, dams, and canals; walled gardens; *lavanderías* (fountains where the Indians bathed and washed clothes); and irrigated fields where vegetables, fruits, grapes, and grains were grown.[16] The near hinterland also contained various industrial work areas and structures, such as pottery kilns, tanning vats, grist mills, etc.[17] In the more distant hinterland were situated fields for dry farming, and open range for grazing cattle, horses, and sheep. Much of the outlying territory was organized into ranchos where livestock was raised and some agriculture undertaken. For example, San Gabriel Mission, one of the largest and most productive missions, boasted seventeen ranchos for horses and cattle, and fifteen ranchos for sheep, goats, and pigs (Phillips 1975:26–27). Mission stations, or *asistencias*, were also established in the outlying hinterland where chapels were built to service the rancho workers. Auguste Duhaut-Cilly (1999:115) described four ranchos of Mission San Luis Rey in June 1827 as each consisting of "an Indian village, a house for the *mayordomo* who acts as manager, suitable storehouses for the harvests, and a fine chapel. Every Sunday these stewards come to the mission to report to the padre on the week's work and on the condition of the rancho." There is also some indication, based on

Figure 2.   View of Mission San Luis Rey by Auguste Duhaut-Cilly, 1827. In the foreground is the neophyte village or rancheria. Duhaut-Cilly (1999:114–115) described the village as consisting "of thatched huts of different shapes but most of them conical, scattered or grouped in no planned order over a large expanse of ground. Each holds one family, and all of them together contained at that time a population of more than two thousand people." (Courtesy of the Bancroft Library, University of California, Berkeley.)

Archibald Menzies's description of the hinterland of the Presidio of Monterey in 1792, that "outposts" were sometimes placed some distance inland, where soldiers were stationed to keep an eye on the movements of the "wild" or "gentile" Indian population (Menzies 1924:294).

The Spanish Crown established three pueblos in Alta California (Los Angeles, 1781, San José, 1797, and Branciforte, 1797). But the recruitment of colonists continued to be difficult, not only because of the isolation of this northernmost frontier, but because of Spain's monopolistic economic policies outlawing trade with any merchants other than those authorized by the Crown.[18] Although the pueblos provided some support to the presidio communities, missions remained the primary suppliers of basic food and goods in the Spanish frontier. When the Franciscan padres sold goods to the presidios, they received credit that could be redeemed in Mexico City through a purchasing agent. This allowed the Fernandinos to purchase goods that could not otherwise be produced in Alta California, including "prayer books, trade beads, woolen blankets, fine cloth, paper products, cooking spices, and wine, chocolate, and rice" (Hackel 1997:117).

With the rebellion in New Spain beginning in 1810, California became even more isolated from Spain, as the supply ships from San Blas rarely sailed anymore.[19] The missions remained the primary economic engine, as the population of the presidios and pueblos became increasingly dependent on the missions for food, goods, and labor. The Fernandinos cultivated trade connections with foreign merchants to obtain specialized goods that could not be produced in Alta California. The friars participated in smuggling cattle products to American and British merchant ships, and they took part in a black market system with the newly arrived Russians at Colony Ross, as discussed later.

With Mexico declaring its independence from Spain in 1821, representatives of the new government arrived in California the following year to take over governance and to win the allegiance of its colonists (Hutchinson 1969:96–123). The new government lifted trade restrictions with foreign merchants, legally opening access to a plethora of goods from around the world.[20] There is some debate among contemporary scholars about the implications of legalized trade for the mission communities, especially for the neophyte populations.[21] However, it is clear that there was tremendous variability in the output of agrarian and livestock products in individual missions (see especially Costello 1989b, 1992). The emergence of the Mexican Republic marked the beginning of the end of the padres' economic and political domination of Alta California. Representatives of the Mexican government questioned the authority of the church and began advocating for the release of mission lands. Resentment also brewed among the Hispanic residents of California, self-identified as the *Californios*, about the stranglehold the Fernandinos had on the best arable land in the coastal zone. Various steps taken in the late 1820s eventually led to the secularization of the Franciscan missions in 1834–36, an issue that I will return to later.

DIMENSIONS OF COLONIAL ENCOUNTERS: THE POLICIES AND PRACTICES OF THE PADRES

The Enculturation Program

The cornerstone of the missionary enterprise in Alta California was a directed enculturation program designed to transform the population of pagan Native Californians into a peasant class of Hispanicized laborers. The Franciscans indoctrinated the neophytes into the Catholic faith, taught them European crafts and trades, and forced them to alter their traditional work habits, subsistence practices, dress, and menu.[22] They viewed these neophytes as *sin razón*, people who had not attained the age of reason, a view that justified their treatment as children dependent on the friars for their temporal and spiritual needs (Monroy 1990:44–45). With the exception of crimes of physical violence (e.g., murder, assault, battery), which were handled by civilian authorities, every aspect of the daily lives of the neophytes came under the controlling scrutiny of the padres.

The padres subjected the neophytes to a rigid schedule (time discipline) of prayers, meals, work, and more prayers, announced by the ceaseless tolling of the mission bells (La Pérouse 1989:81; Monroy 1990:53). The basic daily schedule appears to have varied little during the mission period, as described in accounts of the missions from the late 1700s through the 1820s (Geiger and Meighan 1976:82–83; Golovnin 1979:147; Kotzebue 1830:95–96; La Pérouse 1989:82–91; Lütke 1989:267; Perez 1988:81–82; Schabelski 1993:6) (figure 3). The day typically began with the morning bell at sunup for mass and prayers, followed by a meal of *atole* (a soup of barley meal or other grains); then work commenced and lasted until the bell tolled at noon, when a meal of *pozole* (a thick soup of wheat, maize, peas, and beans) was consumed. The neophytes returned to work after lunch and labored until about sunset, when they went to church for evening prayers, for about an hour, before breaking for a final communal meal of *atole*. About one hour after this meal, the padres locked up for the night those women whose husbands were gone, the young unmarried women, and children over the age of about seven. On Sundays and Feast Days (which could account for ninety-two days of the year), the neophytes did not work (Hackel 1997:122); however, they were required to attend four to five hours of masses and prayers.

The padres employed a variety of coercive measures, including solitary confinement, whippings, stocks, and leg chains, to punish neophytes for infractions against the work schedule and moral code (Archibald 1978:176; Guest 1966:199–204; Jackson and Castillo 1995:81–85; Monroy 1990:85–88). The liberal use of corporal punishment, and the common practice of placing Indians in irons, in the missions and presidios made a very negative impression on many European visitors to Alta California (Duhaut-Cilly 1999:92–95; Golovnin 1979:147–148; Kotzebue 1830:95; Lütke 1989:267–268). In his analysis of Franciscan punishment, Guest (1983; 1989) stresses that whippings usually involved a rope, a lariat, a pliable reed or cane, or a discipline (a whip made of rope, typically with two or more strands thickened with knots) on a person's bare back, usually for no more than twenty-five lashes. However, although the general rule was not to draw blood, the padres implemented the punishment differentially, and some could be quite cruel (see Guest 1966:204–205).

Figure 3. Visit of Jean Francois de La Pérouse to Mission San Carlos de Monterey in 1786. La Pérouse (1989:77) observed that "[b]efore we entered the church, we had passed through a square in which the Indians of both sexes were ranged in a line. They exhibited no marks of surprise in their countenance, and left us in doubt whether we should be the subject of their conversation for the rest of the day." (Courtesy of the Bancroft Library, University of California, Berkeley.)

Neophytes could not leave the mission complexes without the explicit permission of the padres. Those who escaped into the bush were pursued and either persuaded to return through negotiation or brought back by force (Milliken 1995:96–97). The six soldiers stationed at each mission, who comprised the *escolta*, as well as nearby presidio soldiers, served to enforce the mission indoctrination program and helped hunt down neophyte fugitives. They also protected the missions from hostile foreigners and native rebellions.

The Fernandinos focused their enculturation program on young children. Adults who converted to the Catholic faith often maintained their Indian cultural beliefs, values, and identities, which the padres found almost impossible to erase. Consequently, the indoctrination of children began at a young age. The padres separated them from their parents and any elderly relatives. Young girls of between seven and nine years old moved out of their family residences to a dormitory or *monjerio,* where they stayed until married (Monroy 1990:59; Perez 1988:81; Voss 2000). Some young girls worked in elite Hispanic households where they received training in sewing and other domestic tasks (Osio 1996:134). The padres sometimes placed young boys and unmarried men in separate dormitories as well (Archibald 1978:174; Guest 1989:11).[23] The separation of the young children from the elders of their tribes was a calculated move by the padres to accelerate the acculturation process and destroy Indian culture (Sanchez 1995:85).

The spatial organization of the missions facilitated the implementation of the enculturation program and the tight control of the young neophyte population. The padres assigned neophytes to specific residential quarters based on sex, age, and marital status (Archibald 1978:174; Voss 2000). They placed the young and unmarried closest to the tightly secured mission quadrangle but located older, married people outside this central space, usually in the neophyte village. The quadrangle incorporated the women's dormitory, usually built within full view of the padres' quarters. All the rooms on the quadrangle were focused toward the interior patio, and only the padres' rooms looked beyond the mission walls (Sanchez 1995:72). People obtained access to the enclosed patio only through the church, the *convento,* and one or two secure passageways (Costello 1989a:88; Menzies 1924:272; see the eyewitness accounts by Vancouver 1954:24; Zavalishin 1973:380).

The missions resembled penal institutions in many respects, with the practice of locking up some neophytes at night and restricting movements outside the mission grounds, the use of corporal punishment, and the relatively tight control of behavior. Some Russian visitors portrayed them as dungeons or forts where the Franciscans kept the neophytes, especially the children and teenagers, under tight control at all times (Kotzebue 1830:95; Zavalishin 1973:380). Roll call was taken every night at the *monjerio,* and the mother of any girl who was missing would be held accountable for her child's actions and even punished (Pérez 1988:81). Married couples often lived and worked beyond the mission walls, but they had to report for roll call each day before starting work (Sanchez 1995:83, 86). Eulalia Pérez, who worked at Mission San Gabriel, recalled in her interview with Thomas Savage in 1877, that one of her work duties was counting "the unmarried women, bachelors, day-laborers, vaqueros—both those with saddles and those who rode bareback " (Pérez 1988:78). The neophytes could visit their native homelands on furlough for about five to six weeks a year (Guest 1983: 45). During times of food scarcity at the mission, or during the annual acorn harvests, the padres often released the neophytes from the missions for short durations (Kelsey 1985:505).

Native Relocation Program

The Fernandinos resettled coastal hunter-gatherers from dispersed rancherias or village communities into centrally located mission complexes. This policy, known as *reducción* or *congregación*, had a long history in New Spain (see Guest 1978:98; Jackson 1994:13; Jackson and Castillo 1995:6). The padres of Alta California advocated this massive relocation program to facilitate the conversion of natives to Catholicism. Population aggregation allowed the priests to keep close surveillance on natives, in the attempt to control their interactions with gentile (nonbaptized) Indians still residing in the countryside. Furthermore, this program allowed the padres to segregate the neophytes from the immoral and undisciplined influence of the Hispanic colonists, or *gente de razón* (Guest 1978:106–107,113; Servin 1965:136–137).

Some initial experimentation took place in the creation of mission-pueblos by placing selected members of the *gente de razón* into the missions. These proposed mission-pueblos were, as discussed by Francis Guest (1978), to form the nuclei of future urban centers in California. In proposing to desegregate the mission complexes, government officials made an explicit effort to correct some perceived shortcomings of traditional missionary practices that limited the full incorporation of native peoples into Hispanic society, but the proposed blueprints for the mission-pueblo were never implemented in colonial California. Father Junípero Serra's early correspondence suggests that he intended to experiment with the mission-pueblo model by recruiting young men from San Blas and by encouraging (as well as rewarding) intermarriage between Hispanic soldier-settlers and Indian neophyte women in the mission complexes (Palóu 1926b:33–34; Serra 1955a:151).

> It is very important that the missions shall be provided with some peons to cultivate the land, and endeavor to raise some crops for their maintenance and advancement. . . . It seems to me that the easiest way is the one which we have asked for from the beginning and is stated in the letter. It is that young men from the neighborhood of San Blas shall go in the barks in the capacity of sailors. Among them there will be found, in my opinion, without much difficulty, farmers, cowboys, and muleteers. These can be distributed among the missions, six in each one, or at least four, with the condition that the commander of the presidio shall not have the right to take them away during the whole year. (Point 12 of Father Serra's Recommendations to Viceroy Bucareli; March 13, 1773)(Palóu 1926b:18–19)

However, the Fernandinos, dismayed by the poor character and loose morals of the soldiers and settlers who immigrated to the California colonies, quickly scuttled the mission-pueblo program. Repeated problems with soldiers molesting and raping Native California women, and various exposés involving infidelity, induced the padres to shield their neophyte flock from the "scandalous" *gente de razón*.[24] After the abandonment of the mission-pueblo program by the late 1770s, few *gente de razón* resided in the missions, and those that did were employed as the guards, overseers, and managers of the mission workforce and ranches (Guest 1978:107).

The consequence of the Franciscan relocation program was that thousands of coastal peoples were moved from their homelands to foreign settlements in alien territories.[25] This policy of *reducción* involved the aggregation of people from many small polities, often with differing languages and dialects, into large, crowded neophyte communities at the missions. As Cook (1976a:86) emphasized, this process went against the innate centripetal tendency of most native Californians, who enjoyed highly dispersed and fluid settlement patterns. Although the first few neophytes typically came from nearby regions, the padres recruited natives, as the missions grew from several hundred to over a thousand neophytes, from greater and greater distances. By the 1800s many of the missions tapped into interior native communities (e.g., Yokuts, Plains Miwok, Cahuilla) located thirty or forty or more kilometers from the coastal missions. In questionnaires filled out in 1813–15, the padres provided excellent data on linguistic and tribal pluralism, responding that each individual mission community was composed of a multitude of tribes, and that between two and fifteen Indian languages were spoken at each mission (Geiger and Meighan 1976:19–21). Visitors to the missions also commented on the marked ethnic diversity of the neophyte communities (see Duhaut-Cilly 1999:161; Kotzebue 1830:98; Langsdorff 1968:163, 195; Menzies 1924:324).

The padres' relocation program excited considerable consternation among mission Indians, who nurtured a powerful attachment to their ancestral homelands. The magnetism that native lands exerted upon the neophytes astounded the padres. Mission Indians risked severe punishment to return to their cherished hills and parklands, and many left the missions surreptitiously, to die in the lands of their ancestors (see Cook 1976b:80–84; Guest 1979:11–12; Guest 1983:40–45). Guest (1979:12) succinctly summarizes: "from these sources it is abundantly evident that the Indians, however much they might want to join a mission community, did not wish to be separated permanently from their beloved little forest. They did not wish to have to live away from their little *patria chica*, their little homeland whence they had come." Some padres (e.g., Fathers Narciso Durán, Mariano Payeras) recognized that natives who traveled twenty or more leagues from their homelands to enter the missions made tremendous sacrifices, but that people from nearby villages were less prone to run away. Consequently, Father Payeras argued, it was unwise to baptize natives who lived more than twenty-five to thirty leagues away, since they would probably return home sooner or later (Guest 1983:44).

The massive relocation program of the Franciscans was part of an explicit strategy of transforming the neophytes into "civilized" people by disassociating them from their homelands, which played such a central focus in native identity (Margolin 1989:33).[26] By removing the neophytes from the territories of their birth, the fathers alienated them from their mythical landscapes, the graves of their ancestors, and the named rocks and landmarks so central to the construction of native identity.

Although the *reducción* policy remained a cornerstone of missionary practice in Alta California, some neophytes did not have to live in large, multiethnic mission villages. The padres assigned a few Indian workers to outlying mission ranchos or stations. The best-documented ranchos, as noted above, were in the hinterland of Mission San Gabriel and Mission San Luis Rey, where agricultural laborers lived while tending crops, orchards, and livestock. Other neophyte stations or outposts include La Cieneguita near Mission Santa Barbara and Saticoy near Mission San Buenaventura (Johnson 1995:2).

The southernmost missions—Mission San Diego and Mission San Luis Rey—required only a proportion of the neophyte population to reside on-site at any one time, while the remainder dwelled in villages in their native homelands (Carrico and Shipek 1996; Johnson and Crawford 1999; Shipek 1977). In this modified form of *reducción*, only some categories of neophytes (those training for baptism or for specialized jobs, orphans, unmarried girls, widows, the sick or elderly) had to live in the missions. The balance of the neophyte population came to the missions only during festivals, for training or religious services, or to fulfill communal labor tasks (Shipek 1977:69). Using the mission registers, Johnson and Crawford (1999:90) have calculated that 2,034 people, or about half of the neophytes baptized at Mission San Luis Rey, lived in outlying rancherias (Indian villages).

The modified relocation program at Mission San Diego grew out of the difficulties of growing enough food to support the neophyte population of the mission, especially during the early years when droughts and other problems resulted in poor harvests (Shipek 1977:139). At Mission San Luis Rey, the modified *reducción* developed because of the permissive character of Father Antonio Peyri (mission padre from 1798 to 1832), who allowed many of his wards to remain in their homeland villages (Shipek 1977:139–140, 172). As a consequence, the southernmost coastal groups (Diegueño, Luiseño, Cahuilla, and Cupeño speakers) did not experience the full brunt of the relocation program of the Fernandinos. Although the southern Luiseño speakers assigned to Mission San Luis Rey continued to live in their homeland villages, the northern Luiseño-speaking Indians associated with Mission San Juan Capistrano underwent the normal policy of *reducción*, uprooted and forced to live at the central mission (Shipek 1977:140).

Labor Practices

Mission scholars differ in their opinions as to whether the labor system in the missions constituted communal, slavery, or feudal-like conditions (see, for example, Archibald 1978:180–181; Castillo 1989a:117; Cook 1976a:301–302; Farnsworth 1989:231; Heizer 1978c:135; Jackson 1994:130, 135; and Silliman 2001b:386–389). This is not a new debate, as many of the European men who visited the missions also grappled with the issue (Chamisso 1986:243–244; Duhaut-Cilly 1999:115, 167; Kotzebue 1830:79–80; La Pérouse 1989:70, 81; Lütke 1989:267). In reality, the labor system combined some aspects of communal principles and some of enslavement, and is probably best described as a form of forced communal labor (after Sanchez 1995:54–55; Silliman 2001b:387). Cook (1976a:301–302) viewed the system primarily as one of communal labor. According to the Franciscan ideal, individuals contributed labor to a common pool of agrarian and craft activities, from which each individual received support in the way of food, shelter, clothing, and other necessary goods. After the missions had served their purpose, and the neophytes had been transformed into fully indoctrinated Hispanic peasants, the Christian Indians would receive the fruits of their labor by dividing up the land, the built environment, and goods from the mission enterprise.

Of course, the mission system never operated as a truly communal system, since the neophytes did not control access to the means of production (e.g., Sanchez 1995:64). The padres maintained firm control of the labor policies, the management of agrarian and craft production, and the allocation of surpluses, until the secularization of the missions in the 1830s. In exchange for their labor, the padres fed, clothed, and housed the neophytes. But the standard of living in the neophyte dormitories and rancherias was barely tolerable in some cases (see discussion below).

The missions also resembled plantations. The neophytes could not leave the Franciscan lands without permission, and were granted only limited freedom in choosing their occupation. However, their condition was not truly enslavement either, because the padres could not legally sell or own the neophytes. But the Fernandinos did control the Indian labor for extracting surplus from the mission estates, and did "loan" out the neophytes to the nearby presidios and pueblos as laborers, requiring that the *gente de razón* compensate the missions (not the individual neophytes) accordingly (Hackel 1997:125–127; Sanchez 1995:83).

The number of hours a day the neophytes worked varied, depending on the padre in charge, the mission, the labor assignment, and the season of the year. It ranged anywhere from four to nine hours (Cook 1976a:91–94; Monroy 1990:65; Silliman 2001b:387). Everyone labored, regardless of age, with tasks assigned on the basis of the training, gender, age, and attitude of individual neophytes (Hackel 1997:122–123). Young children performed simple tasks, such as scaring birds away from the gardens. Men worked primarily in agricultural and ranching pursuits, in building projects, and at various crafts. After the mid-1790s, skilled craftsmen from New Spain trained some neophyte men as carpenters, soap makers, masons, blacksmiths, leather workers, etc. Women tended to household affairs, raised children, prepared foods, and produced some craft goods, such as baskets and textiles. Hispanic women, working at the missions as housekeepers and caretakers of the dormitories, supervised the domestic industries—for instance, grooming some neophyte women to be seamstresses (Sanchez 1995:78). As Hackel (1997:123) notes, not all labor tasks were gender-segregated (he gives the example of the textile shop at Mission Santa Cruz employing men and women)(see also Silliman 2001b:387–388). The labor system was somewhat flexible so that, during harvests or construction projects, men and women could be temporarily reassigned to large work crews to accomplish a necessary task very quickly. Other work was piecemeal, with neophytes assigned a quota of so many tiles or adobe bricks to be produced each day (Heizer 1978c:128).

The labor demands placed on the neophytes rose substantially after 1810, when Alta California was cut off from New Spain by civil war, and the presidios and pueblos became increasingly dependent on the missions for food and basic goods (Guest 1979:15; Hackel 1997:129). As Father Mariano Payeras observed in 1821, "These poor people will be the most unfortunate and wretched in the world, if they alone, many only recently baptized and uncivilized, have to support so many troops for so long a time. May God grant that some day these troops will be appropriately supplied and that this Lord Governor will consequently cease to long for information of what the Missions possess" (Payeras 1995:299). During the Mexican period (post-1821), when the hide and tallow trade began to dominate the economic activities of the missions, the workload of those neophytes processing cattle products accelerated markedly. The heavy workload was exacerbated by the timing of the hide and tallow trade, which was associated with a significant decline in the overall number of neophytes in the missions.[27]

Social Mobility

The first colonists to Alta California imported from New Spain some of the concepts of the old *casta* system, which classified people into fifty-six categories based on their professed racial histories as delineated by particular admixtures of Spanish, African, and Indian blood. But, although racial distinctions remained important in colonial California, people enjoyed some flexibility in constructing identities and social positions in the new frontier society (Forbes 1983; Haas 1995:30–31; Mason 1998:48–52; Sanchez 1995:56–58). Apart from the Franciscan padres, who were mostly peninsular Spaniards, the majority of the soldiers and colonists in Alta California were mestizos, mulattos, and neophyte Indians from Sinaloa, Sonora, and Baja California. Consequently, it did not serve their interests to support the old *casta* system, which would relegate them to perpetual second-class citizenship. A relatively fluid classificatory system materialized in Spanish California, which emphasized a person's "whiteness" as well as their marriage connections, occupation, wealth, land holdings, and religion. People negotiated social identities throughout their lifetimes, reconstructing and manipulating their family lineages so that they became lighter and more pure ("Spanish") over time. For example, Haas (1995:30) uses census data (1781, 1790) to show how families reclassified themselves into progressively whiter shades over time by cleansing from their backgrounds any hint of African or Indian blood. (See also Mason 1998:52–53.)

The primary social categories maintained in Alta California revolved around the dichotomous constructs of *gente de razón* (people of reason) and *gente sin razón* (people without reason). These categories, used interchangeably with *español* and *indio*, ultimately defined whether a person would be treated as civilized and Christian or as savage and pagan (Haas 1995:31; Sanchez 1995:57–58). However, the line between *gente de razón* and *indio* was not fixed and unyielding but fuzzy, amorphous, and situational, as some native people reclassified themselves as *de razón* through marriage, education, occupation (e.g., skilled craftsperson), residence, dress, speech, or skin color. In 1781, for example, Pablo Rodríguez was classified simply as an *indio*, but "by 1790, probably because he had assumed a new set of characteristics—different clothing, mannerisms, habits of speech— he was categorized as a *coyote* (having an Indian mother and mestizo father). In this new classification, he and his descendants assumed a position closer to that of the Spaniard" (Haas 1995:30). And Sanchez notes:

Acculturated Indians with a trade . . . residing within non-Indian
sites much like the earliest Indian colonists and military scouts
in Alta California, become part of the collectivity of *gente de razón.*
Those Indians acculturated to some extent and with a Hispanic name
but who continue to reside in the *rancherías* or within Indian settlements (like those around Los Angeles in 1836) are still designated as
Indians; this is the case with some caciques, like Chief Juan Antonio
from Jurupa (Lugo, 208). This distinction (Indian versus non-Indian),
the fundamental antagonism within early California society, is the
linchpin around which discourses of identity are articulated. (Sanchez
1995:57)

The colonists viewed most neophytes in the California missions as *indios.* They were apprentices under the tutelage of the padres and in the
process of transforming themselves into civilized and Christian people of
reason. The negotiation of *gente de razón* status by neophytes usually took
place *outside* the social context of the missions. It involved neophyte women
marrying Hispanic colonists (see below) or skilled neophyte craftsmen who
moved outside the mission to practice their trade in pueblos or presidios.
The latter situation resulted from the limited emancipation of neophytes
authorized by Governor José María de Echeandía's decrees in 1827 and 1831
that granted freedom to mission Indians with specialized skills and to married couples residing in the missions for ten or more years.[28]

Although outsiders may have perceived the neophytes in the missions
as simply *indios,* most neophytes were engaged in the active construction
of multiple identities and social positions. They participated in dual and overlapping social hierarchies within the missions, a strategy that offered them
a variety of choices and some degree of social mobility. Despite the best efforts of the padres, the traditional social hierarchies of gentile tribal polities
replicated themselves, in varying degrees, in the neophyte communities (e.g.,
Jackson and Castillo 1995:38). Indian chiefs or captains, members of high-
status families, and shamans and other religious specialists often maintained
their positions of power and status when they entered the missions. This
native hierarchy structured many social relations and status positions
among the mission Indians, even though much of this social action took place
within the clandestine and underground world of the neophyte communities. Since the recruitment of gentile Indians took place throughout the mission period, albeit in fewer numbers by the late 1820s and 1830s, traditional
native leaders were continually being introduced into mission social environments. The padres' own writings provide some of the best evidence of
the pervasive influence of traditional chiefs and shamans in the missions.

The questionnaires completed by the padres from 1813 to 1815 are replete with statements concerning shamans undertaking curing ceremonies and participating in clandestine dances (Geiger and Meighan 1976:47–80). There are also a few references to traditional native chiefs wielding considerable power among the neophytes. For example, the priests at Mission San Carlos remarked,

> Even today they show more respect and submission to their chiefs than to the *alcaldes* who have been placed over them for their advancement as citizens. The chiefs remain known at all times as governors of their tribe even in the event that old age forces them to give the chieftainship over to a successor. They wear no distinctive mark of any kind. In the days of paganism a cloak made from rabbit skins usually distinguished them. The missionary fathers strive to humor them because the contentment of the Indians depends on this. (Geiger and Meighan 1976:126–127)

The padres instituted their own internal social hierarchies within each mission, with the two padres at the top, a small core of *gente de razón* managers who served as overseers, housekeepers, and craft specialists in the middle, and the Indians at the bottom. The padres did not treat all neophytes alike, but subdivided them into positions of status, responsibilities, and privileges depending upon their time in the mission, aptitude, performance in tasks, and level of training or education. Upon first entering the mission, Indians were defined as *catecúmenos* while participating in catechism and doctrinal training to prepare for baptism. Once baptized, they became neophytes— active members of the mission community (Sanchez 1995:60). The neophytes would then be assigned different status positions and perks within the mission hierarchy, depending mainly upon their jobs and social distance from the padres and middle managers. The padres surrounded themselves with bright and progressive native boys who served as servants, translators, pages, and altar boys. Similarly, the middle managers employed Indian assistants who helped oversee and train other neophyte workers (Haas 1995:24–25; Sanchez 1995:84). Some neophytes held positions with formal titles (see Farris and Johnson 1999:8–10; Farris and Wheeler 1998:14). The *yntérprete* served as an interpreter for the padre and aided him in teaching religious lessons to the Indians. The *paje* worked as a house-servant for the padres. The *sacristan* was placed in charge of the sacristy of the church. The *cantor* was the singer in church services. The *enfermero* tended the sick as a male nurse. The *vaquero* filled the high-status position of cowboy and horseman. The *cocinero* was a cook, most likely serving the padres' table. Favored neophytes were not hard to spot, with their special clothing, extra rations of mission food, and access to special foods and drinks (chocolate and teas) and goods (e.g., Skowronek 1998:692). For example, *vaqueros* were issued clothes that resembled those of other *Californio* horsemen and allowed to ride horses with saddles (Hudson 1979:5; Sanchez 1995:78).

A formal system of mission Indian leaders was instituted by Governor Felipe de Neve in 1778, when he issued a decree requiring that each mission elect two *alcaldes* (magistrates) and two *regidores* (councilmen), as part of his plan to prepare the neophytes for self-government once the missions were secularized into Indian pueblos. Although the Fernandinos resisted the implementation of this plan during the first decade or so, by 1796 the *alcaldes* and *regidores* had become fixtures in the neophyte communities (see Phillips 1989). Although the neophytes supposedly selected the mission Indian leaders in free elections, in reality the padres closely monitored the selection process, making sure that only the most trusted and progressive natives were chosen for these positions (Phillips 1975:28; Sanchez 1995:85). The duties of the *alcaldes* have been likened to those of the overseer on a Caribbean plantation (La Pérouse 1989:89): the *alcaldes* maintained order and discipline among the neophytes, informed them about their job assignments, made sure they were not late for work or mass, judged their actions (and informed the padres accordingly), and punished those who transgressed mission rules. The *alcaldes* carried special staffs as an emblem of office, dressed in European clothes, received preferential food rations and goods from the mission storehouses, and were exempt from corporal punishment (Hoover 1977:264; Hudson 1979:5,13).

In the recollections of some elite *Californios*, such as former governor Juan Bautista Alvarado and Mariano Guadalupe Vallejo, the mission Indian hierarchy was perceived as an explicit strategy of the priests to divide and conquer the neophyte population. The policing system maintained internal divisions within the neophyte community and kept an eye on subversive factions and troublemakers within the missions (Sanchez 1995:84–85). As Alvarado stated,

> For the local internal governance (of the mission) the missionaries had organized a policing force composed of the elder neophytes who had been there longest, were married, had families, and were considered morally upright; these were given the title of *alcaldes* (mayors) and had the faith and trust of the missionaries, were protected and instructed by them in the duties entrusted to them (which included) the constant observation and vigilance of all actions and conversations carried out by the other neophytes, reporting and warning anyone that committed some infraction or was remiss in the execution of the communal duties

assigned to them or in any way failed to carry out the padres' orders. This police or spy network was also charged with reporting if anyone had become seriously ill. (Juan Bautista Alvarado, quoted in Sanchez 1995:85)

Glenn Farris (1991:5), in his studies of neophyte family housing at Mission San Juan Bautista and Mission La Purísima, makes the compelling argument that the limited space in the adobe residences was reserved primarily for longtime neophytes who had "achieved a degree of stature and trust in the mission" (see also Voss 2000:51). Farris undertook an innovative analysis in an attempt to identify high-status families who may have resided in the neophyte apartments. Using the baptismal and marriage records at La Purísima, he elicited the names of men and women from nineteen neophyte families who appeared most frequently as godparents (*padrinos* or *madrinas*) or as marriage witnesses (*testigos*). Recognizing that these families probably had considerable clout in the mission hierarchy, he then considered the various offices that the families' men held in the mission. His study demonstrated an association between those men most frequently asked to serve as *padrinos* and *testigos,* and those holding positions of trust bequeathed by the padres (Farris and Johnson 1999:10–19; Farris and Wheeler 1998:15–21).

Some scholars argue that the Indian mission officials eventually undermined or replaced the traditional positions of tribal leadership in neophyte communities (see, e.g., Hoover 1989:397; Hoover and Costello 1985:119–120). That is, Indians who held traditional leadership positions or could trace their lineage to high-status families in precontact times became increasingly marginalized in the missions. There is no doubt that this happened in some cases. But there are other cases where the traditional and the new social hierarchies operated side-by-side.

In some instances, the two hierarchies converged, with traditional chiefs or captains from gentile villages serving as elected *alcaldes* or *regidores.* In an ongoing study of mission records from the Santa Barbara Presidio District, Gerald Gies (2002) and Linda Gies (2002) show how Chumash elites actively worked to maintain their high-status positions within neophyte communities by continuing their pre-mission practice of marrying members of other elite families, by serving as *padrinos* and *testigos* for the children of elite families, and by continuing to foster patron-client relationships with non-elite Chumash neophytes. In another example, James Sandos, citing Steven Hackel's recent analysis of the *alcaldes* at Mission San Carlos, notes that 50 percent of the officials holding office from 1770 to 1833 were appointed from Indian families who maintained access to traditional forms of leadership through kinship and high status (Sandos 1997:211). But Sandos also emphasizes that the selection of the other 50 percent of *alcaldes* exemplifies instances of social mobility, with men who had no prior connections to tribal leadership obtaining positions of power and responsibility at Mission San Carlos. Shipek (1977:147–153, 172) emphasizes that the traditional power structure of native polities remained fairly intact within the neophyte population of Mission San Luis Rey.

Interethnic Marriages

Interethnic marriages with Hispanic soldiers and settlers provided one potential avenue for native women and their children to transform their Indian identity to that of the *gente de razón* (Monroy 1990:107; Weber 1992:307). Indian women who married Hispanic men could join their husbands' residences outside the neophyte communities of the missions. Wives and children produced from interethnic marriages usually took on the baptismal family name of the Hispanic man, providing the opportunity to take on his family's identity as well. Meighan (1987:197–198) suggested that many of the retired soldiers who received land grants for their military service married native women, and these interethnic couples often became the founding members of the elite *Californio* class that would emerge after mission secularization.

Although the Fernandinos practiced a policy of physically segregating their neophyte flocks from most of the *gente de razón*, they were theoretically not averse to interethnic marriages between colonists and Indian neophytes (Kelsey 1985:507; La Pérouse 1989:103). Since all Catholic marriages in Alta California had to be authorized by priests after a review of the background and moral integrity of both partners (see Miranda 1981), the Franciscans exerted considerable control over the approval of marriage partners for both settlers and neophytes. Father Serra initially promoted the marriage of single male soldiers (of whom he approved) with female neophytes at the missions (Castaneda 1997:239; Garr 1972:294; Hurtado 1992). Serra believed that such unions would help civilize the mission Indians by providing good role models at the mission. However, deteriorating relations between the soldiers and priests, and the realization that some soldiers would serve as poor role models for the neophytes, put a damper on this plan. In addition, the Fernandinos soon discovered that soldiers and settlers who married Indian women often did not stay put in the mission complexes but were transferred by officers to other presidios or moved on their own account to new settlements (e.g., Serra 1955a:149–151). The mobility of the Hispanic men soured the padres to this practice of marriage, as they watched their most "progressive" women leave the missions to live with their new husbands (Garr 1972:295–296). Interethnic marriages continued throughout the mission period in California, but they never occurred in great numbers.[29] For example, John Johnson (1995:8) observes that, of the nearly four thousand neophyte marriages performed in the Santa Barbara Presidio District prior to secularization, only four were between Chumash Indians and *gente de razón*.

Unions between neophyte men and women from different polities and language groups may be considered another form of interethnic marriage. Members of one native polity would, I believe, have viewed people from another polity as ethnically distinct, especially if they spoke unintelligible languages and hailed from some other homeland. However, to maintain the distinction between these different kinds of marriage patterns, in the remainder of this book I define *interethnic* unions as those between colonists and Native Californians, and *intertribal* unions as those between members of different Native California polities. This latter form of marriage will be discussed in more detail later in the volume.

Demographic Parameters of Native and Colonizer Populations

Much has been written about the poor health, high mortality rate, and low birth rate of neophytes residing in the Alta California missions (for example, see Cook 1976a:3–55; Hurtado 1988:8; Jackson 1994:83–116; Jackson and Castillo 1995:41–48; Johnson 1989; Kealhofer 1996; Milliken 1995:90–92; and Walker and Johnson 1992, 1994). Four main findings of this demographic research are as follows.

First, detailed analyses of the sacramental registers for individual missions indicate that there was great variation in the crude birth and death rates, net reproduction ratio (net growth of the population), and mean life expectancy at birth for the neophytes within, and between, individual missions. For example, Jackson (1994:83–116) has demonstrated how these demographic variables varied greatly across time and space, depending upon the physical and social environments of the missions, the practices of individual missionaries, and, most importantly, the history of gentile recruitment for each mission. But in spite of this substantial variation, in general the life expectancy of neophytes born into the missions was low, the death rate of the mission populations far exceeded the birth rate, and none of the mission populations were reproductively viable without continuous recruitment of new converts from outlying gentile Indian communities.

The Franciscans, in recognizing the high mortality rate, were distraught that they could not stem the tide of death (see Geiger and Meighan

1976:63–64,75–76). The padres created infirmaries in most missions and put patients on special diets, but the neophytes continued to die in large numbers. In truth, the Indians received inadequate medical care mostly because the Franciscans found medicines and doctors in short supply in Alta California.[30] The Franciscans acknowledged that many more neophytes died than were born in the missions each year and that few of the neophytes raised in the missions lived past twenty or twenty-five years (Geiger and Meighan 1976:62,64,74–75,79–80,105).

The marked decline in the health of neophytes accelerated in the 1800s. This point is evident in the observations made by Europeans who visited the missions from the late 1700s through the 1820s. The early visitors (La Pérouse in 1786, and Vancouver and Menzies in 1792–93) did not describe major health problems, and Vancouver (1954:236) even remarked about the rather good health of the neophyte population: "The scarcity of spirituous liquors, and the great regularity of the inhabitants in food and employment, induces a life of temperance; and consequently, the diseases to which they are liable are seldom of a malignant nature, and in most instances readily yield to the simplest means of cure." However, beginning at least with Rezanov's and Langsdorff's 1806 voyage to Alta California, when they witnessed the measles epidemic at Mission San José, most later visitors emphasized the deteriorating health, high mortality rate, and declining number of neophytes (Chamisso 1986:244–245; Duhaut-Cilly 1999:115; Khlebnikov 1989:390; Kotzebue 1830:101–102; Langsdorff 1968:210; Lazarev 1989:373). The alarming death rate had two major consequences by the first and second decades of the 1800s: to maintain the mission infrastructure, the Franciscans were forced to recruit new neophytes at increasingly greater distances from the missions; and the shadow of defeat, gloom, and death pervaded the daily lives of the surviving neophytes, as well as the attitudes of the padres who tended the sick and dying.[31]

The second demographic point here is that marked gender and age imbalances characterized the mission Indian populations.[32] Children and women usually experienced higher death rates than the rest of the mission population. In times when gentile recruitment waned, the ratio of children and women declined precipitously in many neophyte communities. As Jackson (1994:110–111) summarizes,

> the mission populations had a nearly balanced age structure in the
> 1790s, during a period of active congregation of converts. However, the
> population became unbalanced as a result of high rates of mortality
> among young girls and women and the decline in the number of
> females in periods of limited congregation of converts. In 1832, the

ratio showed a significant imbalance in a number of missions. For example, there were more than two males for every female at Santa Cruz and Soledad missions. In the long run, the deficit in the number of women limited the ability of the mission populations to reproduce, and manifested itself in the declining crude birthrates.

With the high mortality rate of neophyte women, and the imbalance of men and women in most missions, men experienced problems finding suitable marriage partners. As is discussed later, this situation seriously affected traditional marriage patterns and the composition of families in neophyte communities.

The third demographic point is that epidemics of contagious Euro-Asian diseases, such as smallpox and measles, took their toll on mission Indians. But mortality rates from epidemics varied erratically from mission to mission (see Walker and Johnson 1992, 1994). Alta California sustained a different pattern of epidemics than was experienced in the missions of Baja California and northwest Mexico—with relatively few major pandemics spreading across large regions. Most of these pandemics struck after 1800, especially toward the end of the mission period in the 1830s (Cook 1976a:17–20; Jackson 1994:116–119; Kealhofer 1996:68). In considering the demographic collapse of the Alta California missions, and the somewhat limited, but lethal, role played by epidemics, mission scholars have turned to other factors. Chronic diseases, such as respiratory ailments, dysentery, and especially syphilis, have been identified as major culprits in the high mortality rates of the neophytes (Cook 1976a:22–30; Jackson and Castillo 1995:43–44). The padres and visitors to the missions made numerous references to the scourge of syphilis and venereal disease that swept across the neophyte population, and to these diseases' debilitating consequences on adults, especially women (Chamisso 1986:244–245; Geiger and Meighan 1976:74, 105–106; Khlebnikov 1989:390–391; Osio 1996:124). Some scholars argue that the overall effects of syphilis on the high mortality rate and low birth rate of mission Indians have been historically underestimated (see Kelsey 1985:507; Meighan 1976a:7; Sandos 1997:199–201).

Other factors contributing to the chronic high mortality rate at the missions relate to the poor quality of life. Some scholars believe the real killers may have been overcrowding, inadequate ventilation in mission dormitories, poor sanitation, polluted communal water sources, and, in some instances, overwork (Cook 1976a:30–55; Jackson and Castillo 1995:45–50; Kealhofer 1996:69–70; Walker and Johnson 1994:115). Visitors reported the neophyte dormitories and houses to be overly crowded, reeking from the stench of human bodies and raw sewage, and quite cold and damp in the winter months.

The eye is struck by the filth in which they live. It is impossible to enter any of their huts without being immediately covered with hordes of fleas. These huts have floors of bare earth, but they are completely black with filth. The huts for married persons have a place for a fire in the middle which comprises the entire kitchen. The interiors of these dens really differ very little from Kamchadal or Kodiak iurts, although the exterior gives no hint of this. (Mission San Carlos de Monterey; September 1818) (Lütke 1989:263–264)

[F]urthermore they no longer live in huts but in specially constructed stone "cattle-pens." I cannot think of a better term for these dwellings that consist of a long row of structures not more than one *sagene* high and 1½–2 *sagenes* wide, without floor or ceiling, each divided into sections by partitions, also not longer than two *sagenes*, with a correspondingly small door and a tiny window in each—can one possibly call it anything but a barnyard for domestic cattle and fowl? Each of these small sections is occupied by an entire family; cleanliness and tidiness are out of the question: a thrifty peasant usually has a better-kept cattle-pen. (Mission San Carlos de Monterey, 1818)(Golovnin 1979:147–148)

Sheds made of unbaked brick without windows, floors or ceilings occupy most of the square and serve as living quarters for the oppressed American natives, who by nature are weak-minded. The dirt and dreadful stench in these sheds are extraordinary and probably are the primary cause of the premature deaths of those who inhabit these dwellings. (Mission San Francisco de Asís; December 1823) (Lazarev 1989:373)

In an investigation of the high death rate of the missions in 1797, Governor Diego de Borica identified the unsanitary conditions as a primary cause, since he could hardly inspect a dormitory at an unidentified mission due to the stench of human feces (Jackson and Castillo 1995:48).

Cook (1976a:88–90), in researching accusations made by visitors to the missions about the insufferable housing conditions of the neophytes, noted that the relatively small *monjerio* dormitories would have been very cramped if they housed one hundred to two hundred young women. He calculated that each female inmate probably had access to a sleeping area of only 2.0 by .6 meters. Kotzebue (1830:94), in touring neophyte housing at Mission Santa Clara in 1824, exclaimed that "[t]hese are divided into long rows of houses, or rather stalls, where each family is allowed a space scarcely large enough to enable them to lie down to repose." La Pérouse, in making his observations about the neophyte village at Mission San Carlos de Monterey in 1786, remarked:

The Indian village stands on the right, consisting of about fifty huts which serve for seven hundred and forty persons of both sexes, including their children, who compose the mission of San Carlos, or of Monterey. These huts are the most wretched anywhere. They are round and about six feet in diameter and four in height. Some stakes, the thickness of a man's arm, stuck in the ground and meeting at the top, compose the framing. Eight or ten bundles of straw, ill arranged over these stakes, are the only defense against the rain or wind; and when the weather is fine, more than half the hut remains uncovered, with the precaution of two or three bundles of straw to each habitation to be used as circumstances may require. (La Pérouse 1989:79–80)

As Margolin (1989:80) notes in an accompanying footnote, if La Pérouse's estimates are correct, then about fifteen people on average resided in each hut measuring little more than 1.8 meter in diameter. It is probably the case that the deplorable conditions and overcrowding of the neophyte quarters may have been overstated by some visitors. But it seems clear that the living standards of the neophytes were far from ideal, and that the aggregation of sizeable populations at the missions created a significant health risk.

The mission diet is cited as another, but somewhat more controversial, reason for the poor health of the neophytes. Although the padres provided the neophytes three meals a day, the nutritional content of the meals, some scholars argue, was inadequate. Sherburne Cook is the strongest proponent for this claim. In undertaking a lengthy analysis of the caloric value and nutritional content of neophyte meals, he suggested that these "Indians as a whole lived continuously on the verge of clinical deficiency" (Cook 1976a:50). More recent studies temper Cook's initial findings. Some mission scholars emphasize the difficulty of calculating the typical caloric yield of neophyte meals, given the tremendous variation in neophyte food consumption at different missions and over time (Jackson and Castillo 1995:45–47; Monroy 1990:68). Others, such as Kelsey (1985:505–506) and Guest (1983:52–53), stress the diversity and quantity of neophyte foods, highlighting some of the padres' and visitors' accounts of the substantial number of cattle that were slaughtered each week for the meat used to supplement the basic *atole* and *pozole* meals (Geiger and Meighan 1976:81, 85–88; see also Skowronek 1998:697).

Although the neophyte diet was probably less sensitive to seasonal and annual fluctuations than were previous coastal hunter-gatherer subsistence practices, this stability may have been achieved "at the expense of greatly reduced variety and nutritional balance" (Hoover 1989:399–400). This observation is supported by the analysis of stable isotope concentrations in human bone collagen obtained from the skeletons of Hispanic settlers buried in the Santa Barbara Mission Chapel and of neophytes from La Purísima Mission. Although the isotopic levels for prehistoric native peoples from the Santa Barbara region indicate marked consumption of marine resources, the skeletal samples of Hispanic and native peoples from the presidio and mission settings suggest the latter colonial contexts did not emphasize marine foods or maize but rather relied on other kinds of terrestrial resources (Costello and Walker 1987; Walker et al. 1989:354). Furthermore, the comparison of long bone measurements from prehistoric natives and mission neophytes show that the latter were considerably smaller in overall body size. The retardation of body growth among the Santa Barbara neophytes may point to the "nutritional deficiency of the mission diet or the combined effects of poor nutrition and infectious disease" (Walker et al. 1989:354–355).

At least some neophytes augmented the mission food supplies by gathering native plant foods, exploiting marine shellfish and fish, and hunting wild game (e.g., Guest 1983:53). But several mission scholars caution that native foods probably comprised a relatively small part of the overall neophyte diet. Cook (1976a:46–47) estimated that plant and animals from hunting and gathering activities made up about 10 percent. Skowronek (1998:697) suggests that by 1790 wild foods probably constituted more of a treat than a necessity at Mission Santa Clara. He cites David Huelsbeck's findings that wild species at Mission Santa Cruz and Mission Santa Clara probably comprised less than 1 percent of the meat protein available to the neophytes. Thus, according to some scholars, neophytes consumed native foods primarily as luxury items, once the agricultural infrastructure at the missions had been fully developed (see also Jackson and Castillo 1995:45; Langenwalter and McKee 1985:102).

The fourth demographic point is that the collapse of the local native populations took place at the same time that Hispanic numbers slowly increased in colonial California. The initial colonization of Alta California was undertaken by relatively few colonists, primarily Fernandinos and soldiers from northwestern Mexico. The number of Hispanic settlers grew, as colonists were recruited to live in the presidio communities and three civilian pueblos (Costello and Hornbeck 1989; Mason 1984; Phillips 1980). But Hispanic numbers remained relatively low in relation to Indian neophytes. William Mason's (1998:44, 113) detailed analysis of colonial demographics shows that as late as 1825 about 80 percent of the non-Indian population were descended from colonists who had come to Alta California prior to 1790. It was not until after mission secularization in the mid-1830s, at which time the vast mission holdings were broken up into numerous private ranchos, that the non-Indian population really grew, as a consequence of increased immigration. But the true floodgates opened with the annexation of California by the United States in 1846 and the Gold Rush in 1849.

Chronology of Colonial Encounters

The missions served as an instrument of colonization in Alta California for about a seventy-year period (1769 to roughly the early 1840s). The founding dates of the missions ranged from 1769 to 1823, but the majority (eighteen of twenty-one missions) took place before 1800. Thus, several generations of neophytes could have been born and raised within the social and cultural environment of some missions.

BEYOND THE MISSION QUADRANGLES

In visiting the Alta California missions today, it is often difficult to grasp the monumental size of the mission complexes and the challenges faced by the padres in building them. The Fernandinos in a relatively short period constructed a mission system that spanned from San Diego to the greater San Francisco Bay, transforming the anthropogenic landscape of the Native Californians into many thousands of hectares of land for crop and livestock production. The mission complexes were self-contained agrarian communities encompassing a complex infrastructure of religious buildings, craft shops, storage facilities, dormitories, aqueducts, and structures for processing grains, fruits, and meat. Walking around the imposing adobe buildings, we cannot fail to be impressed at the accomplishments of the Fernandinos and the neophyte Indians.

But to appreciate the full extent of the missions, we need to go outside the reconstructed churches and *conventos*, to where we can look in all directions and envision where the Indian neophytes would have been living and working. Sometimes we forget that the neophytes were the very foundation of the mission system. In their initial proposal for colonizing Alta California, the Fernandinos espoused that the new Christian converts would serve as the Church's instrument in building and maintaining the mission complexes, and after only ten years would populate the California frontier as tax-paying farmers working land allocated from the mission estates. But this dream never materialized. In reality, the native peoples who entered these cloisters became laborers in a massive program of agriculture and craft production that fueled the missions as the economic engine of Spanish and Mexican California for the next seventy years or so.

The padres instituted a formidable and repressive system designed explicitly to control and indoctrinate their Indian apprentices. They unleashed an energetic crusade for converting and "civilizing" coastal hunter-gatherers that involved a highly regimented enculturation program, massive relocation, forced labor, differential treatment of neophytes through advancement in the mission hierarchies, and possibilities for interethnic marriage (especially in the early years). They also unleashed a mission system that was highly lethal, with unanticipated mortality rates that devastated local native populations. By spanning several generations of neophytes, the missions produced many Indian children who never really knew the lands of their ancestors. How did the neophytes negotiate this domineering program and engage in survival tactics in interactions with the Fernandinos and mission managers?

4 Native Agency in the Franciscan Missions

Once native peoples made the difficult decision to cross the portals of one of the twenty-one missions in Alta California, they entered an entirely new world, a world of alien social, economic, and ideological practices. In missions structured after monastic retreats, the padres expected the neophytes to follow principles of conduct devoted to self-discipline, religious fervor, fidelity, and sacrifice. Margolin (1989:15) observes that even at the height of monasteries' popularity, very few Europeans ever chose to live in them. Yet the Fernandinos believed that Native Californians—who had little prior experience with agriculture, large aggregated settlements, or Hispanic life ways—would eventually adapt to the regimented life of the missions, a life that most Europeans of the day would have rejected outright as too harsh and inflexible. We can only imagine the amazement and shock that Indians received once they entered these strange, cloistered institutions. The highly controlled social environment must have appeared incomprehensible to people who had enjoyed a previous life of relatively unconstrained movement and freedom.

RECRUITMENT INTO THE MISSIONS

Why did native peoples join the missions? This question has been pondered by scholars of the California missions for more than a century.[1] Much debate has focused on the degree to which the padres exerted force to convert natives to the Catholic faith.

According to the doctrines of the Church and Spanish Crown, the conversion of native peoples to Catholicism was to be voluntary, with each individual supposedly making his or her own decision (Cook 1976a:73; Guest 1979:2). The padres emphasized in their writings that entrance into the

Church was strictly an elective process, and that Indians could move in and out of the mission, prior to baptism.

> I have observed that the pagans who are reduced [to mission life] gladly embrace baptism and with free choice. During the time they are being catechized which can be called a period of probation, they become acquainted with the maxims, laws and precepts of religion. They see the physical labors done by the neophytes and witness as well the punishments administered to delinquents when mildness does not serve to correct them. In a word, from the time of their instruction they know what they will have to do and practice once they become Christians. With a knowledge of all this they ask for baptism when they can with full liberty return to their villages and remain in their pagan state. (Letter of Father Estevan Tapis to Governor Arrillaga in 1805; cited in Guest 1979:4–5)

Natives expressing an interest in joining the Church would receive anywhere from eight days to two to three months of catechism instruction, and at any time during this training, individuals could depart the mission and return to their home villages. However, once the vow to God was made during baptism and they became subjects of the Crown, the neophytes were no longer free to leave the mission compound without explicit permission of the padres (Guest 1966:210; Sandos 1997:205–206).

Even though physical coercion was against the law of the Church and Crown, it probably was used in some cases to recruit neophytes. Russian military officers and merchants who visited the missions after the establishment of Colony Ross believed the Spanish, and later Mexican, soldiers rounded up gentile Indians, using lassos, and barbarously dragged them off to the padres for conversion (Kotzebue 1830:78–79, 108–109; Lazarev 1989:371–372; Lütke 1989:266–267; Schabelski 1993:5; Zavalishin 1973:380; but see Khlebnikov 1989:387). Cook (1976a:73–80) argued that compulsory conversion through force of arms was increasingly employed to recruit neophytes after about 1800. Most of the cases he cited concern punitive expeditions by presidio soldiers who went into the interior (primarily the San Joaquin Valley) in search of neophyte fugitives. Prisoners captured during these raids included the fugitives and any gentiles who assisted them. The latter were supposedly turned over to the priests for catechism training and baptism so that they could enter the missions as neophytes.

Cook's thesis on the coerced nature of neophyte recruitment in the early decades of the 1800s has come under critical scrutiny by Guest (1979). Guest, after examining each case cited by Cook as evidence for compulsory conversion, concludes that there were too many exceptions to this "pattern" of physical coercion, and that Cook selectively used the written documents available. Guest contends that there were only a few cases during the Mexican period when compulsory coercion was probably employed to bring natives to the missions.

If the majority of native peoples, especially during the initial Spanish colonization of Alta California, were not forced at lance point to join the missions, then what compelled them to leave their homelands and settle in neophyte communities? I think part of the answer is that the Fernandinos were excellent salespeople who mounted an aggressive and determined program of recruitment. This program was based on the padres' training at the College of San Fernando, previous experiences in the missions of Sierra Gorda and Baja California (see, e.g., Kelsey 1985:505), and influential writings of the day about theology, philosophy, and missionary practices. The manual of pastoral theology, which laid out an explicit agenda for selling mission life to Indians, played a key role (Guest 1994:266–267).

> First, they were advised to make friends with the Indians, especially the chief and other Indian leaders, by presenting them with gifts: beads, trinkets, brightly colored cloth, and the like. Then, they were to gather about them a group of boys and sing them songs the verses of which contained the principal elements of Christian doctrine. The next step was to teach the boys elementary Spanish, explain to them the meaning of the Spanish words to which the singing had accustomed them, and get from them the equivalent terms in the local Indian tongue. They could then build from there. (Guest 1994:266)

The padres took this advice to heart: the foundation of their recruitment efforts, as they erected individual missions along the coast, involved the exchange of food and goods, especially clothing, to native peoples.[2] The padres orchestrated outdoor ceremonies and gatherings designed to dazzle and attract local Indians, such as during the founding of each Spanish settlement (e.g., Monroy 1990:33–34).

> They made the solemn procession with the Sacred Host around the square that was already marked out and begun for the camp, accompanied by peals of bells and repeated volleys from the cannon on the packet and from the muskets and guns of the soldiers. This function was the cause of great joy and extraordinary pleasure to every one, as may be believed by every Roman Catholic Christian. (Description of the dedication of the church at the Monterey presidio, June 14, 1770; in Palóu 1926a:295–296)

The public spectacle of the missions intensified with the construction of impressive churches containing expansive painted interiors; elaborate furnishings including paintings, silver vessels, and statues; highly stylized masses with incense, music, and choir; and padres dressed in spectacularly ornate vestments. Built with the goal of recruiting native peoples to the Catholic faith, the elaborate frontier churches were designed to overwhelm them. Thus, it is not surprising that local Indians would be attracted initially. Their fascination and respect for the spiritual world would have been piqued by the extraordinary adobe structures and by the padres themselves— strange men dressed in grey habits, who spoke continually to their own God and abstained from sex. Furthermore, the padres were treated (at least in public) with great reverence and respect by the other colonists, who would bow and kiss their hands and robes.

Milliken (1995:221) suggests that the first recruits to join the mission community were motivated by individual situations, pondering what the missions could offer and weighing this against the other choices available. Some of the first recruits probably entered the mission for reasons having little to do with religion or spirituality—children or young teens upset with their families, or people lured by material goods or simply looking for three square meals a day. The padres made a special effort to enlist those young boys most vulnerable to the recruitment efforts into the mission. The young boys felt important at the missions: the Franciscans bestowed upon them gifts and clothing and employed them as translators. Other families made calculated decisions to hand a child over for baptism, thus in their minds forging an alliance with the newcomers; such an alliance might ensure access to nonlocal goods and powerful ritual knowledge.

Still other individuals executed courses of action based on status and gender considerations. Men and women disgruntled with their current social positions had the option of moving into the missions. As Hoover (1989:397) and Margolin (1989:29–30) point out, in some traditional Native Californian societies with rigidly demarcated social status and political positions, the missions beckoned to men and women interested in improving their social position through nontraditional means of attaining prestige and wealth. Monroy (1990:33) argues that Indian women facing patriarchal domination, in some patrilineal hunter-gatherer groups in southern California, came to the missions to escape such discrimination. Some Indian women may also have moved to the missions to escape the persistent sexual abuse and attacks perpetrated by Spanish soldiers. For example, Chumash-speaking women from the Santa Barbara Channel experienced increasing harassment by soldiers by 1776 (see Font 1931:246–253); some may have joined the missions and placed themselves under the protective custody of the padres. In this light, it is significant that the population pyramid for 1782 constructed by Walker and Johnson (1994:112) illustrates that women were among the most frequent early recruits to the Santa Barbara missions.

The spiritual power of the padres intrigued some of the religious specialists, or shamans, in traditional Native California societies. Haas (1995:20) observes that among the first adult converts at Mission San Juan Capistrano were native religious leaders who had joined the mission to gain access to this spiritual power. Similarly, Shipek (1985:489) suggests that native leaders in southern California forged alliances with the padres specifically to obtain access to this new power.

However, following the first few years of the founding of the missions, it must have become obvious to any hunter-gatherer in the nearby environs that these alien settlements were to be avoided at almost any cost. The strict discipline, routinized workday, lack of freedom, wretched living conditions, and chilling mortality rate must have been a substantial challenge to the recruitment efforts of even the most persuasive padre. So why did Indian people join the missions in large numbers even after their repressive regime became widely known? Milliken (1995:219–226) responds that most Indians had little choice. As the prospering missions expanded their agricultural lands and livestock ranges, the effects on local native communities were cumulative, eventually spelling disaster for most.

Traditional native subsistence pursuits became increasingly difficult as livestock and weeds encroached farther and farther upon Indians in the hinterland. The founding of the missionary colonies proved deleterious to the productivity and even survival of those indigenous plant and animal resources exploited by coastal hunter-gatherers (see, e.g., Allen 1998:42–54). Irrigation systems altered the local hydrology, and free-ranging herds of livestock trampled and ate many Indian plant foods. Even more devastating was the introduction of those Old World plants and animals that quickly radiated across the landscape. Archaeological research, including analyses of macroscopic botanical remains in adobe bricks, and pollen, phytolith, and macrobotanical samples from excavation units, indicates that hardy Old World weeds, such as Sow Thistle, Curly Dock, and Red-Stemmed Filaree, began to colonize aggressively the coastal zone of southern and central California, possibly even before the founding, in 1769, of the first mission and presidio in San Diego (e.g., Hendry 1931; West 1989).[3]

Later missions were established in ecological communities already transformed by European weeds, such as Cheeseweed, Red-Stemmed Filaree, Prickly Sow Thistle, Common Sow Thistle, and Sleepy Catchfly (Allen 1998:43–45; Costello 1989a:88; Honeysett 1989:178–179).[4] To make matters worse, Spanish civil authorities issued edicts, such as Governor Arrillaga's command in 1793, requiring that native peoples (both neophytes and gentiles) terminate their age-old practice of burning fields and open woodlands to increase the productivity of wild foods. Thus, as the local coastal landscape became rapidly transformed by alien adobe structures, aqueducts, weeds, and thousands of head of livestock, the ability of local hunter-gatherers to practice their traditional seasonal rounds and subsistence practices became more and more constrained.[5]

Local cycles of drought, and warming seawater temperatures, exacerbated the detrimental effects of the mission agrarian system on the subsistence practices of coastal hunter-gatherers. In a recent study, Larson, Johnson, and Michaelson (1994) marshal an impressive suite of ecological data to demonstrate that abnormally dry conditions and the rising temperature of seawater severely affected the productivity of terrestrial and near-shore maritime environments during the period from 1780 to 1830 along the central California coast. They suggest that the massive movement of Chumash-speaking communities to the missions between 1786 and 1803 was, in part, to minimize the risk of food shortages as the yields of local fisheries and terrestrial wild plants and game plummeted. Here we can see native agency at work— as droughts curtailed wild food procurement, native peoples opted to move into the mission communities to avert local famines. Several eyewitnesses, including Felipe de Goycoechea, the presidio commander at Santa Barbara in the early 1800s, and José de Jesús Vallejo, who lived at Mission San José for thirty-eight years, observed that the number of baptisms increased markedly in local missions during periods of drought, when native foods were scarce (cited in Guest 1979:4,7).

Population decline in gentile villages, resulting from disease and increased violence, curtailed traditional craft pursuits, disrupted trade networks, and terminated the performance of ceremonies and dances that relied on a community of ritual specialists. The debilitating death rate of neophytes in the missions (discussed in chapter 3) no doubt served as a deterrent for gentiles choosing to enter the missions. But it is highly probable that nearby gentile communities also experienced severe population losses. In a preliminary examination of archaeological collections from contemporaneous gentile villages, Meighan (1987:194) argued that the health and mortality of Indian populations in the nearby hinterland was probably comparable to (or even worse than) those of neophytes residing in the missions.[6] Population loss of almost any magnitude would have had catastrophic implications for small-scale Native California polities. Once the population of a native polity dropped below a certain point (through mortality and mission recruitment), the polity would have experienced increasing problems surviving as a functioning social entity. The loss of elders who maintained the social memory and fabric of the group, in addition to the loss of fully initiated individuals who could perform the duties of political and religious leaders, must have devastated gentile polities (e.g., Margolin 1989:31–32; Milliken 1995:221–222). Furthermore, as the native polity's population declined, it would have become increasingly vulnerable to predation from traditional enemies (Milliken 1995:222). As a result, members of these struggling groups were probably forced to join other gentile groups, or move into the missions, for their very survival.[7]

The ultimate consequence of placing missionary colonies in the coastal zone was the structural collapse of local native societies. As gentile villages experienced increasing difficulties in harvesting wild foods and suffered population losses from disease, violence, and outward migration, they no longer could function as viable entities. Under steadily deteriorating conditions, there was probably little choice for most native people but to join the missions. Consequently, in later years it was not uncommon to see mass migrations of entire family groups and village units to the missions. Examples include the movement of entire Huchiun and Saclan villages from the East Bay to Mission San Francisco in 1794 and 1795 (Milliken 1995:129–135), and the immigration of Chumash families into the missions along the Santa Barbara coast in the early 1800s, the deteriorating conditions compounded by drought and warm sea temperatures (Larson et al. 1994). These large-scale population movements indicate that local native polities had reached a threshold where they could no longer function as viable social and political entities. I agree with Randall Milliken: once native communities entered this threshold of structural collapse, they had very few choices—they could either risk starvation or annihilation from enemies, attempt to negotiate membership into one of the gentile polities in the interior, or enter the nearest mission.

NATIVE REACTIONS TO THE FRANCISCAN MISSIONS

Once native peoples made the decision to join a mission, they enacted diverse tactics and social actions to cope with the repressive and structured regime of the Fernandinos. Some social actions involved strategies of active resistance, including uprisings, raiding, assassinations, and fugitivism. Other social actions involved passive resistance, manipulation of relationships with padres, indifference, and outright accommodation and alliance with the mission overseers.

Active Resistance

Many coastal Indians subjected to the Franciscan mission program exhibited considerable resentment toward the regimented daily routine and the domineering practices of the padres. This manifested itself in various forms of resistance and even violence. Jackson and Castillo (1995:73–86) and Castillo (1989c) present the most comprehensive overview of native resistance in the California missions. These authors are careful to distinguish between primary resistance, which took place during the initial encounters between the Spaniards and Indians, and secondary resistance, involving conflict and turbulence that continued to simmer even after the missions had been established for a generation or more (see also Phillips 1975:3). The former involved conventional native warfare organized by traditional Indian political leaders and shamans. The best recorded examples include the attack on the Portolá expedition's camp in San Diego by Diegueño-speaking peoples on August 15, 1769, and the attack on the San Diego mission by as many as eight hundred Diegueño warriors from forty villages on November 4, 1775 (Palóu 1955:76–77, 160–169; Phillips 1975:23). Jackson and Castillo (1995:74–77) also report several Indian revolts that failed because of the effectiveness of the padres' counterintelligence operations. One of these failed plots revolved around a powerful female shaman, Toypurina, who conspired to drive the Spaniards from southern California in 1785.

Secondary resistance typically involved native peoples who had grown up within the mission system, and who often served as resistance leaders in guerrilla-style warfare. Large-scale armed rebellions proved rare, with the major exception of the 1824 Chumash revolt that appears to have been an organized uprising of the neophytes from the missions of Santa Inés, La Purísima, and Santa Barbara. Rather, most of the resistance took the form of attempted murders of padres, fugitivism, and the large-scale raiding of horses, cattle, and mules. Castillo (1989b; 1989c) and Jackson and Castillo (1995:74) also discuss other kinds of passive resistance, such as abortion, infanticide, noncooperation, theft, and foot-dragging, that took place.

The best-documented case of the assassination of a Franciscan friar was recounted by a former Santa Cruz mission neophyte, Lorenzo Asisara. He had been told the story of how Padre Andrés Quintana was murdered by a group of conspirators at the Mission Santa Cruz in 1812 (see Asisara 1989a; Castillo 1989a). Jackson and Castillo (1995:80) and Castillo (1989a) also consider other possible cases where mission Indians poisoned padres in response to cruel treatment and harsh conditions.

Sherburne Cook's much-cited study (1976a:57–64) of mission fugitivism distinguished between temporary and permanent fugitives, with the former consisting of Indians who ran away from the missions but, in many cases, returned of their own volition. The latter represents those neophytes who disappeared and eluded recapture for a period long enough for them to have dropped from the mission rolls. Cook estimated that, prior to 1831, 3400 people, or about one in every twenty-four of the neophytes, had successfully escaped from the mission system. He further noted, basing his conclusion on records of the total number of fugitives (both temporary and permanent) through 1817, that an estimated 4060 neophytes, or about one in every ten mission Indians, had been reported as runaways. Archibald (1978:178) surmises that about 5 percent to 10 percent of the entire neophyte population became runaways at one time or another and eluded recapture, but that a much larger percentage of the mission Indians had made aborted or unsuccessful attempts to escape.

Some of the most famous resistance leaders in Alta California were ex-neophytes who had grown up in the missions and had become fugitives. Many of these leaders had served in positions of responsibility within the mission hierarchy. They proved very formidable adversaries, because they understood Hispanic military tactics as well as the weaknesses in the defenses of the Spanish and Mexican colonies.[8] By the late 1820s and 1830s, armed and mounted raiding bands of escaped neophytes and interior Indian peoples harassed and pillaged missions and private ranchos throughout central and southern California (see Phillips 1975). The raiding became so incessant by the late 1830s and 1840s that no mission or rancho could leave large herds of livestock unprotected. The raiding parties were organized around new types of territorial chiefs, who employed innovative methods to bedevil the missionaries and settlers of Alta California. The raiding was stimulated, in part, by a growing market for California horses and mules, which could be exchanged with traders from Santa Fe, New Mexico, and with British and American trappers venturing into the interior of Alta California (Hurtado 1988:44–46; Monroy 1990:130–131; Phillips 1993:85–87, 160–161).

Daily Practices within the Neophyte Communities

In addition to the better-known accounts of active native resistance, we can generate insights on how neophytes negotiated and mediated the dimensions of colonial encounters within mission communities, by examining the daily practices of individuals and households. We employ three lines of evidence (native texts, archaeology, and selected Franciscan writings) to construct a native perception of the mission system, and to emphasize the diverse responses to the missions exercised through the daily routines of neophyte inmates. These sources portray the neophyte quarters as complex, heterogenous communities marked by underground social practices, clandestine ceremonies, and political intrigue.

There are four native texts used in the analysis of the neophyte communities. Pablo Tac, a Luiseño Indian born in Mission San Luis Rey in 1822, wrote one account.[9] Three other narratives are oral histories written down by Anglo-American researchers who interviewed former neophytes or natives well versed in the stories of the missions. In using these latter sources we need to be cognizant of two issues: one is that they may not be first-hand accounts, as the native speakers may be recounting stories handed down to them by neophytes of their parents' or grandparents' generation; the other issue is that when the events described took place is not always clear—some may have transpired during the days of the Franciscan padres, while others happened in the postsecularization period, when the missions were under the supervision of Mexican administrators (see chapter 8). Since the three native interviewees were born quite late in the mission period or in postsecularization times, most of the stories of the missions under the Franciscans are probably remembrances handed down from earlier generations of neophytes. The interviewees include Lorenzo Asisara, an Ohlone speaker born at Mission Santa Cruz on August 10, 1820, and interviewed by Thomas Savage of the Bancroft history program in 1877, and by E.L. Williams in 1890 (Asisara 1892, 1989a).[10] Another was Julio César, a neophyte born at Mission San Luis Rey, probably around 1824, and interviewed by the Bancroft history program in the 1870s (César 1930).[11] The final account is that of Fernando Librado, a Chumash Indian interviewed by John P. Harrington sometime in 1912–1915.[12]

The primary archaeological studies employed in this section focus on neophyte contexts, especially residential spaces, such as dormitories and houses. The studies include the investigations of the following missions: San Buenaventura (Greenwood 1975, 1976), La Purísima (Deetz 1963; Farris and Wheeler 1998), San Antonio (Hoover and Costello 1985), San Juan Bautista (Farris 1991; Mendoza 2001, 2002), Santa Clara (Skowronek 1998; Skowronek and Wizorek 1997), Soledad (Farnsworth 1987, 1989), Santa Cruz (Allen 1998; Felton 1987), and Santa Inés (Costello 1989a).[13]

The final data set derives from selected writings of the padres, which present scattered glimpses of the daily practices of neophytes outside work and mass. The padres' writings shed light on how natives negotiated two dimensions—the enculturation program and demographic parameters. These snippets suggest the neophytes conducted a separate and secret life

behind closed doors when not at work or mass. The most revealing observations were written by the padres who filled out the questionnaires between 1813 and 1815. They described shamans undertaking curing rituals
in the neophyte quarters, surreptitious dances and ceremonies, the continued practice of many native "superstitions," the use of hallucinogenic
drugs, and "pagan" mortuary customs (Geiger and Meighan 1976:47–51,71–
80,97–100, 119–120).

Enculturation Program: Native Responses

Native Texts   The neophyte narratives speak to the repressive nature of
the Franciscan enculturation program and the controlling influence the
padres had over their lives. Lorenzo Asisara (1989b) testified how much
the padres dominated the lives of the neophytes, and how the temperament
and humanity of the Franciscan fathers varied greatly from individual to
individual. In Asisara's 1877 testimonial, the author's sense of time was
marked by listing the padres and the later mission administrators (after secularization) in rough chronological order. He then evaluated each padre and
mission administrator on the basis of overall treatment of the neophytes—
on, that is, how much they punished the Indians, and whether they were
kind and compassionate or cruel and sadistic. For example, he recounted
stories from older neophytes about how Padre Ramon Olbés "was very inclined to cruelly whip. He was never satisfied to prescribe less than 50 lashes;
even to the little children of 8–10 years he would order 25 lashes given at
the hand of a strong man, either on the buttocks, or on the stomach, when
the whim would enter him" (Asisara 1989b:397). Asisara (1989b:398) also
related how Padre Olbés punished a neophyte couple for not having a baby.
The husband, sent to the guardhouse in a pair of shackles, was forced to wear
cattle horns affixed with leather when he attended mass. The wife (who refused to let the padre examine her reproductive parts) was given fifty lashes
and had to carry around a wooden doll in the neophyte community for nine
days.

In his 1890 interview, Lorenzo Asisara (1892:47) expanded upon his discussion about the somewhat paranoid excesses and intimidating activities
of some padres.

> Sometimes the padres would leave a *real* [silver coin, one-eighth of a
> dollar] in some corner or under the bed, to see if I would take it. I was
> never tempted in that way, but often others were, and then punished.
> It was the custom of one of the padres to go about at night disguised,
> and he would come upon his Indian officers playing cards by the fire.
> One would say during the game, "I play this card!" another some other

card. He would approach nearer and say, "I play this card," showing his hands in the light of the blaze of the fire, when the others would discover by his white hands that he was not one of them.

Julio César (1930:42) remarked as well upon the repressive nature of the Franciscan missions during his youth at Mission San Luis Rey. "When I was a boy the treatment given to the Indians at the mission was not at all good. They did not pay us anything, but merely gave us our food and breech-clout and blanket, the last renewed every year, besides flogging for any fault, however slight. We were at the mercy of the administrator, who ordered us to be flogged whenever and however he took a notion."

César (1930:42) also stated that the missionaries did not really educate the neophytes, but merely led them in rote memorization. "To the question whether we were taught to read and write, I reply that we were only taught to pray and recite the masses from memory. They did not teach me to read the church music. There were singers and instrumentalists, but everything was from memory. I never saw them give a paper with music written on it to any one."

Fernando Librado (1979:17) narrated in some detail the harsh punishments of the mission community.

> In those days punishment for the Indians was performed in a jail just east of the tower of Mission San Buenaventura. In one of the rooms there were the punishment stocks. There were two kinds of stocks in that room. One was shaped of wood to cover the foot like a shoe. It was made from two pieces of wood which opened, and the entire foot was placed into it from toe to heel. These pieces of wood were joined to a ring which went about the knee, and from this ring straps were attached to a belt that went around the waist of a person. Weights were fastened to the straps. As punishment, the priests would work men and women in the fields with these weighted wooden shoes. The priests also sometimes shackled the feet of Indians, or shackled two Indians together at the same time. I remember how the Indians were treated unjustly by the order of the priests.

In describing the spatial organization of Mission San Luis Rey, Pablo Tac mentioned the doorways (e.g., "[a] door which is called the biggest of all. Through here the neophytes enter and leave for work") and walled enclosures and buildings employed to control the movement of neophytes and to maintain restricted access to certain spaces in the mission complex, such as the gardens reserved for the padres (Tac 1958:15–17).

The native narratives provide insights on how neophytes negotiated the repressive enculturation program of the Franciscan missions. These narra-

Figure 4. Neophytes at Mission San Francisco de Asís, as drawn by Louis Choris in 1816. This well-known drawing depicts Indians playing gambling games, probably outside their houses in the neophyte village. Choris was a young artist on the round-the-world voyage of Otto von Kotzebue, commander of the *Rurik*, 1815–18. (Courtesy of the Bancroft Library, University of California, Berkeley.)

tives speak to the critical importance of social bonds established among mission Indians, and the creation of communities within the neophyte villages that became the focus of family life, dances, sharing meals, gambling, and other social actions (figure 4). Lorenzo Asisara (1989b:396, 398–399) made it clear that native gambling, based on the traditional *peon* game (using one black and one white bone) and European cards, was rampant at Mission Santa Cruz. He described how neophytes would make social visits to relatives, where they would spend time eating and gambling. Pablo Tac (1958:21–22) illustrated the social dynamics of a neophyte family, in which the elderly father spent the morning hunting, the elderly mother engaged in domestic work at home, and the grown son and daughter worked in the mission labor force, but all gathered at noon to eat their meal together. Tac also described in some detail the native dances and ball games performed by the neophytes at Mission San Luis Rey, noting "now that we are Christians we dance for ceremony." He recounted the songs, ceremonial regalia, and body movements of three principal dances of the

Luiseños, and also told of a native ball game between the neophytes of Mission San Luis Rey and those of Mission San Juan Capistrano that ended up in a bloody brawl, bringing soldiers out to the playing field to investigate (Tac 1958:22–29).

Fernando Librado presented the most detailed account of the daily life of native peoples in mission communities. Although his recollection pertains largely to Mission San Buenaventura after secularization, it gives, I think, some idea of the kinds of surreptitious activities that took place in the earlier neophyte communities under the Fernandinos. He described social gatherings of natives who came together to play *peon;* to participate in diverse native dances, songs, and ceremonies; to partake in Indian ball games; or to feast (Librado 1979:23, 25–33). Librado also emphasized the two sides of the neophyte community—one public, the other private. For example, when neophyte couples were married, a separate and private "native" ceremony was held inside one of the adobe structures before the Catholic ritual was performed.

> The *smyi* was private and came first, about 9 o'clock in the morning in which the fiesta began. It was held in one of the long adobe-tiled buildings which was west of what is now Figueroa Street. A *ksen* [messenger], who was paid in advance by the father of the boy and the father of the girl, was sent to invite people to the ceremonies. He was dressed well with feathers, bows, and arrows, and he would dodge about as he carried the news of the ceremony, attracting even more attention by his yelling of *yampanak, yampanak.* Invited persons gave presents to the *ksen* also. When the private *smyi* ceremony was over, the young people went to the priest on the afternoon of the same day. Then the "*ush'auwai,*" public ceremony was undertaken. (Librado 1979:28)

He also noted that some dances were performed in front of the entire mission community, but others were observed in the privacy of Indian houses or in the secluded "plaza" spaces (between rows of houses) in the mission village (see Librado 1979:25–33). For example,

> Encarnación [Luhui] danced the *Shutiwishyi'ish* Dance in the adobe house in front of the Mission one afternoon. This house was between the east and middle rows, while the west row bordered the garden wall. The old woman had a little hut of carrizo south of these adobes, and she came from her hut all dressed up. She was naked except for her dancing skirt of feathers, which consisted of two tiers of black feathers and a tier of long feathers below. I think she wore a G-string under her feather apron. She had a woven belt on too, which had three dollar-shaped, red abalone shell ornaments with small stars and half-moons, also of red abalone, in between. Red abalone shell was preferred over blue abalone

because it was flatter, bigger, and more beautiful. Her scant hair was wrapped about the top of her head a couple of times and fastened with a *tsiwin* and *tsux* headdress. Her face was unpainted.

Three old men, whose names I cannot remember, were already seated and awaiting her. They would be her singers. These men used no instruments, but merely placed their left hand over their eyes and slapped their thighs with their right hand. They were to the east of her and kneeling on one knee, and every time a song would end, they cried out.

Lots of people had come to see Encarnación. She merely asked the Indians to join her in her jollification, and many arrived from Ventura and vicinity. Some onlookers gave some things to her, and she gave some of these things to the old men singers. (Librado 1979:26–27)

Archaeological Sources   Like the native narratives, archaeological investigations have stressed the importance of distinguishing public and private spaces when considering the daily practices of neophytes in the missions (Skowronek 1998:687). How the neophytes presented themselves in public, interacted with the padres and other mission managers, and carried on their day-to-day lives in full view of the mission may have been very different from what transpired in the privacy of their own houses or neighborhoods in the mission villages. A common strategy to cope with the coercive elements of the missions was to withdraw into the neophyte communities. Here many Indians performed covert social practices that maintained their connection to the past and renewed their linkages with other tradition-minded neophytes.

Excavations of neophyte quarters and associated social spaces have unearthed a considerable number of artifacts that must have had significant meaning and value to people who self-identified as Indians. These artifacts include: 1) clam and *olivella* shell beads; 2) lithic assemblages consisting of various flaked stone tools and ground stone objects, such as pestles, manos, metates, steatite bowls and ollas, and steatite pipes; 3) bone assemblages of beads, whistles, awls, bird bone tubes (possibly used as shaman sucking tubes), and gaming pieces; and 4) basketry impressions of water bottles, storage baskets, and matting (Allen 1998:63–64,73–88; Deetz 1963; Farnsworth 1987:402–405; Farris 1991:28–38; Farris and Wheeler 1998; Greenwood 1975; Hastings 1975; Hoover and Costello 1985:62–93; Mendoza 2001; Rozaire 1976; Skowronek 1998:686; Wlodarski and Larson 1975; Wlodarski and Larson 1976). There is also good evidence for the modification of European materials (ceramics, glass, roof and floor tiles) into native objects such as pendants, disks, and projectile points (Allen 1998:67, 89; Costello and Hornbeck 1989:314; Farnsworth 1987:410–418; Farris 1991:34–35; Greenwood 1975:471; Hoover 1979:57). For example, at San Juan Bautista, the excavation team of Ruben Mendoza (2001:7) exposed the rim fragment of a copper kettle that appeared to have been salvaged and recycled by neophytes who had meticulously cut it into rectangular pieces.

The faunal and floral assemblages unearthed from neophyte contexts are predominantly the food remains of domesticated animals (cattle, pigs, sheep, horses, dogs, chickens) and agricultural crops (wheat, barley, fava beans), but there is also a fairly consistent presence of traditional native foods. Wild foods recovered include the remains of: marine fishes (rockfish, plainfin midshipman, white croaker, and perch at several missions, as well as yellowtail, bonito, and barracuda at Mission San Buenaventura); shellfish (with mussels dominating plus some clams, abalone, snails, and limpets); terrestrial game (deer, jack rabbits, cottontails, squirrels); birds (quail, turkey, geese, ducks); occasional sea mammals; and a few plants (hazelnuts, black walnuts, wild grapes, and acorns) (Allen 1998:55–61; Farris 1991:39–40; Hoover 1980:144–145; Langenwalter and McKee 1985; McIntyre 1976; Walker and Davidson 1989:168–169). The presence of golden eagles, ravens, and owls may represent evidence of ceremonies performed in neophyte quarters (Langenwalter and McKee 1985:116; Walker and Davidson 1989:169). These birds had important symbolic meanings in the cosmology of many coastal hunter-gatherer groups of California, and birds of prey played especially significant roles in some of their dances, ceremonies, and feasts (e.g., Meighan 1976b:160–161; Raab et al. 1994:254–255).

The analysis of food remains from archaeological contexts provides information on how meat portions were butchered. Although butchering practices varied in the missions examined, it appears that most of the cattle and sheep found in neophyte quarters were usually dismembered using Hispanic practices and tools. That is, based on the cuts of meats and butchering marks on faunal remains, it appears that iron knives, cleavers, or axes were employed (Allen 1998:57; Langenwalter and McKee 1985:111; Walker and Davidson 1989:172–173). Neophytes probably processed these meats under the supervision of the padres or mission managers. The bones associated with neophyte contexts may be meat packages from animals that the padres had the Indian workers kill and prepare for distribution to the neophyte families.

Most of the wild foods (shellfish, fish, and game) found in the native quarters were either harvested by the neophytes using traditional fishing, gathering, and hunting techniques, or traded to the neophytes by gentile Indians. Allen (1998:61–62) describes fish hooks, manufactured from abalone or mussel shells, as well as net weights, recovered at Mission Santa Cruz.

Greenwood (1976:588) points to both archival records and archaeological findings for evidence of pelagic fishing at Mission San Buenaventura using plank canoes. The burial records of Mission La Purísima mention neophytes who died in fishing accidents (Walker and Davidson 1989:169). However, Salls (1989) believes that about 15 percent of the rock fish recovered from Mission Soledad came from deep water environments, and probably required Iberian long-line fishing methods to catch.[14] Interestingly, some neophytes may have shared their catches with the padres, who no doubt would have appreciated fresh fish on Fridays. For example, excavations of deposits associated with the Santa Inés Mission *convento*, including the apartments of the padres, uncovered remains of barracudas, rockfish, and mackerel (Costello 1989a:88; Walker and Davidson 1989:169).

Significantly, much of the manufacture and employment of the native material culture was associated with the private space of the neophyte villages. Areal excavations of the neophyte quarters at Mission Santa Cruz, Mission San Buenaventura, and Mission San Antonio exposed archaeological deposits in the interior of rooms, and sometimes nearby extramural space associated with the front and back yards (Felton 1987:56–58; Gates 1976; Hastings 1975; Hoover and Costello 1985:17–20). The presence of food remains, hearths, fire-cracked rocks, and ground stone tools indicates that neophytes prepared, cooked, and consumed at least some foods in their quarters. Cooking activities at Mission San Antonio took place both inside the rooms and in the adjacent front yards (Hoover and Costello 1985:41), but such activities took place primarily in the rooms at Mission Santa Cruz and Mission San Buenaventura (Allen 1998:63; Hastings 1975:125–134). The spatial distribution of detritus from shell bead production and lithic manufacture also indicates that these activities were centered inside neophyte rooms at Mission Santa Cruz (Allen 1998:73, 82).

It is significant that some adobe room apartments not only contain evidence for processing and consuming native foods but also contain a plethora of native artifacts. Farris (1991:5) argues that these rooms were most likely the abodes of the most progressive and longtime neophytes in the missions. Yet at least some of these families appear to have been living double lives—gaining the trust of the padres during the day and engaging in native activities at night and during their off-hours from work and prayer. For example, in one room (designated the east room of Locus 3) of the neophyte barracks excavated at Mission San Buenaventura, archaeologists found numerous aboriginal artifacts, an abundance of steatite objects, and finely decorated bone whistles. These remains may have belonged to a Chumash shaman or someone of high rank in the local native hierarchy (Greenwood

1975:473; Hastings 1975:125–128). It would be very interesting, in this light, to excavate midden deposits associated with the traditional dome-shaped huts where the "less progressive" Indians resided in the neophyte villages. However, it does not appear that any of these structures have been excavated and fully reported in the archaeological literature.

Although excavations of neophyte apartments yielded the most diverse assemblages of native artifacts, archaeological investigations of other mission contexts have also been revealing. For example, the excavation of the *lavanderías* at Mission San Luis Rey exposed an assortment of artifacts, including bone gambling sticks, pottery gaming disks, hundreds of shell and glass beads, two stone smoking pipes, an array of chipped stone and ground stone tools, Chinese and Mexican pottery sherds, coins, and one Spanish religious medal (Soto 1961:34–36). The investigation of a trash dump, possibly associated with the neophyte housing at Mission San Buenaventura, also unearthed a range of shell and glass beads, ceramic sherds, glass fragments, shellfish, fish, and terrestrial and marine mammal remains. Interestingly, although domesticated animals are well represented, wild species comprise the greatest proportion of the faunal remains. The percentage of marine fish is comparable to that recovered from the prehistoric component of the site (McIntyre 1976:272–274).

Padres' Accounts   The writings of the Fernandinos demonstrate that they were well aware of the widespread extent to which covert activities and social practices took place within neophyte communities, as the following citations from questionnaires filled out in the period 1813–15 exemplify.

> Nevertheless, there are among them some ill-intentioned old persons who inject a dreadful fear into them concerning the devil whom they look upon as the author of all evil. These oldsters make the rest believe that in order to prevent the devil from harming them they should offer him a little flour, which they eat, in a definite tree trunk, in this or that place. With the same purpose in mind, they hold at times secret, nocturnal dances always avoiding detection by the fathers. We are informed that at night, only the men gather together in the field or the forest. In their midst they raise a long stick crowned by a bundle of tobacco leaves or branches of trees or some other plant. At the base of this they place their food and even their colored beads. Then they prepare for the dance bedaubing their bodies and faces. . . . After this they proceed with the dance and continue with it till daybreak. In order to dissuade them from such harmful deception there is no better remedy than preaching and punishment. (Padres at Mission Santa Cruz; in Geiger and Meighan 1976:50)

They are quite fond of gathering for the feast of the bird called *Gavilán* or eagle. The feast consists in hunting said hawk with great eagerness and to the hunt they invite one another. This hunt takes place due to the presence of certain neophytes of this mission who are keen-witted but poor workers when it comes to gathering seeds. These wishing to have a feast resolve to hunt said bird and fool the more simple-minded by telling them that the bird is the being who can free them from their enemies and grant them whatever they ask. These believe this false supposition with such stubbornness that they take as much care of the bird as a most affectionate mother for her son for from the moment they catch it they bring it whatever they have found in the hunt and give it always the better seeds. Then after it has been carefully raised they kill and cremate it. While the remains are in the fire they offer it the seeds and glass beads they collected and anything else they treasure very highly. They hunt another hawk the following year and go through the same performance. The remedy taken to keep them from this foolishness is to station trustworthy Indians to watch this event and to punish those who are caught. (Padres at Mission San Diego; in Geiger and Meighan 1976:47)

Idolatry is still practiced by some Indians. It is being extirpated however, by dint of effort. It would disappear all the faster if the old people and young ones did not live together for the former are the ones who mislead the young. (Padres at Mission San Gabriel; in Geiger and Meighan 1976:57)

Some of the old men pretending to be doctors graduated in the school of their own ignorance, simplicity and rudeness, would relate a long series of fabulous stories, full of ridiculousness and extravagance regarding the creation of the world and its government. The boys and young people took much delight in them and they would even pay some old men to recite these stories. Many times neophytes with good sense who possessed true Christian sentiments assured me that they knew the futility of such stories. So whenever they saw boys in such circles one or more would warn them. (Padres at Mission San Buenaventura; in Geiger and Meighan 1976:58)

The padres noted that the consumption of native foods was a common practice in the private space of neophyte residences.

The neophytes in their houses have plenty of fresh and dried meat. In addition in their homes they have quantities of acorns, *chia* and other seeds, fruits, edible plants and other nutritious plants which they do not forget and of which they are very fond. They also eat fish, mussels, ducks, wild geese, cranes, quail, hares, squirrels, rats, and other animals which exist in abundance. Owing to the variety of eatables which they keep in their homes and being children who eat at all hours it is not easy to compute the amount they daily consume. (Padres at Mission San Buenaventura; in Geiger and Meighan 1976:86)

The number of meals these Indians eat is beyond count for it can be said that the entire day is one continuous meal. Even at night when they awaken they are wont to reach out for the first thing at hand and eat. . . . Besides the mission food the Indians are also very fond of the food they enjoyed in their pagan state: those from the mountains, venison, rabbits, rats, squirrels or any other small animal they can catch; those from the seashore enjoy every species of sea food. (Padres at Mission Santa Barbara; in Geiger and Meighan 1976:86)

But in private, in their own houses they prepare their seeds which are of good quality and in abundance such as acorns, sage, *chia*, pine nuts and others. They know how to endure hunger but because they have a hearty appetite they eat at all hours. (Padres at Mission San Antonio; in Geiger and Meighan 1976:87)

However, they are free to eat in their huts and so they eat day and night nor is there any way of making them use moderation. They eat rats, squirrels, moles, shellfish and all living things except frogs, toads and owls which are the only animals they are afraid of. (Padres at Mission San Carlos; in Geiger and Meighan 1976:87)

Relocation Program: Native Perceptions

Native Texts   The native texts offer some insights into the challenges of being forced to live with peoples from a multitude of polities, many of whom spoke mutually unintelligible languages and some of whom were recognized as traditional enemies. Asisara (1892:46–47) recounted the location of different Indian "tribes" and languages on the central California coast, before the groups were aggregated at Mission Santa Cruz. He emphasized that members of distant groups could not understand each other, and that some were antagonists who had until very recently been fighting with "bows and arrows." Fernando Librado (1979:4–5) observed how the foods and customs of the Tulareños Indians (Yokuts speakers from the Central Valley) differed from those of other neophytes in the San Buenaventura Mission.

The native narratives confirm that not all neophytes were resettled at the mission centers but, rather, flexibility existed in the placement of people across the landscapes of some mission estates. Julio César (1930:42) recounted various outlying ranches associated with Mission San Luis Rey, noting that most had sizeable settlements of mission Indians. Furthermore, he observed that the padres visited those rancho settlements with chapels only about every eight days (or at least once a month). Consequently, workers in these outlying villages were outside the direct daily control of the missionaries, although mission overseers were stationed at these settlements to keep the Indians in line. Tac (1958:17–20) also mentioned the multiple ranchos where mission Indians lived in the hinterland of Mission San Luis Rey.

Archaeological Sources   Archaeological research indicates that, during periods of intensive native recruitment to the missions, the relative percentage of native artifacts (such as chipped stone and ground stone tools, bone tools, and shell ornaments) increased in neophyte residential contexts (Farnsworth 1989:241–245). Conversely, during those times when mission records indicate that gentile recruitment waned, the relative percentage of native artifacts decreased. In Farnsworth's analysis of the artifacts from neophyte quarters in three missions (Mission Soledad, Mission San Antonio, Mission La Purísima), the number of native artifacts dropped when gentile recruitment attenuated, but never fell below about 30 percent of the total neophyte assemblages (see Farnsworth 1987:603–620; Farnsworth 1989:241,246). Farnsworth's research shows that the presence of native artifacts in neophyte contexts cannot simply be explained by the resettlement of gentile Indians into mission communities. There is strong evidence that, even in times when few gentiles were recruited, some neophytes maintained many conventional *indio* practices.[15]

Labor System: Native Craftspeople and Slackers

Native Texts   The native narratives define the jobs that the padres expected the neophytes to perform. Asisara recounted (1892:45–46) that mission Indians served as textile workers (weaving blankets), blacksmiths, tanners, and fieldworkers at Mission Santa Cruz. He noted that women served as seamstresses, prepared wool for the weavers, and also worked in the fields. Tac (1958) also described native men laboring as gardeners, shoemakers, and blacksmiths, and women as textile workers at Mission San Luis Rey. Colonial records document complaints made by neophytes to civil authorities about the abusive labor practices of some padres; for example, Governor Diego de Borica's investigation on why two hundred neophytes fled Mission San Francisco in 1796 resulted in native testimonies about the long hours they worked, as well as complaints about unfair punishment and inadequate food (Guest 1966:208–212).

Archaeological Sources   As Skowronek summarizes (1998:697–698), no systematic investigations by archaeologists and physical anthropologists have yet been undertaken on the physical duress inflicted on the neophytes by the labor regime of the Fernandinos. Paleopathological examinations of neophyte skeletons from mission cemeteries can provide many insights into the labor practices of the mission Indians, and into whether these Indians suffered long-term health risks from their jobs. Such studies conducted on native populations in other areas of the country have yielded much information about long-term impacts of colonial labor programs (e.g., Larsen 1994).

Archaeological research indicates that neophytes incorporated indigenous practices into daily work routines. Although they employed Hispanic tools and technological methods, to varying degrees, in their labor, the neophyte workers maintained native artifacts and methods whenever possible. In the excavation of the tanning vats at Mission La Purísima, Deetz (1963:166–172) reported that native peoples employed chipped stone tools and rib bone beamers (from cow bones) for working hides. Although the use of these native objects is today typically explained by the general paucity of metal tools at the missions, I believe that this usage also displays native agency and preferences in action. Deetz (1963:186) emphasized continuity, too, in the native artifacts and technology associated with women at the missions, especially for those tasks involving food preparation and domestic work. Manos and metates (and impressions of baskets, steatite tools, bone awls, plugged abalone shells, as well as aboriginal ceramics in southern California) are commonly found in mission archaeological excavations (Deetz 1963:186; Greenwood 1976:171–172; Hollimon 1989; Skowronek 1998:694–695; Wlodarski and Larson 1976:59–60). These objects, used by many generations of coastal hunter-gatherers before European contact, demonstrate strong connections with the past. Significantly, mission Indians employed some of these native tools to process both native and non-native foods (such as wheat and barley). For example, the carbonized seeds of wheat, barley, and fava beans detected by Farris (1991:40) in his testing of the neophyte quarters at Mission San Juan Bautista, suggest that neophytes employed traditional methods of cooking plant seeds (such as the use of parching baskets) to prepare some European crop foods in their own homes.

Archaeological research also shows that the expertise and job performance of neophytes varied greatly. Hackel (1997:123–124) comments that at least some neophyte laborers became experts at their trades, especially after they were allowed to apprentice with seasoned craftsmen from New Spain, beginning in the mid-1790s. Otherwise, he observes, how can we account for the construction of the region's impressive adobe and wood churches, the spinning and weaving of the cloth used to clothe the people of Alta California, and the production of the leather, wood, and ceramic goods

used by the soldiers and settlers in the presidios and pueblos? Native laborers accomplished all these tasks by their skill and sweat—but there is
also archaeological evidence of shoddy workmanship by the neophytes (Costello and Hornbeck 1989:314). This point is epitomized by Julia Costello's
excavation and interpretation of the ceramic kiln at Mission San Antonio,
where a sizeable mound of tile wasters was uncovered near the mouth of
the kiln (1985; 1997:213–214). Her comparative analysis with other kilns
in New Spain indicates there was associated with this kiln an exceptionally
large number of broken tiles, suggesting either on-the-job training, infe-
rior skills in firing ceramics, poor clays, or intentional damage of tiles through
substandard production. Costello also observes that native workers incom-
pletely mastered the production of lime at Mission Santa Inés (1989a:94).
These findings raise the possibility that either some neophytes engaged in
a passive form of resistance by intentionally being slackers in their labor
or the mission managers were constantly rotating new recruits into these
occupations.

Social Mobility: Native Accommodation and Resentment

Native Texts   The texts provide a much-needed native perspective of the
mission social hierarchy—especially of how mission Indian officials interacted with the broader neophyte communities. The dual social hierarchies
of the missions created frictions and tensions within the neophyte villages.
Considerable mistrust, apprehension, and resentment existed between Indian *alcaldes* and neophytes (especially traditional native leaders) who did
not hold formal mission offices.

Asisara intimated (1989b:396) that the *alcaldes* were the eyes and ears
of the padres in the neophyte community at Mission Santa Cruz. In one instance, the *alcaldes* informed a padre that a neophyte named Dámaso had
missed work and had been gambling all afternoon. The padre subsequently
ordered the *alcaldes* to punish (whip) Dámaso on the stomach.[16] However,
according to this secondhand story, before the Indian officials could obey, a
mutiny broke out in the men's dormitory, with the residents pummeling
the *alcaldes* with pieces of tiles and rocks. In his 1890 interview, Asisara was
even more blunt about the oppressive nature of the missions and the subversive role the *alcaldes* played in the neophyte community.

> The Indians at the mission were very severely treated by the padres,
> often punished by fifty lashes on the bare back. They were governed
> somewhat in the military style, having sergeants, corporals, and
> overseers, who were Indians and they reported to the padres any
> disobedience or infraction of the rules, and then came the lash without

mercy, the women the same as the men. The lash was made of rawhide.
I was never punished, except a few slaps for forgetfulness. (Asisara
1892:46–47)

César (1930:42) also observed the special status that the *alcaldes* held in
the missions: they, along with the *vaqueros*, were the only neophytes allowed to ride horses.

Librado recounted the important status of the *alcaldes* (also referred to
as judges) in the Mission San Buenaventura Indian community: "An old Indian named [Captain]Luis Francisco was a judge [alcalde] at Mission San
Buenaventura. There were four judges, a mayordomo, and a corporal. This
was the board that made all the dispositions as to the ways of proceedings,
such as work and so on. When a band of workers had a good foreman, the
Indians would call him mayordomo" (Librado 1979:13). He also related that
some Indians advanced quite high up in the colonial hierarchy, as one educated and honest man, the captain Juan de Jesús, became the administrator
general of Mission San Buenaventura.

Tac (1958: 20) described the special treatment the padres received at the
apex of the mission hierarchy.

In the Mission of San Luis Rey de Francia the Fernandino Father is
like a king. He has his pages, alcaldes, majordomos, musicians, soldiers,
gardens, ranchos, livestock. . . . The pages are for him and for the
Spanish and Mexican, English and Anglo-American travelers. The
alcaldes to help him govern all the people of the Mission of San Luis
Rey de Francia. The majordomos are in the distant districts, almost all
Spaniards. (Tac 1958:20)

He also considered the duties of the *alcaldes* and the somewhat coercive role
they played in the neophyte community of San Luis Rey.

The Fernandino Father . . . appointed alcaldes from the people themselves that knew how to speak Spanish more than the others and were
better than the others in their customs. There were seven of these alcaldes, with rods as a symbol that they could judge the others. The
captain dressed like the Spanish, always remaining captain, but not
ordering his people about as of old, when they were still gentiles. The
chief of the alcaldes was called the general. He knew the name of each
one, and when he took something he then named each person by his
name. In the afternoon, the alcaldes gather at the house of the missionary. They bring the news of that day, and if the missionary tells them
something that all the people of the country ought to know, they return
to the villages shouting, "Tomorrow morning. . . ."
  Returning to the villages, each one of the alcaldes wherever he goes
cries out what the missionary has told them, in his language, and all

the country hears it. "Tomorrow the sowing begins and so the laborers go to the chicken yard and assemble there." And again he goes saying these same words until he reaches his own village to eat something and then to sleep. In the morning you will see the laborers appear in the chicken yard and assemble there according to what they heard last night.

With the laborers goes a Spanish majordomo and others, neophyte alcaldes, to see how the work is done, to hurry them if they are lazy, so that they will soon finish what was ordered, and to punish the guilty or lazy one who leaves his plow and quits the field keeping on with his laziness. They work all day, but not always. (Tac 1958:19–20)

Archaeological Sources   Neophytes accorded higher status and greater responsibility by the padres may have left behind archaeological signatures of their differential access to Hispanic luxury goods and trade commodities, and of greater elaboration of their residential quarters. Unfortunately, detailed studies of the intraspatial patterning of neophyte villages and individual residences are only in their infancy. There are many problems to consider in undertaking such microscale analyses, including the reuse of rooms during both the mission and postmission periods, the association of artifacts with particular residents, and sorting out the microstratigraphy of floors and refuse deposits. Despite these difficulties, there are promising leads. The differential distribution of imported goods in mission Indian quarters is cited as possible evidence for status differences among the neophytes, and as material evidence of those individuals and families closely aligned with the padres (Hoover and Costello 1985:41; Skowronek 1998:689). For example, Hoover (1977:264; 1979:56) notes that one of the rooms excavated in the neophyte barracks at Mission San Antonio contained a high proportion of glass beads and imported pottery uncovered on a tile floor. Some of the floor tiles were incised with geometric designs of circles, crosses, and crossed diagonal lines—design motifs that Hoover believes may have been inspired by Christian symbolism. Although the original occupants of this tiled room are not known, Hoover suggests that whoever resided here enjoyed some degree of status differentiation, and that perhaps here was the household of an *alcalde* or overseer.

Deetz (1963:182–183) presented a similar archaeological pattern for the neophyte family barracks at Mission La Purísima. In the excavation of rooms in the linear adobe structure, he observed that all of the rooms contained dirt floors except for Rooms 3 and 4. In this apartment suite, the field crews unearthed a plastered floor, remains of whitewashed walls, and a range of exotic goods, including a cello string, wine glass, wine bottles, fine porcelain, stirrup and spur rowel, and relatively few native artifacts. He interpreted these archaeological remains as probably the residence of an Hispanic soldier, but it is equally possible that it was occupied by the family of an Indian official. More recently, Julia Costello has refined Deetz's original hypothesis by suggesting that this room may have been occupied by a Hispanic *enfermera* (nurse), Guadalupe Briones, who was hired to work in the adjacent infirmary in 1817 (Farris and Wheeler 1998: 1,8–9). Additional areal excavations are needed in other mission settings to identify and evaluate contexts used by high-status neophyte families or Hispanic workers or managers assigned to live in the neophyte family quarters.

Archaeological investigations indicate great diversity in the kinds and quality of ceramics associated with neophytes of the different missions. Costello (1992:67–68) shows that nearly 50 percent of the ceramics associated with Indian populations at Mission San Buenaventura and Mission San Antonio were produced in the missions, but only 4 percent of the ceramics at Mission La Purísima were local wares. In contrast to those of the former two missions, La Purísima neophyte residences exhibited high frequencies of English wares (55 percent) and Chinese wares (22 percent), frequencies not unlike what is found in the padre or Hispanic quarters. She also observes a general tendency for the proportion of English ceramics to increase significantly after 1810.[17] Furthermore, she argues that some of the nonlocal ceramics associated with neophyte quarters were probably actively purchased or obtained by the Indians, while others tended to be older wares that were heirlooms, cast-offs, or materials scavenged from other mission contexts.

Interethnic Unions: Silence from the Native Community

Native Texts   The native texts provide little information on marriages that took place between neophyte women and Hispanic men.

Archaeological Sources   There has been little archaeological investigation of possible interethnic households in the mission complexes. However, most of the Indian women who married Hispanic soldiers and settlers moved out of the *monjerío* dormitory and probably left the neophyte community, eventually resettling outside the missions. It would be instructive to try and trace an interethnic couple who moved to a nearby presidio or pueblo settlement, and undertake an archaeological investigation of the couple's residence.

Demographic Parameters: Native Encounters with Death

Native Texts   The horrific mortality rate experienced by the neophytes must have presented a terrifying and deeply disturbing situation for the Indians residing at the missions. Tac (1958:19) lamented the rapid population decline of his people, the Quechnajuichom. "In Quechla not long ago there were 5,000 souls, with all their neighboring lands. Through a sickness that came to California 2,000 souls died, and 3,000 were left." Librado detailed how native doctors attended to the suffering of the sick, attempting to nurse them back to health through curing rituals and through application of indigenous medicines (Librado 1979:57–60,68–73). He described the common use of charms with powers to protect and heal. He also identified some people within the native community as "poisoners" who were blamed by the community for the illness and death of particular individuals (Librado 1979:38,40–45). He noted that dances were performed to celebrate the recovery of a sick person (Librado 1979:45). Finally, Librado (1979:76) described the mortuary ceremony of Salvador, an old man who had been in charge of the mission looms. A traditional ceremony was held at the house of his surviving wife, with mourners offering baskets of food. The grieving family and friends threw corn meal, beans, and chia to the four directions, in the afternoons for three days, after which they burned the baskets of the dead man.

Archaeological Sources   Excavations have unearthed artifacts believed to have been used in indigenous curing ceremonies. These include types of charmstones, bone and stone tubes, bone whistles, and rock crystals that appear to be regalia associated with shamans and Indian doctors (Allen 1998:86; Costello and Hornbeck 1989:315–316; Farnsworth 1987:412,416; Hastings 1975:125; Hoover and Costello 1985:92; Skowronek 1998:686). Archaeological work also indicates that some neophytes were accorded special treatment at death, deviating from standard Catholic burials. The padres oversaw the Christian burial of the Indians and followed the prescribed Catholic customs of the day. That is, neophytes might be wrapped in a shroud and/or placed in a wooden coffin. They were buried on their backs with hands clasped over the chest (Skowronek and Wizorek 1997:80–81). However, in some cases, mourners placed native grave goods, especially shell and glass beads, with the deceased; such cases indicate the observance of mortuary protocols whose roots extend thousands of years into prehistory.

In fact, there is considerable variation in the mortuary practices concerning individuals from the few neophyte cemeteries that have been archaeologically investigated. As Skowronek and Wizorek (1997:81) have recently summarized, previous archaeological investigations at Mission La Purísima revealed only one grave with associated grave goods—specifically, glass beads (see, e.g., Humphrey 1965)—but excavators at the third mission cemetery (1781–1825) at Mission Santa Clara discovered eleven individuals associated with more than 6,000 shell beads and 484 glass beads (see, e.g., Hylkema 1995). Recent mitigation work at the fifth mission cemetery (1826–51) at Mission Santa Clara recovered 2,347 wire and drawn glass beads, and more than 100 shell beads, including clam disk beads, clam tubular beads (*Tivela*), three types of *Olivella* beads, and abalone pendants (Skowronek and Wizorek 1997:81–84).

Padres' Accounts   The padres recognized that neophytes commonly conducted illicit ceremonies and curing rituals in the mission colonies.

> There are certain keen-witted neophytes but poor workers who convince others that they know how to cure [illnesses]. They called them *Quisiyay*, that is to say, wizards. They "cure" in this manner: as soon as he knows that someone is ill, he goes to the sick person or the relatives of the sick person call the *Cusiyay*. He places a stone, a piece of wood or a hair in his own mouth then puts his mouth to the affected part and begins to draw or suck on that part. When he withdraws he shows the patient what he had placed in his mouth and convinces him that was the object causing him harm. (Padres at Mission San Diego; in Geiger and Meighan 1976:71)

> There are no physicians among the Indians. There are sorcerers and wizards who are consulted and paid by Indians suffering from serious and desperate maladies. These counsel the Indians to use a certain bitter herb cooked and this is taken in liquid form or by way of injection. . . . When their illness causes pain in a definite area their principal remedy is to scarify it with sharp stones and to suck or extract blood from that area. (Padres at Mission San José; in Geiger and Meighan 1976:79)

The padres also admitted that unauthorized native rituals took place as part of the burial rite of neophytes.

> As Christians they are buried according to the ritual of the church. Nevertheless, in secret they cling to their pagan practice. As a sign of mourning the father, mother, child, husband or wife, or brother or sister cut off their hair. If scissors are lacking they burn it bit by bit. Moreover they throw ashes over their entire bodies, weep bitterly, abstain from food, and the old women smear their faces with pitch. Since the effects of this remains for months they look like Ethiopians. It is also their habit to go to the woods to drown their sorrow. (Padres at Mission San Carlos; in Geiger and Meighan 1976:99)

> What I omitted to say was that on the pyre on which they burn the corpse, they throw seeds, beads and other trifles they possess. The neophytes do the same thing at the burials in the cemetery when the mis-

sionary fathers are not looking. (Padres at Mission San Luis Rey; in Geiger and Meighan 1976:119)

Chronology of Colonization: Persistence of Native Practices

Native Texts The narratives indicate that indigenous practices and cere-monies did not become rarer over the seventy-year period of the missions. In fact, a significant finding of Librado's account is that many native cus-toms continued to be practiced in mission communities after secularization (Librado 1979).

Archaeological Sources Farnsworth employs archaeological data to eval-uate changes in the degree of native acculturation throughout the mission period. He reasons that if the enculturation program of the padres was suc-cessful, then one would expect increasing evidence over time for the trans-formation of Indians into Hispanic peasants. But such is not the case (Farnsworth 1992:30–31). Within any neophyte community, there was con-siderable diversity in the use of Hispanic technologies and objects, proba-bly varying from residence to residence and even from individual to indi-vidual. As noted above, the diversity and quantity of "native" objects also varied in relation to the number of gentiles recruited to join the mission. As Farnsworth demonstrates, the percentage of native objects in neophyte contexts increased somewhat during periods of heavy gentile conversion, and vice versa: "Therefore, it seems that with a lower ratio of Indians to Spanish and fewer 'pagan' Indians being baptized, the missionaries were able to influence the Indians more during the mission's early years than during the following years of rapid population growth which resulted in greater continuity of traditional Indian activities in the population" (Farnsworth 1992:31–32).

He also argues that the pressure to embrace Hispanic customs and life ways may have actually decreased markedly after 1810, when Alta California became cut off from Spain. According to Farnsworth and others (see Horn-beck 1989:427–432), the padres became increasingly focused on agricultural and livestock production, exchange with foreigners, and manufacture of lo-cal goods.

> During this period, the missions changed emphasis from attracting, controlling, and acculturating the California Indians to exploiting their labor for economic production. The missionaries still required a certain degree of Spanish culture, especially in the male population, which com-posed the prime labor force, for they had to be able to carry out the introduced European agricultural tasks, industrial processes, and crafts

needed to produce the missions' wealth. However, in other aspects of their lives—except in religious practices, greater continuity of Indian traditions could be tolerated. As long as the Indians carried out Christian religious activities—not those which the missionaries associated with pagan rituals—and did the tasks assigned to them, the missionaries did not attempt to introduce other aspects of Spanish culture as energetically as before. The result was a decline in the intensity of cultural exchange and increased continuity of traditional culture. (Farnsworth 1992:34)

Thus, after about 1810 at least, some of the padres became more tolerant of indigenous practices and customs if these did not disrupt the religious and economic activities of the missions. This observation suggests that social actions within the neophyte communities may have been less scrutinized than in previous years. Farnsworth concludes that, when the padres began to place less emphasis on the indoctrination of the neophytes, the mission Indians were able to maintain material cultures in which up to 40 percent of the objects represented direct continuity with their prehistoric life ways (Farnsworth 1987:618).

NATIVE NEGOTIATIONS
WITHIN THE MISSION COMMUNITIES

The analysis of native texts, archaeological findings, and selected writings by the padres demonstrates how neophytes employed strategies of social agency to cope with the repressive and overly structured regime of the Franciscan mission system. By focusing on the daily practices of neophytes, we see how native peoples negotiated and mediated the padres' "intended" colonial structures. For each of the seven dimensions of colonial encounters, we track what really happened in the missions—how some natives responded to the Franciscan policies by accommodation, how some remained ambivalent, and how others withdrew into the neophyte communities and participated in an underground native economy and social organization.

The major findings of this chapter are threefold.

First, the neophyte communities were heterogenous in composition and highly complicated in social organization and practices. The people composing the neophyte villages hailed from diverse polities, spoke mutually unintelligible languages, and may sometimes have regarded one another as traditional enemies. Considerable tension existed among neophyte factions within the villages, especially between those natives who toed the line and became trusted accomplices of the padres and those who maintained some social distance from the Fernandinos. One can see this in the dimensions of colonial encounters—the simultaneous operation of mission Indian officials and traditional native leaders, the presence of skilled craftspeople and slackers, the existence of *enfermeros* and shamans, and the rise of "progressive" Indians with access to Hispanic goods and trade commodities alongside neophytes who performed native ceremonies and social practices in the privacy of their homes.

Second, in examining the social practices and activities of neophytes, it is important to differentiate between the public and private spaces in the missions. Social actions enacted in front of the padres and mission managers differed from those that took place behind closed doors. We should not conceptualize the social organization of the neophyte villages as simply a dichotomous confrontation between the progressive and the traditional neophytes. It appears that some of the *alcaldes* and other Indian office holders, in whom the padres placed their trust, led double lives, portraying themselves as devout Christians during the day and participating in pagan practices at night. The discovery of native foods, tools, ornaments, and ceremonial regalia in some adobe apartments, where these mission Indian officials probably resided, suggests that the social situation was quite complex. Thus, some neophytes worked their way up the mission hierarchy by manipulating the padres through outward appearance and actions, though in reality they maintained many former beliefs and values, and still identified as *indios*.

Third, there is a tendency among contemporary scholars to view the neophytes as broken, despondent, and spiritless people. There is little question that many mission Indians were in deep shock and under considerable psychological stress. But by considering the native texts and archaeological sources, another kind of image emerges. In spite of the repressive missionary system and chilling mortality rates, there were, one discovers, neophyte villages that were still active and socially viable entities. To be sure, factions, strife, and tensions crackled across the heterogenous neophyte communities. But the neophyte quarters also served as the focus of family life—and of communal or factional gatherings that involved dances, feasts, gambling, ceremonies, and games. There is evidence, too, for discrete residential subgroups[18] in some neophyte villages, and for the active creation of vital Indian communities within the mission complexes.

My findings emphasize that an underground world of Indian daily practices took place in the neophyte communities. It was here that many neophytes escaped the frustrating and confusing world of the missions and padres. In these neighborhoods, sequestered between the houses and behind closed doors, these neophytes ate communal meals with relatives and friends, told stories of the old days, and employed parts of their own material culture in familiar social settings. Such "native" material objects probably took on added significance in these neophyte quarters, becoming vested with the symbolic values and meanings of Indians who had become lost in a new colonial domain.

The implications of discovering socially viable neophyte communities that retained Indian identities and many native practices will be discussed, after a consideration of native and merchant interactions in the Russian frontier.

5   Russian Merchants in California

A visit to Fort Ross State Historic Park after touring the Franciscan missions to the south is most instructive. Although Colony Ross differed in many ways from the Spanish settlements of Alta California, the contemporary presentations of the two colonial frontiers are similar. Park visitors walk through reconstructed buildings and interpretive displays that highlight European culture in colonial California. Whether by visiting a mission quadrangle or by viewing Russian log houses, we gain an appreciation of how foreign architecture and artifacts first took root in the frontier areas and how European life ways underwent multiple transformations in this new environment. The California Department of Parks and Recreation has superbly reconstructed the imposing palisade walls of the Ross settlement, which were fortified with two impressive blockhouses erected on the northwest and southeast corners. The blockhouse cannons guard the palisade today and constantly thrill children, who aim them toward imaginary ships sailing along the horizon. The reconstructed, thick redwood walls encompass a secure quadrangle containing the chapel, officials' quarters, Kuskov House, and Rotchev House.[1] It was here that the manager of the settlement, its chief clerk, and other high-ranking officials of the Russian-American Company administered the colony.

But, like that of the mission quadrangles, much of the story of Colony Ross needs to be told from a vantage point outside the stockade complex. This is where the majority of the colonists lived, worked, recreated, and procreated, and it is here that interactions with their Indian neighbors unfolded. In order to repopulate the park with images of native peoples and colonial workers, we must rethink our vision of the colonial hinterland. The landscape outside the stockade abounds with archaeological remains, and there are many stories to be told. Recent archaeological research on these hinterland sites, in combination with native oral traditions and archival documents, has enhanced and even transformed our interpretations of Colony Ross.

THE RUSSIAN-AMERICAN COMPANY

The maritime fur trade, fueled primarily by Asian demand for sea otter pelts, launched Russian exploration and settlement in North America. The renowned Vitus Bering and Alexeii Chirikov expedition of 1742–43, which made landfalls in southeastern Alaska, the Aleutian Islands, and Bering Island, first reported that Alaskan waters teemed with sea mammals. In short order, Siberian merchants and investors financed voyages to harvest sea otters (and other marketable furs) from the "Eastern Sea" beyond Kamchatka (Crowell 1997a:33). Word quickly spread that Chinese elites would pay dearly for the fine furs, which they employed as decorative trim for their robes and as warm clothing. The opening of the Chinese market presented extraordinary opportunities for Russian and other European merchants, who could make their fortunes trading furs for teas, silks, spices, nankeens, porcelains, and other valued Asian goods.[2]

Although the number of Russian companies in the North Pacific fur trade proliferated following the Bering-Chirikov voyage, sharp competition and rising expenses soon weeded most out. As hunters exterminated sea otters near the Siberian coast, the costs of mounting longer trade voyages and of maintaining outposts on distant Pacific islands became prohibitive to all but the few most successful merchants. In 1799, Tsar Paul I conferred upon the Russian-American Company an exclusive Russian monopoly for the exploitation of resources in North America, as well as the rights to be the sole Russian agency for founding and administering colonies in the Americas. Modeled after other commercial monopolies of the day (e.g., the Hudson's Bay Company, the East India Company), it was run as a quasi-private mercantile corporation, financed primarily by private stockholders. The tsar and various departments of the Russian imperial government closely monitored the Company, and the tsar's family owned stock in the fur trade conglomerate (Fedorova 1973:131–133; Gibson 1976:10; Tikhmenev 1978:56).

The board of directors, elected by stockholders, headed the corporate administration of the Russian-American Company, in St. Petersburg, Russia.[3] They hired the "chief manager" (or "chief administrator") to direct the Company's operations in Russian America, and he served in the capacity of governor of the colonies.[4] His duties were to manage the administrative counters or districts, enforce Russian laws, negotiate with foreign traders, entertain important visitors, and hire much of the workforce (Dmytryshyn et al. 1989:xxxviii-xl). Headquartered in the commercial and administrative capital of Russian America, the chief manager's offices moved from Kodiak Island to New Archangel (Sitka), Alaska, in 1804.

The Russian-American Company established an impressive commercial empire spanning the entire North Pacific (map 8). From the early 1770s to 1867, Russian merchants and fur traders founded more than sixty Russian settlements in the vast region from the Kurile Islands (north of Japan), to the Aleutian and Kodiak archipelagos, mainland Alaska, California, and for a brief time, Hawaii (Fedorova 1973:272; Mills 2002). After acquiring monopoly rights in 1799, the Company took over administration of all Russian settlements in the North Pacific. This immense colonial territory was divided into seven administrative units, known as counters. The chief manager appointed a manager for each counter, as well as other key personnel, who reported directly to his office in New Archangel. The counters included: Kurile (Kurile Islands), Atkhinsk (the Western Aleutian, Near, and Komandorskie islands), Unalaska (the eastern Aleutian and Pribilof islands), Kodiak (the Kodiak archipelago and Alaskan Peninsula), Sitka (the northwest Pacific coast), Mikhailovsk Redoubt (the Norton Sound region and the Kuskokvim and Kvikpak River basins), and Ross. (See Dmytryshyn et al. [1989:xl].)

The Russian-American Company depended on native peoples to harvest sea otters, fur seals, and other valued sea mammals from the waters of the coastal counters. From their earlier experiences in the Siberian fur trade, the Russians brought to North America the practice of subjugating native peoples and forcing them to pay a tax or tribute *(iasak)* in furs. The early exploitation of sea otters on the Aleutian Islands and Kodiak Island, Alaska, involved military force and the taking of women and children as hostages to insure that local native leaders paid their *iasak* (Crowell 1997a:11–16). This form of tribute-taking was banned by Catherine II in 1788, but it was replaced by the mandatory conscription of native peoples to hunt on behalf of Russian companies. After the Russian-American Company received its imperial monopoly, the practice continued of drafting men, between the ages of eighteen and fifty, from the Aleutian Islands and Kodiak Island to serve a three-year period working for the Company. Native workers were paid on commission or received daily or yearly salaries in scrip, a parchment token exchanged for goods from the company store (Tikhmenev 1978:144).

The native hunters conscripted by the Russians were among the most sophisticated and effective sea otter hunters in the world. Trained from childhood to become skilled hunters, they employed lightweight *baidarkas* (small

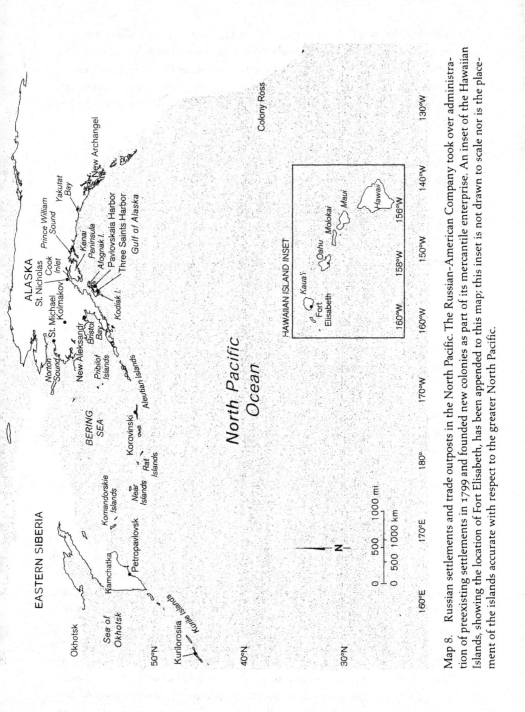

Map 8. Russian settlements and trade outposts in the North Pacific. The Russian-American Company took over administration of preexisting settlements in 1799 and founded new colonies as part of its mercantile enterprise. An inset of the Hawaiian Islands, showing the location of Fort Elisabeth, has been appended to this map; this inset is not drawn to scale nor is the placement of the islands accurate with respect to the greater North Pacific.

skin kayaks) to pursue sea otters in kelp beds and along shallow, rocky intertidal waters. Using lethal barbed-bone projectile points attached to darts, which were fired with great accuracy from bows or throwing sticks, the native workers systematically harvested thousands of sea otters and other commercially valued sea mammals across coastal waters of the North Pacific (Ogden 1941:11–14).

RUSSIAN COLONIZATION OF CALIFORNIA

In March 1812, the serenity of the Kashaya Pomo homeland was abruptly shattered by a cacophony of many strange tongues and the steady chopping of redwood timber, reverberating across the rugged coastal landscape. What Spanish colonial administrators had feared for many decades had finally come true—the Russians had extended their colonial domain southward from the North Pacific and now encroached into Alta California territory. Under the able leadership of Ivan Kuskov, a workforce of twenty-five Russians and eighty Native Alaskans began digging the foundation ditch and erecting the stout palisade walls of the settlement soon to be dedicated by Russian-American Company officials as Ross. The new settlement, perched on a windswept marine terrace overlooking a small cove, was located only 110 kilometers north of the Presidio of San Francisco. Thirty-six years after the founding of the first presidio and mission on San Francisco Bay, Spanish settlers woke to find new neighbors almost on their doorstep. With the coming of the Russians, the colonial landscape and frontier dynamics of northern California were transformed forever.

Why did the Russians come? They came to exploit the rich resources of the region, primarily its sea otters and agricultural land. The expansion of Russian colonial activities into California began in the early 1800s, when sea otter populations in the cold northern waters (along the Aleutian and Kodiak archipelagoes and Prince William Sound) declined precipitously from overhunting.[5] At the same time, American and British ships plied the Northwest coast, ladened with manufactured goods, such as cloth, metal hatchets, glass beads, knives, and in some cases even guns and alcohol, which they traded to autonomous native hunters in return for furs (Crowell 1997a:7, 10–11; 1997b:14–15; Ray 1988:338–342).[6] As fierce competition among the traders depleted the availability of furs in the North Pacific, American and British merchants began to look southward for new sources of sea otters. They quickly discovered, however, that their system of bartering with local natives did not work very well south of Trinidad Bay, because most Native Californian groups did not actively hunt sea otters in great numbers (Ogden 1941:43–44).[7]

The exploitation of thousands of sea otters along the coastal waters of California began in earnest when a mutually advantageous agreement was reached in 1803 between an American merchant and Chief Manager Aleksandr Baranov.[8] In short supply of ships and sailors, the Company accepted the offer of the enterprising Yankees to transport its hunting teams of Native Alaskans and Russian foremen to California waters on American ships. In return, the Company received half of the catch, when the Americans returned to New Archangel after the hunt. These "contract" hunting ventures proved so successful that the Company entered into nine additional contracts with American skippers from 1806 to 1813.[9]

In addition to the profitable hunting of sea otters, California attracted the Russians because of its seemingly inexhaustible agrarian potential. In 1806, Nikolai Rezanov, Councillor of the Tsar, made his celebrated voyage to Alta California to purchase foodstuffs for the North Pacific colonies. Rezanov wrote glowing accounts of the agricultural productivity of the Franciscan missions and became a strong advocate for establishing a Russian base in northern California.[10] The advantages of developing an agricultural enterprise in California, as well as of creating formal trade relations with the Franciscan padres, were not lost on the Company.[11] The Russian enterprise experienced many hardships in supplying and sustaining its hunting colonies in the North Pacific with foodstuffs, especially imported foods (grains, beef, sugar, fruit) for its European work force. Efforts to raise wheat, barley, and beef in the North Pacific proved fruitless, and the high costs of shipping goods from Mother Russia to its colonies became a major profit drain.[12]

Reconnaissance work for establishing a California colony began in earnest in 1808 and 1811, when Chief Manager Baranov sent Ivan Kuskov south, purportedly to hunt sea otters. But while Company hunters scoured local waters for sea mammals, Kuskov surveyed the coastal territory north of San Francisco Bay to evaluate possible locations for the new colony.[13] Even though Bodega Harbor presented the best port facility in the region, it had two strikes against it—it lacked suitable timber for building a settlement, and the harbor itself was quite shallow, only accommodating small ships during low tides (Fedorova 1973:135; Khlebnikov 1976:107). Instead, an exposed marine terrace on the coast further north of Bodega Harbor was selected as the administrative center for the new colony, primarily because of its defensive location and its proximity to redwood, fir, laurel, and oak trees. Construction of the Ross settlement began in March 1812, and on August 30, 1812, it was officially dedicated as a Company colony.

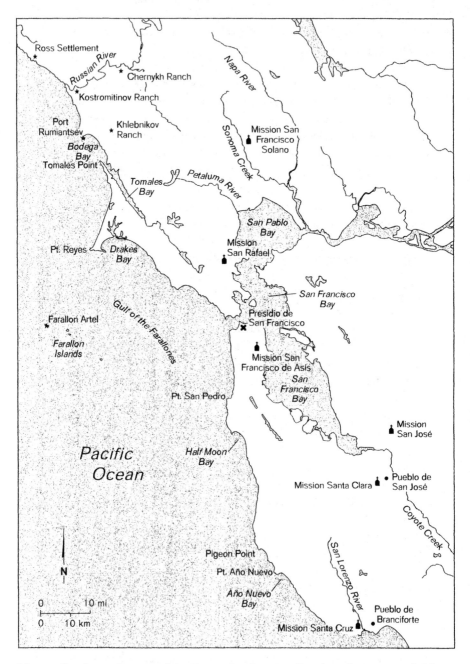

Map 9.   Russian settlements of the Greater San Francisco Bay Area that comprised Colony Ross or the Ross Counter. Also shown are the northern Franciscan missions and Presidio de San Francisco.

Figure 5.   View of the Ross settlement as observed by Auguste Duhaut-Cilly in 1827. This drawing illustrates the mercantile village that grew up around the original stockade built by Ivan Kuskov and his men. The Ross chapel is visible in the center of the picture, with outlying houses and gardens extending north, east, and west of the old stockade wall. (Courtesy of the Bancroft Library, University of California, Berkeley.)

COLONY ROSS

The Ross Counter included the administrative center of Ross, a port facility at Bodega Harbor (christened Port Rumiantsev by the Russians), at least three outlying ranches (founded after 1833), and a permanent hunting camp (map 9). The spatial organization of the colony facilitated three major economic enterprises—harvesting California sea otters and fur seals, producing grain and beef, and manufacturing goods primarily for trade with the Franciscan padres.

The stout stockade wall built by Kuskov and his men belied the true profession and character of the Ross settlement—that it was primarily a mercantile village (see Parkman 1996/1997). Houses, industrial workshops, warehouses, corrals, and barns sprang up beyond the palisade enclosure (figure 5). The village of Ross, nestled on a small flat plain overlooking the rocky coastal terrain with ample views of the nearby forested hills, represented a charming spectacle to visitors. The Russians built many fine buildings, using a plank-and-post construction technique or assembling redwood log houses on rock foundations.[14] Carpenters finished the structures with fine glass windows, gabled roofs, and rain gutters, giving the settlement a "European" appearance.[15]

The stockade demarcated an enclosed section of the broader Ross settlement, a section reserved for the offices and houses of the elite Russian managers, living quarters for unmarried Russian workers and distinguished visitors, and a gated compound where valued goods (fur pelts, trade merchandise) were warehoused for safekeeping. But outside the enclosure was where the majority of the colonists lived and worked (map 10). Many of the lower-class Russian workers, ethnic Siberians, and Creoles resided in the nearby Russian Village, or *Sloboda*, which consisted of numerous residential structures, gardens, and orchards, as depicted in period illustrations and by eyewitness observations (Farris 1993a).[16] Native Alaskan workers, primarily Alutiiq and Unangan peoples, resided, when not hunting sea otters, in a residential area south of the stockade complex.[17] A range of households populated the Native Alaskan Neighborhood: single Native Alaskan males, Native Alaskan couples and families, and interethnic couples (Native Alaskan men and Native Californian women). North of the stockade was the Native California Neighborhood, with at least six hamlets or residential compounds. Here Miwok and Pomo peoples resided while serving as laborers for the Russians.[18] The Company recruited native peoples primarily from Kashaya Pomo and Bodega Miwok groups, along with some Southern Pomo and Central Pomo peoples.[19]

The majority of the settlement's industrial and manufacturing activities were concentrated in workshops south and southwest of the stockade complex, primarily along Fort Ross Creek and Sandy Beach Cove (see Allan 2001). Company workers constructed an industrial complex that included: a tannery equipped with six redwood vats for tanning, dressing, and preparing hides and skins to be made into boots, shoes, and other leather products; a well-equipped carpenter's and locksmith's shop; a blacksmith's shop with a forge; a cooper's shop; and a workshop for manufacturing or repairing brass, copper, and tin objects (Duflot de Mofras 1937:7,251–252; Vallejo 2000:12–13; Watrous 1998:14–15; Wrangell 1969:207). Craftspersons produced redwood barrels, rowboats, wheels, and cooking implements for trade with Hispanic California, and also repaired rifles, locks, and other items for Spanish and Mexican clients. Two mill-driven machines crushed tan-oak bark, harvested from the nearby forest, for use in the tannery (Watrous 1998:15). The industrial zone also boasted a shipyard, with a shipway where ships and small boats were built, along with a landing and small wharf (Allan 2001; Tikhmenev 1978:134,228).[20]

The Company devoted the nearby environs of the Ross settlement to

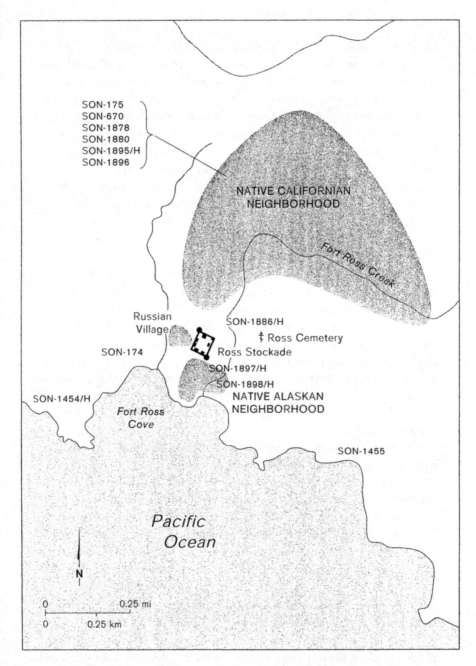

Map 10.   The spatial layout of the Ross settlement. Shown are the Ross Stockade and outlying ethnic neighborhoods (Russian Village, Native Alaskan Neighborhood, Native Californian Neighborhood). The map is based on archival documents and archaeological
research. (From Lightfoot, Schiff, and Wake 1997:xii.)

garden plots, fruit orchards, wheat and barley fields, and open range for cattle, pigs, sheep, and horses. The agrarian infrastructure included corrals and barns for the animals, threshing floors and windmills for processing wheat and barley crops, and granaries for storing the processed grain.[21] Russian workers planted gardens close to the settlement, typically near houses or in small plots near Fort Ross Creek, where in some years employees raised excellent crops of lettuce, cabbage, beans, peas, potatoes, melons, pumpkins, beets, radishes, and watermelons. At least two orchards were planted a short distance north of the stockade complex.[22] Company managers placed fields of wheat and barley in nearby tillable land. All of the garden plots, orchards, and fields had to be fenced to keep free-range livestock out. During the dry season, the livestock would search for fodder as far as twenty-one kilometers from the stockade (Wrangell 1969:209).[23]

Bodega Harbor served as the principal port of the Ross Colony (map 9). It was situated twenty-nine kilometers south of the Ross settlement, and travelers took at least five or six hours to cover the ground on horseback, using a beaten trail over perilous coastal cliffs and steep hills; this was about the same time it took to paddle between the settlements in *baidarkas* (Duhaut-Cilly 1999:181–184; Golovnin 1979:160; Payeras 1995:331–332; Schabelski 1993:10; Watrous 1998:15). The Russians built Port Rumiantsev on the southwestern extension of Bodega Harbor (now known as Campbell Cove). The settlement consisted primarily of storage facilities, a bathhouse, and a few residences.[24]

In the first few years, the Company focused on sea otter hunting and trade with Spanish California. It established a hunting camp, or *artel*, on the Farallon Islands in 1812 (map 9); the *artel* served as a base for pursuing local sea otters, fur seals, and sea lions, and for harvesting seagull feathers, meat, and eggs.[25] Extensive sea otter harvests were also mounted in northern California waters from spring until fall (Golovnin 1979: 162,166; Khlebnikov 1976:108,131). Native Alaskan hunters paddled fleets of *baidarkas* north to Trinidad Bay, and south along the Sonoma and Marin coasts, portaging their lightweight boats across the Marin headlands to San Francisco Bay. The hunts were quite successful, for the number of sea otters had declined significantly in these waters by the late 1810s and early 1820s.[26]

The Company turned to manufacture and agricultural production in the 1820s and 1830s, in an attempt to turn a profit in California. They expanded the industrial sector, enhancing the shipbuilding enterprise through the mid-1820s, and boosting the production of small boats, furniture, leather goods (specifically, shoes and boots), and bricks, for the Alta California trade and beyond (Gibson 1976:116; Khlebnikov 1990:101,135). In efforts to make

Ross the "granary to the colonies," the Company intensified efforts to produce wheat, vegetables, and beef for export to their North Pacific settlements.
They increased the amount of land under cultivation in the hinterland of
the Ross settlement.[27] In the early 1830s, Company managers established
three ranches in fertile pockets of interior land between the Ross settlement
and Port Rumiantsev (map 9). The pockets included the Kostromitinov Ranch,
near the confluence of the Russian River and Willow Creek; Khlebnikov
Ranch, about eight kilometers inland of Bodega Harbor in the upper Salmon
Creek Valley; and the Chernykh Ranch, situated about sixteen kilometers
inland (between the modern towns of Occidental and Graton) on Purring-
ton Creek (Tomlin and Watrous 1990:16–17). A fourth ranch appears to have
been in operation near Bodega Harbor, but not much is known about this endeavor (Gibson 1976:118–119; Vallejo 2000:5). The Kostromitinov, Khlebnikov, and Chernykh Ranches encompassed 40½, 28, and 83 hectares, respectively, of fields, orchards, and pasture land, and each contained bathhouses,
kitchens, barracks, "commodious quarters for the Indians," and officers' quarters surrounded by gardens (Duflot de Mofras 1937:7,253–254).[28]

HISPANIC AND RUSSIAN INTERACTIONS IN CALIFORNIA

Hispanic and Russian interactions in colonial California can only be described as a classic love/hate relationship, like two partners locked in a marriage gone bad. Neither side believed the other could be trusted, and they
continually placed each other under close surveillance. Tensions and frictions
characterized most of their close confrontations, yet they became economi-
cally dependent on each other, and when they cooperated in joint ventures,
mutual benefits resulted for all involved.

The governments of Spain and, later, Mexico never officially recognized
Colony Ross as a legitimate settlement, and continually protested Russia's
encroachment into California territory. From the outset, Spanish civil administrators met the construction of the Ross settlement with consternation.[29] This began a protracted effort by the Alta California governors, the
viceroys of New Spain, and the Madrid government to dislodge the Russians from Colony Ross.[30] Tensions between the colonial neighbors were
exacerbated by the systematic poaching of sea otters in Spanish waters.
Whenever the opportunity presented—even when Company ships visited
Spanish ports to trade—the Russians dispatched Native Alaskan hunters
into Alta California waters.[31] Since the Spanish colonists lacked ready access to boats to pursue the sea otter hunters, colonial administrators ordered

mounted patrols to ride along the coastline, searching the near-shore waters for any signs of *baidarkas*. When they spied hunters in an area, the nearest presidio was alerted, and Spanish soldiers ambushed Company employees when they came onshore to take on water. This method must have worked well, as a number of Russians and Native Alaskans were taken prisoner (Bancroft 1886a:308; Hutchinson 1969:25; Khlebnikov 1990:91; 1994:12; Ogden 1941:61–63; Russian-American Company 1989c:332–334). Most were jailed, at the presidios of San Francisco, Monterey, and Santa Barbara, where they were put to work as laborers until the Company negotiated the ransom of prisoners (see Bancroft 1886a:312–315; Khlebnikov 1994:102).[32]

At the same time that Spanish administrators disputed the Company's right to found Colony Ross, the Spaniards participated in regularized trade with the Russians. The Spanish governors of Alta California found themselves in a tough and conflicting situation (see Hutchinson 1969:28–29; Spencer Pritchard 1990:84). On the one hand, they were sworn to uphold the laws of the Spanish Crown, which forbade commerce with foreign merchants. On the other, they recognized that trade with the Russians provided much-needed revenue and manufactured goods for the people of Alta California.[33] The Fernandinos were favorably inclined to trade with the Russians from the very beginning (Bancroft 1886a:66, footnote 5; Rezanov 1989a:117); they were quick to acknowledge that this trade represented a means of exchanging surplus agricultural products for manufactured goods that could not be obtained in Alta California or even from New Spain. With the supply ships from San Blas sailing irregularly after 1810, many of the *gente de razón* and missionaries probably viewed the establishment of nearby Ross, and its access to European and Asian goods, as somewhat of a blessing.[34]

What emerged over time was an informal protocol: when Russian ships arrived in Alta California ports, the captain of the vessel or the Company representative on board met with the governor (or, if the governor was not available, with the nearest presidio commandant), outlined the reasons why trade should be undertaken in Spanish California in this particular case, and requested permission to sell his cargo. The governors granted permission on a case-by-case basis, with reasons then informally circulated as to why an exception could be given in this instance.[35] Russian negotiations usually involved sizeable "gifts" to the governor and other key officials, as well as the payment of significant "taxes" and "duties," which fluctuated from ship to ship (Lütke 1989:262).

Colony Ross became the focal point of trade between the Company and the northern missions of Alta California. Spaniards in northern Alta California depended on the Ross Colony to make and to repair an array of iron implements.[36] Special orders could be placed at Colony Ross or with Company ships, resulting in the delivery of almost any conceivable merchandise, such as cooking utensils, wheels, longboats, etc. (Wrangell 1969:210). As Spencer Pritchard details, the 1821 trip of the *Buldakov* to San Francisco carried

> several items for Governor Sola, such as one "delicate writing desk," "forty-four packages high quality white thread," and "one box containing two dozen small cups." On that same ship, Mariano Estrada received two *arrobas* of ammunition he needed, while the padres at Mission San Francisco obtained the one thousand one-inch nails they ordered, along with two new sets of candlesticks. That same year the *Golovin* brought treated canvas for *Comandante* Luis Arguello's barge, needles and thread for the presidio troops, and even "one pair small scissors for Mrs. Chepita." (Spencer Pritchard 1990:88)

By 1818 a system was in place to notify the Franciscans about the arrival of Russian ships, what the ships were selling, and what they needed in the way of foodstuffs (Spencer Pritchard 1990:88). The Franciscan padres traded for some goods specifically earmarked for Indian neophytes. These goods included ticking, which was used as clothing because of its durability (Khlebnikov 1994:203). The Russian merchants were also careful to import special candles for the Franciscan churches, candles that could be not taller than .9 meters and about 4 centimeters in diameter (Khlebnikov 1994:206–207).

The construction of Mission San Rafael (1817) and Mission San Francisco Solano (1823), ostensibly to keep the Russians from settling on the north side of San Francisco Bay, stimulated increased trade across the Hispanic and Russian frontiers. The Russians helped supply materials and goods used in the construction of the two missions, and visits took place on a regular schedule between Colony Ross and the missions (Farris 1989a:4; Gibson 1976:185). Spencer Pritchard notes that one padre from San Rafael made a weekly trip to Ross by muleback to obtain brandy, and that some other fathers opened charge accounts with the Russians (Spencer Pritchard 1990:87).

Hutchinson (1969: 96–105) provides an excellent discussion of the newly inaugurated Mexican government's reaction to the nearby Russian colony, when the new government took over administration of Alta California in 1821–22. The lifting of the trade embargo turned out to be a curse for the Russian-American Company, which had enjoyed a virtual commercial monopoly in Alta California under Spanish colonial rule. The Company now had to compete directly with American and British merchants, as well as with American whalers seeking fresh provisions—competition that raised the prices of Mexican products and lowered the selling value of Russian goods (Khlebnikov 1994:110).[37] However, since the Americans and British were primarily interested in trading with Mexican California for hides and tallow, the Russian settlements in the North Pacific remained the primary market for mission-grown grain during the 1820s and early 1830s (Duhaut-Cilly 1999:169). The Russians received special treatment by the Mexican Californians; for example, small boats and *baidarkas* (skin boats that held cargo and/or up to thirty people) that ferried trade goods from the Ross Colony were not subject to inspection, and the boats did not have to pay any of the duty or anchorage fees. By 1826, the Company was permitted to retain a permanent commercial agent in Alta California, who oversaw a well-stocked warehouse of goods in Monterey and purchased grain and other agricultural products for the North Pacific colonies (Gibson 1976:183; Spencer Pritchard 1990:90–92).

In addition to trade, the Russian-American Company also negotiated another commercial venture with Mexican California: a contract system that allowed the legal hunting of sea otters in Alta California waters. In 1823, an agreement was reached with Mexican officials to split the catch equally between the Mexicans and Russians (Khlebnikov 1976:110–111). Almost immediately, the merchants dispatched twenty-five *baidarkas* from Ross to hunt in San Francisco Bay, and during a two-month period these hunters captured about three hundred sea otters (Lazarev 1989:378–379). Under various licenses with the Mexicans, the Company sent its Native Alaskan hunting teams to Alta and Baja California throughout the 1820s. To make the most of this business endeavor, the Company, it appears, systematically short-changed the counts of otter pelts reported to Mexican authorities (see Khlebnikov 1990:159). In the 1830s, the Russians experienced difficulties in renewing their licenses, as the Mexican government reserved the right to hunt for its own naturalized citizens (many of whom were from the United States) (Ogden 1941:95–119). For the most part, the Russian-American Company was shut out from hunting sea otters in Alta California waters in the 1830s and 1840s—at which time the yields decreased dramatically as hunters with guns exterminated the few remaining animals (Ogden 1941:120–152).

With the collapse of the sea otter trade and the breakdown of an agreement with the Mexican government to allow the Russians access to fertile agricultural land along the Russian River, the Company decided to close down its unprofitable operation at Ross.[38] The merchants reached an agreement in 1839 with the Hudson's Bay Company, which would provide wheat, beef, and other foodstuffs to Russian colonies in the North Pacific at a reasonable price. In 1841, Company officials negotiated a deal with Johann Sutter, owner of an extensive Mexican rancho in the Sacramento Valley, who agreed to purchase the Company's assets in California for thirty thousand dollars in cash and produce. On January 1, 1842, the managerial staff and remaining Russian, Creole, and Native Alaskan workers boarded the last Company ship to depart Port Rumiantsev for New Archangel, ending a chapter in California history (Watrous 1998:20).

DIMENSIONS OF COLONIAL ENCOUNTERS: THE PERSPECTIVE OF THE RUSSIAN MERCHANTS

Enculturation Program

The Russian-American Company did not mount any concerted effort to enculturate local natives in European values, meanings, or life ways. The merchants implemented no substantive policies or practices for intentionally transforming the material culture, dress, menu, ceremonies, or belief systems of indigenous communities (Farris 1989b:489; 1992:16). The reason they made so little effort to "civilize" or "proselytize" local peoples at Colony Ross stems primarily from the profitmaking nature of their enterprise: the Company had little to gain from the conversion of Pomo and Miwok Indians at Colony Ross. However, I feel that two additional factors—the inaction of the Russian Orthodox Church and the geopolitics of colonial California—also contributed to the lack of any kind of formal enculturation program in the Russian frontier.

Even though the Tsarist government mandated that the Company support the missionary efforts of the Russian Orthodox Church (Osborn 1997:5–6), in reality few priests preached in Russian America until the middle of the nineteenth century (Rathburn 1981:12). Only a single priest served the widely dispersed Russian settlements in North America in 1816, and by 1825 the number had only increased to five (Gibson 1992:20).[39] The entire Russian colonial domain in America could boast of only four churches and five chapels in 1833 (Osborn 1997:7). Although Unangan, Alutiiq and Tlingit peoples in some Alaskan counters received considerable attention from devout missionaries, other native peoples were ignored (Black 2001; Kan 1988:506–509; Rathburn 1981:13–15; Veltre 1990:180–182). Colony Ross never had a permanent priest assigned to it. The missionary enterprise in Russian America expanded greatly in 1840 when the Russian Orthodox Church appointed the energetic Ivan Veniaminov bishop of Alaska; the number of clergy, missions, and native schools soon increased significantly (see Dmytryshyn et al. 1989:xlii; Kan 1988:509–511). But by this time, the doors were closing on the Ross Colony.

The colonists at Ross were members of the extensive Sitka parish, but the priests who served this parish made only three recorded trips to California. The first documented visit was in 1832, when the Orthodox priest Alexei Sokolov and subdeacon Nikolai Chechenev traveled to Ross to serve mass and to perform many necessary church rites for Company employees.[40] Father Veniaminov conducted his inspection of the Ross Colony in July 1836, when he compiled a confessional list, administered sacraments of marriage, performed baptisms, and collected census data (Veniaminov 1992). The final visit of an Orthodox priest was by Father Andrei Sizykh in 1841, traveling on board the *Elena*, in preparation for closing down the Ross settlement (Osborn 1997:249).

Russian Orthodox services did take place at Colony Ross even in the absence of ordained priests. The colonists built a beautiful chapel at Ross in the 1820s from local subscriptions and from donations by visiting sailors (Gibson 1992:22; Khlebnikov 1990:147). During the extended periods when no Orthodox priest visited Ross, a designated layperson authorized by the bishop in Alaska administered marriages, baptisms, and funerals. Supply officer Fedor Svin'in performed many of these vital functions for the colonists at Ross.[41] It is not clear who took over the position of observing church rites at Ross after Svin'in passed away in 1832 (Osborn 1997:251). However, when Father Veniaminov visited the Ross settlement in 1836, he remarked on the poor condition of the chapel, its inadequate support by the colonists, and the colonists' low attendance at church services (Veniaminov 1992:22). Furthermore, he discovered a number of colonists "living in sin" with "unlawful" or "illegitimate" Indian wives (Osborn, 1997:374–407): the Company men, that is, lived with one woman while legally married to another, and/or their Indian wives were not baptized members of the Russian Orthodox faith.

If some members of the Ross congregation endeavored to convert local Indians to the Russian Orthodox faith, they appear to have had little success. In the two censuses he compiled (in 1820 and 1821), Ivan Kuskov counted 65 Native Californians (9 men and 57 women) as part of the Ross settlement (Istomin 1992). As detailed below, the Company held 8 of the men as prisoners, and all but one of the women resided in interethnic households with colonial men. None of these Miwok and Pomo peoples appear to have been members of the Russian Orthodox Church.[42] In his visit to Ross in 1832, Subdeacon Nikolai Chechenev reported the presence of 39 baptized Native Californian adults and children (Osborn 1997:189). In gathering information for his 1836 census (information later updated for the 1838 census), Father Veniaminov listed between 18 and 23 women (the number depends on how duplicate names are counted) and 8 of their children as baptized members of the church (Osborn 1997:407–408); in his 1836 journal, he wrote that 39 "converted Indians" resided in the Ross Colony (Veniaminov 1992:22). Two Native Californian men, identified as Company employees (i.e., Murav'ev Ieromin, Zakharov Irodion), were probably also baptized members of the Russian Orthodox Church (Osborn 1997:423). Thus, at any one time probably no more than about 30 to 40 Indians, primarily women and children, were recognized by priests as members of the Russian Orthodox Church.[43]

The business orientation of the Russian-American Company provided little motivation to civilize local natives, and this hands-off approach was probably amplified in light of the Company's relations with Spanish California. In an attempt to prove their legitimate right to colonize the Ross Counter, the merchants "purchased" land from local Indian groups (Kotzebue 1830:121–122). Claiming that such groups, and not the Spanish, were the lawful landowners of the region, they sent Company representatives to meet with Indian chiefs of the Bodega Miwok and Kashaya Pomo prior to founding settlements at Bodega Harbor and Ross, respectively.[44] In September 1817, the Russian-American Company held a ceremony at Ross with several local Indian leaders to cement their political alliance and to show gratitude to the Indians for "ceding to the Company land for a fort, buildings and enterprises, in regions belonging to Chu-gu-an [the local leader], [land] which the inhabitants call Med-eny-ny [Métini]" (Hagemeister 1989:296). The Russian representatives drew up a "treaty" that documented the ceding of Kashaya Pomo land to the Russian-American Company. The document was signed in the presence of the native leaders by six Russian officials including Leontii Hagemeister, Ivan Kuskov, and Kirill Khlebnikov.

The treaty became a propaganda piece employed by the Russians to legitimize the founding of Colony Ross. The Company stressed that the Indians who had granted permission to establish the colony lived side by side with the Russians in peace and friendship. Company officials broadcast to visiting dignitaries from Russia and other European countries that the Company treated the local Indians equitably and had not adversely impacted them.[45] Company agents and sympathetic visitors often played up the differences between how well the Russians treated the local Indians and the use of force by "cruel" or "tyrannical" Franciscan missionaries to convert the neophytes to Catholicism (see, e.g., Duflot de Mofras 1937:5; Golovnin 1979:167; Kotzebue 1830:79–80, 124–126; Tikhmenev 1978:140).

Another possible factor in the Company's hands-off approach toward

the Bodega Miwok and Kashaya Pomo was the maintenance of trade relations across the Russian and Hispanic frontiers. Although some Russian
agents made disparaging remarks about the Franciscan mission program, the
Company was careful not to initiate activities in the Ross Counter that might
upset the most ardent supporters of Russian trade in Alta California—the
Fernandinos. In 1817, the board of directors wrote to Chief Manager Baranov about the continued liability of keeping a certain Dr. Georg Schäffer
(who led the abortive Russian colonization of Hawaii) in the Company's
employment. In the text of this letter, the directors raised serious concerns
about letting Dr. Schäffer found a "school" (perhaps a mission?) in the Ross
Counter.

> If, however, you still have a use for him [Dr. Schäffer] you may keep
> him on as a doctor, but do not let him establish a school or a distillery
> at the Ross settlement. It is too early to do either of these things, and
> will continue to be until the Russians have become firmly entrenched
> there and the Spaniards accept us as their neighbors.
>
> This is especially true since in California for the most part the monks
> dominate the entire local administration. If we established a school
> they would view our enterprising settlement with entirely different
> eyes than is now the case. . . .
>
> Keep the Ross settlement in such condition the Spanish will have
> no reason to consider it anything more than a simple *promyshlennik*
> [Russian worker] outpost. Meanwhile, under this cover, build up agri-
> culture, livestock breeding, poultry raising, the planting of fruits and
> vegetable and establish plantations. Improve the settlement itself with
> necessary buildings. (Russian-American Company 1989a:239–240)

Thus, it appears that the main administration of the Company was appre-
hensive about developing a competing missionary program in California that
would potentially raise the ire of the Franciscan padres.

The merchants implemented a general policy toward the Kashaya Pomo
and Bodega Miwok that allowed these Indians to continue their traditional
cultural practices in the Ross Counter, as long as the practices did not adversely affect the daily schedule of mercantile operations. However, several
accounts indicate Ross managers subjected their workers to strict rules and
discipline, and maintained close supervision over Company facilities, land,
and commercial enterprises (Bancroft 1886a:632–633; Khlebnikov 1990:188).
"There appears to be great order and discipline at Ross, and although the
governor is the only officer, one notes everywhere the signs of close supervision. After being busy all day in their various occupations, the colonists,
who are both workers and soldiers, mount guard during the night. On hol-
idays they pass in review and drill with cannon and musket" (Duhaut-Cilly

1999:185). Managers imposed rules over the admittance of Indians inside the Ross stockade, primarily to safeguard goods stored in the warehouses and to protect the administrative buildings and residences of the elite Russians; they also forbade local Indians to hunt livestock in the open range beyond the stockade (Khlebnikov 1990:194). Infractions of the rules by natives, especially transgressions against colonists, such as murder or battery, resulted in imprisonment. The managers sent some Indian prisoners to Sitka, but most remained in the Ross settlement (Istomin 1992; Osborn 1997:409). Retribution usually involved hard labor for the Company, as opposed to floggings, stocks, or capital punishment (Farris 1997a:190).

Some visitors to the Ross settlement were astounded at the lack of progress the Russians had made, even after many years of close contact, in "civilizing" the natives. When Cyrille LaPlace, the captain of a French vessel, visited the Ross settlement in 1839, he chided Alexander Rotchev, the Company manager, for the backwardness of the Indians living in a nearby hamlet. "Mr. Rotchev, seeing my astonishment that the contact with the compatriots (Russians) had not modified more the ways and habits of the natives, assured me that these people, just like their counterparts in New Archangel (Sitka), obstinately refused to exchange their customs for ours" (LaPlace 1986:68).

Rotchev, however, did confide to LaPlace that the local natives were slowly changing over time.

Also one sees their tastes change more each day to the varied articles of adornment, dress and other things with which are paid the services which they provide to the colony. Thus one could hope that if the company retains this establishment for long enough, the natives will be led little by little to submit to the yoke of civilization. (LaPlace 1986:68)

But Rotchev emphasized that the Russian colonists would continue to respect the "freedom and religious beliefs" of the Kashaya Pomo and Bodega Miwok no matter how "absurd" they were (LaPlace 1986:68).

Native Relocation Program

The Russian merchants did not implement a formalized native relocation program in the Ross Counter. However, population aggregation did take place as some native women established interethnic households with colonial men at Ross. And in the 1820s and 1830s, Kashaya families and individuals living in outlying ridge-top settlements moved on a seasonal basis to the Native California Neighborhood to work as agricultural laborers. But most of the Kashaya population continued to reside in the hinterland well beyond the Ross settlement.

Company managers granted their Native Alaskan workers remarkable leeway in where they sited their residences, in the architectural styles they employed, and in the layout of the structures and the overall village plan (Blomkvist 1972:107; Tikhmenev 1978:134). Similarly, the Russians permitted the Kashaya Pomo and Bodega Miwok residing in the Native Californian Neighborhood or near Port Rumiantsev considerable latitude in where they placed their settlements, how they built their houses, and how they conducted their daily affairs. Company administrators and Russian and European visitors left behind a small corpus of writings about local Indian settlements. They described in some detail the traditional thatched conical houses where men, women, and children relaxed, gambled in small groups, or involved themselves in manufacturing or repairing woven baskets, bows and arrows, and fishing nets. The visitors also observed the preparation of native foods consisting of shellfish, fish, game, parched grains, and acorn "porridge," the latter cooked in watertight baskets using red-hot stones (Golovnin 1979:168–169; Kostromitinov 1974:7–18; LaPlace 1986; Lütke 1989:275–278; Matiushkin 1996:5; Schabelski 1993:10).

Cyrille LaPlace wrote a detailed observation of a Kashaya village located a short distance north of the Ross stockade. His observations, made in 1839 during the waning years of Russian colonization, highlight how intimately the Indians were still connected to their prehistoric roots.

> Also, from this moment I could move freely in the huts and admit myself thus to the secrets of their interior. This interior was hardly hidden, it is true, because the habitations of these poor people consisted without exception of miserable huts formed of branches through which the rain and wind passed without difficulty. It was there that all the family, father, mother, and children spent the nights lying pall-mall around the fire, some on cattle hides, the majority on the bare ground, and each one enveloped in a coverlet of wool which served him equally as a mantle during the day, when the weather was cold or wet.
>
> Such was the costume of the men who surrounded me, that it seemed to me all of them were nearly nude, except the chief and several young men, that without doubt the presence of the governor, for whom they showed a profound respect, had decided to wear European shirt and pants. I was disappointed. I would have preferred to see them in their native ceremonial costume with their martial spirit and truly dignified air, which I was later able to verify when this same chief who welcomed me at his house came to visit me the next day. . . .
>
> The majority were busy with housekeeping, preparing meals for their husbands and children. Some were spreading out on the embers some pieces of beef given as rations, or shell-fish, or even fish which these unhappy creatures came to catch either at the nearby river (Fort Ross Creek?) or from the sea; while the others heated the grain (wheat?)

in a willow basket before grinding it between two stones. In the middle of this basket they shook constantly some live coals on which each grain passed rapidly by an ever more accelerated rotating movement until they were soon parched, otherwise the inner side of the basket would be burned by the fire. Some of these baskets *(paniers)*, or more accurately these deep baskets *(vases)* seemed true models of basketmaking, not only by their decoration but by the finishing touches of the work. They are made of shoots of straw (?) or compact gorse so solidly held together by the threads, that the fabric was water-resistant, as efficiently as baked clay and earthenware. (LaPlace 1986:66–68)

There are Russian accounts of curing ceremonies, of feasts, and of ritual dances celebrated by the Kashaya and Bodega Miwok. For example, in 1818 Russian naval officers and a painter, Mikhail Tikhanov, witnessed firsthand a shaman attending to a dying Bodega Miwok leader in the presence of the grieving wife and family members (Golovnin 1979:169; Matiushkin 1996:5).[46] Kostromitinov (1974:10–12) observed feasts in which chiefs invited Indians from the region to partake of delicacies, storytelling, and songs and dances. He even described ritual activities relating to the Kuksu and Old Ghost ceremonies, ancient observances handed down over countless generations and held as annual commemorative celebrations. The Kuksu ritual involved elaborate dances and songs that impersonated the Kuksu (or Guksu) and other spirit creatures; the dancers, singers, and drummers of the Old Ghost gatherings impersonated the spirits of recently deceased kin in a mourning ceremony.[47] But Kostromitinov also noted that the Indians concealed most ritual remembrances from the Russians. "They only grudgingly answered questions we asked them concerning these rites, and for this reason it was impossible to learn further details" (Kostromitinov 1974:10).

None of the available Russian accounts (correspondence of the main administration, Company journals, etc.) indicate that the Company forced the Bodega Miwok or Kashaya Pomo to relocate their permanent residences to Port Rumiantsev or Ross. The basic Company policy encouraged most Kashaya and Bodega Miwok, with the exception of native women living with colonial men in interethnic households, to stay in their own villages (Farris 1989b:489). This policy even applied to the Indian refugees from northern San Francisco Bay who moved into the Russian frontier to escape the Franciscan mission system. Native peoples displaced by the construction of Mission San Rafael and Mission San Francisco Solano were encouraged by Company management (Ivan Kuskov) to relocate along the southern boundary of the colony, providing a buffer between the Russians and their Hispanic neighbors (Matiushkin 1996:6).

Although the general policy was not to resettle Indians in Russian settlements, the merchants did support the seasonal occupation of Indians in the Native Californian Neighborhood, as well as in the outlying ranches, when they served as agricultural laborers. And when the Company was shorthanded during the agricultural season, the managers could be very brutal in forcing local Indians to live and work at Ross (see below). However, after they served their time, the Indians were supposedly paid, then released so they could return to their home villages.

Labor Practices

The merchants instituted a labor regime at Colony Ross that involved four categories of Indian workers: prisoners *(kaiurs)*, colonial spouses, Company employees, and seasonal laborers.

Prisoners　The *kaiur* class of laborers derived from the colonization of the North Pacific by Russian fur hunters in the late 1700s. When they ruthlessly conquered Kodiak Island and subjected its inhabitants to Russian rule, the fur hunters forced the Alutiiq leaders to turn over all their slaves and war captives, and these outcasts became laborers for the colonists. When the slave laborers, called *kaiurs* (a Kamchatka word for hired laborer), began to decline in number by the early 1800s, their ranks were filled by individuals who had committed offenses against the Russian-American Company (Davydov 1977:190–193). The Company assigned *kaiurs* to all its settlements in the North Pacific, and most managers apparently had several allotted as servants and manual laborers.

When the Russian-American Company founded Ross, its managers employed *kaiurs* as unpaid workers for building projects and other labor-intensive undertakings. Ivan Kuskov, in his 1820 and 1821 censuses, listed eight Native Californian men serving time for crimes against the Colony. These men included Vaimpo and Chichamik (accused of the "murder of Kodiaks and some others"), Kapisha (convict worker), Vekvekun (captured as one of the "murderers of the hunter Andrey Kalag"), Yovlo (serving time for the murder of a Kodiak), and Chilan, Yogokoiy, and Chil'lya (sentenced as convict laborers for the killing "of the best three horses") (Istomin 1992: 14–22). The Company sent Vekvekun to Sitka on the *Buldakov* in 1820, along with the horse killers Chilan and Yogokoiy. Kapisha, a Coast Miwok man, served his sentence (with his Kashaya Pomo wife, Vayamin) on the Farallon Islands *artel* (Istomin 1992:14, 30). Three other men (Genvar, Maletin, and Zhak), possibly Native Californians, were listed as sent to Sitka between 1838 and 1840 to serve sentences for unspecified crimes (Osborn 1997:409). The prisoners completed their sentences by performing hard labor for the Company, although some were released because of illness or old age.

Colonial Spouses   It is not clear whether Native Californian women who established joint residences with Native Alaskan, Creole, or Russian men were drafted into mandatory service for the Company. I believe they were. Company managers maintained some control over the Native Californian women at Ross. Kuskov explicitly stated in his 1820 and 1821 censuses that, when interethnic households split up, women were either "allowed" or "released" to return to their "native place" or "motherland" (Istomin 1992:6–7). Native Californian women at Ross were involved in work details that supported a range of Company harvesting and manufacturing projects. The merchants stationed some Indian women and their Alutiiq husbands on the Farallon Islands *artel* (Istomin 1992:5, 25). Some Native Californian women learned to make "Aleut handicrafts, such as sewing the whale gut *kamleika* [waterproof outer garment] and other things" (Lütke 1989:278). Native Californian wives probably worked for their Native Alaskan spouses in preparing pelts, tanning hides, and sewing together the sea lion hides for making or repairing *baidarkas*. Company officials also taught the "Indian wives of the Aleuts" to weave wool in the production of cloth at Ross (Golovnin 1979:166).

Company Employees   The censuses compiled by Kuskov (1820–21) and Veniaminov (1836 and 1838) list a few Indian men as Company employees. There is no record of what kind of compensation these individuals received for their work, but I suspect the Company paid them, like other full-time workers on the payroll, minimal annual salaries. The 1820–21 censuses identified the Kashaya man Iik as working in the Ross kitchen of "his free will" (Istomin 1992:28–29). The 1836 census recorded Zakharov Irodion as a California Indian laborer working at Ross (and he continued to live at Ross until 1841, when he sailed to Sitka with other Company employees) (Osborn 1997:409, 423). Murav'ev Ieromin, not listed in either the 1836 or 1838 censuses, was Native Californian and served as a Company employee in 1841, relocating to Sitka later in the same year (Osborn 1997:409, 423).

Seasonal Laborers   The Company employed the majority of Native Californians as seasonal laborers. The merchants hired them to perform specific tasks, negotiating with native workers about compensation on a case-by-case basis. Kostromitinov (1974:8) observed, over his many years at Ross, that "they sometimes demand a great deal for work performed by them, sometimes, on the other hand, very little."[48] The Russian managers paid the seasonal or short-term laborers "in kind" for services, giving them food, to-bacco, beads, and clothing (Khlebnikov 1990:193–194; Kostromitinov 1974:8–9; LaPlace 1986:68–69; Wrangell 1969:211). The seasonal laborers toiled in various industrial enterprises at Ross and Port Rumiantsev—for instance, hauling clay for making bricks (Wrangell 1969:211). It is likely that the mer-chants used the seasonal laborers to cut timber for building ships, which the laborers then had to transport over the rugged terrain to the shipyard at Ross (see, e.g., Lightfoot et al. 1991:17). However, the primary work falling upon the shoulders of Indian laborers was agricultural—tilling the soil, cul-tivating plants, harvesting grains (by hand), transporting wheat and barley crops to granaries, and threshing and grinding the grain into flour (see Gib-son 1976:119; Khlebnikov 1976:119; Wrangell 1969:210–211). Kashaya Pomo and Bodega Miwok workers also tended livestock, especially when other Russian or Native Alaskan herders were unavailable for this duty (Khlebnikov 1976:119; 1990:141). Khlebnikov (1990:141) reported in 1824 that he did not trust the seasonal laborers to tend the herds, believing that the laborers were probably driving "the animals off into the countryside," thereby contributing to the loss of cattle and sheep in the Ross Counter.

Labor practices involving California Indians changed dramatically over time. In the early years of the Ross settlement (ca. 1812–20), the merchants placed relatively few labor demands on local Indians. The commercial agenda focused primarily on sea mammal hunting, and the merchants re-settled large gangs of Native Alaskan hunters at Ross to perform this work. Consequently, the principal California Indians laboring in the colony at this time included the *kaiurs*, the handful of Indians serving as Company em-ployees, and probably the native women living with Native Alaskan, Creole, or Russian men. Relations between the colonists and local natives were probably at their best during the first years of contact (Lightfoot et al. 1991:24).

With the reorientation of the colony's commercial agenda in the 1820s and 1830s as a result of overhunting, labor shortages emerged, since more bodies were needed for new manufacturing enterprises (e.g., brick produc-tion, ship building) and for increased agricultural production. By the late 1820s and early 1830s, relations between Company managers and the local native population began to deteriorate. Visits to the Ross settlement by In-dians, especially by Native Californian men, became rarer and rarer (Ban-croft 1886a:299, footnote 11; Farris and Beebe 2000:iv-v). At this time, the program of agricultural intensification caused a significant need for seasonal workers, and the Russians exploited local Indian groups as cheap and necessary labor (Dmytryshyn et al. 1989:xlviii). Not surprisingly, the Russians experienced problems in recruiting an adequate workforce. The native workers were often mistreated, working long hours for very little compensation—compensation that consisted primarily of "bad" food (Wrangell 1969:210–211). To make matters worse, the Russians mounted armed raids against distant Pomo communities to capture agricultural workers. Wrangell (1969: 210–211) described one such raid, in which the Russians drove Indian men, women, and children almost seventy kilometers to Ross "like cattle" with their hands tied. There they were forced to work, without their household possessions, for about two months.

The demand for seasonal laborers increased even more in the early 1830s, with the founding of the three interior ranches. However, the abusive treatment of native workers may have been curtailed somewhat, after Chief Manager Wrangell's visit to Ross in 1833. In observing the blatant exploitation of the Indian workers, he issued immediate orders to compensate them more fairly in the future.

> In the aforementioned proposal I have authorized providing the Indians and the Aleuts the best food, as against formerly, and especially paying the Indians somewhat more generously for work. . . . It goes without saying what consequences there must be in due course from such actions with the Indians, and will we make them our friends? I hope that the Factory, having received permission from me to provide the Indians decent food and satisfactory pay, will soon see a change in their disposition toward us, and the Main Administration will of course recognize these increased expenses, justifiable and useful, as against the former expenses. (Wrangell 1969:211)

By the late 1830s, local managers implemented some of these new initiatives. For example, at the Khlebnikov Ranch, a cook was hired to feed the agricultural workers, and one of the Native Alaskan archers was instructed to hunt "wild goats and deer to feed the Indians" (Selverston 1999:3).[49]

Another factor that may have lessened the labor crunch in the Ross Colony in the 1830s was the influx of ex-neophyte workers from the northern missions of Alta California, following secularization in 1834. Neophyte fugitives from the missions had represented a potential source of labor for Company managers earlier. But there is little evidence that the merchants recruited them to work at Ross before the secularization of the missions.[50] If the Company employed escaped neophytes as agricultural laborers, it risked the alienation of its most favored trade partners, the Franciscan fathers. In fact, some level of cooperation took place between the Russian managers and Spanish/Mexican colonial administrators so that neophyte fugitives who committed crimes in the Russian frontier could be returned to Alta California. This point is made by Khlebnikov in a letter to the new Ross manager, Paul Shelikov, in 1824.

> Spanish Indians, considering themselves Christians, often come to Fort Ross or are under the fort's protection. Sometimes they come to beg. There is no need at all to allow them to stay, because they will only quarrel with the missionaries. If one of the Indians steals something or kills livestock and is caught, the guilty party is to be kept at Ross in shackles and put to work. Then, when a ship comes, he is to be sent to Monterey or San Francisco to the local authorities with an explanation of his offenses. (Khlebnikov 1990:194)

With the secularization of the northern missions, the Russians began using ex-neophytes from Mission San Rafael and possibly Mission San Francisco Solano as agricultural laborers (Jackson and Castillo 1995:95). In his inspection tour of the missions in 1839–40 for the Mexican California government, William Hartnell reported that the administrators of the San Rafael mission told him "that in the Russian fields there are many Mission Indians whom they [the mission administrators?] claim" (Jackson and Castillo 1995:190 fn34). The presence of ex-neophyte workers in the Russian frontier may explain why an adobe house, rather than the standard timber structure, was constructed at the Khlebnikov Ranch sometime in the 1830s (see Selverston 1999:3).

Social Mobility

The Russian merchants imposed a colonial hierarchy in the Ross Counter that defined the status, work, pay, and residential arrangement of all its workers. Although they used several factors to define an employee's position in the Company (e.g., level of education, job skills, overall motivation), ethnicity was the primary variable employed in defining four major "estates" or classes: 1) "Russians," 2) "Creoles," 3) "Aleuts," and 4) "Indians" (Fedorova 1975:11–15; Khlebnikov 1990:187–194; Wrangell 1969:210–211).

The Company divided Russian workers into three groups (Fedorova 1975:15). At the apex of the hierarchy were "the honorable ones," who served as Company administrators and/or military officers. "The semi-honorable ones" comprised the next step, as clerks, soldiers, navigators, and laborers. The third group, "colonial citizens," was made up of Russian workers who remained in Russian America after retiring from service in the Company.

The Company classified Creoles, the offspring from Russian men and native women, as a separate "estate." Creoles were generally not accepted by either the Russian or Native American communities (Fedorova 1975:13–14). The Company educated some Creole men in Russia, and they served in important positions as officers on Company ships, and as middle-level managers, clerks, and skilled craftsmen (Spencer Pritchard 1991:43). Although some Creole workers at Ross made a modest wage, they were paid less than members of the Russian estate, even for performing the same jobs (see the salary scale for workers at Ross, in Khlebnikov (1994:165). Khlebnikov (1990: 63–64) justified this discrepancy by noting that Creoles had been raised and trained at the Company's expense.

Native Alaskans from the Aleutian Islands, Kodiak Island, and Prince William Sound were classified collectively as "Aleuts." Most Native Alaskans stationed at Ross were Alutiiq peoples, drawn primarily from Kodiak Island but also from the upper Alaska Peninsula, sections of the Kenai Peninsula, and Prince William Sound. The other Native Alaskans included some Unangan (or Aleut) peoples from the Aleutian Islands, Tanaina workers from Cook Inlet, and Tlingit laborers from southeastern Alaska (Istomin 1992). Native Alaskans served as general laborers, porters, fishers, commercial sea mammal hunters, and skilled craftspersons (Lightfoot et al. 1991:16–20; Murley 1994, 1998). They worked on commission (being paid per sea otter pelt) or received daily or yearly salaries in scrip, a parchment token that could be exchanged for goods in the Company store (Tikhmenev 1978:144).

The Company reserved the "Indian" estate, the lowest rank in the colonial hierarchy, for local Native Californians employed as seasonal laborers or as spouses for the Ross colonists. The "Indians" working or living at Ross included nearby Kashaya Pomo and Bodega Miwok peoples as well as men and women from Southern Pomo and Central Pomo tribes to the north and east of the settlement, primarily along the Russian River. The 1820–21 Kuskov censuses identified the homeland of the women residing in interethnic households as "from the Great Bodega" or "Bodegan" (Coast Miwok or Bodega Miwok), "from the vicinity of Ross" (Kashaya Pomo), "from the Slavianka (or Russian) River" (either Kashaya Pomo or Southern Pomo), and "from the Cape Barro-Dearena (Point Arena)" (Central Pomo) (Istomin 1992:5–6). Chief Manager Wrangell's description of the native group that was captured and marched about 70 kilometers to Ross in 1833 indicates they were either Southern Pomo or Central Pomo. Also members of the "Indian" estate were the ex-neophyte laborers from the greater San Francisco Bay region who relocated to the Ross Counter after 1834.

The Russian-American Company did not establish a separate or dual social hierarchy for its "Indian" workers. That is, unlike the Franciscan padres, the merchants did not create new leadership positions for Native Californian workers outside those already extant in traditional tribal societies. The single exception was the designation of the "chief *toion*" who served as the spokesperson for local tribal groups, as discussed below. The Company tended to rely on Russian, Creole, or Native Alaskan employees to supervise task groups composed of local native workers.

But although the "intended" policy of the merchants was not to transform local native political structures, Russian colonization had a significant impact. A practice the Russians imported to California from their North Pacific colonies was to work closely with recognized leaders of native groups in contracting for labor. This practice effectively institutionalized status differences that existed within native groups and probably enhanced the political power of some prominent Indian families and leaders. Archaeological research and native oral traditions indicate that, prior to Russian contact, the Kashaya were organized into multiple small polities or village communities, each associated with its own suite of political and ceremonial leaders defined primarily by kin relations (Lightfoot 1992; Lightfoot et al. 1991:43–119). When they founded Colony Ross, the merchants encouraged one leader, known as the "chief *toion*," to become the designated spokesperson for the entire Kashaya Pomo in matters concerning the Russian-American Company. This action greatly increased his status, power, and name recognition among the colonists and local natives.

In her analysis of such political transformation, in which the leader of one local group became the recognized "tribal" authority, Jean Kennedy (1955:19) suggests that "[t]he adoption of a single chief gives evidence of the effect of the Russian centralization of authority." As she points out, the earliest recognized "chief" of the Kashaya tribe was known, in the oral tradition of the Kashaya Pomo, as "Toyon." This name probably derived from the Russians, who identified "native administrators" as *toions* in their colonies (Kennedy 1955:18–19). In fact, *toion* is, according to Leonid Shur, a "Yakut word meaning 'leader'" that Company officials applied to Indian chiefs or influential tribal elders throughout Russian America (Shur 1990:204, glossary). Russian negotiations with the Bodega Miwok probably stimulated a similar consolidation of political power, with Company representatives recognizing Valenila (aka Velenila) of the Port Rumiantsev area as the "chief *toion*" of all Bodega Miwok people.[51]

The "treaty" between Company agents and local Kashaya representatives in a ceremony held at the Ross settlement on September 22, 1817, clearly shows how the Russians favored one native leader over the others. In the full text of the treaty, below, the chief, Chu-gu-an, is probably the "Toyon" identified in Kashaya Pomo oral tradition.

On September 22, 1817, the Indian chiefs Chu-gu-an, Amattan, Gem-le-le and others, appeared at Fort Ross by invitation. Their greetings, as translated, extended their thanks for the invitation.

Captain Lieutenant Hagemeister expressed gratitude to them in the name of the Russian American Company for ceding to the Company land for a fort, buildings and enterprises, in regions belonging to Chu-gu-an, [land] which the inhabitants call Med-eny-ny. [Hagemeister] said he hoped they would not have reason to regret having the Russians as neighbors.

Having heard [what was] translated for him, Chu-gu-an and a second, Amattan, whose dwelling was also not far off, replied, "We are very satisfied with the occupation of this place by the Russians, because we now live in safety from other Indians, who formerly would attack us and this security began only from the time of [the Russian] settlement."

After this friendly response, gifts were presented to the toion and the others; and to the Chief, Chu-gu-an, a silver medal was entrusted, ornamented with the Imperial Russian seal and the inscription "Allies [soiuznye] of Russia" and it was stated that this [medal] entitles him to receive respect from the Russians, and for that reason he should not come to them without the medal. It also imposes on him the obligation of loyalty and assistance, in case this is needed. In response to that he and the others declared their readiness and expressed their gratitude for the reception.

After the hospitality, when [the Indians] departed from the fort, a one-gun salute was fired in honor of the chief toion.

We, the undersigned, hereby testify that in our presence the chief toions responded in exactly this way. (Dmytryshyn et al. 1989:296–298)

Some flexibility existed for "Indians" to move up the colonial hierarchy at Ross. Native peoples could creatively manipulate their social practices and identities to take on new roles, jobs, and responsibilities in the colonial community. The boundaries among the colonial "estates" were not rigid and impermeable. In reality, the imposed colonial estates were composites of diverse peoples who often hailed from different homelands, spoke different languages, and maintained distinctive ideologies and worldviews. Since these broad ethnic categories existed primarily in the minds of the Company managers, the cultural practices associated with each estate in the colonial hierarchy were somewhat enigmatic. There was considerable latitude for the creation of invented traditions at Ross (e.g., Upton 1996:5). To be recognized as a member of the Russian, Creole, Aleut, or Indian estates, "it was imperative that you 'talk the talk' and 'walk the walk' in the eyes of the Ross managers" (Lightfoot et al. 1998:205).

Sannie Osborn (1997:172) makes this point in describing how native peoples could be reclassified as Creoles.

> In practice, not all persons designated as Creoles were of mixed ancestry. Some individuals of entirely native descent were designated as Creole because of their occupations or positions within the Company hierarchy. After 1821, Native Alaskans who became naturalized citizens by pledging allegiance to the tsar could be also considered Creoles (Oleksa 1990:185). And, others who were Creole by definition, were listed as Russian on the basis of the social position of their father (Black 1990: 152). Perhaps more importantly, being a Creole was "more a matter of the spirit, a state of mind, a question of self-identity." (Oleksa 1990:185)

Upward social mobility within the colonial hierarchy at Colony Ross could be pursued by Native Californian men and women through two distinct pathways. The first was restricted primarily to native men who chose to become Company employees. In contrast to "Indian" seasonal laborers who worked at Ross intermittently, scheduling work around other hunting and gathering activities in the broader region, Miwok or Pomo men serving as Company employees were obligated to labor year-round for the Ross managers. Even though not much is known about the "Indian" employees, it seems reasonable that they became members of the Russian Orthodox Church and probably downplayed their "Indian" identities in the colonial community. As full-time employees, they hitched their destinies to the Company, which meant they could be redeployed to other Russian colonies in the North Pacific at any time.[52] The other pathway for social mobility was followed by some native women in interethnic households.

Interethnic Unions

The general policy of the Russian merchants was to support pluralistic relationships in their North Pacific colonies—primarily to increase the population of Creole people who would eventually enter the service of the Company (Fedorova 1973:206; 1975:11). With regard to Russian California, the Company's board of directors wrote in 1818 that interethnic marriages, especially between the "Aleuts" and "daughters of the Indians," were mutually beneficial because they created "family ties" between the newcomers and the indigenous population (Russian-American Company 1989d: 307–308). Company agents were pleased to solidify their political alliances with the Kashaya Pomo and Bodega Miwok through a network of marriage and kin relations. This practice also ensured the creation of Creole offspring who could serve as future laborers at Ross.

In the wake of the political alliance forged between the Russian-American Company and local Indian groups in the 1817 "treaty," interethnic marriages or unions became common between colonial men and Native California women. Valenila and Chu-gu-an, as well as other lesser *toions* of the Bodega Miwok and Kashaya Pomo, contributed to the political alliance by offering their daughters as mates to Ross employees (Golovnin 1979:163; Kotzebue 1830:124). By supporting these interethnic unions, the local leaders made a calculated move to enhance their political influence and regional power base by establishing kin relations and social obligations with the foreigners. Indian families probably extended the full social responsibilities of kin relations to their alien in-laws (Golovnin 1979:163). These obligations may have extended to the construction of houses for the mixed ethnic couples, assistance in performing various chores, sharing of food, circulation of trade goods, and participation in local ceremonies (e.g., Tikhmenev 1978:140). In turn, it was traditional for Alutiiq men to give presents to the father and mother of the bride, and to bring their in-laws choice portions of meat and other valued goods (Davydov 1977:182; Merck 1980:108).

The Kuskov (1820–21) and Veniaminov (1836, 1838) censuses, recently published by Alexei Istomin (1992) and Sannie Osborn (1997), respectively, provide longitudinal data for examining the nature of interethnic unions in the Ross Counter during the 1820s and 1830s. These data indicate that interethnic households were common at the Ross settlement, especially during the early years. In the censuses of 1820–21, the majority of the households at Ross with two or more people were composed of Native Californian women, colonial men, and their children. Of the 95 households counted, 56 were composed of Native Californian women residing with colonial men. The majority of the women lived with Native Alaskan men (50), followed by Russian men (5) and a Creole man (1). In the Veniaminov censuses of 1836 and 1838, there is a marked decline in the number of interethnic households containing Pomo or Miwok women. Of the 73 households with 2 or more members, only 20 now included Native Californian women. Furthermore, the composition of the mixed-ethnic relationships changed dramatically: the majority of the Native Californian women (11) now resided with Russian men. Only 4 women dwelled with Native Alaskan men, with the rest cohabiting with Creole spouses (3), Yakuts spouses (1), and an unidentified man (1).

Russian accounts emphasized the brittleness of many of these interethnic affairs, with couples often separating after only a short time together. Khlebnikov (1990:194) recounted in 1824 that "[a]ll the Aleuts have Indian women, but these relationships are unstable, and the Aleuts and the Indians do not trust each other. An Indian woman may live for a number of years with an Aleut and have children, but then, acting on a whim, will drop everything and run off to the mountains." Kostromitinov (1974:10) described conventional marriage rites among the Kashaya Pomo as relatively informal, with separations not uncommon if the couples were unsuited living together. Native Californian women entering into conjugal relationships with colonial men viewed these marriages as relatively open and flexible social arrangements, which could be quickly dissolved when one or both partners became dissatisfied. For example, none of the fifty-six couples involving Native Californian and colonial men in the early 1820s remained together by the time Father Veniaminov recorded the 1836 and 1838 censuses (Osborn 1997:213, 297). The longest documented relationship lasted thirteen years—Paraskeva (listed only as an "Indian wife") and Isai Adamson, a Finnish cooper, appear to have stayed together from 1823 to 1836 (Osborn 1997:385). The great majority of the other interethnic unions lasted a much shorter time.

In cases of divorce or separation, the colonial men (or even Ross managers) typically decided the status of the children, with male offspring frequently joining the father's household in the Ross village or returning with him to Alaska. Female offspring tended to remain with their Indian mother at Ross or accompanied her back to her native homeland (Istomin 1992:7).

The colonial hierarchy at Ross may have become more fluid and permeable over time, at least with respect to marriage partners. In a previous analysis of the 1820–21 census data, Lightfoot, Wake, and Schiff (1991:21) have shown that most interethnic associations tended to take place between the same or adjacent ethnic classes or estates. That is, most of the Native Californian women at Ross interacted primarily with Native Alaskans, while the Native Alaskan women resided primarily with other Native Alaskan men or Creole men, and the Creole women lived with Creole or Russian men. Only one Creole woman dwelled with a man below her estate (a Native Alaskan *toion*). Linguistic information corroborates these patterns teased from the census data. Studies of the Kashaya Pomo language indicate a common practice of borrowing Native Alaskan words (Kari 1983:1–3; Oswalt 1994:102–104). Furthermore, an analysis of Russian loanwords incorporated into the Kashaya Pomo language suggests that some of these words originated from Aleutian or Alutiiq speakers (Oswalt 1957:245–247; 1994:102–103).[53] Lightfoot, Wake, and Schiff (1991:22) conclude by recognizing that social relationships cross-cut the colonial hierarchy, but that "the closest interactions took place primarily between people of the same or adjacent ethnic classes. In reality, the Kashaya Pomo and Coast Miwok workers probably had very little interaction with the 'honorable' Russian managers of the colony. Rather their social relations extended primarily to the native Alaskans, and to a lesser degree with the Creoles and lower class Russians." The 1836 and 1838 census data suggest that this rather tightly structured hierarchical network of interactions had by that point undergone some changes, at least with respect to the marriage patterns of Native Californian women. The great majority of Indian women now lived with Russian, Yakuts, and Creole men (n = 15, or 75 percent of the 20 interethnic households), indicating that access to the men of the upper estates was no longer as restricted as in the early 1820s.

Some Native Californian women took advantage of the more permeable nature of the colonial hierarchy in the late 1820s and 1830s and actively created innovative kinds of colonial identities. An important component in the construction of new colonial identities at Ross was conversion to the Russian Orthodox faith, as native women could not be legally married so long as they remained outside the Orthodox congregation. As noted above, little evidence exists for the conversion of Native Californians until the 1830s. At this time, a cohort of thirty to forty baptized women and children lived at Ross. According to the Veniaminov census records, a few of the adult women were legally married to colonial men, although the majority were widows, heads of single parent households, or single females (Osborn 1997:368–412). I believe that baptism, the acceptance of a Russian Christian name, and outward observances of Orthodox practices were fundamental practices in the transformation of a native woman's identity at Ross. As a member of the church, a woman became integrated into the broader colonial community, and she had the opportunity to redefine her social position and marriage status accordingly.

Some Native American women were apparently successful at crafting new colonial identities in the late 1820s and 1830s, eventually becoming incorporated into the colonial hierarchy and sailing to Sitka on Company ships with their families. They joined the Russian Orthodox Church and married Russian or Yakuts men, and the Company recognized their children as members of the Creole estate. Katerina Stepanova, identified only as a California Indian, accompanied her Yakuts husband, Petr Popov, and two daughters, Matrena and Irina, to Sitka in 1829. In 1831, census records list her eldest daughter as fourteen years old and in Sitka, and her youngest as seven years (Osborn 1997:384). Three women whose interethnic families are listed on the 1836 and/or 1838 censuses accompanied their Russian husbands to Sitka in 1841 when the Company sold the Ross Colony. These included Matrona and her "peasant" husband Foma Arzhelovskii, and their two Creole daughters Anis'ia and Agrafena; Fedos'ia and her "peasant" husband Onufrii Kuznetsov, daughter Varvara, and three sons Nikolai, Gavriil, and Petr; and Afanas'ia and her "peasant" husband, Trifon Akad'ev (Osborn 1997:376–377).

Luker'ia, a young unmarried baptized woman, also accompanied the Company employees to Sitka in 1841 (Osborn 1997:408). The passage of Luker'ia to Alaska indicates it was possible for a California Indian woman to engage in upward social mobility without entering into an interethnic relationship with a colonial man. Like the two California Indian men who became Company employees (Murav'ev Ieromin and Zakharov Irodion), native women could choose to enter the church, develop close affiliations with the colonists and the Russian-American Company, and move up the colonial hierarchy.

Demographic Parameters

Throughout the occupation of the Ross Colony, the Russian-American Company maintained a relatively modest population of Russians, Creoles, and Native Alaskans in its California outpost. Table 2 presents the population figures for the colony, with numbers broken down into subtotals for foreign (colonial) adult men and women, subtotals for Native Californian adult men and women, and a grand total for adults and children. Keep in mind that it is not always clear whether the population estimates reported by observers refer only to the Ross settlement or to the entire Ross Counter. The number of foreign adults stationed in Russian California fluctuated between one hundred and two hundred people, with the peak population between 1820 and 1830.

Very little information is available on population trends of those Miwok and Pomo peoples residing in the hinterland of the Ross Counter from 1812 to 1841. Unlike the Franciscans, who religiously recorded the number of baptisms, marriages, and deaths at each mission, Company officials were not meticulous in detailing demographic observations of the Kashaya Pomo or Bodega Miwok. Census data collected on local Indians dealt almost exclusively with those closely associated with the Ross settlement, primarily *kaiur* laborers, Company employees, women residing with colonial men, and baptized women and children. The population estimates in table 2 do not, with the exception of Wrangell's 1833 observations, include Indians who worked at Ross as seasonal laborers.

Only rough estimates are available for the number of native people in the Native Californian Neighborhood, and none really exist for the Kashaya population in outlying homeland villages. The population of Indian laborers at Ross fluctuated on a seasonal and yearly basis. With agricultural intensification in the 1820s and 1830s, the number of Indians residing in the Native Californian Neighborhood swelled from spring to fall with seasonal laborers "recruited" from outlying communities. The number of agricultural workers reportedly increased from 100 in 1825 to about 150 in 1833 and 200 in 1835 (Gibson 1976:119). In August 1839, during the height of the harvest, LaPlace observed "several hundred" Indian workers in the vicinity of the Ross settlement (e.g., Native Californian Neighborhood) (LaPlace 1986:65).

The increasing exploitation of native laborers during the 1820s and 1830s took place at a time of general population decline among the Kashaya Pomo and Bodega Miwok peoples. Unfortunately, the exact rate and magnitude of this decline are not known. It is clear that several lethal epidemics swept across the North Bay region from the late 1810s through the 1830s. Kostromitinov (1974:7) observed that many Native Californians north of San Francisco Bay "were exterminated by the pestilences which raged during the years of 1815–22." In 1828, a measles epidemic killed twenty-nine Creoles and Native Alaskans at Colony Ross, but the merchants failed to record the number of Native Californian casualties (Gibson 1976:128). In 1833, another measles epidemic disabled most of the payroll, and killed many local peoples (Gibson 1976:128). Osborn (1997:229) cites evidence for possible smallpox outbreaks at Colony Ross in 1835 and 1838. Russian-American Company correspondence indicates that, when Chief Manager Kupreianov visited California in 1838, he noted that

> the mortality at Ross was not great although the "greater part of the Indians bore signs of it." Although the Russian settlement at Ross may have escaped the worst of the 1838 smallpox epidemic, Kupreianov commented that the disease had "spread to the tundra" [outlying areas] and was rumored to be killing off significant numbers of Indians as well as being severely felt at the Spanish missions and ranches. (Osborn 1997:229)

During the period 1836–40, a suite of epidemics of measles, chickenpox, whooping cough, and smallpox struck the Company's colonies from the Aleutian Islands to California (Fedorova 1973:161; Tikhmenev 1978:198). The numbers of Pomo and Miwok fatalities at Colony Ross are unknown.

Medical care at Colony Ross was not much better than that practiced in the Franciscan missions. Tikhmenev (1978:161), in writing the Company's official history, reported that prior to 1821 the mercantile giant employed no trained physicians in Russian America, and the workers cared for the infirm using "treatments learned from medical handbooks." The main administration did send medicines and smallpox vaccine to its colonies in 1808

TABLE 2. Population of the Ross Counter

Ethnic Group	1812	1818	1818–19	1820	1821	1830	1833	1836	1838
Russians									
Men	23	26	21 or 27	38	24	35	41	46	49
Women						2	4	1	1
Yakuts									
Men				5	5			5	2
Women								2	1
Creoles									
Men				8	6	21	10	10	12
Women				9	6	32	15	18	17
Native Alaskan									
Men	80	102	75 or 78	116	79	61	42	24	22
Women				5	14	51	15	5	6
Hawaiians									
Men				4	3				
Women									
Foreign (Colonial) Subtotal	103	128	96 or 105	185	137	202	127	110	110

Ethnic Group	1812	1818	1818–19	1820	1821	1830	1833	1836	1838
Native Californian									
Men				8	4		35	4	4
Women				48	34		37	36	25
Native Californian Subtotal				56	38		72	40	29
Total Adults (Foreign, Native Californian)				241	175	202	199	150	139
Children									
Male				38	29		54	65	77
Female				37	32		40	45	47
Children (All) Subtotal			96 or 105	75	61		94	110	124
Grand Total	103	128		316	236	202	293	260	263

SOURCES: 1812 (Fedorova 1973:135); 1818 (Golovnin 1979:162); 1818–19 (Gibson 1976:12); 1820 (Osborn 1997:187); 1821 (Osborn 1997:188); 1830 (Khlebnikov 1994:71); 1833 (Wrangell 1969:210); 1836 (Osborn 1997:192); 1838 (Osborn 1997:193).

to vaccinate colonists and "as many natives as possible" (Tikhmenev 1978:161). Moreover, the Russians are credited with the earliest efforts to control smallpox in California, as they delivered the first "smallpox lymph" to government officials in Monterey (McKenzie 1996:3). When Chief Manager Kupreianov visited Colony Ross in 1838, he reported that a shipment of smallpox vaccine had been received in 1837, along with orders to vaccinate anyone not yet inoculated (Osborn 1997:229).

Chronology of Colonial Encounters

A notable characteristic of Russian colonization in California was its relatively short duration. The colonial enterprise endured for only twenty-nine years (1812–41), roughly half the duration of the Franciscan colonial program. The shorter time means that only one to one and one-half generations could possibly have been raised in this mercantile setting. The number of children resulting from unions between colonial men and Creole, Native Alaskan, and Native Californian women increased steadily in the 1820s and 1830s (see table 2), however; had the colony survived another ten to twenty years, a substantial wave of people would have been raised in Russian California.

CULTIVATING A POSITIVE IMAGE

So how well did the Russians treat their indigenous neighbors? The mercantile motives of the Russian-American Company shaped the policies and practices for interacting with local Indian peoples. The Ross Counter received little assistance from the Russian Orthodox Church, in part because the Sitka parish was severely understaffed, but also because the Company did little to promote the permanent assignment of an Orthodox priest in its California colony. The Main Administration and Ross managers had no intention of establishing a competing missionary program in California that might alienate their Franciscan trade partners. The absence of Orthodox missionaries at Colony Ross allowed the Company to institute an unbridled commercial agenda for Russian California. The "intended" colonial structures included no formal enculturation program, no formal native resettlement program, an abusive labor regime, the perpetuation of an intimidating colonial hierarchy divided into four ethnic "estates," the promotion of inter-ethnic unions, and the presence of a moderate number of foreign administrators and workers who never intended to reside permanently in California. We can only speculate how some of these dimensions of colonial encounters (e.g., the enculturation program, exploitation of native workers, and interethnic cohabitations) might have differed if the church had permanently assigned a priest to Colony Ross.

The Russian-American Company worked hard to cultivate an image of the fair treatment of Pomo and Miwok natives, to legitimize its colony in California. Correspondence from the Main Administration and colonial agents stationed at Ross repeatedly stressed the good rapport the Russians had with their Indian allies who had given them permission to settle Port Rumiantsev and Ross. The carefully groomed image of the Russian-American Company remains with us today, as the Russian merchants continue to be identified as the "kinder, gentler" colonials in California (e.g., Heizer and Almquist 1971:11–12,66; Spencer-Hancock and Pritchard 1980/1981:311). And their treatment of native peoples did differ significantly from that in the Franciscan missions. But it is time to look closely at the teflon coating of the Russian merchants. Their colonial program was, in its own way, no less harsh or disruptive to local natives than that of the Fernandinos in Alta California.

6 Native Agency in the Ross Colony

"In the old days, before the white people came up here, there was a boat sailing on the ocean from the south." So begins a Kashaya story about the first glimpse of a foreign sailing vessel, probably one of the ships captained by Cabrillo, Drake, or Vizcaíno that slowly tacked northward along the coast. The sighting inspired considerable wonder and anxiety among the Kashaya, as they believed it was a "big bird floating on the ocean." They promised to hold a feast and dance in honor of the "big bird person" if it would not destroy their world. According to the story, the great bird did not stop to wreak havoc on them but continued to sail north beyond the horizon. The Kashaya were convinced that the strange creature left them alone because of the promise of a great feast and dance, which they celebrated as soon as the vessel disappeared (see Oswalt 1966:245–247).

When the "big birds" returned more than two centuries later, the Kashaya were not so fortunate. The sailing vessels that poked along the coastline did not evaporate into the ocean, but eventually anchored offshore. As the Russian merchants disembarked, they appeared to emerge from the ocean depths, and thereafter became known as the "Undersea People" in local oral tradition.[1] The Undersea People settled on tribal lands known as Métini, and we can only imagine the number of feasts and dances the Kashaya held in hopes of sending them on their way.[2] When it became clear that the Russian colonists were not about to sail northward into the horizon, the initial shock of the local Indian leaders was probably replaced with a mixture of pragmatic determination and foreboding. Chu-gu-an, Amattan, Gem-le-le, and other Kashaya leaders capitalized the best they could on this foreign intrusion. By allowing the Undersea People to live as neighbors, the sagacious chiefs used the colonists as powerful deterrents to the continued northern expansion of the Franciscan missionaries and Spanish soldiers, and as protection from raids by hostile Indian groups. But what price would be paid for this alliance with the Undersea People?

INCORPORATION INTO THE ROSS COLONY

Previous Spanish colonization of Alta California colored the initial encounters between the Russian merchants and coastal hunter-gatherer groups of northern California. The Russians pursued good relations with local Indian leaders, knowing full well that the Indians' acquiescence to the founding of the Ross Colony was critical for legitimizing the Company's colonial venture in California. The Bodega Miwok and Kashaya Pomo peoples, in turn, viewed the Undersea People as the lesser of two evils: allying with them might serve to block further Spanish expansion into northern California, keeping the Franciscans and soldiers out of their tribal territories (see, e.g., Farris 1989b:488).

Company agents and Russian naval officers recorded the animosity that Bodega Miwok and Kashaya Pomo peoples felt toward the Spanish, and later Mexican, colonists. Although we must be careful about the political motivations of these Russian accounts, we may well believe that genuine apprehension gripped most local peoples who feared that the Franciscans might expand northward and force them to join the mission system. It was no secret that the missions were lethal to the health and well-being of coastal hunter-gatherers. The Pomo and Miwok interacted with scores of neophytes fleeing the missions of the greater San Francisco Bay, who resettled in the Russian frontier (e.g., Farris 1992:15). Kostromitinov (1974:7) observed that large Indian villages once dotted the greater Bodega Bay region but that, after the founding of Mission San Rafael and Mission San Francisco Solano, the population had drained from the area: natives had been moved to the missions, emigrated to the Russian frontier, or succumbed to lethal diseases. Matiushkin made the following observation on his visit to Port Rumiantsev in 1818.

The Spanish had expanded their hunt for people to Tomales Bay itself. By now all the Indian bands fled for safety under the guns of Fort Ross or to Port Rumiantsev, where they think that four falconets and three Russians can defend them from the Spanish. Last year when a large number of people gathered at Fort Ross and asked for his protection, Kuskov persuaded them to settle in the forests and mountain gorges and then to attack the Spanish unexpectedly. The savages followed his advice and settled in the forests that are visible from Port Rumiantsev, toward Tomales Bay. Once the Spanish became aware of this, they gave up their pursuit. (Matiushkin 1996:6)

Golovnin (1979:163) also observed the deep hatred that local Indians had for the Spaniards, during his 1818 sojourn at Ross.

Local native animosity toward the Franciscans and Hispanic soldiers continued during the Mexican period. Schabelski (1993:9), traveling north from Mission San Rafael to the Ross settlement in the latter months of 1822 or in early 1823, described how neophyte fugitives ran from him when they mistook him for a Spaniard. He also witnessed a group of thirty Indian auxiliaries from Mission San Rafael chasing escaped neophytes near the Russian River—activities that no doubt must have alarmed the Bodega Miwok and Kashaya Pomo. In his 1824 trip to Ross, Kotzebue observed an Indian village, not far from Port Rumiantsev, defiantly resisting the Spaniards.

> On the north-east was a high mountain thickly covered with fir trees, from amongst which rose dark columns of smoke, giving evidence of Indian habitations. Our soldiers said that it was the abode of a chief and his tribe, whose valour had won the respect of the Spaniards; that they were of a distinct class from the common race of Indians; had fixed their dwellings on this mountain on account of its supposed inaccessibility; were distinguished by their courage, and preferred death to the dominion of the Missionaries, into whose power no one of them has ever yet been entrapped. (Kotzebue 1830:119)

During his 1833 tour of the Ross Counter, Ferdinand Wrangell (1974:2) met Indian refugees on the Russian River who feared falling into the "hands of Spaniards who quite often go out to hunt Indians in order to convert their prey to christianity." Wrangell's group then spent the night gambling at a village composed of neophytes "who had fled the missions and now were living in impenetrable forests beyond the plains before us" (Wrangell 1974:3). These groups were not shy about voicing their hatred of the Hispanics (see also Wrangell 1969:212). Mariano Vallejo, in his 1833 inspection of the Russian frontier, also noted the hostility that the Indians of the Sonoma Coast displayed toward the Mexicans, and attributed this attitude to the past injustices of the missionaries and soldiers (Hutchinson 1969:220; Vallejo 2000:3–9). The local antipathy for Mexicans intensified when, in the mid-1830s, some Indian groups (i.e., Satiyomis) on the Russian River (near present-day Healdsburg) became embroiled with Vallejo and his troops from Sonoma in a bloody war (see Farris 1989a:14; 1992:15).

Russian-American Company agents took full advantage of the geopolitics of colonial California by offering the Bodega Miwok and Kashaya Pomo economic incentives, friendship, and, most important, guarantees of protection from the Spaniards and later from the Mexicans and their Indian auxiliaries. During the ceremonies surrounding the signing of the 1817 treaty, Hagemeister reported to the Company's main administration that the native leaders "unanimously expressed their satisfaction that the Russians had settled among them, thereby creating a barrier against attack by distant Indians who live near the Spanish presidio of San Francisco" (Russian-American Company 1989d:307).[3] Golovnin emphasized in 1818 how Valenila (also known as Velenila), the Indian leader at Bodega Harbor, wanted the protection of the Russians.

> This chief, called Valenila, definitely wanted more Russians to settle among them in order to protect them from Spanish oppression. He begged me for a Russian flag, explaining that he wanted to raise it as a sign of friendship and peace whenever Russian ships should appear near the shore. In view of all this, it would be contrary to justice and reason to assert that the Russians occupied land belonging to someone else and settled on the shores of New Albion without having any right to do so. (Golovnin 1979:165)

Thus, the Bodega Miwok and Kashaya Pomo peoples were initially incorporated into the Ross Colony as political allies. As noted in the previous chapter, local Indian leaders, such as Valenila of Bodega Harbor and Chu-gu-an, Amattan, and Gem-le-le from the vicinity of Ross offered their daughters as mates to the Ross employees, cementing the alliance with the Company and establishing kinship ties with the foreign colonists. In addition, for the Russians the Bodega Miwoks served as an early warning system, announcing any northern intrusion of the Spaniards, Mexicans, or potentially unfriendly foreigners into the Ross Counter (Khlebnikov 1990:194).

NEGOTIATING THE ROSS COLONY

Active Resistance

Extant colonial records and native texts are quiet when it comes to the topics of armed rebellion, assassinations, and widespread livestock raiding on the Russian frontier. I am not surprised that incidences of active resistance were rare during the first few years of the Russian and Pomo/Miwok alliance. But I am somewhat amazed that this "inactivity" continued into the 1820s and 1830s when relationships with the Undersea People began to unravel under the growing demands for agricultural labor. Company documents record that local Indians stole livestock and murdered colonists (Gibson 1976:130–131; Khlebnikov 1976:119; 1990:141), but the thieves pilfered most of the cattle, horses, and sheep individually while the animals were grazing in free-range land some distance away from the Ross stockade; this theft did not involve large-scale livestock rustling by armed and mounted raiders. Most of the murders committed against the colonists involved Native Californian men fighting with Native Alaskan workers (e.g., Istomin 1992:14–15; Osborn 1997:245); this, I think, probably relates to tensions that bubbled to the surface when a large cohort of Indian women lived with Native Alaskan men during the early years of Colony Ross. And unlike the conspiracies to assassinate abusive padres in the Franciscan missions, no native plots to murder the Russian managers have yet come to light. Why was the Russian frontier seemingly immune to armed revolts, assassination of managers, and large-scale raiding of livestock, by way of contrast to the Hispanic missions and ranchos?

Perhaps the lack of violent resistance stemmed from the presence of a well-armed Russian militia capable of pursuing anyone causing trouble in the Ross Counter. However, these were not professional soldiers but mercantile workers trained, in off hours, to use arms; it seems curious that a part-time militia of armed civilians would be a greater deterrent to native violence than the veteran Spanish and Mexican soldiers serving in the missions and presidios. Colony Ross may have been spared large-scale livestock raiding because, unlike the Spanish and Mexican settlements celebrated for their equestrian prowess and horse breeding, Ross was not renowned for its horses. And since horses were the primary commodity that Indian raiders in the Central Valley sold or exchanged to foreign middlemen (American trappers, New Mexican traders), there may have been little incentive to travel to the more isolated Russian colony to mount such raids.

Daily Practice in the Ross Counter

An important consideration in understanding why violent resistance was less common at Colony Ross than at the Franciscan missions is the impressive range of strategies deployed by local Indian peoples to mediate the adverse impacts of Russian colonization. I contend that the Pomo and Miwok peoples who participated in the Russian frontier had more options available than did Indian neophytes trapped in Franciscan missions. The local Indians in the Ross Counter took advantage of some Russian colonial practices, while at the same time they maintained powerful connections to homeland villages in the distant hinterland where they could disappear at a moment's notice.

My discussion of native agency at Colony Ross will focus on the Kashaya Pomo. Their experiences at Colony Ross have been recorded in a number of native stories. In addition, considerable archaeological work has been undertaken on village sites associated with the Kashaya in the Fort Ross State

Historic Park. Unfortunately, the same cannot be said for the Bodega Miwok: native stories on Miwok and Russian contacts have yet to be recorded in any detail, despite the recent publication of Isabel Kelly's interviews with Tom Smith and Maria Copa (see, e.g., Collier and Thalman 1996). And almost no archaeological work has been conducted on colonial-age sites in the Bodega Harbor area.

Kashaya accounts of Colony Ross derive from oral traditions passed down from people who observed firsthand the Russians and their mercantile enterprise. These observations were transmitted from one generation to another through the verbal presentation of stories. The native texts employed in this section were transcribed in the late 1950s by Robert Oswalt while he was undertaking linguistic fieldwork among the Kashaya Pomo. As a linguistic anthropologist trained at U.C. Berkeley, Oswalt was primarily concerned to collect native stories to analyze the structure and historical connections of the Kashaya Pomo language. However, he soon realized that he had tapped into a very important source for understanding the history, culture, and life ways of the Kashaya Pomo people. Consequently, he continued to collect additional stories, a task that went well beyond his linguistic study. In preparing his seminal monograph, *Kashaya Texts*, in 1966, he transcribed word by word eighty separate stories in Kashaya, translated them to English, and organized them into four main sections—myths, the supernatural, folk history, and miscellany.

The native texts cited here are from the folk history section of *Kashaya Texts*, and they derive from two key consultants—Herman James and Essie Parrish. There is little question that most of these stories are anchored in real events that took place at Colony Ross. Glenn Farris (1988; 1992) researched two versions of a story of tall, mounted strangers passing near the Ross settlement as told to Robert Oswalt by James and Parrish. Both stories document the Kashaya's unique perspective on the men, women, and children of a Hudson's Bay Company brigade that filed across the Métini landscape in April 1833. Farris (1997d) provides additional historical detail and ethnographic information to some stories told in *Kashaya Texts*.

In his late seventies when interviewed by Oswalt, in 1958 and 1959, Herman James had learned much about Kashaya encounters with the Russians from his maternal grandmother, Lukaria. She had grown up in the Métini region, and was reported to have been about eight years old when Ivan Kuskov and his men founded the Ross settlement (Oswalt 1966:9). Lukaria helped raise Herman James (born in 1882), and they remained very close until her death, in 1908. The name "Luker'ia" is mentioned three times in the list of baptized Indians prepared by Father Veniaminov in 1836 (Osborn

1997:408). The name is recorded once as the daughter of "Mavra," and the other two times as the name of a grown woman—one of whom ended up in Sitka in 1841. I feel pretty confident that one of the two baptized adult women listed as Luker'ia by Veniaminov was Herman James's grandmother.

Essie Pinola Parrish was in her late fifties and a very influential religious leader of the Kashaya Pomo when Oswalt began his linguistic fieldwork. She too had been raised by a maternal grandmother, and had eagerly learned stories about the old ways from her and from other elderly relatives. Her maternal grandmother had been born about ten years after the Russian-American Company left California, and was raised in the northern periphery of Kashaya territory (Oswalt 1966:9).

Thus, Herman James and Essie Parrish provided two different Kashaya perspectives on the Russian merchants. Herman James's stories derived directly from a woman who had grown up under the Russian colonial program, who had probably lived at the Ross settlement, and who had converted to the Orthodox faith. Essie Parrish heard stories transmitted down from the generation prior to her grandmother's, and these accounts probably reflected the world view of the Kashaya residing in the northern hinterland of the Ross Colony.

Archaeological investigations at the Fort Ross State Historic Park provide yet another perspective on Kashaya engagements with the Ross colonists. Recent fieldwork has been undertaken in the hinterland of the Ross stockade by a collaborative research team involving archaeologists from the California Department of Parks and Recreation, elders and tribal scholars of the Kashaya Pomo tribe, and faculty and students at U.C. Berkeley. The research objectives concern the long-term implications of the mercantile labor program and the multi-ethnic dynamics of Colony Ross upon the Kashaya Pomo.[4] As of the fall of 2003, the project has completed an intensive pedestrian survey of the Fort Ross State Historic Park and initiated excavation work in the Native Alaskan Neighborhood, the north side of the stockade complex, the Native Californian Neighborhood, and the more distant hinterland.

Recent investigations of the Native Alaskan Neighborhood provided considerable information about the Native Alaskan workers and their families, and also focused on Native Californian women who resided with Native Alaskan men in pluralistic households. Our excavations unearthed architectural remains of houses, associated extramural space (including fence lines of redwood posts), discrete trash dumps ("bone beds") in abandoned houses, and broad vertical exposures of the midden deposits at the base of the marine terrace (see Lightfoot et al. 1998; Lightfoot and Schiff 1997; Lightfoot, Schiff, and Holm 1997).

Since the early 1950s, archaeological excavations have been conducted immediately north of the Ross stockade wall, where the material culture of Native California peoples has been exposed. Although some of the stone tools are prehistoric (remnants of extensive low-density lithic scatters), the majority of the lithics, manufactured goods, and faunal remains date from the early to middle nineteenth century (Ballard 1997:127–130). Archaeological fieldwork in this area reveals information about native peoples living very close to the stockade, most probably Native Californian women cohabiting with Creole or Russian men (see Ballard 1997:133–134).

Archaeological investigations of the Native Californian Neighborhood, which involved both surface survey and some excavations, have contributed to our understanding of Kashaya families and individuals living near the Ross settlement, mainly as seasonal agricultural laborers in the 1820s and 1830s. Some of these sites exhibit evidence for occupation in post-Russian times, when the Kashaya worked for William Benitz, a rancher who eventually took over control of the Ross lands. In addition to surface collections and mapping at CA-SON -175, -670, -1878, -1880, -1895/H, and -1896,[5] limited excavations have been undertaken at CA-SON-670 (Noller and Lightfoot 1997; Stillinger 1975) and CA-SON-1896 (Parkman 1990). In the summer of 1998, a collaborative team of Kashaya, state park, and U.C. Berkeley scholars initiated a multi-year field program at Meʔtini Village (CA-SON-175), a program involving topographic mapping, geophysical survey, surface collection of archaeological materials, and excavation (Parrish et al. 2000).

Mapping, geophysical survey, surface collection, and excavation have also been completed at Tomato Patch Village, an archaeological site with an impressive view of the Sonoma coast from atop a high ridge about five kilometers southeast of the Ross stockade. Analysis of materials from this village indicates that it dates to late prehistoric times and was inhabited at the time of the occupation of Colony Ross. The site provides excellent comparative information on the daily practices of native peoples in the more distant hinterland of the Ross settlement. Antoinette Martinez's (1997; 1998) investigation of the large depression, three smaller house depressions, and midden deposits at the site suggests that this village may have accommodated Kashaya who wanted to be close to relatives residing near the stockade but still maintain a physical and social distance from the colonists. She also entertains the idea that the village may have served as a labor camp or even as a refuge after the Russians abandoned Colony Ross (Martinez 1998:134).

Enculturation Program: Native Persistence

Native Texts Native narratives emphasize the reluctance of the Kashaya to accept any cultural innovation not in keeping with what they perceived to be a proper "Indian" virtue. Several themes in the native accounts illustrate how the Kashaya viewed foreign innovations and the strict discipline maintained on the Russian frontier.

A common theme is the strong resistance asserted by the Kashaya to any attempt to pressure them to accept the cultural practices of foreigners.[6] Text 55, "The First White Food," told by Essie Parrish, describes what happened when either the Undersea People or later "whites" (or possibly both?) attempted to tame the Kashaya Pomo by offering food of "civilized society."

> It was also there at Métini that the white people first discovered the Indians—having come up, they found them. After they discovered the Indians, they wanted to domesticate them. In order to feed them food, in order to let them know about white man's food, [the white men] served them some of their own white food.
>
> Never having seen white men's food before, they thought that they were being given poison. Having given [the Indians] their food, they left and returned home but [the Indians] threw it in a ditch. Some they buried when they poured it out. They were afraid to eat that, not knowing anything about it—all they knew was their own food, wild food. They had never seen white people's food before then. That is what our old people told us. This is the end. (Oswalt 1966:251)

The belief that non-Indian foods may have been poisoned says much about the Kashaya's perception of foreigners. Like other Native Californian tribes, the Kashaya believed that shamans, bear doctors, and other potentially evil people murdered innocents through poisons. By equating foreigners with malevolent persons, the Kashaya narratives make a powerful statement that the newcomers could not be trusted.

Another common theme in stories is the benefit of maintaining and preserving Kashaya indigenous practices threatened by the continued encroachment of the Undersea People. In Text 63, "Two Underseas Youths Freeze to Death," recited by Herman James in September 1958, two young colonists were harvesting black birds ("coot") near the modern town of Jenner when a cold rainstorm froze them to death. After Company employees found their bodies and returned them to their grieving mothers, the local Kashaya remarked how Kashaya clothing was superior to that of the foreigners.

> Because of that, the Indians said that cold was a terrible thing. Even if he wore a lot of clothes, a person would die if he got drenched in the rain. "When the body's blood grows cold, one becomes numb," said the

Indians. They [Indians] wore a bear skin underneath so that the cold could not get in. Even the rain couldn't penetrate that bear skin or panther skin—or the buckskin that they wore in summer time. That's why the Indians never sickened from the great cold, even when the rain beat against them. [The Russians] asked why it didn't happen to them [the Indians]. Then they told the undersea people. (Oswalt 1966:275)

The Kashaya narratives also illustrate how these Indians maintained their traditional cultural practices even while incorporating new foods, tools, or raw materials into their daily lives. In Text 56, "The First Encounter with Coffee Beans," told by Essie Parrish in September 1958, the Kashaya employed their own way of preparing seeds when first given coffee beans and a grinder.

> As before, a white man gave them coffee to drink—gave it in a sack. At that time, a long time ago, they ground the coffee themselves. He gave them a grinder too. When he had done so, he taught them [how to use it]. But [the Indians] didn't do it—they still didn't know what it was for. Even though he showed them, they didn't understand what it was for. They didn't want to drink it either.
> She boiled it too. Just the way they used to cook their acorns, that's how she boiled [the coffee beans], thinking they would become soft— she boiled them whole. She let it boil and boil—let it boil all day long. She tested them with her fingers but they never did get soft—they weren't cooked. Then, saying that they must have been bad, that they were just like rocks, she poured them out.
> This is the end. (Oswalt 1966:251)

In Text 60, "Grain Foods," Herman James recounted how the Undersea People involved the Indian people in agricultural work—harvesting crops and threshing wheat. The story also revealed how local Indians would harvest grain (presumably wheat) for their own consumption, using traditional native practices. "They also used to tell that the Indians in their different fashion also gathered grain when it was ripe by taking a tightly woven packing basket and knocking [the grain] so that it would fall into that. When they filled [the baskets] they too would store that at their houses. They too [had] a lot, a lot like that for winter, and pinole too" (Oswalt 1966:267).

In the same story, Herman James also revealed how the Kashaya eventually consumed wheat flour but maintained the use of their traditional pinole, as well: "Then they found out; they saw how they, the undersea people, stored their own kind of food. At that time, the Indians didn't yet know much about flour. Later on, when [the Russians] had lived there a while, [the Indians] ate flour too. And they also still ate pinole in their own way" (Oswalt 1966:267–269).

The Kashaya narratives indicate that the Kashaya did not attempt to hide their "Indian" cultural practices from the purview of colonists and European visitors—in contrast to the secrecy that permeated many aspects of neophyte daily life in Franciscan missions. This point is corroborated by accounts of colonists and visitors who toured Indian villages near the Ross settlement and Port Rumiantsev (see chapter 5).

There is, however, at least one reference to an adoption of foreign ways that may have had a significant impact on the world view of the Kashaya. In Text 58, "The Last Vendetta" (September 1958), Herman James tells the story of a man from the Métini region who was killed by another native man from the "forest depths." There then ensued the revenge killing of the murderer by the victim's family, who pursued him to a village deep in the interior. At the end of the text, Herman James recounts that such killings ceased when Indian people became members of the Orthodox church.

> Into what we call a 'cross-house' [= church] some people drifted in.
> Some people drifted into the church belonging to the undersea people.
> Thereafter there was no more killing of people—what was called
> enemy-killing.
>   My grandmother told this, saying that she herself saw and heard it.
> From where they were living, men set out and killed a man. Then my
> grandmother said, "Thereafter the Indians didn't kill each other. They
> lived peacefully." This is true. (Oswalt 1966:259)

This story reflects the personal experience of Luker'ia (Herman James's grandmother), who probably had converted to the Russian Orthodox faith. The narrative not only states that some Kashaya became practicing Christians but that, under Russian colonial domination, fighting between coastal and interior native polities may have decreased substantially.

Yet another theme in the Kashaya narratives is the strict discipline maintained by the Russian-American Company at Ross. There are two native texts that speak to the punishments meted out to Indians and colonists alike. In Text 61, "The Wife Beater," Herman James emphasizes how the Company did not tolerate domestic violence or the abuse of Indian women.

> One time there was a man and an Indian woman living there [Métini]
> together. Once, early in the morning, he arose cranky. He growled at
> his wife. He got meaner and meaner, and suddenly grabbing an axe, he
> cut her head with it.
>   At that time, the undersea people already lived there. They already
> had a sheriff then, and when they told him, he led him [the husband]
> away. He was shut up at a place where a little house was standing. They
> locked him up for about one week.

Then, in the woods, they cut off small hazel switches to whip him with. They brought them to the settlement. They laid them there.

Then, leading the man out, they made him stand at a certain place. So that he couldn't run away, they had tied his hands, tied his feet, and stood him up. Next they started in to whip him. When one [switch] wore out, they took another, and thus whipped him for half a day. He fell down unconscious. Then they carried him home. (Oswalt 1966:269)

Herman James continues his story by telling how the man recovered from the whipping but his wife moved out and left him, not returning to him even after he recanted his bad behavior to an assembly of people.

In Text 62, "The Suicide of a Wife," Herman James told another story about the mistreatment of an Indian woman by her husband, an Undersea man, and the swift retribution of the Company. The couple had been quarreling, and when the man left for work he told his wife, "If I find you here at home, I will kill you." Subsequently, she finished eating her meal, dressed in her "good, new clothes," and walked over to the nearby coastal cliff with her eldest daughter in tow.

"What are you going to do?" she [the daughter] asked her mother. "I am going to die today," she replied to her daughter. "No," said the daughter. "Who would take care of us?" "Your father growled at me so much that I can't go home any more," [the mother] said.

Then the child grabbed her dress. When she did so, [the mother] didn't listen. After a while, she suddenly threw herself way down onto the gravel beach. When that happened, when she threw herself down, the child let go.

Then she ran home and told. The others came, carried her up, and laid her down over at her house. The next day they buried her—at that time they already buried people [no longer cremated them].

Then her husband arrived home and she wasn't there. Subsequently, they locked him up as a prisoner—the undersea people did. One week later, they took him out, led him off a little way from the houses, and arrived at the place where they used to whip people. Then they whipped him; they whipped him for almost a whole day. When they did so, he fainted and fell to the ground. He didn't regain consciousness; he died. Then they buried him.

This is also a true event that was told to me. [My grandmother] really saw it herself. This is all. (Oswalt 1966:271)

Luker'ia, in recounting Texts 61 and 62 to her grandson, was obviously impressed by the discipline maintained at the Ross settlement—especially the Company's protection of native women associated with the colony. Spousal abuse appears to have been severely punished by Ross managers.

Luker'ia told Herman James that she witnessed the punishment of the Russian worker who harassed his Indian wife. The perception that the Company would risk killing one of its own workers as punishment for such harassment probably contributed to the movement of native women to Ross. If native women believed the Company provided some protection from abusive men, this may have contributed to decisions to resettle at Ross to establish interethnic households or to join the church. That the Indian woman who committed suicide in Text 62 was buried, not cremated in the tradition of the Kashaya, may indicate her conversion to the Orthodox faith. Although this is speculative, I think that native women who converted to Christianity probably received deferential treatment by Ross managers and may have been placed under the guardianship of the Company.

Archaeological Sources   The findings of the archaeological investigations corroborate native texts that accentuate how the Kashaya mediated encounters with the colonists through Indian world views and cultural constructs. As active agents in confronting the Russian colonial program, the Kashaya deflected any subtle attempts by the Undersea People to force adoption of foreign practices. Cultural change most certainly took place, but it was very much directed by the Kashaya.

Variation marks the kinds of archaeological remains found in the Native Alaskan Neighborhood, the north side of the Ross stockade, the Native Californian Neighborhood, and Tomato Patch Village (see Ballard 1995:143–159; Martinez 1998:154–168). The differences are useful for understanding how individuals and families devised unique strategies for negotiating the colonial world, whether by working as seasonal agricultural laborers, living with colonial men, or maintaining low profiles in the hinterland. Yet a common thread connects the archaeological sites. Each place is characterized by a resounding "Indian" identity that permeates how the Kashaya manufactured and used materials, how they processed, cooked, and consumed foods, and how they organized and maintained space. The roots of these daily practices penetrate back through many generations of Kashaya families.

The common "Indian" signature of the material remains include: chipped stone flakes, tools, cores, and debitage; ground stone tools, such as handstones, pestles, millingstones (slab and basin), hammerstones, and net weights; fire-cracked rocks and battered cobbles; various kinds of bone tools; large quantities of shellfish remains, including mussel, chiton, turban snail, clam, and abalone; and remains of large ungulates, such as deer and elk, with the bones processed to extract marrow (see Ballard 1995; Martinez 1998; Schiff 1997a, b; Wake 1995, 1997a, b, c). The ubiquitous presence of fire-cracked rocks of varying size indicates that conventional methods of cooking had been employed in the Native Alaskan Neighborhood, North Wall Site, Meʔtini Village, and Tomato Patch Village (e.g., Lightfoot, Schiff, Martinez et al. 1997:400–408; Martinez 1998:159). Kashaya chefs used earth ovens or open hearths to cook many meat dishes, and they heated stews or soups in watertight baskets using red-hot cooking stones.

The Kashaya perpetuated a similar pattern of use in how they organized and maintained space in prehistoric settlements and colonial-age villages (Lightfoot et al. 1991:116–119). Local Indians spatially segregated residential areas from midden or trash areas. Villages were laid out with houses in upslope locations. The house structures were regularly cleaned of debris so that only an occasional lithic tool is found in the residential areas. The Kashaya situated their midden deposits downslope, where they discarded shellfish remains, animal bones, ash, fire-cracked rocks, cooking rocks, and other trash. Archaeological findings at Tomato Patch Village indicate the house structures were regularly swept clean, with refuse dumped either outside the residences or in a separate downslope midden area—where today the accumulation of materials is more than a meter deep (Martinez 1998:133–135). The center of the site consisted of a very large pit depression, most likely the remains of a semisubterranean structure used for purifying steam baths, ceremonies, and dances. This area was also kept very clean.

A similar spatial pattern is emerging at Meʔtini Village[7] just north of the Ross stockade. Recent fieldwork involving geophysical survey and intensive surface collection indicates that the village space was segregated into a "clean" zone and refuse-filled space. The western and northern sections of the village, centering around the large depression, contained very few artifactual or faunal remains. Today the Kashaya believe—based on oral traditions—that this large surface depression once served as a ceremonial "round house" where dances, purification rituals, and prayers took place. In contrast to this "clean" zone, the entire eastern section of the site was composed of midden deposits full of shellfish remains, animal bones, ash, fire-cracked rocks, and cooking stones.

Archaeological research at the above sites suggests that Kashaya men and women reproduced their conventional cultural practices when confronted with the Russian colonial program. But in their entanglements with Company managers and the multi-ethnic workforce, some aspects of Kashaya material culture underwent significant transformations.[8] Archaeological findings highlight changes in the Kashaya menu: the Kashaya in colonial contexts consumed beef, mutton, and pork (Wake 1995, 1997b, c). Also, new material media, such as ceramics, glass, and metal of European and Asian manufacture, were widely adopted, as indicated by their common occurrence in archaeological assemblages (Ballard 1997; Silliman 1997). The Kashaya produced a greater range of native crafts, especially in the Native Alaskan Neighborhood where Native Californian women probably produced *kamleikas* (waterproof pullovers) and birdskin parkas (Lightfoot, Schiff, Martinez et al. 1997:408).

Yet although new foods and material media were introduced, the Kashaya incorporated them into day-to-day practices according to "Indian" values and meanings. They treated beef, sheep, and pigs like any other large ungulates—the meat butchered and cooked as if deer or elk. Even seals, sea lions, and other marine mammals, a minor component of the menu of the Kashaya in prehistoric times, were processed and cooked in the same way as large terrestrial game by Native Californian women living with Native Alaskan men (Lightfoot, Schiff, Martinez et al. 1997:406–407).

The Kashaya also used ceramic, glass, and metal artifacts in a distinctly "Indian" way. There is little indication, for example, that iron nails, glass window panes or vessels, or ceramic plates, saucers, and tea cups served their original "European" function as architectural elements or tablewares in Kashaya residences (Farris 1997c:131–132; Silliman 1997:169–171). Instead glass, ceramic, and metal items were used as raw materials for producing a range of native artifact forms, including glass flakes and projectile points; ceramic beads, pendants, gaming pieces, and amulets; and fish hooks and metal tools (Ballard 1995; Silliman 1997). The highly fragmented and disorganized nature of the ceramic, glass, and metal pieces found in native contexts strongly suggests that these materials were probably scavenged from other sources (Russian trash dumps or the industrial zone) at Ross and then recycled into useful native artifacts (Lightfoot, Schiff, Martinez et al. 1997:409).

Glass beads, primarily drawn, hot-tumbled, undecorated monochrome and polychrome varieties, became a major constituent of all the archaeological sites. However, these glass artifacts may have simply replaced clamshell disk beads and other forms of shell beads, and as such continued to express Indian identities in colonial contexts (Martinez 1998:129). The Kashaya used glass beads as ornaments for baskets and clothing, and these objects probably signified status and wealth to the Indians, in the early years of colonization. Native agency is evident in the glass bead assemblages from the Ross region: the colors represented (primarily white and red, with varying percentages of black, green, and purple/blue) follow the traditional, and symbolically charged, color preferences of the Kashaya (Martinez 1998:109; Ross 1997:192–196).

New forms of landscape modification resulted from employing Indian cultural conventions in new colonial settings. Native Alaskan men employed their practice of filling and leveling abandoned house structures with rock rubble and dirt to create new surfaces in the Native Alaskan Neighborhood. (This matter is presented in some detail in Lightfoot, Schiff, Martinez et al. 1997:410–412.) Their Native Californian spouses then used these prepared surfaces as places for dumping refuse from nearby houses and associated extramural spaces. Thus, the Kashaya world view of order and hygiene was incorporated with Alutiiq conventions to produce an innovative cultural landscape in the Native Alaskan Neighborhood.

Relocation Program: Incorporation of Foreigners into the Native Landscape

Native Texts   As recounted in their own history, the Kashaya were not involved in a major resettlement program at Colony Ross. In fact, they depict the exact opposite as happening. The Undersea People invaded their land and moved near their extant villages in the Métini region. From a Kashaya perspective, it is incorrect to portray native peoples as participants in the colonial enterprise, since it was the colonists who became incorporated into the broader Kashaya landscape. This point was made in Text 64, "Tales of Fort Ross," told by Herman James.

> This, too, my grandmother told me. She also really saw this herself. I am going to tell about the land at Métini. They lived there. Where they originated, where our ancestors originated, at Métini, is the place where they first lived. They lived there for a long time.
>
> Then, unexpectedly, they detected something white sailing on the water. It later proved to be a boat, but they didn't know what it was— the Indians hadn't seen anything like that before. Then it came closer and closer, and unexpectedly it landed, and it proved to be a boat. They turned out to be undersea people—we Indians named those people that.
>
> Having landed, they built their houses close to where the Indians were. After staying for a while, they got acquainted with them. They stayed with them. The Indians started to work for them. They lived there quite a while; having lived there for thirty years, they returned home. (Oswalt 1966:277)

With the rapid exploitation of the Indian cultural landscape by the Undersea People, agricultural production and livestock raising, Kashaya stories make clear, took over much of the Métini landscape. The usurpation of the land had significant implications for local natives. In Text 59, "Hunting Sea Otter and Farming," told by Herman James in September 1958, the Kashaya remembered when much of the native landscape was shrouded in agricultural fields: "With that they bought wheat to plant where the fields stretch out at Métini. The whole land was covered; that was their business now. By growing they learned how to grow the food, all the things they ate. They lived there a long time. That was the only way they prospered" (Oswalt 1966:265). Herman James painted a similar picture in Text 60, "Grain Foods" (introduced above): "Where the land lies stretched out, where all the land is at Métini, they raised wheat which blanketed the land" (Oswalt 1966:267).

Another important perspective gleaned from Kashaya oral tradition is that only part of the native population resided near the Ross settlement and its agricultural core at any one time, with many families dispersed across the interior forests and outlying coastal reaches. In Text 63, the story of "Two Undersea Youths Freeze to Death," Herman James recounted that when the Undersea People looked for the lost Russian children they searched all over the Métini region. "They looked everywhere; even over where the Indians were living [apart from the Russian settlement]. There was nothing. They didn't find anything. 'They must still be way off to the south,' they said. 'Let's go search'" (Oswalt 1966:275). In "The Last Vendetta," Text 58 (described above), some native families dwelled away from the Ross settlement in the "forest depths." This particular story described fighting between a family from Métini and another in the "forest depths." They evidently knew each other, as indicated by their conversations. I assume they were members of different polities and kin groups who spoke the Kashaya language.

Archaeological Sources   Archaeological research indicates that some native aggregation took place at the Ross settlement, especially in the 1820s and 1830s when seasonal agricultural laborers resided in the near hinterland. But the occupation of six or so sites in the Native Californian Neighborhood hardly constitutes a major resettlement program, especially since some of these sites may have had occupation spanning back to late prehistoric times. Furthermore, individuals and families apparently responded differently to Russian recruitment efforts. Small, residential compounds erected in the Native California Neighborhood suggest that entire village units did not move intact to Ross (Lightfoot et al. 1991:115–118).

Kashaya stories and archaeological research concur that a significant component of the native settlement pattern was maintained in the outlying fringes of the Ross Counter, often in relatively inaccessible locations on the tops of steep wooded ridges (see Lightfoot et al. 1991:43–55).[9] I believe an important component of local native agency in confronting Russian colonialism was to maintain Kashaya settlements both near to and far from the

Figure 6.   Indian camp near Fort Ross (1886) by Henry Raschen. This night scene portrays a small village of Kashaya Pomo preparing an evening meal around a glowing fire. Although painted forty-five years after the Russians sold Colony Ross, this painting gives us an idea of what the outlying Kashaya settlements may have looked like. Raschen observed two Kashaya-style redwood bark houses and the entrance to a semisubterranean structure. The center of the picture depicts a man on horseback with a rifle. (Courtesy of the California Historical Society; FN-31558.)

Ross settlement (figure 6). Kashaya people had the choice of moving near the mercantile colony to work for or live with colonial men, or residing in the rugged coastal hills, which offered greater physical and social distance from the colonists. This settlement system provided the Kashaya with considerable flexibility. They could have circulated back and forth between the Ross settlement and the more distant hinterland, their movement depending upon current Company policies, local relations with the colonists, work opportunities, timing of wild food harvests, and even love interests. Families constructing thatched houses in the Native Californian Neighborhood, or women moving into interethnic households at Ross, might decide to stay in close proximity to the Russian colonists for only a short while, before disappearing into the nearby woodlands when seasonal work ended or when relations with spouses soured.

Labor Practices: Much Work for Little Pay

Native Texts Kashaya perceptions of the labor regime at Colony Ross stress the hard work involved in the stages of harvesting and processing grain crops, as well as the inherent dangers of working for the Undersea People. Text 60, the story on "Grain Foods," provides considerable detail on the kinds of labor performed by Indian workers.

> My grandmother told me this too about what the undersea people did. What I am going to tell about now is how they ground their flour when they raised and gathered wheat. . . . When it was ripe everywhere, then the people, by hand, cut it down, tied it up, and laid it there. Then, in a sea lion skin, they dragged it to their houses.
>
> They had made a big place there, with the earth packed down hard by wetting—there they threw down what they had tied up. Next they drove horses down there. The person who drove the horses around there in a circle was one man who took turns with various others. When it was that way [threshed], when it had become food alone, they put it in sacks. While loading it in sacks, they hauled it off in stages where their storehouse was. They filled that place up with lots—many sacks.
>
> In order to make it turn into flour, they had something that spun around for them in the wind—they called it a "flour grinder." When they got ready to grind with that, they poured [the wheat] down in there to be ground, while tossing the sacks up—that they did all day long. Then they filled the sacks with flour, and hauling it away as before, they piled it up in a building. There was a lot for them to eat in the winter. (Oswalt 1966:267)

The story continues with a poignant remembrance of a native woman who died while working around the windmill during its operation.

> Once, while a woman was walking around there, she happened to get too close while the wind was turning [the grindstone]. At that time, women's hair was long. [The woman's hair] got caught and turned with it. The woman, too, was spun around, all of her hair was chewed off, and she was thrown off dead.
>
> They picked her up, carried her home, and cremated her—at that time they still cremated. That is the way it happened; the flour grinder snared the woman and she died. (Oswalt 1966:267)

In Text 59, "Hunting Sea Otter and Farming," Herman James recounted how perilous it was to serve as a Company employee, especially hunting sea otters in the northern latitudes where ships disappeared and men often starved or froze to death. The story highlights the Kashaya's awareness of how dangerous it was to labor on hunting expeditions, as well as their foreboding image of the rugged, cold environment of Alaska.

Then they sailed up to that place. That land in the north was a cold place. We Indians called it Ice Country [Alaska]. After staying a while, they sailed southward. They were transporting south many skins— many otter skins. They say it was six months before they showed up.

Once in a while they ran out of food; they saw hard times. Many times that happened to them but they didn't listen [profit from their mistakes]. They sailed off for long periods and sold those skins. Loading up the boats, they sent them off to some other place. When they sold [the skins] they made quite a lot of money. . . .

After a while it got so that they couldn't sail up there because of the ice. They say that in that country the ice was like houses floating around, it was so cold. It was like mountains rising from the sea. Once in a while when a boat was bumped by one, it was smashed to pieces. When that happened the people drowned and froze stiff from the cold. One time when that must have happened to a boat, the undersea people—there were perhaps twenty in the boat—were all drowned. They were never found, never heard from again; they were never to return again.

They still didn't listen but still sailed off to gather and shoot the many [otter], and, having loaded up the boats with them, sail off to their home—which was Métini. One time, after a while, as I said before, the route where they were accustomed to sailing up turned out to be closed off by ice rearing like mountains. . . . When they were sailing along the way, they too ran out of food—the food ran short. Starving, they sailed along.

When they didn't show up from there, the other undersea people from Métini set out to search; they already knew what had happened to them when they didn't show up for so long. Now they set sail. They found [the lost ship] when it had sailed about half way back. Some of the men had already died—starved—only the few stronger ones were sailing the ship. The ship that had sailed out from Métini was carrying a lot of food, for they had known the others would be starving. They gave them a lot of food. (Oswalt 1966:261–265)

Archaeological Sources Although native narratives underscore the hard work and dangers of laboring for the Russian-American Company, archaeological research points to the stingy remuneration paid to Indians. Indian workers housed in the Native Alaskan Neighborhood, along the north side of the Ross stockade, in the Native Californian Neighborhood, and at Tomato Patch Village had limited access to manufactured goods stockpiled at Colony Ross. The Company shipped a wide assortment of textiles, ceramic, glass, and metal goods from Asia, Europe, and the United States to Ross, but primarily for trade with Alta California.[10] Few of these items were apparently earmarked as pay to native workers. Most of the manufactured goods recovered by archaeologists from Native Californian contexts appear to have been not new but, rather, recycled after being discarded or handed down by other Ross employees. The single major exception to this is the glass bead assemblage. It is the brightly colored beads, along with the food remains from cattle, sheep, and pig, that comprise the archaeological findings of goods or rations most likely used to compensate Indian workers. Yet the beads were primarily inexpensive embroidery varieties (Ballard 1995; Martinez 1998; Ross 1997), and the beef rations provided these workers often included "low-utility" or "cheap" cuts of meats (Wake 1995; 1997b:293, 297). In the case of Tomato Patch Village, there is little evidence that beef, mutton, or pork rations were given at all (Martinez 1998:146–151).

My interpretation of the archaeological record is that the Russian-American Company provided little direct support or assistance to the seasonal laborers or to the native women residing in interethnic households. Russian correspondence indicates that native women and children residing in the Native Alaskan Neighborhood experienced food shortages when their spouses were away and were forced to support themselves as best they could.[11] The situation for seasonal laborers was probably even worse. Native persons associated with the Ross settlement had to supplement their meager rations with wild foods. They harvested shellfish from nearby inter-tidal habitats; fished for cabezon, ling cod, and rockfish from the shore; captured ducks, geese, and possibly even shorebirds such as gulls; hunted the deer and small game to be found in the surrounding area; and gathered locally available seeds and nuts (Ballard 1995:146–147; Gobalet 1997; Schiff 1997b; Simons 1997; Wake 1997b). But native peoples living close to the Ross stockade experienced increasing difficulties in undertaking traditional hunting and gathering activities. With agricultural fields blanketing the area, timbering activities in the nearby woods, and industrial enterprises along the waterfront, they were severely limited in their ability to harvest local wild foods.

The overall neglect of native spouses and Indian workers by the Russian-American Company probably energized the maintenance of close connections with kin and friends in the greater Métini region. Not only did the outlying Kashaya settlements provide refuge for local Indians when interactions with foreigners turned bad at Ross, but kin and friends in the distant hinterland must have provided stone tools, obsidian, venison, acorns, and other goods for those living near the Ross settlement. In turn, people in outlying communities who sustained supportive social bonds with native spouses and seasonal workers at Ross assured themselves access to many European and Asian goods. European observers were astounded at how quickly goods paid to seasonal workers (e.g., tobacco, clothing, food, glass beads) disappeared from sight, usually after intensive bouts of gambling (see LaPlace 1986:69–70).[12] Where the goods ended up is unclear, but there is no evidence for hoarding among the native workers at Ross. Presumably gambling, gift-giving, and other social practices redistributed many of the goods to members of the broader Pomo community in the "forest depths," some distance from the Russian outpost (Lightfoot et al. 1991:150–151).

Upward Social Mobility: An Exception Rather than the Rule

Native Texts Kashaya stories, as far as I know, do not celebrate any native person—whether Company employee, colonial spouse, and/or Christian convert—moving up the colonial hierarchy. There is no mention of native peoples constructing new colonial identities and downplaying their Indian values. In Text 58, "The Last Vendetta," Herman James mentioned the importance of the "cross-house" (church) for bringing peace to native groups in the greater Métini region (Oswalt 1966:259). But the story, as originally told by Luker'ia, gave no hint that an Indian who joined the Orthodox faith would necessarily enjoy greater social mobility at Ross.

Archaeological Sources Archaeological investigations to date have not revealed much evidence for upward social mobility involving Indians who created new colonial identities or who manipulated the boundaries of colonial "estates." No archaeological studies have yet been undertaken in the residential quarters of Indians who were known Company employees or baptized members of the Orthodox church. Our primary research on social transformations has focused on Native Californian women who joined interethnic households in the Native Alaskan Village Neighborhood.

Interethnic Unions: Native Identity in Domestic Settings

Native Texts A Kashaya story about marriage with foreigners emphasizes the perils of this kind of relationship, and its brittleness. Text 62, "The Suicide of a Wife," described the unhappy ending of the relationship between an Undersea man and an Indian woman. After the colonist threatened to kill her, she threw herself off the nearby cliff, in front of her eldest daughter. The Company subsequently whipped the abusive husband to death, as punishment (Oswalt 1966:271).

Archaeological Sources   The principal question that directed our archaeological research of interethnic households in the Native Alaskan Neighborhood was whether these pluralistic contexts promoted significant cultural change among Native Alaskan men and Native Californian women. The results of our four-year field investigation, presented in detail elsewhere (Lightfoot et al. 1998; Lightfoot, Schiff, and Wake 1997), are only summarized here. We found evidence for cultural innovations in these households, in a menu that was neither wholly Native Alaskan nor wholly Native Californian but instead combined the consumption of large terrestrial game, domesticated animals, and sea mammals. The residents of interethnic households engaged new raw materials (ceramic, glass, metal) in the production of native artifact forms, and practiced an expanded range of native crafts. They adopted metal tools to butcher meats and to carve and shape bone tools. Kashaya conventions of cleanliness and trash disposal were combined with Alutiiq customs of covering trash areas with new surfaces, daily practices that produced innovative landscape modifications.

But there is little indication that native residents implemented strategies of upward mobility or that they forged new ethnic identities. When exposed to new foods, ceremonies, and craft goods, the female spouses viewed these primarily from within a Native Californian perspective. Our investigation suggests that Kashaya conventions and organizational principles were largely followed in the day-to-day domestic practices of interethnic households. The residents butchered terrestrial and sea mammal meats in similar ways, and they cooked the meat in earth ovens. They cleaned house floors and associated extramural spaces according to Kashaya principles of cleanliness and order, with refuse being tossed into discrete trash deposits. Native Californian material culture, such as millingstones and chipped stone tools, were the primary household domestic equipment recovered. In fact, an "Indian" signature permeated the organization of domestic space associated with the interethnic households.

Our archaeological study concluded that Native Californian women exerted their own identities within interethnic households, while making accommodations and some concessions to their respective spouses. Culture change took place, but it was very much an indigenous project directed by Californian women at the scale of the household and by Alaskan men at the scale of the broader village layout. Native women were largely successful in reproducing their indigenous cultural categories in domestic contexts and in generating new kinds of cultural practices that basically "fit" within their perceptions of what constituted proper Kashaya behavior. Consequently, we unearthed little evidence for social mobility—strategies that would have transformed the identity of Native Californian women into members of the Native Alaskan "estate."

Demographic Parameters: Death, Disease, and Abuse

Native Texts Physical abuse, anguish, and death are the focus of many Kashaya stories recounting native interactions with the Undersea People. Some of these narratives, as described above, revolve around the abusive treatment of Kashaya women who suffered from domestic violence (Texts 61, 62) and work-related accidents (Text 60). Other narratives recite, for instance, the outbreak of violence between Indian families from "Métini" and the "forest depths" (Text 58), the death of two Undersea boys due to exposure and foolhardiness (Text 63), and the lethal dangers of laboring for the Company in Alaskan waters (Text 59). The Kashaya's perception of the mercantile colony is not flattering—it depicts a mostly troubled time of hard work, suffering, and uncertainty about the future. However, although there are occasional references to individuals becoming sick during the Kashaya's encounters with the Undersea Peoples, there are no references to major pandemics decimating local Indian communities, in any of the narratives.

Archaeological Sources The most definitive study on the demographic parameters of the Ross Colony was undertaken by Lynne Goldstein and Sannie Osborn as part of the archaeological and archival investigation of the Fort Ross Cemetery (Goldstein 1992, 1995, 1996; Osborn 1997).[13] This project discovered 131 graves within the formal grounds of the Russian Orthodox cemetery, of which records on 89 persons (39 listed by name) were found through archival research. None of the individuals buried in the cemetery have been identified as belonging to the "Indian" estate (see Osborn 1997: 266, 293). Most Kashaya men and women who died while living or working at Ross were probably buried in outlying native villages. The major exception may have been women (and a few men) who chose to become baptized members of the Russian Orthodox church, as well as some of the children of interethnic unions between Kashaya women and colonial men. A significant finding of the project was the relatively large number of women and children buried in the cemetery, but poor preservation of the skeletal remains limited the ethnic identity of individuals.

The archaeological survey of the Fort Ross State Historic Park provides data on long-term trends in the settlement patterns and population dynamics for the Métini region over an eight-thousand-year span (see Lightfoot et al. 1991:57–119). Unfortunately, the survey data do not provide detailed population estimates for the Métini region, but rather provide coarse-grained trends in the growth and decline of native peoples' use of the area over time. Thus, there is no evidence for any major demographic collapse when European exploration first took place along the California coastline in the sixteenth and early seventeenth centuries, or immediately after Russian colonization in the early nineteenth century (Lightfoot et al. 1991:148–150). However, the temporal resolution is too crude to evaluate whether major changes took place in the Kashaya population between 1812 and 1841.

Timing of Colonialism: Maintaining Indian Practices

Native Texts   Native accounts are largely quiet about any significant changes in Kashaya world views or cultural practices during three decades of interactions with Undersea People.

Archaeological Sources   Archaeological research at the Native Alaskan Neighborhood, the area north of the Ross stockade wall, the Native California Neighborhood, and Tomato Patch Village is remarkable for the strong "Indian" signature of the archaeological remains throughout the period of Russian colonization.

NATIVE RESILIENCE ON THE RUSSIAN FRONTIER

The intended policies and practices of the Russian-American Company presented local Indians with many options for coping with the merchants and their multi-ethnic workforce. The Kashaya Pomo rarely resorted to active or violent resistance in Russian California. Instead, they instituted more subtle tactics ranging from accommodation through various kinds of passive resistance and almost total avoidance of the Russian merchants.

Accommodation to the colonial program usually involved some form of manipulation of the colonial hierarchy by taking advantage of the fuzzy boundaries separating colonial estates, or classes. Two major pathways existed for native social mobility at Colony Ross. One entailed native men becoming full-time Company employees; the other involved indigenous women marrying colonial men, converting to the Russian Orthodox faith, taking on Russian Christian names, and consciously working at shedding "Indian" cultural practices in public. Another possible pathway was for single native women to move to the Ross settlement; there, they maintained their own households, took on the vows of baptism, and became active members of the Russian Orthodox congregation. However, Company records, native narratives, and archaeological findings indicate that relatively few men or women opted for these pathways.

The majority of the Kashaya worked aggressively to maintain Indian cultural values and belief systems in the ever-changing colonial setting of Colony Ross. Some native women entered into relationships with colonial men, but these women in interethnic households steadfastly asserted their Indian identity. Other Kashaya peoples chose, or were coerced, to work as seasonal laborers for the Company, yet fit the Company's work schedule into their seasonal round of hunting and gathering activities. When not toiling for the merchants, they hunted wild game, fished, and gathered food beyond the heavily impacted zone of logging, agricultural, and livestock grazing around the Ross settlement. Still other Kashaya maintained low profiles in the inaccessible corners of the greater Métini landscape, establishing homes in the forest depths and keeping a wary eye out for Russian overseers and labor "recruiters."

The Kashaya's dogged resistance to foreign cultural practices is evident in European accounts, native texts, and archaeological findings. Yet significant cultural transformations touched everyone in the Russian frontier. This process of culture change was, however, an indigenous project, as local natives directed the kinds of innovations they adopted and employed in day-to-day practices. They selected or modified new cultural practices that harmonized closely with Kashaya values and meanings. However, we should not view their struggle to conserve native life ways (i.e., tools, tool production, cooking practices, and the organization of residential space) as simply a case of cultural persistence. These mundane artifacts and routinized activities took on new meanings in the Russian frontier (see Lightfoot and Martinez 1995). In the course of enacting their day-to-day practices in the Ross Colony, native peoples continually created strong Indian identities; these identities were unambiguously broadcast to any family members, friends, colonists, or European visitors in the Russian frontier.

In conclusion, a critical component of native agency in the Ross Counter was the sustenance of a regional settlement system that allowed people the flexibility of living both "near" and "far" from the colonists. Native men and women could choose to participate in the Russian colonial program and move to the Ross settlement as spouses and laborers, but when relationships with the colonists soured, they had the option of slipping away and reestablishing residences in the distant hinterland. It was prudent for Indian peoples living near Ross to maintain strong ties with family members and friends in the outlying periphery, as they served as an extended support network. I believe that the conspicuous assertion of Indian identities in the daily lives of many of the men and women living near Ross was important in signaling their close connection to people in the woods. In turn, the native men and women at Ross served as important insiders to outlying Indian groups, keeping an eye on the colonists, relaying news about their latest movements and plans, and providing ready access to foreign goods through gambling, gift-giving, and exchange.

7 Missionary and Mercantile Colonies in California

The Implications

How did the missionary and mercantile colonies in California contribute to the divergent outcomes that reverberate to this day in the state's Indian communities? This question will be addressed through a comparison of the seven dimensions of colonial encounters outlined in the preceding chapters for the Hispanic and Russian frontiers. By examining how native peoples negotiated the "intended" colonial structures of the Franciscan padres and Russian merchants, we can better understand how the variations in these entanglements led to significant changes in local tribal organizations, social relations, and Indian identities. The cultural transformations that unfolded were not haphazard developments or random events; rather, the changes that took place in Indian cultural practices are components of broader social processes that underscored how native peoples confronted and mediated the policies and practices of missionaries and merchants.

Some scholars may be uneasy with the emphasis on cross-cultural comparison and social processes that make up this chapter. Most students in anthropology today are trained with a healthy dose of historical particularism and very little grounding in the comparative method.[1] In part, this sharpening of focus is a pragmatic response to the burgeoning increase in scholarship, which grows geometrically each year. But it also reflects a theoretical shift away from studies of cultural evolution and cross-cultural generalizations, which once dominated the field, to more postmodern trends that emphasize historical individualism, practice, and agency. In the current celebration of cultural diversity, some will question any search for generalizations that claim to make sense of the tremendous variation in native and colonist encounters. Yet in recognizing the unique historical paths of people in pluralistic frontier settings, we do not need to turn our backs on the study of broader social processes that can make sense of unfolding cultural transformations. I attempt to chart a middle course in this chapter, one that navigates the deep complexities of native agency and individual histories but also emphasizes the consequences of peoples' decisions, in confronting colonial structures, that contributed to long-term processes of culture change.

COMPARING THE DIMENSIONS
OF COLONIAL ENCOUNTERS

Enculturation Programs

What were the consequences of the Franciscan padres and Russian merchants implementing differing enculturation programs among coastal hunter-gatherer peoples? The Fernandinos created an enculturation program that intended to convert natives into good Catholic peasants; Company agents made little effort to indoctrinate local Indians in Russian values, meanings, or life ways.

There is no question that the directed enculturation program of the Franciscan padres had a tremendous impact on coastal Indians in southern and central California. The padres obligated the hunter-gatherer peoples to become full-time agriculturalists and ranchers, taught them new crafts, enforced a strict time-managed routine, and introduced new foods and material culture. These "directed" innovations resulted in significant transformations in the life ways of the neophytes. We can no longer characterize second- and third-generation Indians who grew up in the missions as truly hunter-gatherer peoples. They lived in fully sedentary villages (often in alien adobe structures), relied primarily on agricultural foods, worked in craft shops and in the fields, and participated in Catholic ceremonies. They probably had little direct connection to their ancestral homelands, and they participated in cultural practices that their prehistoric successors would have found alien and maybe even repugnant.

But in recognizing the significant changes that took place among neophytes, the question remains whether the padres were successful in transforming the majority of the neophytes from *indios* to Hispanic peasants. That is, by the time of mission secularization in 1834, had the padres been successful in disconnecting their Indian wards from their prehistoric roots and transforming them into something totally new? True, some native women had married colonial men, and they (and especially their children) may have constructed Hispanic identities outside the missions. But these women appear to have been few. In reviewing the pertinent native texts, archaeological findings, and padre accounts in chapter 4, I have argued that what transpired among the majority of neophytes in the Franciscan missions was the continuous reworking of new forms of Indian identities.

Some mission scholars emphasize that the Franciscans were largely unsuccessful at transforming coastal hunter-gatherer populations into devout Catholics who readily adopted Hispanic values and life ways (e.g., Castillo 1994:280–281; Farnsworth 1987:79–86; Guest 1966:209; Hurtado 1988:25; Jackson and Castillo 1995:34–37; Osio 1996:66–67). Natives did incorporate elements of Hispanic culture and Catholicism into their lives, but those elements that they chose conformed largely to extant native values and world views (e.g., Farnsworth 1987:98–102; Haas 1995:28; Hoover 1989:398; Jackson and Castillo 1995:33–37; Shipek 1977:153–154). The routinized participation in Catholic masses and celebrations most certainly had an impact on neophytes. But as Graham (1998:29–30) points out, the Christian faith is highly malleable, with indigenous peoples in other colonial contexts appropriating the symbols and meanings of this new religion and recombining these with elements of their own belief system. This process of syncretism allowed neophytes to adopt various teachings and symbols of the Catholic faith, then transform these into Indian cultural practices in form and meaning.

The construction of new forms of Indian identities in the missions took place in the underground world of the neophyte villages. Behind closed doors, native peoples produced and employed Indian material culture in their daily lives. They executed a schedule of dances, feasts, ceremonies, curing rites, and games in their own quarters that was vested with symbolic meaning. In examining the diverse range of "Indian" objects unearthed in neophyte spaces, I feel native peoples were clearly reaching back to their ancestral past and maintaining a strong sense of Indian identity within the missions. Although significant culture change had taken root, the neophytes actively constructed identities that distinguished them from the padres and other Hispanic foreigners.

The continuous re-creation of Indian identities within the neophyte quarters is supported by the padres' own admissions. Four decades into the colonial enterprise, some Franciscans were quite candid about their failure in transforming neophytes into Catholic peasants. The padres lamented that the neophytes still continued to employ many pagan practices in the missions, that Catholicism had only been superficially adopted, that native curers and "sucking doctors" still attended the sick, and that Indian shamans organized dances and ceremonies among the neophytes in secret locations (Geiger and Meighan 1976:47–51,71–80).

Although the Russian-American Company did not support a formal program of directed culture change per se, the Company's mercantile policies and practices had significant impacts on local Indians. The Russians introduced coastal hunter-gatherers to foreign goods, foods, cultural practices, and economic activities, not the least of which were agriculture and industrial manufacture. Pomo and Miwok peoples participated in the cultivation of wheat and barley, tended livestock, and worked as manual laborers in shipbuilding and brick production. Eyewitness accounts, native texts, and archaeological findings clearly demonstrate that culture change took place among local Indians in food ways, use of new kinds of raw materials, and modifications of the cultural landscape.

But when introduced to cultural values and beliefs other than their own— whether Russian in origin or derived from the multi-ethnic workforce— the Kashaya Pomo displayed stiff resistance. They asserted this cultural antagonism while living with colonial men or while toiling in the Company's agricultural fields. By directing the course of culture change in their own lives during such engagements with the Russian merchants, the Kashaya incorporated new ideas and materials into their daily life ways yet carefully molded these practices according to Kashaya world views and cultural conventions. Thus, like the neophytes, the Kashaya were actively participating in the reshaping of their own Indian identities in the Russian frontier.

Native Relocation Programs

What were the consequences of the fact that the Franciscan padres and Russian merchants implemented different kinds of native relocation programs among coastal hunter-gatherer peoples?

The Franciscans instituted a program of *reducción* that entailed the massive movement or relocation of native peoples from dispersed villages into centrally located missions. By the end of the mission period, thousands of Miwok, Ohlone, Esselen, Salinan, Chumash, and Gabrielino peoples had been removed from their native settlements and relocated thirty kilometers or more from their tribal homelands. The Luiseño and Diegueño peoples had experienced a modified version of this program at Mission San Diego and Mission San Luis Rey, where the padres had allowed many families to remain in their homeland villages; Julio César's recollection of Mission San Luis Rey emphasized that some outlying ranchos contained Indian "towns" with overseers and chapels.

The Russian-American Company did not institute a formal program of native relocation, although some native men and women moved to the Ross settlement. As a consequence, the Kashaya peoples actively maintained villages in the homelands of their ancestors. They instituted an innovative regional settlement system in the Russian frontier: although some Kashaya lived near the Ross settlement, interacting on a daily basis with the colonists, others sustained strategically located villages in the inaccessible, distant "forest depths."

The massive relocation program of the Franciscan mission system, I would argue, had important consequences for neophytes. The padres created novel and distinctive social arenas by removing people from the villages of their homelands and relocating them to the missions. The overall effects of the relocation program probably varied from mission to mission. The least impacted neophytes were those associated with the two southernmost missions, who maintained their home villages. In the other missions, the padres aggregated together peoples from many tribal polities, who spoke mutually unintelligible dialects and languages, but even in these missions, the residential arrangement for neophytes varied. The Franciscans dispersed some individuals to outlying outposts or agricultural stations, such as those in the hinterlands of Mission San Gabriel, Mission Santa Barbara, and Mission San Buenaventura (Costello and Hornbeck 1989:312–313; Johnson 1995:2). Even among those Indians residing in large mission villages, some persons established smaller neighborhoods or discrete residential subgroups within the broader neophyte communities (see Johnson 2001:58–60; Johnson and McLendon 2000:649), but within the large, polyglot mission communities, natives were still forced to interact closely with members of other tribal groups while at work, during communal meals, in religious services, and in the women's and men's dormitories. The massive scale of the Franciscan relocation project must have had significant implications for neophyte identities and for the construction of social boundaries in mission communities. Furthermore, although the Fernandinos allowed their wards to return periodically to their homelands, the forced resettlement of thousands of Indians into a foreign territory could only have alienated them—both physically and spiritually—from the mythological landscape and graves of their ancestors.

The Russian colonial program presented native peoples with flexible residential options, which had different consequences for the Kashaya than had the missionaries' program upon most neophytes. By sustaining native settlements both near to and far from Ross, the Kashaya could choose to participate in the mercantile program or to distance themselves from their colonial neighbors. The outlying hinterland villages provided a refuge from colonial encounters where a continued sense of Kashaya community could be created. Here, family members celebrated the landscapes of their ancestors, visited named landmarks mentioned in their oral traditions, and made pilgrimages to places that dramatized the creation and well-being of their people. The Kashaya men and women who made the trek to the Russian settlements entered a new world of strange tongues and alien cultural practices, but even the agricultural encampments near the Ross settlement were not nearly so diverse in ethnic composition and languages as were most neophyte villages. The encampments contained mostly Kashaya peoples, with some Bodega Miwok and Southern Pomo speakers.[2] Most important, the Kashaya living near the Ross settlement could choose to relocate back to their ancestral lands at the end of the agricultural season, or when they tired of their colonial spouses. This afforded them a luxury that most neophytes could only dream about—that of leaving the colonial "front line" and re-immersing themselves in the world of coastal hunter-gatherers.

Labor Practices

What were the consequences of the labor practices instituted in the Franciscan missions and Colony Ross on coastal hunter-gatherer peoples? At one level, the labor regimes to which missionary and mercantile colonies introduced native peoples were very different. The Franciscans employed a combination of communal principles and enslavement. Although the neophytes had little choice but to labor, the padres provided them with three meals a day, clothing, and housing in the mission complex. In contrast, the Russian-American Company supposedly introduced local Indian people to a market economy, where they were "paid" for their labor. Russian managers employed native spouses of colonial men, hired a few men as full-time Company employees, and recruited local men and women to work as seasonal laborers in agricultural and industrial enterprises. (The Company, of course, could always depend on convicted *kaiur* laborers to perform the most difficult and appalling tasks in the colonial community.)

At another level, the labor regimes in both colonial frontiers were quite similar. The Franciscan padres and Russian merchants both exploited natives as inexpensive labor. Although much ink has been spilled over the padres' unjust treatment of Ohlone, Chumash, and other neophyte laborers, the investigation, in chapter 6, into Pomo and Miwok work conditions indicates that these laborers worked long hours for the Russians, sometimes under unhealthy or dangerous conditions, for very little pay—glass beads, tobacco, clothes, and "bad" food. Some natives were physically coerced to work.

The primary differences in the labor regimes of the Franciscan missions and the Russian-American Company are three. First, native people working for the Russians were given more freedom to come and go. When the laborers completed their tasks, they could return home to their villages. (It is not clear, however, whether they could choose to leave during the planting or harvesting seasons without provoking some kind of retribution from their colonial overseers.) Second, the Franciscans were committed to providing their workers with food and housing (even if substandard in some cases). In contrast, the Company made little concerted effort to support its workers, beyond the payment of rather meager food rations and goods for services rendered. The Ross managers were somewhat schizophrenic when it came to local Indian peoples. On the one hand, they quickly punished colonial men who abused native women at the Ross settlement. On the other hand, they distanced themselves from the Indians' daily lives, even when Indian women suffered from food shortages. The Company's policy of general neglect over the conditions of its colonists' Indian spouses and its seasonal workforce was probably an important reason for most Kashaya men and women on the colonial front line to maintain strong bonds with family and friends in the "forest depths." Third, in the missions some neophyte men received specialized training as carpenters, soap makers, masons, blacksmiths, leather workers, and *vaqueros*. In contrast, most native workers in the Ross Colony performed unskilled manual labor; skilled artisans in the mercantile colony were recruited and trained primarily from the ranks of Native Alaskans, Creoles, and Russians, although a few Native Californians worked as Company employees and probably served as apprentices to master craftsmen.

The mission and mercantile labor regimes had slightly different consequences for Indians in the Hispanic and Russian frontiers. That the Franciscan mission program allowed some neophytes to become highly skilled craftspeople proved beneficial for these neophytes when they eventually left the missions, and they were among the first emancipated from the missions during the early experiments (1826–27) with secularization. The most significant consequence of the differences between the two labor regimes, however, involved native peoples' participation in coastal hunter-gatherer activities. The Indians at Colony Ross performed seasonal work for the Russians and yet maintained, during the remainder of the year, a modified schedule of hunting and gathering in the distant hinterland. The Franciscan labor regime did not provide this flexibility, as work was expected from the neophyte charges throughout the year, six days a week—except on feast days and Sundays, when they participated in church rites. Although there were occasional forays permitted to hunt, fish, and gather wild foods, the neophytes were forced by the padres to turn their backs on traditional hunting and gathering pursuits. However, archaeological findings of wild foods in neophyte quarters indicate that clandestine operations in the near hinterland (and/or exchange with gentile tribal peoples on the periphery) certainly continued when possible.

Social Mobility

What were the consequences of the differing policies and practices concerning the social advancement of native peoples in the Hispanic and Russian frontiers? The Franciscan missions and Colony Ross were characterized by similar colonial structures. A person's status, pay, and overall treatment were defined primarily by perceived ethnic identity, with Indians always at the bottom. But the boundaries separating Indians from other colonial identities were not fixed and immutable in either case, but could be manipulated and massaged. Native men and women could launch strategies of social advancement if ambitious, pragmatic, or just plain desperate.

Similar pathways existed for upward social mobility in the missions and in the Ross settlement. To move up the colonial hierarchy, native people were expected by the padres and merchants to adopt, at least in public, highly visible cultural practices of the colonists (dress, food ways, work practices, etc.). At the same time, the natives were expected to downplay the cultural practices of their past and to distance themselves from outward signs of Indian heritage. The pathways for social advancement in the missions involved neophyte women marrying Hispanic men, neophyte workers (primarily men) becoming master craftspersons, and native men taking on important Indian offices in the mission hierarchy. At Colony Ross, native women could also advance up the colonial hierarchy by marrying colonial men, or could advance through becoming members of the Russian Orthodox Church and by taking on Russian Christian names. Social advancement for native men was largely limited to joining the Russian-American Company as full-time employees.

However, important differences underscored the incorporation of native peoples into the colonial hierarchies of the missions and of Colony Ross. While the padres supported a separate system of Indian officials, first instituted under Governor Felipe de Neve in 1778, the Russian merchants depended on traditional native political organizations for labor recruitment and discipline. The padres selected (or had elected) certain trusted Indians to serve in leadership positions, granting them considerable authority and power over other neophytes and showering them with special privileges and rewards. As discussed in chapter 4, the *alcaldes* indeed maintained control over other neophytes, making sure they reported to work and often serving as spies for the padres. The creation of this system of Indian officials produced dual or overlapping social hierarchies in many neophyte communities, where traditional tribal leaders and mission Indian officials often endured side by side. In some cases, the tribal leaders and mission Indian officials came from the same high-status families. This appears to have been the case for some Luiseño and Diegueño leaders in the two southernmost missions. But conflict and tension did arise between members of old prominent Indian families and "upstarts" from lower-status families who became *alcaldes* and *regidores,* in other missions. These tensions became exacerbated when Franciscan padres tried to actively dampen and diffuse the power of traditional tribal leaders in neophyte communities.

A significant consequence of the overlapping hierarchies in Franciscan missions was the creation of new kinds of factional groups. The aggregation of native peoples from many different homelands into mission settlements undoubtedly produced fissures within the neophyte communities. These cracks widened further with the creation of a suite of political offices for favored neophytes. With the promotion of mission Indian officials, not necessarily tied to traditional political organizations, there developed factional groups that cross-cut conventional tribal polities. Such fractures in mission neophyte communities erupted, separating those neophytes who were loyal to the priests and those who were not. Fissures also formed between native *alcaldes* chosen by priests and traditional headmen, and shamans who represented traditional native power structures (e.g., Milliken 1995:94, 182–184). In other cases, native tribal leaders assumed positions of authority in the mission hierarchy; they probably began building bases of power that extended well beyond the membership of their old polities. Thus, one outcome of native agency in response to the colonial hierarchical structure was the development of deep divisions and fissures within neophyte communities, divisions that no longer followed conventional tribal or polity boundaries.

The Russian-American Company did not create a separate system of Indian officials to administer and oversee its native laborers. Company mangers depended upon traditional Indian leaders to recruit laborers and to help maintain morale among the native workers. Some native leaders enhanced and even institutionalized their tribal positions of authority by working with the Russian-American Company. In this way—and particularly through the creation of *"chief toions"* by Company managers—the Russians helped initiate significant transformations in the political structure of local Indian polities.

Interethnic Unions

What were the consequences of pluralistic households in the Hispanic and Russian frontiers? Since interethnic unions between native women and colonial men took place in both frontiers, we can evaluate their comparative roles in promoting cultural transformations in mission communities and in the Ross Counter. As discussed above, one way that pluralistic households may have stimulated culture change was by serving as a major pathway for the social advancement of native women and their children. In the Franciscan missions, a neophyte woman could marry into the *gente de razón* class, take her husband's name, and assimilate into an Hispanic household. At Colony Ross, native women could also marry Russian, Creole, or Native Alaskan men and take on new colonial identities through the adoption of alien cultural practices and by joining the Russian Orthodox Church. In both the mission and mercantile colonies, the most significant cultural transformations probably revolved around the offspring of interethnic couples, offspring who faced many choices in the construction of their identities. By associating with their paternal side, they could move up the colonial hierarchy and assume new frontier identities.

Although I recognize the potentially significant consequences of interethnic unions in colonial contexts, I believe they played a fairly minimal role in stimulating culture change in neophyte communities. As I outlined in chapter 3, after the first few years of Father Serra's experimentation, the padres became very protective of their neophyte wards and allowed relatively few of the girls and young women to become involved with Hispanic men. Consequently, the number of interethnic marriages in these communities remained consistently low until the secularization of the missions (e.g., Castaneda 1997:241; Hurtado 1988:23,25,170; Mason 1984:133–134). More important, neophyte women who married into the *gente de razón* class inevitably removed themselves from the neophyte communities when their husbands were redeployed to new posts in Alta California.

Although the frequency of interethnic unions was greater in the Russian frontier, their role in stimulating culture change among local Indian groups was also fairly minimal. The Russian-American Company viewed colonial marriages as a way of cementing their political alliances with local native groups, and as a means of increasing their work force. Given the relatively large number of young women residing with colonial men at Colony Ross, especially in the early years, some of the women must have served as cultural brokers; that is, they must have facilitated the introduction of novel cultural practices, languages, and beliefs into the broader Kashaya community. But I have found little evidence that these unions had any long-lasting consequences on the cultural practices or belief systems of the Kashaya Pomo.

Most of the unions were, as discussed in chapter 5, quite fragile, typically lasting only a short period before native women returned to their home villages. Archaeological investigations of pluralistic households in the Native Alaskan Neighborhood indicate that innovations in diet, craft production, and landscape modification were created by Native Californian women and Native Alaskan men, but the overwhelming archaeological signature unearthed in our investigation was that of native women reconstituting their Kashaya identities in the practice of day-to-day activities centered in the domestic sphere (e.g., Lightfoot et al. 1998; Lightfoot, Schiff, Martinez et al. 1997). My general impression in examining Russian accounts, native narratives, and archaeological findings is that most native women who had relationships with colonial men at Ross chose to be staunch activists in promoting Kashaya beliefs, meanings, and world views.

Although the potential existed for native women to take on the identities of the ethnic "estates" of their husbands through baptism in the Russian Orthodox Church and by entering into "legal" marriage, the number of documented cases is very small. Furthermore, most of the local native women who assumed new colonial identities at Ross did not remain connected to their Indian families and friends for long. As happened in the Franciscan missions, native women most closely identified with the colonial hierarchy and the Christian faith left the area—in this case, the Ross Counter. Inevitably the Company would reassign the woman's husband and "Creole" children to another North Pacific colony; as a consequence, few of the native women who closely identified with the Russian colonizers remained in Kashaya country after 1841.

Demographic Parameters

What were the consequences of demographic changes in native and colonial populations in the Hispanic and Russian frontiers?

The most significant change in the Franciscan missions was the abysmally high mortality rate for neophytes. As I summarized in chapter 3, none of the neophyte communities that housed Miwok, Ohlone, Esselen, Salinan, Chumash, and Gabrielino peoples were reproductively viable in the long term. The death rate overshadowed the birth rate, infant mortality was continually very high, and the number of women of marriageable age declined markedly relative to the number of men. This demographic pattern had dire consequences for the continuation of traditional native polities within the missions. The entire population of some polities declined to only a few hundred people, and such small-scale entities were highly vulnerable to demographic collapse. The loss of a few men and women would have jeopardized the transmission of folk tales, myths, and ritual information to successive generations of neophytes. Furthermore, with significant and sudden population loss, there would not have been sufficient qualified or fully trained men or women to serve in critical leadership positions or to perform clandestine dances and ceremonies for polity members in the missions. Thus, we can imagine that among the survivors in the missions, the transmission of cultural knowledge about certain specific polities became splintered and fractured over time.

The very high mortality rate of young women in the mission communities must have had significant consequences not only for the propagation of new members of traditional native polities but also for the continuation of conventional marriage patterns. The demographic catastrophe left men of marriageable age with relatively few potential marriage partners. Under these conditions, traditional rules of marriage that connected specific families within polities or across nearby political boundaries became unworkable. To find mates and produce families, neophytes were forced to search for new sources of eligible marriage partners, seeking beyond their traditional tribal world.

As mortality rates increased, the padres recruited fresh converts from polities located at greater and greater distances, to take the place of the dead. This recruitment practice brought successive waves of neophytes into the missions, and the new recruits periodically reinvigorated the neophyte communities with new Indian oral traditions, cultural practices, political organizations, and ritual systems from their respective polities and homelands. The neophyte villages became bubbling cauldrons of cultural fusion where fresh insights on Indian life ways merged with those already extant there. In addition, the recruitment practice brought young women from distant polities into the missions, women who would serve as marriage partners for single neophyte men.

Less is known about the specific population parameters of the Indians residing in the greater Métini region. During the 1820s and 1830s, several major epidemics consumed native populations on the Russian frontier, and I suspect the Kashaya Pomo population must have been severely impacted. How this suspected demographic decline must have affected the transmission of cultural knowledge and the availability of marriage partners among the Kashaya Pomo is not known.

Chronology of Colonial Encounters

What were the consequences of the differing temporal dimensions of colonial encounters in the Franciscan missions and and at Colony Ross? The Fernandinos subjected coastal hunter-gatherers to their colonial program for about seventy years, but the Russian merchants administered their colony for only twenty-nine years. The longer chronology of the Franciscan missions facilitated the restructuring of native polities and the revamping of Indian social relations within neophyte communities. In the neophyte families that survived the unhealthy conditions, several generations grew up in the regimented social environment of the missions. Coastal hunter-gatherers entering the missions prior to 1800 underwent significant transformations over time, with succeeding generations becoming increasingly disenfranchised from their native polities, homelands, and tribal pasts. By the time of mission secularization in the mid-1830s and early 1840s, few living members of some neophyte communities had actually experienced life in one of the precolonial coastal native polities.[3]

In contrast, the shorter time span of the Russian colonization implied that only one to one-and-one-half generations of local Indians had been exposed to the pluralistic mercantile colony. I feel this shorter chronology facilitated the reproduction of Kashaya cultural practices in the Ross Counter. Children born after 1812 grew up with parents and grandparents who had experienced life before the Russian-American Company. The generation raised under the Russian flag would not have begun producing offspring until the 1820s, and these children would have been in their early teens when the Company sold its California colony in 1841. Consequently, a generation of elders familiar with precontact times grounded the Kashaya's experiences within the mercantile colony, and these elders retained a corpus of cultural knowledge for teaching Kashaya children about the history, religion, and life ways of their people.

REPRODUCTION OF INDIAN IDENTITIES
IN COLONIAL CALIFORNIA

A major finding of this book is that the majority of native peoples in the Franciscan missions and Colony Ross continued to reproduce their Indian identities through several decades of colonial encounters. The processes and outcomes involved in the creation of Indian identities varied markedly within and across the Hispanic and Russian frontiers. Yet immediately following mission secularization in the mid-1830s and 1840s, and the closing of the Ross Counter in the early 1840s, most peoples of local native ancestry still recognized themselves as "Indians" and not as Hispanics, Mexicans, Russians, Creoles, Native Alaskans, or some other colonial identity. This observation is based on the following two considerations.

First, in analyzing the dimensions of colonial encounters involving social mobility and interethnic unions, I have argued that various pathways existed in the Franciscan missions and Colony Ross for advancing up the respective colonial hierarchies. But in most cases native men and women who opted to follow these pathways had to distance themselves from their Indian heritage and actively engage in the construction of colonial identities. My findings suggest that a relatively small number of native people made this leap into the worlds of the padres and merchants.

In considering identity formation and social advancement in the neophyte communities of the Franciscan missions, it is important to distinguish between those strategies that involved social advancement up the hierarchy of Indian offices controlled by the padres, and those strategies that involved the transition from *indios* to *gente de razón*. Native people who chose to become *alcaldes* and other prominent Indian officials did not, I believe, have to sacrifice their Indian identities; the broader matrix of colonial society still considered the *alcaldes* and other Indian officials in the missions *indios*. However, this was not the case for those men and women attempting to break into the *gente de razón* class.

As already noted, the number of neophyte women who married colonial men and relinquished their native identities was never large. The other pathways for moving up the colonial hierarchy were also not well trod. Only a small group of masons, tile makers, carpenters, *vaqueros*, etc., successfully integrated themselves into Mexican Californian settlements in 1826–27.[4] This resulted in part from the tight control the Franciscans maintained over their neophyte charges. But I think it goes beyond this: eyewitness accounts suggested that many neophytes eligible for the program chose not to take advantage of it, and that most men released from the missions did not end up emulating the life ways or behavior of proper Hispanic settlers but rather retained many "Indian" characteristics (see Hutchinson 1969:128–131).

A similar pattern has been outlined for native peoples who pursued strategies of social advancement in the Ross Counter. Although Pomo and Miwok peoples could have manipulated various pathways for advancing up the mercantile colonial hierarchy, only a relatively few men and women succeeded in distancing themselves from their Indian heritage. In reviewing the dimensions of colonial encounters, I have stressed that only a small number of people engaged in the construction of new colonial identities through interethnic marriage, baptism, acceptance of Russian Christian names, and/or incorporation into the Russian-American Company as members of its full-time workforce.

The second consideration indicating that most peoples of local native ancestry still recognized themselves as "Indians" and not some other colonial identity is the following. When we turn to the archaeological record, there is excellent evidence for native people actively promoting their Indian identities throughout the colonial period.

The case for this in the Franciscan missions has been definitively made by Paul Farnsworth in his pioneering comparison of Mission Soledad, Mission San Antonio, and Mission La Purísima (Farnsworth 1987; 1989; 1992). He critically evaluated the common perception that culture change among the neophytes should have increased over time, as they became more and more Hispanicized from the late 1700s through the early-to-mid 1800s. Farnsworth conducted a detailed analysis of ten categories of archaeological remains by employing different measurements of imported, hybrid, and traditional (native) artifacts, measurements he used in the creation of "acculturation profiles." His findings indicate that the specific acculturation profiles for the Esselen-, Salinan-, and Chumash-speaking peoples in the missions varied across space and time. However, the overall trend detected by Farnsworth not only contradicts the common perception of increasing Hispanicization but suggests that native peoples maintained or even expanded their traditional cultural practices after the first decade of the nineteenth century (Farnsworth 1992:35). As noted in chapter 4, Farnsworth attributes the perpetuation of native material culture to several factors: the participation of the padres in the hide and tallow trade; declining emphasis by the padres on the enculturation program; and the significant influx of gentile Indians recruited into the missions from the San Joaquin Valley.

A similar case for the continued construction of Indian identities in the Russian frontier was made in chapter 6. Indeed—and it is another significant finding of this book—the archaeological assemblages unearthed from native contexts in the missions and at Colony Ross show many similarities. Of course, in recognizing these rather "coarse-grained" resemblances, I do not want to downplay the many discrete differences in the material culture of individual sites in the missions or the Ross Counter. Archaeological remains from neophyte contexts vary from mission to mission and across time, especially during periods of massive recruitment when the padres resettled waves of gentiles into some missions (e.g., Costello 1992; Costello and Hornbeck 1989; Farnsworth 1987:602–620; Farnsworth 1989:241–246). Variation also underlies the archaeological assemblages from different native contexts across the Métini landscape (i.e., the Native Alaskan Neighborhood, the area north of the Ross stockade, Native Californian Neighborhood, and Tomato Patch Village). But even with these caveats, I am struck by the overall similarities between the archaeological remains from native villages in the Ross Counter and those from the missions where extensive excavations of neophyte quarters have taken place (i.e., Santa Cruz, Soledad, San Antonio, San Juan Bautista, San Buenaventura, and La Purísima).

In my discussion (in chapters 4 and 6) of the artifact assemblages from neophyte quarters and from Ross villages, we saw many concordances in the materials represented (stone, bone, and shell artifacts, glass beads), the diversity of native food remains recovered (deer, sea mammal, fish, shellfish), and the employment of traditional native practices to prepare and cook meals. Although in the mission areas, Hispanic cultural practices influenced some elements of technology and menu, neophytes continued to use native artifact forms and manufacturing techniques with strong links to their prehistoric past. This is especially evident in the chipped stone tools, ground stone tools, shell fishhooks, shell and bone beads, bone tools, bird-bone whistles, and rock crystals (probably used in Indian rituals). Similar remains have also been unearthed in native contexts both near and far from the Ross settlement.

Excavations of neophyte quarters indicate that European-introduced foods (cattle, sheep, wheat, corn) were cooked alongside native foods, such as deer, sea mammals, geese, ducks, rock fish, shellfish, hazelnuts, and possibly seaweed (e.g., Allen 1998:55–62; Hoover and Costello 1985). The neophytes prepared and cooked some new foods, such as wheat and barley, according to traditional native prescriptions (e.g, Farris 1991:40). This point is amply supported by the large quantities of fire-cracked rock recovered from neophyte quarters (Allen 1998:88): this rock debris resulted from neophytes cooking food in watertight baskets, hearths, and earthen ovens. We found a similar pattern at Colony Ross, where new foods, such as beef, mutton, and even sea mammals, were prepared according to time-tested Kashaya conventions for cooking large terrestrial game. The Kashaya cooked these meat dishes in underground ovens, over coals, or in stews simmered in watertight baskets using the "hot rocks" method.

Another striking similarity is how Indian peoples in the missionary and mercantile colonies used European objects, such as glass bottles and ceramic containers, as sources of raw material to produce native forms. Remnants of glass and ceramic containers recovered from archaeological deposits in the Santa Cruz neophyte barracks and in native villages at Colony Ross are very fragmentary; few reconstructable vessels are present (Allen 1998:67; Farris 1997c; Silliman 1997). This pattern suggests that native peoples scavenged and recycled broken but useable foreign objects from trash dumps, in both colonies. However, instead of using the objects in the European fashion as ceramic and glass tableware, the people transformed them into native objects such as pendants, beads, scrapers, and projectile points.[5] Glass beads are another significant constituent of the archaeological assemblages in both the Hispanic and the Russian frontiers. Yet they do not signal a disconnection with the precolonial past, as native peoples employed glass beads as they had shell beads over many previous centuries.

Perhaps the most significant finding is that the organization of space in domestic contexts in both the missions and Colony Ross followed Indian precepts and conventions. Here I rely on some of my previous work on identity formation and practice theory, to make the point that the ordering of daily life often serves as a microcosm of the broader organizational principles and world views of individuals (Lightfoot et al. 1998; Lightfoot and Martinez 1997); how people conduct mundane domestic tasks, how they dispose of refuse, and how they structure space can tell you much about their identities and social relations in colonial worlds. Most interesting, with regard to the mission colonies, is that the built environment for some neophyte families changed from circular thatched houses to rectangular adobe rooms — something that was completely alien to them. However, Allen's (1998:53) recent analysis of the Santa Cruz neophyte quarters indicates that the organization of space within the square-room barracks was based on native dictates and practices. For example, the neophytes placed fire pits in the center of the room, a placement similar to their customary practice in circular native huts. They also established secondary fire pits, which appear to have been "Indian" adaptations to the light and heat requirements of the rectangular floor space (see also Voss 2000:51). We detected a similar pattern of "Indian" use of domestic space at Colony Ross. In chapter 6, I discussed how the organization and maintenance of space in native villages followed Kashaya cultural values and conventions that had their roots in prehistory. Even more interesting is that Kashaya perspectives on cleanliness and hygiene were imposed, in the domestic context of pluralistic households, by native women residing with colonial men.

In sum, it appears that most native persons caught within the Franciscan missions and Colony Ross maintained a strong sense of "Indian" values and meanings that continued to direct their lives throughout their encounters with colonists. Individuals and families broadcast their sense of "Indianhood" despite the unsettling colonial worlds crashing around them. However, in the process of reproducing Indian identities in colonial contexts, native peoples did not simply replicate themselves as clones of their precolonial ancestors. Culture change was inevitable, just as it had been throughout more than twelve thousand years of prehistory. Native peoples incorporated new innovations and cultural practices into their daily life ways, as they confronted the Franciscan padres and Russian merchants. The peoples emerging at the end of the colonial period were not the same "Indians" who viewed the first Spanish and Russian buildings taking shape on the California landscape (e.g., Allen 1998:6, 94–97; Farnsworth 1989:237). Nevertheless, indigenous values and meanings directed the processes of cultural transformation that unfolded across both frontiers.

The construction of Indian identities differed greatly between that of the men, women, and children in Franciscan missions and that of those at Colony Ross. In the missions, the celebration of "Indianness" tended to take place behind closed doors. In the underground "Indian" world of the neophyte quarters, families and friends engaged in the manufacture of native tools and ornaments, the cooking and consumption of native foods, and the veneration of native ceremonies. During the day, neophyte workers and Indian officials accommodated themselves to the padres' rigid schedule of labor, church services, and communal meals. But at night and in spare moments during the work day, mundane native cultural practices—conducted out of sight of the padres and their spies—became vested with symbolic value as people connected to the world of their ancestors.

In contrast to this secrecy, archaeological work at native villages in the Métini region indicates that the Kashaya openly broadcast their Indian identities to the colonial world through the performance of daily routines, the organization of village space, the construction of native houses and extramural features, and the prominent erection of sweat lodges or assembly houses where they held curing ceremonies and dances.

NEW SOCIAL FORMS AND TRIBAL RELATIONSHIPS

By considering the interplay of the different dimensions of colonial encounters, it is possible to examine the rise of new social forms and tribal relationships in colonial California. I identify three broad social processes in the outcomes of native engagements with colonial structures in the Franciscan missions and Colony Ross. The first process, associated with the Miwok, Ohlone, Esselen, Salinan, Chumash, and Gabrielino speakers of the northern missions, is characterized by the fragmentation of traditional native polities, the emergence of new kinds of social organizations, and the creation of Indian identities no longer tied to individual polities but more to a specific mission community. The second process involves the continuation of traditional native polities, leadership positions, and ritual systems, as described for the Luiseño and Diegueño speakers of Mission San Luis Rey and Mission San Diego. The third process is evident at Colony Ross, where the members of autonomous Kashaya Pomo polities coalesced to create a true "tribal" organization.

Polity Fragmentation and the Creation of "Pan-Mission" Identities

Demographic decline and the native relocation program of the northern missions are critical factors for understanding what happened to many of the Miwok, Ohlone, Esselen, Salinan, Chumash, and Gabrielino peoples. As discussed above, high mortality rates devastated small coastal hunter-gatherer polities, especially those encompassing only a few hundred people. Demographic collapses evident in mission populations contributed to the loss of elders and ritual knowledge, to the inability to field enough people to sponsor dances and ceremonies, to problems in finding eligible and experienced people to fill tribal leadership positions, and even to difficulties in recruiting new members. Thus, the unrelenting death toll in the missions would have contributed to the implosion of many small political entities and the amalgamation of new forms of tribal life. Furthermore, if the population of a native polity dropped much below two or three hundred in number, then traditional tribal marriage networks would have collapsed, leaving young men to search for new sources of marriage partners (see, e.g., Hantman 1983:43–49; Wobst 1974, 1976). I suspect that an increasing number of intertribal marriages—marriages, that is, between members of different polities—resulted. It is true that some neophytes attempted to continue precontact marriage patterns within the missions. Johnson (2001:58–59, 67) notes that Chumash Islanders brought into the Santa Barbara missions from about 1814 to 1816 were able maintain some degree of social distinction and marriage networks within neophyte communities (see also Johnson and McLendon 2000:649). But I think this kind of social exclusiveness would have been difficult to maintain in the long run, given the appalling mortality rates. Although intertribal marriage was an important institution in creating and maintaining political alliances in precontact times, the number of such unions and the linkages made by them among peoples of different homelands increased greatly in neophyte communities.

An important factor that interlinks with demographic decline and the creation of new forms of marriage networks is the massive relocation program that herded together hundreds of native peoples from diverse polities and homelands into the northern mission communities. In these large aggregated communities, arranged intertribal marriages were sometimes resorted to in an attempt to stop bloodshed and conflict among members of hostile polities brought into the missions; for example, Milliken (1995:79,

188–189) describes how intertribal marriage was employed to end the state of warfare among various Ohlone-speaking polities in the San Francisco Bay Area. In some cases, this resort involved the marriage of well-established neophytes with newly recruited Indians who had a history of hostility with mission Indians.

The padres of the northern missions also encouraged nontraditional marriage practices by pressuring single men and women to marry outside their native polities, and even, in some cases, by choosing marriage partners for them. The Fernandinos were well aware that one way to stem population decline in the missions was to increase the birth rate and pray that children would survive. Consequently, they often coerced young men and women to marry, and widows (and widowers) to remarry after their spouses died (Jackson and Castillo 1995:57). Padres even instigated mass marriages following baptisms, in which they lined up men and women to find prospective marriage partners.

> Men and women were . . . ranged in separate lines in the presence of the mission people, and harangued by the padre, with the aid of an interpreter, on the merits and responsibilities of marriage. Each person was asked whether he or she wished to be married, and every one saying aye was ranged in a separate line of his or her sex. Any man or woman who admitted having sexual connection was placed apart to be married to her or him with whom that connection had been, to be married whether they were willing or not. The rest of the men were then asked, one by one, which of the women opposite they chose to marry. If the selected women showed unwillingness to accept the man, he had to choose again. (original Bancroft 1888:227–228; quoted in Milliken 1995:134)

Milliken (1995:134–135) describes a number of these mass marriages at the missions of Santa Clara and San Francisco, during a period of intensive neophyte recruitment in 1794–95. Although many couples renewed existing marriages, some no doubt took on new spouses from the existing neophyte community.

Given the large number of young women dying in the missions, this would, I suggest, have increasingly compelled single or widowed men to marry eligible women from more distant tribal lands as they entered the missions. This marriage practice would have resulted in the creation of innovative kinship ties and social obligations between men and women from different polities, language groups, and homelands. Milliken (1995:178–179) documents several cases where women from distant nations willingly married well-established men in the neophyte community at San Francisco. In examining these cases, he suggests "[m]arriage to a neophyte apparently was an important way for a vulnerable woman and her powerless tribal relatives to establish a secure place for herself within the Mission San Francisco community" (Milliken 1995:178). There are other cases of newly recruited Indian women marrying well-established neophyte men after their original spouses from the native homeland died. For example, five of nine Indian women from tribes along the eastern San Francisco Bay (primarily Saclan and Jalquin) quickly married long-time neophyte men in Mission San Francisco, after their husbands had been killed (Milliken 1995:181–182). Milliken (1994:174–176) also documents intertribal marriages of Ohlone men and women, including widows and widowers, with "fresh" Yokuts-speaking recruits brought into Mission Santa Clara and Mission San Juan Bautista from native homelands along the San Joaquin River.[6]

Another important factor in the development of novel social forms and tribal relationships in neophyte communities was the creation of new kinds of factional groups. I have already discussed how the formal system of Indian offices created fissures within the neophyte communities (e.g., between those neophytes who supported the new political hierarchy of the missions and those who remained loyal to traditional Indian leaders). Other kinds of native political organizations also emerged with the rise of armed raiders, composed of escaped neophytes and interior Indians, who attacked missions and private ranchos throughout central and southern California by the late 1820s and 1830s (Hurtado 1988:43–46; Phillips 1975:41–46,163; 1993:97–105,164). Some of the most famous resistance leaders and raiders were ex-neophytes who had grown up in the missions. The rise of these neophyte rebels underscores the break-up of traditional native polities and the construction of new kinds of political organizations that took their place.

In summary, new social forms and Indian identities emerged with the development of innovative marriage patterns and the rise of novel forms of factional groups in large, pluralistic neophyte communities. Johnson's detailed analysis (1997:259–260) of the Indians of Mission San Fernando indicates that by the end of the mission period many families petitioning for land from the mission estate were composed of husbands and wives from different linguistic backgrounds or mixed parentage. "These facts illustrate the 'melting pot' process that occurred at the missions as intermarriage and living in community brought together peoples who had once possessed distinctive cultural differences" (Johnson 1997:260). Native people's affiliation with traditional native polities began to dissolve, especially among second-

or third-generation neophytes born in the missions. What replaced the ancestral political structures was a complex and fractured system of social affiliations and kin relations that cut broadly across neophyte communities. Neophytes were no longer identified by their particular tribal polity, but by other signifiers such as their advancement up the mission hierarchy as Indian officials, their positions in underground ceremonial and political organizations, their membership in different factional groups, and their connections to other neophytes through blood, marriage, and friendship.

Multi-scalar Indian identities arose in the missions. At the same time that neophyte communities became fractured into multiple, cross-cutting networks of social relations, a more generalized sense, I believe, of mission Indian identity unfolded. That is, in addition to the construction of individual identities predicated on kin ties, social connections, political positions, and factional groups within neophyte communities, native peoples were now identified by the missions where they were raised. Old distinctions based on ancestral homelands, native polities, or language became less relevant to neophytes who grew up in the missions. The only "homelands" that many second- and third-generation neophytes had ever really known were the mission estates. Allen (1998:41, 97) makes a similar interpretation for the neophytes at Mission Santa Cruz, after examining the archaeological remains associated with two different neophyte dormitories. She argues that individual tribal memberships in the missions probably became blurred, with the development of a more "amalgamated group" of neophytes. Hurtado (1988: 69–71) offers a similar interpretation for native workers in a colonial rancho in central California (Sutter's New Helvetia rancho), where a parallel process of depopulation and changing marriage patterns weakened traditional family ties and tribal affiliations.

Continuity of Native Political Organizations and Ritual Systems

A different conjuncture of native agency and colonial structures led to divergent outcomes in the two southernmost missions. The padres of Mission San Luis Rey and Mission San Diego instituted modified relocation programs in which only a portion of the outlying native populations moved to the missions. The majority of the native peoples remained in their home villages, with their political structures more or less intact. Father Antonio Peyri and other padres at these two missions allowed traditional leaders to retain their power and authority in return for their cooperation. Rather than implementing a separate system of Indian officials, as in the northern missions, these padres allowed that the extant native political hierarchies be perpetuated and incorporated into the mission system. Native leaders and members of their families served as midlevel managers or intermediaries between the missionaries and their polities (Carrico and Shipek 1996:200; Shipek 1977:152–172).

Florence Shipek (1977) details how the maintenance of native political structures and the continued occupation of homeland villages enabled local peoples to conserve some aspects of traditional hunting, fishing, and gathering activities. Seasonal rounds continued to be practiced, with native peoples harvesting, processing, and consuming a range of wild foods. The more varied and nutritious menu, coupled with the less crowded and healthier villages, resulted in a lower mortality rate than that experienced by native people in the dense, overly congested neophyte communities of the northern missions (Shipek 1977:65–73). Although mortality rates remained high, especially during years of periodic drought or erratic rainfall, the general picture was one of lower crude death rates, and more balanced male/female sex ratios and child/adult ratios (see Shipek 1977:67–71, appendix). Johnson and Crawford (1999:90) believe that the decentralized settlement pattern of Mission San Luis Rey allowed the neophyte population "to have escaped some of the devastating consequences of introduced diseases that ravaged more concentrated mission settlements."[7] Marriage patterns no doubt changed in the southernmost missions, but they probably did not involve the traumatic restructuring of marriage networks that occurred in the northern missions.

Through negotiations with the padres of the southernmost missions, native peoples perpetuated, to some degree, many traditional practices involving local native polities, transmittal of leadership positions, economic practices, and ceremonial cycles. But the Luiseño and Diegueño peoples were not immune to culture change. Significant transformations took place: the adoption of new agricultural practices (irrigation), crops (wheat, olives, fruit trees), and livestock; the mastery of new crafts; the ability of some natives (especially native leaders) to converse in Spanish; and the incorporation of aspects of Catholic symbols and rituals into native belief systems (Carrico and Shipek 1996:200–203; Shipek 1977:140–154).

A critical difference between the neophyte communities of the northern and southern missions concerns the reorganization of native polities and tribal relationships. In the southern missions, neophytes incorporated changes into a preexisting structure of political hierarchies and social relations. The identities of Luiseño- and Diegueño-speaking peoples remained, I suspect, rooted to the individual polities and villages where they were born, in contrast to the more generalized "pan-mission" identities that materialized in the northern missions.

Coalition of Autonomous Polities into a "Tribal" Organization

Native entanglements with the mercantile colonial program of the Russian-American Company resulted in a third social process. As detailed earlier, significant differences characterize how the dimensions of colonial encounters unfolded in the Russian frontier and in the Franciscan missions. The key dimensions underlying the divergent outcome for the Kashaya Pomo people are aspects of the relocation program, social mobility, and demographic parameters.

The Russian merchants allowed local Indians to maintain villages in their respective homelands; they encouraged them to reside near Russian settlements only when working for the Company or living with colonial men. The Kashaya Pomo responded by maintaining and establishing a network of villages and residences situated near to and far from the Ross settlement. This allowed Kashaya men and women to rotate between the colonial "front lines" and the back country, and men and women residing in the distant hinterlands of the colony could follow a full suite of hunting and gathering activities.

The Company did not create a separate system of native offices, but instead relied on extant native leaders to serve as intermediaries between the Russian merchants and local polities. However, this Russian colonial program differed from that of the southern missions in that the former followed a time-honored practice of promoting one or two prominent leaders to represent all of the Indians when dealing with the Company. The Russians afforded such a leader the opportunity to enhance political stature and influence by becoming the spokesperson for the entire population speaking the Kashaya Pomo language. The promotion of the chief *toion*, or Toyon, to represent the Kashaya people kicked off a process of political consolidation among the previously autonomous polities.

This process was facilitated by changes in the demographic structure of the Kashaya population. Russian sources indicate that epidemics hit local native populations, but the magnitude of demographic decline is unknown. However, given the small size of the autonomous precontact polities (village communities), any significant population downturn may have created problems for individual polities in staffing leadership positions and in maintaining enough knowledgeable men and women to participate in dances and ceremonies. Under conditions of population stress, the political maneuvering of the Toyon (a.k.a. Chu-gu-an) was enhanced, as he was evidently able to persuade other smaller, struggling polities to consolidate within a larger political entity. Political consolidation also facilitated the finding of marriage partners within the broader group. This was especially true for young men, who no doubt were grumbling about the difficulties of finding suitable mates in the 1810s and 1820s, when relatively large numbers of women lived with colonial men.

One consequence of Kashaya women establishing pluralistic households at Ross was the production of large families. The existence of colonial men greatly expanded the number of potential mates available to Kashaya women. Since most of these relationships did not last long, and a woman might have multiple liaisons, a sizeable number of offspring resulted. When parents split up, the children were either divided between the parents or went home with their mothers. Since girls tended to be sent home with their Indian mothers, according to the Kuskov census of 1820 and 1821, apparently a large group of young females were raised in Kashaya villages. Some researchers have argued that mixed-blood offspring tended to be less susceptible to Euro-Asian pathogens (e.g., Settipane 1995:9–10). If this is true, then an unanticipated effect of the Kashaya women's affairs with colonial men may have been the creation of a more robust and healthy population. In any event, this cohort of mixed-blood females would have entered the following generation's pool of eligible mates and helped to maintain the newly emerging Kashaya "tribe" as a demographically viable entity.

In sum, the outcome of Kashaya agency in the Russian frontier was the creation of a broader "tribal" organization brought about by the confederation of previously autonomous polities under the unified leadership of Toyon. It represents one of the few native groupings in California that would be recognized by anthropologists as a real tribe—as, that is, a distinct social group with a common language and territory, and united under a single system of leadership. Thus, there emerged a broader Kashaya Indian identity, during the twenty-nine years of Russian colonization, that eventually eclipsed peoples' associations with precontact polities.

CONNECTIONS TO HOMELANDS

How native peoples relate to their ancestral homelands says much about how they shape their native identities and cultural practices. The very essence of being an Indian for many tribal peoples in western North America is rooted in the sacred landscapes of their ancestors (Basso 1996; Momaday 1974; Spicer 1962). As Keith Basso (1996) has so poignantly penned for the Western Apache, the sense of place and the sense of self are very much intertwined. Cultural landscapes are imbued with deep meaning and history, with specific places serving as portals to the past. Here one can feel the presence of the recently deceased and can still hear them talking and laughing; one can even imagine the ancient ones of long ago walking across the same sacred ground. The mere mention of a place name can serve as a mnemonic peg for recalling stories of past peoples and events formative in the construction of local Indian identities (1996:62–64). And Edward Spicer demonstrates that the construction of Indian identities during colonial times in the American Southwest was very much tied to the maintenance of a land base: "[a] major influence in all cases, however, was the conditions affecting the relationship of Indians to the land. At the time of the entrance of the Spaniards all the Indians held in some form a belief in a sacred and indissoluble bond between themselves and the land in which their settlements were located" (Spicer 1962:576). Those native groups who maintained residences in their traditional homelands were the most successful in asserting their distinctive tribal identities throughout several centuries of confrontations with Spanish, Mexican, and American colonizers (Spicer 1962:576–578).

Viewed in this light, native peoples' connections to their ancestral lands must have influenced the construction and reproduction of Indian identities and cultural practices in colonial California. Clearly, limited access to the ancient homeland constrained people from walking the paths of their forebears, from visiting old village sites and the graves of their ancestors, and from appreciating the grasslands, forests, creeks, and landmarks that figured so prominently in their folk tales and native histories. The Fernandinos evidently understood this; by removing the neophytes from the lands of their ancestors, the padres intentionally severed their ties with the past (see, e.g., Margolin 1989:33). The long-term implication of the Fernandinos' strategy was to accelerate the processes of polity fragmentation, to give rise to new social forms, and to create new kinds of Indian identities in the northern missions.

The alienation of many of the Miwok, Ohlone, Esselen, Salinan, Chumash, and Gabrielino from their homelands became magnified as new generations were born and raised in the missions. Their connections to tribal lands became increasingly fuzzy. I can envision the creation, under these conditions, of new kinds of ceremonies, ritual knowledge, myths, legends, and folk tales from people amalgamated from diverse polities, language groupings, and homelands. Indians born and raised in the neophyte communities might construct "pan-mission" identities that vested the broader landscapes of the missions with new meaning and symbolism. Local places would become mnemonic pegs for recounting the hardships and tragedies of the missions, as well for recalling upbeat times of love, friendship, and family in the neophyte quarters.

In contrast, since they could maintain residences in ancestral homelands, native people in the southernmost missions and the Russian frontier were reminded of their tribal pasts whenever they scanned the horizon or kicked over an artifact. The opportunity to visit places steeped with stories and archaeological remains would have made the past come alive for children of the Luiseño, Cupeño, Diegueño, and Kashaya Pomo. The intermeshing of daily practices in places vested with tribal meaning reinforced a strong sense of Indian identity for these people.

The dispersed settlement system of the Kashaya, which penetrated deeply into the most sacred places of the tribal landscape, facilitated the teaching of traditional life ways, values, and belief systems to children. For example, a child born and raised near the Ross stockade who began showing distinctive signs of non-Indian behavior could be shipped off to relatives in the "forest depths." Here the child would be immersed in Kashaya history and cultural practices. This might involve a good dose of storytelling and of exploring the rocks, streams, and hillsides mentioned in myths and folklore, visiting the ancient sites of ancestors, undergoing ritual purification, or participating in hunting and gathering activities. The ability of native men, women, and children to leave the hustle and bustle of the Ross settlement and plunge themselves into the reflective quiet of the distant forests may have been important in maintaining a proper perspective of what it meant to be Kashaya.

UNANTICIPATED FINDINGS

Before undertaking this comparative analysis, I expected that the rigorous enculturation program of the Franciscan padres, in contrast to the system of the Russian merchants, was the most significant factor for understanding the differing outcomes for the cultural identity of coastal hunter-gatherers in southern and central California. It all seemed pretty straightforward. The Franciscan program of directed culture change would have led to the increasing Hispanicization of neophytes, over time, in contrast to the seemingly laissez faire policies of the Russian-American Company, which would have essentially left the culture of the Kashaya Pomo intact. Furthermore, I thought that interethnic unions might have served as catalysts for culture change, contributing not only to the Hispanicization of neophyte women, but to the establishment of a web of households across the Hispanic and Russian frontiers where cultural innovations would be spawned and nurtured.

But the findings of this study suggest an alternative scenario of the dynamics of colonial encounters in the Franciscan missions and Colony Ross. The enculturation program of the Fernandinos was apparently not that successful in converting the majority of the neophyte population into Catholic peasants, nor did interethnic unions play much role in the Hispanicization of native women or in stimulating many cultural innovations. Only a relatively few men and women made the transition from *indios* to *gente de razón* before the missions were secularized; a similar pattern is found at Colony Ross, where only a small number of native men and women distanced themselves from their native heritages and took on colonial identities.

What we discovered was that native entanglements with the "intended" colonial structures of the Franciscan padres and Russian managers resulted in the widespread re-creation of Indian identities and cultural practices throughout colonial California. But in the Indians' daily practice of reproducing themselves and their cultural constructs, significant cultural transformations took place. Depending upon the specific conjunctures of native agency and colonial structures, new kinds of Indian identities, social forms, and tribal relationships emerged. By considering the interplay of the seven dimensions of colonial encounters, we have identified three basic social processes in the outcomes of native engagements with the missionary and mercantile colonies.

The first process involved the breakdown of individual polities, the development of new kinds of social relations and marriage networks, and the creation of more generalized Indian identities. Although the specific cultural forms and processes varied from mission to mission, this general pattern was associated with many of the Miwok, Ohlone, Esselen, Salinan, Chumash, and Gabrielino peoples. The key dimensions underlying these changes were native responses to the massive relocation programs, demographic decline, creation of separate Indian offices, and the chronology of the colonial encounters. Sequestered within the neophyte neighborhoods of the mission complexes, native peoples coped with the adversities of the rigid colonial regime by creating new social relations with individuals from distant polities and homelands, by allying themselves with novel factional groups, and by maintaining Indian cultural practices, which involved the gathering together of family and friends.

The second process was characterized by the greater continuity in traditional structures of native political hierarchies, social relations, economic practices, and identities that unfolded among neophytes in the hinterlands of Mission San Luis Rey and Mission San Diego. The key dimensions of colonial encounters underlying this pattern were the maintenance of villages in traditional homelands, the aggressive posturing of native leaders who served as intermediaries between the mission and local Indian communities, and the lower overall mortality rate. By taking advantage of the modified relocation program and the willingness of some of the padres to work with them, leaders of some Luiseño and Diegueño polities helped conserve Indian life ways; thus these ways were among the least affected in colonial California.

The third process was the consolidation of formerly autonomous polities into the emerging tribal organization of the Kashaya Pomo. The key dimensions of colonial encounters underlying this pattern were the maintenance of villages in traditional homelands, the designation of a chief *toion* by the Russian-American Company, moderate to heavy population decline, and the short chronology of colonial encounters. The toyon responded to the Russian mercantile program by convincing other leaders of nearby polities to unite under his leadership. Members of the newly emerging Kashaya tribe instituted a dispersed settlement system that allowed men and women the choice of participating in various mercantile enterprises or keeping a low profile in the "forest depths." The coalition of the Kashaya into a unified tribal system provided a more robust organization for weathering some of the problems associated with Russian colonization. The larger population base was helpful in coping with demographic fluctuations and insuring the availability of marriage partners. It also ensured that a sufficient number of knowledgeable people would be available to staff political offices and ritual positions, to apprentice youngsters in the ways of hunting and gathering, and to teach the Kashaya language to future generations.

As we shall see, the cultural transformations underpinning the three social processes became critical factors in the federal recognition of California Indian tribes. In the aftermath of the Hispanic and Russian frontier period, only some of the innovative native identities, social forms, and tribal relationships would be recognized as "truly Indian" by government agents, anthropologists, and other gatekeeping authorities.

8 The Aftermath

Native peoples endured tremendous difficulties following the collapse of the mission and mercantile colonies in the 1830s and early 1840s. The United States annexed California, the Gold Rush came and went, coastal cities mushroomed almost overnight, and thousands of foreigners displaced Indians from their lands. By the early 1900s, some prominent anthropologists claimed that Indians from a broad swath of coastal California had become largely extinct. These pronouncements had profound consequences for descendant communities. Indian groups perceived to have "melted away" were mostly ignored by early ethnographers, and tended not to receive land allotments from the federal government. Today, these groups remain "unacknowledged" tribes having no legal status with the United States. In contrast, those coastal peoples identified by anthropologists as members of viable Indian communities experienced very different histories. Intensive ethnographic research resulted in a plethora of monographs and articles, which were widely disseminated among scholars, government agencies, and interested lay people. The majority of these higher-profile groups eventually received federal land grants and are today recognized by the United States government as legitimate tribes.

The study of colonial entanglements provides the necessary historical context to understand why anthropologists in the early twentieth century claimed the widespread extinction of coastal California Indians. Taking a page from Fernand Braudel and other *Annales* scholars who advocate for the study of cultural processes over the long run, I hold that the social forms and tribal organizations that emerged from native engagements with the mission and mercantile colonial programs became structures (of the *longue durée*) that both shaped and directed future developments for the coastal peoples of southern and central California. In this chapter I examine how the social processes associated with the Indians of the northern missions, southernmost missions, and Colony Ross continued, with some modifications, into the later nineteenth and early twentieth centuries. Anthropologists who initiated fieldwork in coastal California responded very differently to these ongoing cultural transformations: although able to incorporate native groups from the southernmost missions and Colony Ross into anthropological constructs of Indianhood, they mostly failed in accommodating descendant communities from the northern missions. Berkeley anthropologists, in particular, had difficulties working with native peoples whose original polities had fragmented, and whose daily lives by the early 1900s centered around nontraditional social forms and new kinds of Indian identities.

AFTER THE FRANCISCAN MISSIONS AND COLONY ROSS

What happened to coastal native peoples after the mission and mercantile colonies collapsed and the people became ensnared in a host of new colonial structures and practices?

I can only present a brief sketch of what happened.[1] Suffice it to say, with the break-up of the massive mission complexes beginning in 1833–34, and the replacement of Franciscan padres with the Zacatecans and later parish priests, several options opened for neophyte peoples. They could work for settlers at the ranchos and pueblos, join gentile Indian groups in the interior, or establish their own Indian pueblos or villages near old missions or in the coastal hills and mountains. Similar options also existed for native peoples in the Russian frontier after Colony Ross was sold in 1841 to Johann Sutter, a rancho owner from Sacramento Valley.

The complex legal process involving the secularization of the Franciscan missions is covered in a number of excellent studies (e.g., Bancroft 1886b:301–362; Hutchinson 1969; Jackson and Castillo 1995:87–106; Neri 1976; Servin 1965). The Mexican Congress initiated the break-up of the vast mission holdings by passing the mission secularization law for Alta and Baja California in August 1833. Under this law, the Franciscan missionaries would relinquish control to secular priests, who would establish a parish at each mission (Hutchinson 1969:161–164).[2] Each neophyte family head and all males over twenty-one years were supposed to receive a plot of land for a home and another plot for cultivation. Furthermore, the cattle, seeds, and tools constituting the mission estates were to be divided up among them. Mexican officials appointed administrators to oversee the mission property, recognizing that the redistribution of land and other assets would take place over multiple years (Sanchez 1995:130–138). However, relatively few of the ex-neophytes received land grants, and those with land did not maintain ownership very long. Prominent *Californio* families soon consolidated most of the mission land into extensive ranchos.

In many respects, the large number of ranchos carved from the mission lands in the 1830s and 1840s provided the greatest degree of continuity for many neophyte families, following secularization (Greenwood 1989; Hornbeck 1978; Phillips 1993:107; Silliman 2000). In exchange for labor in the hide and tallow trade and in agricultural production, the Indians were allowed by the rancho owners to reside on rancho lands, where they received protection, food, and some goods. The establishment of Indian rancherias (native villages) on these private ranches provided one option for keeping ex-neophyte family units together in the coastal region of southern and central California (Monroy 1990:187).

The workforce of Mexican ranchos was not restricted to ex-neophytes or nearby gentile Indians, but incorporated native peoples from the old Russian frontier. After the closing of Colony Ross and its purchase by Sutter, the Ross settlement became the headquarters of a Mexican rancho eventually owned and operated by William O. Benitz. The Kashaya Pomo continued to inhabit their indigenous homeland, and most resided at the Benitz Rancho, where they maintained an Indian rancheria a short distance from the old Ross settlement. Other Kashaya Indians lived and worked at the Kruse Rancho not far from Salt Point, and at Captain Stephen Smith's Rancho near the town of Bodega, where Bodega Miwoks also resided. Census figures indicate that the Indian rancheria on Benitz's property housed anywhere from 100 to 162 people, but the Indian population on the Kruse Rancho numbered only about 20 to 30 (Kennedy 1955:76–82; Lightfoot et al. 1991:121–122).

Former mission Indians also resettled near civilian pueblos, such as Los Angeles, Monterey, and San Juan Capistrano, where they were incorporated into the local workforce as day laborers, field hands, or domestic servants (Johnson 1995:4; Phillips 1980). The majority of the household servants, most of whom were women, lived in the homes of their employers, while many of the men worked in the fields and lived in separate households (Hurtado 1992:198–202). Some of the native women married non-Indians, and these mixed couples comprised fourteen percent of the households sampled in Los Angeles in 1860 (Hurtado 1992:200).[3] Phillips (1980:436–448) stresses that the Indian workers of Los Angeles experienced massive social disintegration during the period of the 1840s through the 1860s, when many suffered and died from diseases, alcoholism, and violence.

Some ex-mission Indians joined extant tribal groups in the interior (Johnson 1995:4). Many neophytes recruited to the missions from tribes in the San Joaquin Valley and southern deserts probably returned home after secularization. Ex-neophytes descended from coastal polities also disappeared into the interior. Some would have resettled with spouses from the interior (e.g., Yokuts-, Serrano-, Cahuilla-, and Cupeño-speaking peoples) whom they had married in the missions. Others requested protection and shelter from interior peoples, which compelled the latter to make social adjustments to incorporate non-kin persons into more inclusive native polities (Phillips 1993:95–98). Over time, these new members, especially the children of intertribal unions, probably embraced the identities and cultural practices of their adopted group.

There is evidence for the depopulation of some parts of the San Joaquin Valley following a devastating malaria epidemic in the early 1830s, and ex-neophytes may have contributed to the repopulation of the area (Phillips 1993:94–95, 105). They may have joined refugee communities headed by a new breed of charismatic and politically savvy Indian leaders, many of whom grew up in the missions (Monroy 1990:196–199; Phillips 1975). These bands became notorious for raiding horses, mules, and other livestock from ranchos in Mexican California and exchanging these to American trappers and New Mexican traders for trade goods (Phillips 1993:158–164). The new territorial chiefs enhanced the power and the size of their raiding forces by incorporating ex-neophytes. The active recruitment of displaced natives resulted in novel political organizations that cross-cut Indian languages, homelands, and former polities (see Phillips 1975:45, 163). Merrill (1994) describes similar kinds of multi-ethnic bands in northern Mexico, where new social and political structures arose to integrate people from diverse homelands and backgrounds, a process that created new frontier identities.

Ex-neophytes also remained near some missions and worked for the *mayordomos* or administrators who supervised the mission property and goods after secularization (Monroy 1990:126–127). Johnson (1995:3,6; 1997: 258–259) notes that the emancipation of neophytes did not happen overnight; through the early 1840s, neophytes had to apply to be *licenciados* through the recommendation of mission administrators. It was not until Governor Pío Pico issued his *Reglamento* in 1845 that all neophytes were unconditionally released from the missions. One mission, San Juan Capistrano, was converted into a Mexican pueblo and the property divided up between ex-neophytes and *Californios*. Each family received a house lot, one or more plots of land for producing crops, and access to the pueblo communal property for raising livestock and other agricultural products (Haas

1995:53–56). Other former mission Indians established their own pueblos or villages in the near or distant hinterland of the missions (see below).

Unfortunately, most Indian groups failed to obtain legal title to the land they occupied (see Garr 1972:300–307; Haas 1995:56–60; Johnson 1995:5–11). A few fortunate ones petitioned and received Mexican land grants, such as those bestowed in the hinterland of Mission San Diego, Mission San Luis Rey, Mission Santa Barbara, and Mission San Fernando (see Farris 1997b; Haas 1995:39–40; Johnson 1995:10; 1997:259–260; Johnson and Crawford 1999). But as the population of non-Indians continued to increase, especially after the Gold Rush, it became increasingly difficult for ex-neophytes to maintain their villages and properties. Non-Indians flooded into the coastal zone and literally pushed Indians off lands having good pasture, arable soils, and dependable water sources. (Historical overviews of this process occur in government reports of 1874 and 1883 [Ames 1979; Jackson and Kinney 1979].) This difficulty held even for those Indians who received Mexican land grants. They rarely had the legal or financial resources to support their land claims to representatives of the United States government, to relevant state and local agencies, or in court when sued by wealthy Anglo-American neighbors. The end result was similar—native villages were pushed farther and farther into marginal and relatively inaccessible areas in the coastal hills and mountains.

In postsecularization times, no matter what option chosen, almost all native peoples suffered tremendously, especially during the dark years of the 1850s through the 1870s.[4] Whether they ended up in ranchos, on the outskirts of pueblos, in their own villages near mission centers, or in coastal hills and mountains, they experienced horrific mortality rates due to violence, mistreatment, overwork, disease, and alcoholism. Cook's demographic analysis indicates that population loss during American colonization from 1848 to 1865 was three times as severe as during the entire pre-American colonial period (Cook 1976a:346). For example, Charles E. Kelsey's report to the Commissioner of Indian Affairs in 1906 estimated that about thirty-four thousand neophytes were released during mission secularization (1834), and that by about 1900 only three thousand descendants were still alive (C. E. Kelsey 1979:125).

The sharp demographic plunge was exacerbated by the uncertain living conditions of coastal Indians, who had become a class of landless peons. *Californio* and Anglo-American settlers constantly encroached on Indian-occupied lands and residences, forcing many groups to relocate to ever more remote places in the hinterland. By the 1860s and 1870s, conditions had deteriorated to the point that coastal native communities and villages did not hold legal title to any land to call their own. This problem would come back to haunt many when they later attempted to obtain legal status as federally recognized tribes.

FEDERAL LAND ALLOCATIONS

The abortive history of Indian reservations proposed, created, and then rescinded in California by agents of the United States government is covered in detail elsewhere (see Castillo 1978; Forbes 1982; Heizer 1972; Parman 1994; Phillips 1997; and Rawls 1984). For my purposes, it is sufficient to note that none of the attempts to establish reservations from 1851 to 1870 (including the original eighteen unratified treaties and Edward Beale's early experiments with "military" reservations) provided any secure land base for the coastal Indians of southern and central California. The Mendocino Reservation established on the north coast in 1856 (and abandoned in 1867) did incorporate Northern Pomo, Central Pomo, and Coast Miwok (including Bodega Miwok) peoples, but there is no record that the Kashaya Pomo who worked and lived on the Benitz Rancho were sent there (Barrett 1908:48; Kennedy 1955:80–81).

By the 1870s, the plight of the former Mission Indians had become so grim that the federal government was forced into action. In January 1870, an executive order created the San Pasqual Pala Reservation in southern California, but a controversy erupted among local white landowners and the land was quickly returned to public domain (Castillo 1978:114). In 1873, John G. Ames, a special agent to the Commissioner of Indian Affairs, was dispatched to evaluate the "number, location, and condition of the so-called Mission Indians of Southern California." He made a number of recommendations to purchase land for some native groups and to provide them with clothing and agricultural implements (Ames 1979:51). Between 1875 and 1877, new executive orders were issued that established thirteen separate reservations, totaling 52,000 hectares (130,000 acres) of land, for the homeless so-called Mission Indians in southern California (Castillo 1978:114).

In the 1880s and 1890s, pressure from influential non-Indians and humanitarian organizations continued to be exerted on the federal government to assist the Mission Indians (see Rawls 1984:206–209). After publishing *A Century of Dishonor* (1885) about the deplorable treatment of American Indians, Helen Hunt Jackson focused her attention on the Indians of southern California. Working for the U.S. Department of the Interior and as a writer for *Century Magazine*, she investigated the status and condition of the Mission Indians, making forceful recommendations to purchase land, in her 1883 report to the Commissioner of Indians (Jackson and Kinney 1979). The following year, she published the best-selling novel *Ramona*, which highlighted the unjust treatment of Indian survivors by land-hungry Anglo-American settlers. Jackson's reform movement certainly heightened the visibility of southern California Indians (Rawls 1984:206; Stewart and Heizer 1978:705; Thomas 1991:123–125).[5] Fourteen more reservations were granted by an act of Congress in 1891 (Act for the Relief of Mission Indians), amended in 1898, to provide land for the Mission Indians (Castillo 1978: 116); this act conferred trust-patent status to the new reservations (Rawls 1984:211; Shipek 1978:610).

The Indian reservations awarded in southern California between 1880 and 1898 were placed within the traditional territories of Luiseño, Cupeño, Diegueño, Serrano, and Cahuilla peoples (Shipek 1978:612–613). As Castillo (1978:114) points out, not all "Mission Indians" receiving land allocations had been subjected to the colonial program of the Franciscans. Some of the reservations were located well beyond the farthest reaches of any mission lands, in desert lands where Cahuilla and other peoples only marginally affected by the missions and Franciscan recruitment efforts received land allocations. But it is significant that, when we examine the spatial distribution of land grants within the hills and mountains of the coastal zone, we see that the majority are in the near and distant territories of the two southernmost missions—San Luis Rey and San Diego (see map 3).

I think the placement of land grants in southern California epitomizes how the legacy of colonialism resonates in Indian communities to this day, with regard to federal recognition. The boundaries of the federal land grants were fixed so that they included or were placed near extant Indian villages (Castillo 1978:114). Native communities selected for protection included some of the original villages of neophytes who maintained residences in their native homelands under the modified relocation program of Mission San Luis Rey and Mission San Diego (Johnson and Crawford 1999:90–92). For example, Julio César (1930:45) mentioned Pala as one of the Indian villages associated with a mission rancho in the hinterland of Mission San Luis Rey, and it was the centerpiece of one of the 1875 land grants.

The outlying villages of the ex-neophytes and their families in the hinterland of the southernmost missions made significant impressions on humanitarian workers (such as Helen Hunt Jackson) and government agents alike. Clearly the historical connection between the contemporary Indian communities and their colonial/ancestral villages and homelands struck a chord with non-Indian officials. The reports of Ames (1979) and Jackson and Kinney (1979), written in 1873 and 1883 respectively, described the old mission chapels and structures at some of the villages, such as Pala (Ames 1979:69).

> In many of the villages are adobe chapels, built in the time of the missions, where are still preserved many relics of the mission days, such as saints' images, holy-water kettles, &c. In these chapels, on the occasions of the priest's visits, the Indians gather in great numbers, women sometimes walking two days' journeys, bringing their babies on their backs to have them baptized. There are also in several of the villages old Indians, formerly trained at the missions, who officiate with Catholic rites at funerals, and on Sundays repeat parts of the mass. (Jackson and Kinney 1979:84)

Although these native settlements experienced many difficulties with encroaching whites (see Ames 1979; Jackson and Kinney 1979), they maintained viable and sizeable Indian communities through the dark years of the 1850s and 1870s. The estimated Luiseño and Diegueño populations in the 1880 census were 1,120 and 731 respectively, mostly distributed in mission-era settlements in coastal valleys where federal land allocations were made. Jackson and Kinney (1979:75) stressed that these counts surely underestimated the local native population because they did not systematically include Indians who lived near coastal urban centers.

Although federal officials established Indian reservations for some of the ex-neophytes of the two southernmost missions, they allocated no federal lands, between the period of 1870 and 1900, to any of the Indians associated with the northern missions or Colony Ross. The single exception is a small plot of land acquired for the Chumash-speaking "Santa Ynez" community (see map 3). Johnson (1995:10–11; 2001:59) details how aggressive settlers forced the ex-neophytes from Santa Inés mission lands in 1855. These Indians relocated to the Canada de los Pinos estate, owned by the Catholic church. Here they established the settlement of Sanja de Cota on a creek not far from the old mission. This land parcel was acquired by the U.S. government and recognized as a federal reservation by 1901 (Grant 1978:507; Shipek 1978:612).

Significantly, by the 1880s the federal government no longer classified the ex-neophytes of the northern missions as Mission Indians.

> The term "Mission Indians" dates back over one hundred years, to the time of the Franciscan missions in California. It then included all Indians who lived in the mission establishments, or were under the care

of the Franciscan fathers. Very naturally the term has continued to be applied to the descendants of those Indians. In the classification of the Indian Bureau, however, it is now used in a somewhat restricted sense, embracing only those Indians living in the three southernmost counties of California, and known as Serranos, Cahuillas, San Luisenos, and Dieguinos; the last two names having evidently come from the names of the southernmost two missions, San Luis Rey and San Diego. (Jackson and Kinney 1979:75)

The federal government's snubbing of ex-neophytes from the northern missions cannot be attributed to their sudden disappearance. Nor can it be explained by their complete integration into nearby Hispanic communities. A similar process took place in the hinterlands of the northern missions as had transpired among the ex-neophytes of Mission San Luis Rey and Mission San Diego. That is, some Miwok, Ohlone, Esselen, Salinan, Chumash, and Gabrielino peoples established viable native villages near the old missions and in their distant peripheries. A description of examples of ex-neophyte communities reported in the hinterland of northern missions during the late nineteenth century follows.

Johnson (1997) describes what happened to Chumash, Gabrielino, and Tataviam Indians from Mission San Fernando after secularization. Some ex-neophytes petitioned for Mexican land grants, establishing households or small communities at nearby places, such as Rancho El Encino and Rancho El Escorpíon, or at the former mission rancho of San Francisco Xavier. Other families petitioned to remain on mission lands. A large number moved to Tejon, where the Sebastian Military Reservation was created in 1853. Even when the federal government closed the reservation in 1864, many continued to live on the ranch as *vaqueros*, shepherds, and agricultural laborers.[6]

Johnson (1995) presents a succinct overview of the Indian settlements established in the Santa Barbara region. At Kamexmey, near San Buenaventura, and Qwa' near Goleta Estero, Chumash Islanders established "traditional" Indian communities consisting of tule houses, sweat lodges, acorn granaries, and shrines. Here native rituals and ceremonies were practiced, as were fishing, canoe-making, and bead production (Johnson 1995:7). In addition to Kamexmey, two other Indian rancherias are clearly marked, on an 1855 map, along the Ventura River near Mission San Buenaventura. Another Indian community survived for many years south of Mission San Buenaventura, within the city limits of Ventura. The Indian barrio of La Cieneguita, near Mission Santa Barbara, remained a vibrant community for several decades after secularization, until it was terminated by land sales and population loss (Johnson 1995:9–10).

A sizeable rancheria thrived near old Mission San Carlos a short distance from Monterey (Jackson and Kinney 1979:88). Helen Hunt Jackson described it in her book (Jackson 1902:154–155) *Glimpses of California and the Missions,*[7] and appealed to the federal government in her and Abbot Kinney's 1883 report.

> In conclusion, we would make the suggestion that there are several small bands of Mission Indians north of the boundaries of the so-called Mission Indians' Agency, for whom it would seem to be the duty of the Government to care as well as for those already enumerated. One of these is the San Carlos Indians, living near the old San Carlos Mission at Monterey. There are nearly one hundred of these, and they are living on lands which were given to them before the secularization act of 1834. (Jackson and Kinney 1979:88)

Robert Louis Stevenson (1892:104–107) penned the following poignant description of the San Carlos Indians in his book *Across the Plains.*

> Their lands, I was told, are being yearly encroached upon by the neighbouring American proprietor, and with that exception no man troubles his head for the Indians of Carmel. Only one day in the year, the day before our Guy Fawkes, the *padre* drives over the hill from Monterey; the little sacristy, which is the only covered portion of the church, is filled with seats and decorated for the service; the Indians troop together, their bright dresses contrasting with their dark and melancholy faces; and there, among a crowd of somewhat unsympathetic holiday-makers, you may hear God served with perhaps more touching circumstances than in any other temple under heaven. An Indian, stone-blind and about eighty years of age, conducts the singing; other Indians compose the choir; yet they have the Gregorian music at their finger ends, and pronounce the Latin so correctly that I could follow the meaning as they sang. The pronunciation was odd and nasal, the singing hurried and staccato. (Stevenson 1892:105–106)

Helen Hunt Jackson and Abbot Kinney also mentioned two native communities in the near hinterland of Mission San Antonio and Mission San Miguel, as well as the Indian village of "Santa Suez" near Santa Barbara (Jackson and Kinney 1979:88).[8]

Gary Breschini and Trudy Haversat (2002) detail the distinct possibility that southern Ohlone- and Esselen-speaking peoples took advantage of the rugged southern Coast Ranges to establish refugee communities. Employing archival records, local stories, and archaeological findings, they make a convincing case that the upland terrain of the southern Monterey–Big Sur coastline supported runaway neophytes from nearby missions (e.g., Mission San Carlos de Monterey, Mission San Antonio, Mission Soledad). For example, excavations at Isabella Meadows Cave (CA-MNT-250) unearthed a burial of a native girl with shell and glass beads that probably dates around 1825. Local lore indicates that "wild" Indians continued to live in the remote, inaccessible areas until 1850 or later (Breschini and Haversat 2002:40–41).

In the 1840s, at least one thousand ex-neophytes from Mission San José, and possibly more from Mission Santa Clara, moved to an extensive refuge area, in the East Bay region of the San Francisco Bay Area, that extended north from the old mission to the town of San Leandro. Here they established an extensive settlement system of villages containing mission survivors (Field et al. 1992:424). Eventually some of the native people retreated into the far eastern hinterland of the San Francisco Bay, settling in the Diablo Range and Livermore Valley in locations where prehistoric villages once stood (Leventhal et al. 1994:308). By the early 1860s, some of the Indians had moved south of what is now the town of Pleasanton to establish a new community on land ceded to them by Agostin Bernal, a local rancher. At the "Alisal" rancheria (also known as Verona Station), Ohlone and other Indian descendants constructed multiple houses and at least one sweat lodge. They intermarried with the Bernal family, participated in hunting and gathering activities, and provided labor for livestock raising and crop production (Field et al. 1992:424–426; Leventhal et al. 1994:309). The rancheria remained an active native settlement for several decades. Here residents performed a plethora of ceremonies, combining the 1870s resurgence of the Ghost Dance with other traditional central California rites such as the Kuksu Dance and World Renewal Ceremony. The Ohlone community experienced a revitalization not only in their celebration of ceremonies and dances, but also in the singing of tribal songs, the use of sacred language, and the production of many Indian crafts (Field et al. 1992:425–426; Forbes 1982:88; Galvan 1968:12; Leventhal et al. 1994:310). Ohlone-speaking people also occupied small rancherias in nearby areas, now the towns of Niles and Sunol, and in the hinterland of Mission San Juan Bautista (Field et al. 1992:425; Leventhal et al. 1994:310–311).

Indian communities of the old Russian frontier also survived into the late nineteenth and early twentieth centuries (figure 7). It is not clear what happened to the Bodega Miwok community, which had prospered under the leadership of Valenila in the heyday of Port Rumiantsev. Two hundred and fifty Bodega Miwoks were reportedly sent to the Mendocino Reservation in 1856. But when Samuel Barrett began his ethnographic fieldwork in 1903, only a few had returned to Bodega Bay and its environs (Barrett 1908:48, 303–307; see also Kelly 1978). The Kashaya Pomo remained in the vicinity of the old Ross settlement until the late 1860s, when William Benitz sold

Figure 7. Indian group (Pomo) [n.d.], by Henry Raschen (1854–1937). The painting illustrates a small encampment of men and women involved in a gambling
game, probably in the 1880s. The location of the camp is not known, but the painting may depict Kashaya Pomo in the vicinity of Stewarts Point. A man and woman
play the traditional hand game for what appear to be strings of clam disk beads, as
well as for baskets and tanned skins. A woman stands among a group of spectators
holding a string of clam disks. In the background is a conical house, with one woman
carrying a burden basket, and another fixing a meal. The Kashaya women wear
dresses, cloth shirts, scarves, necklaces, and shoulder blankets, while the male gam-
bler sports a jacket and bandana. No children or young adults are depicted. (Oil
on canvas, 35.25 in. × 55.125 in. Courtesy of the Oakland Museum of California,
A78.143; lent by the Mann Family Trust; photo by M. Lee Fatheree.)

his property to James Dixon and Dixon's partner Lord Charles Fairfax. In
establishing a commercial timber operation at the former Russian colony,
Dixon and Fairfax forced the majority of the Kashaya to vacate the Benitz
rancheria by about 1870. Most of the Kashaya relocated to Charles Haupt's
ranch, about thirteen kilometers southeast of Stewarts Point. Married to a
local Indian woman, Haupt allowed the Kashaya to establish the thriving
village of Potol on his property (Lightfoot et al. 1991:122). Other Kashaya
families continued to reside in the greater Ross region in small rancherias,
and they reoccupied one of their former villages (duʔk̓ašal, also known as
Abaloneville) (Kennedy 1955:89; Oswalt 1966:4).

In sum, the allocation of federal land grants to coastal Indian groups from

1870 to 1900 was limited primarily to the isolated mountain valleys (and desert places) where the ex-neophytes of the two southernmost missions continued to reside. Other native communities in the near and distant hinterland of the northern missions and Colony Ross received no land allocations. The single exception is the Santa Ynez reservation in Santa Barbara County. To address the questions of why land grants were not forthcoming to the Indians of the northern missions, and of how the Kashaya were eventually awarded their own trust land, we need to turn to the fledgling field of anthropology at the turn of the twentieth century and the supporting role it played in actions leading to the federal recognition of California tribes.

ANTHROPOLOGY AND TRIBAL RECOGNITION

As discussed in chapter 2, Alfred Kroeber and his colleagues at the University of California, Berkeley, created the conceptual foundation for studying the languages, culture areas, and polities of California Indians, in the first three decades of the twentieth century. From the outset, this influential group did not treat all Native Californians alike. They were quite selective about whom they chose to study, and significant biases resulted in the ethnographic coverage of the state. The criteria for undertaking field research revolved around the primary mission of the ethnographic program—reconstructing the original aboriginal cultures of California.

Berkeley anthropologists recognized that the "memory culture" methodology worked best with native groups whose contact with whites had been relatively recent (i.e., since the time of the Gold Rush) and where elders could recall the cultural practices of precolonial times. In large part, Kroeber and his U.C. Berkeley colleagues chose to work with native peoples who conformed fairly closely to the basic tenets of the "tribelet" model. They interviewed, that is, elders who could still recall small-scale village communities where members spoke the same language and practiced a specific repertoire of cultural practices, food ways, and ceremonies. Consequently, they devoted much effort to studying native groups in northern California, some areas of the state's Central Valley, the foothills and mountains of the Sierra Nevada, and a few groups in California's southern deserts.

Berkeley anthropologists ignored, for the most part, Indians residing within the former domain of the Hispanic frontier; the anthropologists' response concerned these native groups' longer period of contact and the general perception of marked culture change. In his *Handbook of the Indians of California*, Kroeber drew a solid dark line around the "limits of complete missionization," and graphically showed (as blank white space) that native groups within most of the coastal region of central and southern California were almost entirely extinct (with, e.g., only 0–1 percent surviving in 1910) (Kroeber 1925:887) (see map 11). Within this extensive area, Berkeley anthropologists refrained from undertaking any concerted fieldwork—they rarely ventured into their own backyard to interview native elders. But, in truth, this boundary line turned out to be highly permeable.

Kroeber believed that, in spite of the many decades of intervention by the Spaniards, Mexicans, and Anglo-Americans, the "memory culture" methodology could still be employed among selective native communities of the deep southern coast. Among the Indians associated with Mission San Luis Rey and Mission San Diego, the ethnographers found functioning Indian communities with elders who could recall some vestiges of tribelet organizations, who still spoke the native languages, and who could describe traditional social organizations (e.g., patrilineal lineages or clans, totemic moieties) and ceremonies. Kroeber felt this region of "knowledgeable" elders had a higher rate of Indian survivorship than had the rest of the central and southern California coast. He estimated that 10–19 percent of the southern Luiseño had survived as of 1910, and that 20–29 percent of the Diegueño were alive in 1910 (map 11).

Thus, it is clear that Kroeber acknowledged the potential to work with some, but not all, native groups who had been drawn into the Franciscan missions. As Kroeber (1925:888) elaborated:

> First of all, it is established that the tribes that were completely devoted to mission life are gone. Many are wholly extinct; the most fortunate may amount to one-hundredth of their original numbers. In the extreme south, among the Luiseño and Diegueño, there seems to be an exception. It is not real; but due to the difficulty just mentioned: data are lacking to enable a separation of the wholly missionized from the partly missionized Luiseño and Diegueño. Both groups have therefore been treated as units.

In a later publication, Kroeber (1936:105–106) remarked that good information still existed among some southern California groups.

> In the Southern area there may also have been a pair of interrelated, nearly contiguous, and yet differentiated climaxes, among the Coast Chumash and Coast Shoshoneans. The difficulty in coming to a decision is that our knowledge of the Chumash is almost wholly archaeological, their cults and society remaining a terra incognita; whereas for the Shoshoneans there exist excellent cult and society data from the Juaneño and Luiseño, who, however, declare that they derived their

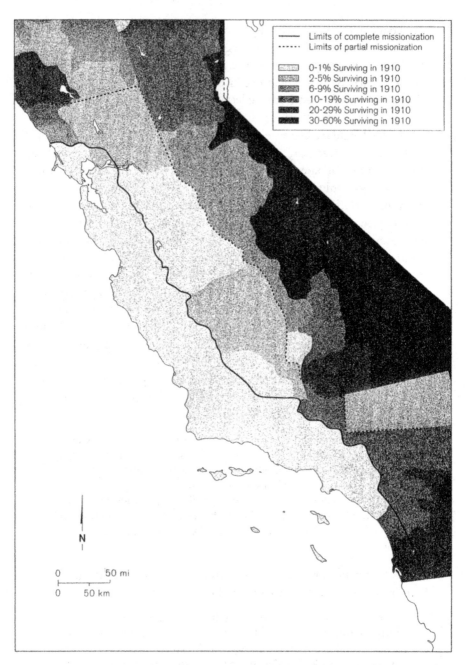

Map 11.   Indian survivors of central and southern California. Kroeber calculated Indian survivorship as the percentages of Indians alive in 1910 in comparison to 1770 populations. Also shown are areas of "complete missionization" and "partial missionization" as estimated by Kroeber. (Adapted from Kroeber 1925:887.)

most elaborate cults from the Gabrielino of Catalina island and the fronting mainland. These Gabrielino have perished with about as little record of their intangibles as the Chumash.

Kroeber mounted a concerted effort to undertake ethnographic fieldwork among the Luiseño and Diegueño to reconstruct their "original" aboriginal cultures. Kroeber dispatched a few of his graduate students to complete this work. He also collaborated with colleagues working in the area, or obtained ethnographic notes from astute but nonanthropologically trained observers (such as Philip Sparkman, whose notes were acquired by Kroeber after Sparkman's murder in 1907).[9] These studies were published as seminal monographs or extensive articles in the *University of California Publications in American Archaeology and Ethnology* and *University of California Anthropological Record* series (see, for example, Drucker 1937; Du Bois 1908; Gifford 1918; Kroeber 1908, 1917; Sparkman 1908; Spier 1923; Strong 1929; and Waterman 1910).

In contrast, little fieldwork was undertaken, under the auspices of the Berkeley ethnography program, among the Indian descendants of the northern missions. This area, for the most part, remained terra incognita in the celebrated University of California publications.[10] Kroeber did some exploratory interviews with elders of central coast groups. He met with some Ohlone and Chumash speakers in 1901 and 1902, as part of his ambitious salvage program to describe the structure of all the Indian languages in California. But he did little else in this area in later years (see, e.g., Johnson 1988:8; Ortiz 1994:124–125).

Although Berkeley fieldworkers neglected the denizens of the central and (most of) the southern coast, other fieldworkers did not. John P. Harrington and, to a lesser extent, C. Hart Merriam initiated extensive interviews with various members of Ohlone, Esselen, Salinan, Chumash, and Gabrielino groups. Harrington began his work with the Chumash in 1912, producing more than two hundred thousand pages of field notes on Chumash languages, ritual beliefs, folklore, and cultural practices, and in the 1920s he initiated concerted research on Ohlone speakers from San Jose to Monterey (Bean 1994; Johnson 1988:8–9; Johnson 2001:55; Ortiz 1994:100). His field research indicates that a very extensive body of knowledge had been retained by elders on their native material culture, belief systems, and life ways. Many continued to broadcast their Indian identities to outsiders. Population estimates for the Ohlone, Esselen, Salinan, and Chumash peoples during the period 1900–1920 (e.g., Cook 1976a:236; Edwards and Kelsey 1979:99–109; Mason 1912:116–117) indicate that many of the "hinterland" Indian communities (described above) of the late nineteenth century were still extant at this critical time of early ethnographic research.

Although Kroeber turned his back on Indians in his own neighborhood, he observed no moratorium on working north of San Francisco Bay, in the area of the historic Russian frontier. In 1903, he sent his first doctoral student, Samuel Barrett, to work among the Pomo as part of the newly created *Ethnological and Archaeological Survey of California*. Kroeber estimated that the percentage of Pomo people surviving from 1770 to 1910 ranged from 20–29 percent (among the northern groups) to 2–9 percent (for the Kashaya Pomo) (see map 11). Although Barrett visited Indian consultants from across the Pomo linguistic area (which had been divided into seven separate languages), he spent time particularly with the Kashaya Pomo, taking copious notes about their language, life ways, and material culture, and even about the location of their ancestral villages (see Barrett 1908). Thus, the first dissertation produced by the high-profile ethnographic program at U.C. Berkeley focused on native peoples who had been closely tied to the Russian mercantile colonial program. Barrett's fieldwork was followed by that of other Berkeley ethnographers, linguists, and geographers, such as Edward Gifford (1967; 1937), Edwin Loeb (1926), Omer Stewart (1943), Fred Kniffin (1939), Mary Jean Kennedy (1955), and Robert Oswalt (1957; 1966; 1971; 1988).

A Consideration of the Biases in Fieldwork Coverage

The politics and personalities of early anthropologists in California exacerbated the neglect of the central and most of the southern coast by Berkeley scholars. A bitter rivalry festered between Kroeber, the celebrated founder of California's first homegrown field program, and Harrington, an "outsider" affiliated with the Smithsonian Institution. The resulting "turf wars" influenced decisions about where fieldwork would be undertaken. Since Harrington commenced intensive work among the communities of Chumash and Ohlone descendants in the 1910s and 1920s, Kroeber was careful not to duplicate his efforts (Bean 1994:xxiii). As Robert Heizer reminisced in the mid-1970s,

> I have also heard it said, by people who neither knew Kroeber nor what they were talking about, that Kroeber really fell down on the job by failing to work with these Central California groups. It is true that Kroeber and his students neglected the Chumash and Costanoans, but this was done because Harrington made it quite clear that he would resent Kroeber's "muscling in," and since there was plenty else to be done, Kroeber did not press the issue. Harrington may have felt that he

had Kroeber bluffed, but when the issue was finally raised it was
Harrington who backed down. (Cited in Bean 1994:xxiv; original
Heizer 1975:233–234)

It is unfortunate that Harrington did not share his ethnographic field notes
with others (especially Kroeber and his colleagues). Harrington published
very little on the massive data base he recorded on the native peoples of the
central and southern coast. His findings remained relatively obscure until after his death, in 1961, when his notes first became available to other researchers. As Kroeber (1936:106, footnote 4) summed up the situation, John P. Harrington, "an unusually able worker, has rescued invaluable records from the
last surviving Chumash" but had "so far published little."

But the neglect of the central coast by Berkeley anthropologists was more
than simply institutional rivalry. From the outset, an important consideration for choosing native peoples to study was whether the ethnographers
felt that memory culture methodology could be employed successfully, and
on whether some remnants of past tribelet organizations could be reconstructed. The ethnographers selected field sites based on the potential of
exposing "pristine" aboriginal cultural practices. The mere existence of a
native community or Indian elder was not enough—the critical criterion
was whether the native informant could present a perspective on the past
that allowed the anthropologists to filter out the effects of Western civilization and to reconstruct the original, "authentic" tribal entity. As Les
Field recently wrote, Kroeber employed an "essentialism" that identified
Indian peoples by a particular constellation of discrete traits. Ethnic iden-
tification of Indian peoples in California was defined "in terms of a set of
essences, typically including language, modes of self-presentation such as
jewelry, clothing, and body ornamentation, and ritual performances, especially ones that can be labeled religious" (Field 1999:194). Kroeber and
friends used the "essences" of aboriginal cultures to construct a classification of native groups in California based on their distinctive languages, cultural practices, material culture, and ritual knowledge. A serious problem
with this essentialist approach was what to do with essences or traits that
might have become mixed or tainted from encounters with others. The
memory culture methodology provided little leeway or guidance for working with groups whose "original" cultural matrix had undergone significant
transformations.

Given the difficulties that Berkeley anthropologists experienced in grappling with Indian cultures that had been "diluted" by contact with others
over time, the spatial pattern of their ethnographic fieldwork became in-

tertwined with the legacy of colonialism. Ethnographers in the early 1900s surveyed a cultural landscape along the central and southern coast that had been molded by native peoples' participation in the Hispanic and Russian frontiers. The divergent outcomes that resulted from native engagements with colonial policies and practices affected how Kroeber and his colleagues perceived the opportunities, in these given areas, for employing the memory culture methodology.

Berkeley ethnographers believed it was worthwhile to consult with Indian descendants of the two southernmost missions to salvage information on their aboriginal cultures. Culture change was clearly evident among the Luiseño and Diegueño communities in the early 1900s, as evidenced by modern agricultural practices, adobe structures, outward acceptance and participation in Catholic ceremonies, and political organizations influenced by reservation politics and government intervention. But there was also a clear connection to the past (see Shipek 1977). By maintaining Indian villages in their ancestral homelands, and perpetuating Indian political structures under the Franciscan padres, enough knowledge of traditional values and cultural practices remained that early anthropologists believed much could be learned about past tribelet organizations by interviewing tribal elders. That is, the strong continuity with the past provided ethnographers with a window for obtaining information on tribelet ceremonies, clans, lineages, moieties, and material culture (see, e.g., Strong 1929). Furthermore, the creation of a network of small to moderate-size Indian reservations in southern California provided a highly accessible enclave of elders for the Berkeley ethnographers to interview.

Kroeber and his colleagues must have been positively giddy about the possibility of working with the Kashaya Pomo. Of all the California groups, the Kashaya Pomo epitomized, to an early twentieth-century anthropologist, what a large tribelet or small "tribe" should look like. The Kashaya people spoke a single language, recognized an overarching "tribal" political structure, could point to the boundaries of a well-defined territory, and continued to embrace many cultural practices that outsiders would clearly identify as "Indian." While living at the village of Potol on Haupt's ranch, the Kashaya harvested wild foods from the nearby region, including shellfish, fish, acorns, seaweeds, and venison. Indian foods also played a central role when the group came together for feasts and ceremonies. Two earth-covered dance houses, and a later above-ground board dance house, were eventually built at Haupt's ranch, and the Kashaya community observed a seasonal cycle of ceremonies and dances (Kennedy 1955). "Indian" material culture (e.g., redwood slab houses, baskets, clam disk beads) was still clearly in evidence in 1903, 1904, and 1906, when Barrett conducted his dissertation fieldwork among the Kashaya (Barrett 1908).

By way of contrast, the descendant communities of the Ohlone, Esselen, Salinan, Chumash, and Gabrielino peoples represented a conundrum for Berkeley ethnographers. The memory culture methodology was clearly not adequate for making sense of native groups whose cultural "essences" were considered impure or mixed as a consequence of culture contact. What could these anthropologists do with peoples whose "original" tribelet polities had long since collapsed and fragmented into new social forms? What could they do with peoples who had constructed novel cross-tribal relationships through marriage and friendship? What could they do with peoples who now recognized a more generalized construction of Indian identities?

Evidently they could do very little.[11] When Kroeber went to work with the Ohlone community of Alisal, near Pleasanton, he found not just Ohlone speakers but a complex admixture of Ohlone, Yokuts, Patwin, Miwok, and Esselen peoples who had been intermarrying and living with one another since the days of the Franciscan missions.[12] Today this cultural fusion is viewed in a positive light: "Under such circumstances, the cultural and political richness of the intertwined and intermarried families living at *Alisal*, among whom Ohlone, Yokuts, and Miwok languages were spoken, produced a ritually and ceremonially syncretic cultural revival," noted Leventhal et al. (1994:310). But in the days of Kroeberian anthropology, such cultural admixture was a real liability; it did not fit the conceptual model of small-scale, homogeneous tribelets. Kroeber would later remark that these kinds of groups could be considered "ethnographically extinct," because you could "no longer learn from living informants the speech and modes of life of the ancestors of these informants" (Kroeber and Heizer 1970:3).

The Implications of Early Ethnographic Fieldwork

At the same time that Berkeley anthropologists undertook their fieldwork and defined the "essences" of what constituted "real" California Indian groups, the federal government initiated another phase of allocating land grants to landless Indians. Through the tireless efforts of the Northern California Indian Association, Congress was persuaded to appropriate $100,000 to purchase lands and provide services for California Indians (Edwards and Kelsey 1979; Rawls 1984:209). During the period from 1906 to 1930, a total of thirty-six federal land grants, ranging in size from about two to a little over one hundred hectares, were allocated to native groups in sixteen northern California counties. However, none of these lands were allocated to homeless Indians in southern California (Castillo 1978:118). The only Indian survivors of the old Hispanic and Russian frontiers to receive land were the Kashaya Pomo, in 1914; their sixteen-hectare property, bought for $1,100, is located about five kilometers east of Stewarts Point on Miller Ridge in Sonoma County (Kennedy 1955:96). It appears that the federal government continued to assist the Luiseño and Diegueño Indian communities, as at least four additional Indian rancherias received federal trust status between 1910 and 1939 (Shipek 1978:612–613), yet the Indian descendants of the northern missions received nothing.

In fact, the inability of some native groups to obtain federal land grants by the early 1900s was the kiss of death.[13] This was especially true along the coastal strip between San Francisco and Los Angeles, where continued urbanization and rising property values would, by the 1930s, force native peoples off their lands. These fragile Indian communities, once pushed, or evicted, from previously unoccupied land, were destined to falter and splinter into small family groups. Thus, if a land base had not been obtained by an Indian group by about 1930, that group was almost certainly doomed to remain in limbo as one of the many "unacknowledged" tribes in California.

In a recent paper, Les Field (1999) argues that a prominent anthropologist such as Alfred Kroeber must have had a profound impact on the process of tribal federal recognition in California. The consequences of ethnographic fieldwork, he states, can be traced back to the allocation of land grants during the period from 1906 to 1930. Three federal Indian agents (Charles E. Kelsey, Charles E. Ashbury, and John J. Terrell) made recommendations to the federal government for purchasing lands for specific Indian groups. At least one of the agents (Charles E. Kelsey), Field shows, was greatly influenced by the research and findings of anthropologists. Not only did anthropologists present informed opinions about what should constitute a legal Indian group or "band," but the detailed monographs and articles they wrote could be used to support the legitimacy of purchasing land for specific Indian groups. In the political arena of tight funding, in the early 1900s, anthropology publications provided a line of evidence employed by federal Indian agents to justify prioritizing some groups for land allocations. The cause of a native group was not helped if it had received no attention from anthropologists—or, even worse, had been referred to in the authoritative literature as "extinct" or as having "melted" away.

> Again, the manner in which the published materials of academic anthropologists coincided with the disempowerment of these bands and their destiny as unacknowledged tribes is pertinent. The authoritative anthropological literature of the time minimized the cultural identities of many groups that appeared on the list and even claimed that some of them

had become culturally extinct, among them the numerous Ohlone peoples, the Esselen people, the Coast Miwok, many of the Central Valley Yokuts, the Yosemite area peoples, and others located in the coastal and gold-mining areas and therefore most heavily impacted by various regimes of colonialism. (Field 1999:198)

There exists a rather strong correlation between those native groups of the central and southern California coast receiving land allocations from the federal government and those Indian peoples intensively studied by Berkeley anthropologists. In the case of the Luiseño and Diegueño peoples, the prior existence of Indian reservations in southern California helped attract Berkeley anthropologists; the resulting publications and dissemination of information about these peoples caused, I believe, a positive synergy in which their status as legitimate Indian groups continued to be enhanced over time. It is probably no accident that additional land allocations were made to these southern California groups after a flurry of seminal Berkeley publications began appearing, in 1908 (e.g., Du Bois 1908; Kroeber 1908; Sparkman 1908; Waterman 1910). Similarly, it is probably not a coincidence that the Kashaya Pomo were allocated their rancheria a short time after Samuel Barrett and other U.C. researchers began working with them.

The unacknowledged status of most Ohlone, Esselen, Salinan, Chumash, and Gabrielino peoples today is related, in part, to ethnographic practices of the early 1900s. Because Kroeber and other prominent anthropologists viewed them as either culturally extinct or as cultural admixtures, they ignored these groups and turned their full attention to more "pure" Indian groups in other parts of the state. John P. Harrington from the Smithsonian Institution filled this void; however, in retrospect, this turned out to be an unfortunate turn of events for the central coast Indians: given the animosity between Kroeber and Harrington, once the latter claimed the central coast as his ethnographic territory, future Berkeley students would shy away from the region as long as Kroeber directed the University of California at Berkeley ethnographic program. Harrington proved a tireless and meticulous fieldworker, and his extensive field notes are today providing anthropologists and Indians with a plethora of information on native cultural practices of the central coast. But his secretive behavior and refusal to publish or share his field data did little to help the cause of local Indians in the early decades of the twentieth century. He kept his volumes of field notes—which could have provided critical information about the deep histories of central coast peoples—locked away, while decisions were being made about federal land grant allocation.

What the Indian peoples of the central coast desperately needed in the early 1900s was such a vocal and effective advocate as Helen Hunt Jackson. Had some highly visible ethnographic reports been forthcoming on their unique histories and cultures, they might have been in contention to receive federal land allocations; without such legitimizing support, they were doomed to oblivion and second-class status. As a consequence, many exneophyte communities of the northern missions had no land to call their own in the late nineteenth and early twentieth centuries. They continued to split apart, eventually breaking up into smaller family units.[14] If land had been obtained at this critical time in their history, the circumstances of the central coast Indians would be very different today. In considering the history of the Chumash people at the Santa Ynez rancheria, we can see what a significant difference a small land base can make—what a difference it *has* made in the continuation of this vibrant Indian community.

THE BIGGER PICTURE

Federal Indian policies in the late 1800s and early 1900s were diverse, conflicted, and mostly detrimental to Indian culture. At the same time that land was allocated to some homeless California Indians,[15] government agents initiated a program to reduce the land base of tribes across the country and to assimilate them into mainstream America. With the passage of the 1887 General Allotment Act,[16] Congress authorized the break-up of communal reservation lands into individual and family allotments of 32-hectare (80-acre) and 65-hectare (160-acre) plots to promote the supposed benefits of private ownership. Although some of the original California reserves in southern California were subjected to the 1887 Act (specifically, the Rincon, Morongo, and Pala reservations), the overall impacts of the privatization of reservation land were felt more widely among Indian tribes in other states (Castillo 1978:117; Parman 1994:1–10; Rawls 1984:211). Other government initiatives quickly followed (e.g., the Indian Appropriation Act of 1907), aimed at facilitating non-Indian access to tribal lands through leasing and purchase of allotments and through sale of surplus reservation land (Kelly 1988; Parman 1994).

These changes in the trust status of reservation lands were part of a broader package of forced assimilation that included prohibitions of native ceremonies and dances, of traditional curing practices, and even of Indian dress and language (Berthrong 1988:262; Castillo 1978:120). The cornerstone of this assimilation program was the government day- and boarding schools where Indian children were taught the virtues of Anglo-American life ways. Most of these government schools stressed a vocational (manual labor) curriculum that taught agricultural and ranching skills to boys and housekeeping duties (cooking, sewing) to girls (Berthrong 1988:262; Hagan 1988:58). Like the old Franciscan missions, the government boarding schools were designed to separate Indian children from their tribal relatives to facilitate the children's enculturation into the Anglo-American mainstream. This program of forced assimilation (privatization of reservation land, persecution of Indian religions and customs, de-emphasis of Indian languages) directed federal Indian policies until the 1930s, when significant reforms were made under Indian Commissioner John Collier and the Indian Reorganization Act of 1934. With the advent of a new policy of cultural pluralism, local tribal governments were revitalized, granted more autonomy, and allowed greater economic development (see Nash 1988; Parman 1994:89–106).

I find it ironic that, during the period when the federal government supported such a rigorous assimilation policy (from about the 1880s to approximately 1930), land grants to homeless California Indians were based on perceptions of how closely they conformed to being "real" Indians. It appears that federal Indian agents selected the most traditional groups for land allotments, with the idea that these groups would then be subjected to the assimilation program of the Bureau of Indian Affairs; native peoples already exhibiting clear signs of acculturation or cultural admixture received little attention from these agents. Therefore it is not surprising that early anthropological research played a critical role in the decision-making process for land allocations to Native Californians. Kroeber and his U.C. Berkeley colleagues crystalized ideas of Indianhood extant in the late 1800s and early 1900s into a cohesive model of how Native Californians were supposed to look and behave.

This tribelet model has greatly influenced our conceptualization of California Indians. It assumes that Indian peoples would be organized into small, autonomous polities, would speak their native languages, would participate in traditional ceremonies and dances, and would maintain some core of "Indian" material culture and food ways. As outlined throughout this book, some coastal native peoples fit this conceptual image better than did others, and the fit depended mostly on the outcome of a people's encounters with Franciscan missionaries and Russian merchants. Those peoples that fit the tribelet model were rewarded with land, tribal sovereignty, and government support, while those that did not were forced to split into small family groupings and retreat into coastal urban centers to survive.

9 Conclusion

The central thesis of this book is that we need to take a long-term diachronic perspective on the rise and fall of colonial frontiers in order to understand the status of Indian communities today—to know why some native groups are federally recognized and others remain unacknowledged. California offers a tremendous opportunity for examining how native entanglements with missionary and mercantile colonies produced a diverse range of multicultural experiences that reverberate among Indian populations to this day. Although both the Hispanic and Russian colonial regimes exploited Indian people, the ultimate goal of each was quite different: the Franciscan padres attempted to convert and civilize the Indians; the managers of the Russian-American Company used them as political allies and then as laborers in a final bid to wring profits out of its California mercantile enterprise. Native people swept into the Franciscan missions were subjected to an energetic crusade of conversion and civilization, a massive resettlement program, forced labor, scrutiny under Indian *alcaldes,* and the demographic disaster of catastrophic mortality rates accompanied by highly skewed sex ratios. Indians in the Russian frontier did not encounter formal enculturation, or resettlement programs per se, but they faced a challenging labor regime, poor working conditions, declining population, and heavy recruitment of native women to live with colonial men.

There are many benefits to undertaking cross-cultural comparisons of native peoples who encountered different kinds of colonial regimes. Comparative studies provide the broader cultural context necessary for understanding the range of native responses to colonization, for examining similarities and differences in the outcomes of native and colonial entanglements, and for identifying larger social processes in how natives negotiated missionary and mercantile colonies. But it is a daunting task to implement such a study. It is challenging enough to master the literature and resources of and about native peoples who were exposed to one colonial regime, without taking on an entirely new frontier of scholarship. Like most scholars studying colonialism in North America, I was perfectly content to focus my attention on one colonial program, Colony Ross, thereby maintaining my status in the field as a midsize fish in a relatively small pond. Yet to address the question of why some native groups became federally recognized and others did not, I decided to launch a comparative analysis of Colony Ross and the Franciscan missions. Although this venture proved most stimulating and insightful, I must confess that the extensive scholarship and rich literature on Spanish and Mexican California literally overwhelmed me on occasion.

A significant finding that I have made in developing my cross-cultural approach for comparing the Hispanic and Russian frontiers is that we need to broaden our conceptual thinking of what constitutes California's colonial history. This realization goes beyond the fact that most histories of colonial California relegate the Russian-American Company and its multi-ethnic workforce to a few peripheral paragraphs, in tomes of many hundreds of pages; rather, my point is that writers of most colonial histories continue to portray their subjects from a European perspective drawn largely from archival documents. Also, although native oral histories and native oral traditions are beginning to receive some attention, the findings of hundreds of archaeological projects across the state remain largely ignored. We need to reconceptualize the writing of colonial histories, so as to provide a firm foundation for the inclusion of these diverse data sources. I believe that the systematic integration of historical documents, native narratives, and archaeology will alter some of our current perceptions about California's past; not only will traditional historical scenarios be reevaluated and new and provocative interpretations be generated, but we will see the construction of multiple histories from the distinct vantage points of the pluralistic populations who made up California colonial communities.

The cross-cultural comparative approach employed in this book revolves around the triumvirate of historical anthropology, multidimensional analysis, and a long-term diachronic perspective. The holism of historical anthropology draws on sources from ethnohistory, ethnography, native texts, and archaeology to construct a more balanced and multi-voiced perspective of the past. It is the most powerful approach for studying the past outside of H.G. Wells's time machine. In this approach, European written accounts are employed primarily to construct the "intended" colonial structures of the Franciscan padres and Russian managers. Native texts and archaeological findings are then used to examine how these colonial structures were actually negotiated in the practice of daily living by native peoples. The extensive research undertaken on archaeological sites in the Hispanic and Russian frontiers over the last twenty-five years proved similarly indispensable to my study; using the practice-based perspective of archaeology, I was able to synthesize new insights on the organizational structure, food ways, material culture, and ceremonial rituals of Indian communities in the missions and at Colony Ross.

The multidimensional aspect of the comparative approach is its structure around seven dimensions of colonial encounters, which serve as the primary variables in my analysis of the Hispanic and Russian frontiers. I consider how native peoples mediated in practice the structures of domination unleashed by missionary and mercantile agents by examining the enculturation programs, native relocation programs, social mobility, labor practices, interethnic unions, demographic parameters, and chronology of colonial encounters. The diachronic aspect of the comparative approach not only considers colonial encounters among Indians, missionaries, and merchants, but extends the analysis into the colonial aftermath when tribal peoples confronted federal Indian agents and anthropologists in the late nineteenth and early twentieth centuries.

Using this comparative methodology, I trace the distinctive outcomes for the coastal hunter-gatherer peoples associated with the southernmost missions, the northern missions, and Colony Ross. The specific conclusions of my study are as follows.

I find—in contrast to some scholars—little evidence to support the assertion that the coastal Indians of central and southern California had become culturally extinct or entirely "Hispanicized" as a consequence of their colonial experiences. Instead, indigenous peoples reproduced their Indian identities and cultural practices across the Hispanic and Russian frontiers. Yet, in this process, significant cultural transformations emerged among native groups as they created new kinds of Indian identities, social forms, and tribal relationships. The interplay of key dimensions of colonial encounters—native relocation programs, demographic parameters, social mobility, and chronology—provides an analytical framework for understanding why divergent forms of Indian organization took place. Specifically, I outline three basic processes of culture change that unfolded in the California frontiers.

The first process involves the massive resettlement program, initiated by the padres of the northern missions, that wrenched Miwok, Ohlone, Esselen, Salinan, Chumash, and Gabrielino peoples from their homelands and assembled them together in sizeable neophyte villages. These new communities were created by literally throwing together strangers from different homelands, language groupings, and polities. The combination of population aggregation, chilling mortality rates, competition between traditional native leaders and new Indian officials, and successive generations of neophytes being born and raised in the missions had significant consequences for these hunter-gatherer peoples. What emerged were new marriage patterns that linked people from distant polities and homelands, the rise of novel forms of factional groups, and the creation of social affiliations and kin relations that cut broadly across neophyte communities. Neophytes no longer identified themselves by particular tribal polities or ancestral homelands; instead, they took on more generalized Indian identities linked to the missions in which they grew up. Yet my analysis suggests that the mission Indians maintained strong and vital Indian communities behind the closed doors of the neophyte quarters, where they partook of Indian foods, games, ceremonies, and ritual observances.

The second process commenced among the Luiseño and Diegueño Indians associated with Mission San Luis Rey and Mission San Diego. Here, the Fernandinos implemented a modified native relocation program that not only allowed many Indians to maintain their residences in ancestral homelands but presented opportunities for native leaders to retain their status and power in their neophyte communities. These developments, in combination with a less drastic demographic collapse than in other neophyte communities, and a greater continuity of traditional marriage patterns, presented the opportunity for native peoples to perpetuate, to some degree, local native polities, leadership positions, economic practices, and ceremonial cycles. Significant transformations did take place with respect to the adoption of new agricultural practices, the mastery of new crafts, the gain of fluency in Spanish, and the incorporation of some aspects of Catholic symbols and rituals into native belief systems. But rather than adopting a more generalized "pan-mission" identity, the southernmost Indian peoples apparently maintained close associations with their polities and with the villages and homelands where they were born.

The third process involves the consolidation of formerly autonomous polities into the emerging "tribal" organization of the Kashaya Pomo. Local native peoples responded creatively to the Russian-American Company by maintaining residences both near and far from the Ross settlement. This settlement system allowed Kashaya men and women to rotate back and forth between being on the "front line" with the colonists and disappearing into the back country. At the same time, a prominent Kashaya leader, Toyon, enhanced his political stature and influence by becoming the spokesman to the Russian-American Company, an event that began the political consolidation of formerly autonomous polities into a united tribal organization. Population loss due to epidemics and other hardships probably accelerated these political and social transformations. What emerged during the twenty-nine years of Russian colonization was a new, more inclusive, Kashaya "tribal" identity that eclipsed in territory and population any of the precontact polities.

The new Indian identities, social relations, and tribal forms that took shape in the California frontiers became long-lasting structures that influenced how anthropologists, federal administrators, and the general public would perceive and respond to native peoples in the late nineteenth and early twentieth centuries. Although many factors influenced decisions about the federal recognition of individual Indian communities, a critical issue, as I have argued, was how gate-keeping authorities conceptualized "real" California Indian tribes. Here is where Alfred Kroeber and his colleagues at U.C. Berkeley played such a significant role, in classifying Californian Indians by language, culture area, and polity. For they constructed a tribelet model that envisioned traditional California Indian societies as small-scale entities in which members spoke the same language, lived in tightly defined communities, participated in a shared set of cultural practices (food ways, dances, ceremonies), and manufactured and used similar forms of material culture—and this tribelet model became, by the early 1900s, the yardstick for evaluating the authenticity of Indian descendant communities. Not only did this model influence where Berkeley ethnographers would conduct their research within the state but it also determined which groups would be labeled as "culturally" extinct.

Although Kroeber and his colleagues recognized that significant culture change had taken place among the Luiseño, the Diegueño, and the Kashaya Pomo, they observed enough community cohesion and "traditional" cultural practices to classify these as bona fide Indian groups. Kroeber dispatched graduate students from U.C. Berkeley to work with elders of these groups and to write ethnographic studies. The seminal publications that resulted continue to be used today, and they most certainly enhance the status and authenticity of these Indian peoples in contemporary California.

Such was not the case for the Indian survivors of the northern missions. The Indian groupings that emerged among the Miwok, Ohlone, Esselen, Salinan, Chumash, and Gabrielino peoples consisted of multi-ethnic communities and polyglot families, practicing a more generalized sense of Indianhood. These new forms of native organization varied so diametrically from the tenets of the tribelet model that Kroeber and other scholars believed groups thus organized could no longer be classified as indigenous. Instead, the scholars argued, the "real" Indians of these peoples had become extinct or "melted away" to live with other Indians or in Hispanic communities.

The pronouncement of Indian extinctions by authoritative anthropologists could only have hurt the chances that the Indian groups concerned would ever be recognized by the federal government. Although the Kashaya Pomo tribe was awarded a rancheria during the federal allotments of 1906–1930, and some southern California groups received recognition and increased their land holdings, the majority of the Indian survivors of the northern missions would never receive federal land allotments. Thus, if descendant communities in coastal California had not obtained a land base by the 1920s or 1930s, the chances of their receiving federal recognition were very slim. As outsiders continued to pour into the central and southern coasts, the surviving Indian communities were pushed from their land; the upshot was that most Indian settlements broke apart, people were forced to disperse, and communities fissioned into ever smaller family units.

Today, the Indian descendants of the northern missions face a very difficult task, in petitioning the Bureau of Indian Affairs for federal recognition: they must prove that they have maintained themselves as politically and culturally autonomous entities since the dawn of European colonization. But the findings of this book urge that we take into account the multiple and complex processes of change that transformed native peoples in the California frontiers; any consideration of Indian identities and tribal recognition in California must address the outcomes of native encounters with Franciscan padres, Russian merchants, Hispanic colonists, and Anglo-American settlers over the last 250 years. We should not expect that the complex, multicultural colonial experiences of native peoples would necessarily result in the discrete, small-scale, tightly integrated, native communities that Kroeber envisioned in his tribelet model. Although recognizing the important and pioneering contributions that Kroeber and other early ethnographers made to our understanding of Native Californians, we must rethink the legacy of viewing Indians as a static, traditional people. Native societies, both today and in the past, are dynamic and continually in transformation in relation to ever-changing social conditions. Constructing a more encompassing and inclusive historical perspective on California Indians means appreciating the many roads these people have traveled in getting to today.

Notes

1. With the passage of the California Native American Graves Protection and Repatriation Act of 2001 (California State Assembly Bill No. 978), the current two-tiered hierarchy of Indian tribes will probably become more complex once the new act is implemented. I predict that a three-tiered status system will unfold in California. Federally recognized tribes will maintain their high-status position. These extant corporate entities, along with an unknown number of "unacknowledged" tribes (the specific "acknowledged" tribes have yet to be named), will be recognized by the state of California. At the bottom of this pecking order will be those tribes not recognized either by the Bureau of Indian Affairs or by the State of California.

1. DIMENSIONS AND CONSEQUENCES OF COLONIAL ENCOUNTERS

1. In focusing on missionary and mercantile colonies, my intention is not to minimize the significant differences within each colonial institution or to ignore the deep antagonisms between the religious and secular communities within the Spanish frontier. I recognize that presidios and pueblos also incorporated native peoples as laborers, and that this is a critical research issue. But the Franciscan padres were given the primary responsibility for integrating Indians into the Spanish colonial system and this will be a primary focus of this book. I also recognize that other colonial institutions, such as ranchos, were created to integrate native peoples as laborers in colonial California, but my comparison will highlight the missionary and mercantile colonial programs.

2. Some government administrators viewed missions as potential sources of colonial citizens who would help populate the new colonies. It was expected that Christian Indians would serve as laborers and domestic servants, pay taxes, and even participate in militias to help protect colonial provinces from hostile forces. See Weber (1992:112).

3. There is a wealth of information on the varied missionary colonies of the French, British, Spanish, Russians, and Americans in North America. Some of the more readable accounts of Protestant, Catholic (Franciscan, Jesuit), and Russian Orthodox missionary activities, which provide details not presented here on the similarities and differences of their evangelical efforts, are in Axtell (2001), John (1996), Kan (1988:506), McEwan (1993), Milanich (1995:178–212), Taylor (2001), Weber (1992), and White (1991).

4. In using the term *mercantile* in this work, I refer to colonial activities pertaining to or connected with merchants or trade. Specifically, I am concerned primarily with commercial enterprises involved in the terrestrial and maritime fur trade in North America. My use of mercantile should not be confused with the more specific meaning of *mercantilism*, employed by economists and historians, that speaks of an integrated system of policies of protectionism, balance of trade, and political unification in the development of European nation states in the sixteenth, seventeenth, and mid-eighteenth centuries. I recognize that there is considerable debate about the meaning and usefulness of the concept of mercantilism (e.g., whether such integrated policies ever existed, how much they differed from later laissez faire practices, and whether the term should be avoided). See Coleman (1969), Harper (1969), Heckscher (1955, 1969), Judge (1969), Magnusson (1994), Minchinton (1969), and Wallerstein (1980:37). It is not my intent to enter into this debate, but only to note that some aspects of orthodox mercantilism may or may not apply to the fur trade companies mentioned in this work.

5. The movement of fur traders into the western United States and Canada took place rapidly. British and American fur companies continually searched for pristine rivers and creeks where new outposts could be established near untapped beaver dens. As local regions became hunted out, traders felt constant pressure to move into new territories before competitors did. In relatively short order, strings of trade outposts and rendezvous sites materialized across western North America, many hundreds of kilometers from the nearest "white" towns. The Lewis and Clark expedition in 1806 passed no fewer than eleven separate parties on the Missouri River who were trading for furs, with Arikara, Sioux, and Pawnee peoples (Swagerty 1988:361). By the mid-1830s most tribes in the intermountain West and the Northern Plains had access to trade outposts, placed in strategic locations on major rivers and their tributaries. See Ray (1988:336–338, 344–346) and Swagerty (1988:366, 369–370).

6. Most fur-trade companies were dependent on native producers to provide furs, hides, and robes. Although some native peoples incorporated fur trapping in their traditional seasonal round, other natives became procurement specialists dependent on white traders for goods and even food. See Kardulias (1990), Whelan (1993), and Wolf (1982). Still others served as day laborers or employees of fur-trade companies, paddling canoes, carrying freight, or providing supplies to outposts. See Swagerty (1988:365).

7. Although missionary and mercantile colonies were founded on different principles in regard to how native people were viewed and administered, these

colony types were not mutually exclusive. Colonial administrators sometimes dispatched priests to work with native peoples in mercantile colonies—as happened in New France, where the Jesuits worked side by side with traders. This also took place in Russian America, where fur companies supported, at least in principle, the missionary program of the Russian Orthodox Church. However, tensions often arose between the agents of the cloth and fur traders, because of their fundamentally divergent goals for colonialism and because they often disagreed in policy and practice on the treatment of native peoples. See Taylor (2001:107, 417) and White (1991:56–70). Missionaries accused mercantile companies of injustices stemming from the sexual abuse of native women and the exploitation of both men and women as expendable laborers. Merchants, in turn, often viewed the clergy as a hindrance to mercantile enterprises, especially when the priests attempted to protect their neophyte flocks from abusive labor practices. See, for example, Kan (1988:507).

8. The Bureau of Indian Affairs (2002:46328–46331) lists 108 federally recognized Indian entities for California. The count includes as three separate entities: the Capitan Grande Band of Diegueño Mission Indians of California; the Barona Group of Capitan Grande Band of Mission Indians of the Barona Reservation, California; and the Viejas (Baron Long) Group of Capitan Grande Band of Mission Indians of the Viejas Reservation, California. For a description of each federally recognized Indian group, see Kammeyer et. al. (2002:53–61).

9. The 2002 *Field Directory of the California Indian Community* (Kammeyer et al. 2002:41–46) presents a partial list of California Indian tribes who have either petitioned for federal recognition or remain unacknowledged. Of the eighty-one unacknowledged native groups listed in either category, thirty-nine groups, or a little under half, appear to be descendant communities of former mission Indians. For more information on contemporary Ohlone, Esselen, and Salinan descendant communities, see Field et al. (1992), Leventhal et al. (1994), Sayers (1994), and Yamane (2002:205–220).

10. These accounts provide periodic windows for observing the California colonies through time, beginning with the early visits of Jean Francois Galaup de La Pérouse in 1786, George Vancouver and Archibald Menzies in 1792–93, and George Langsdorff and Nikolai Rezanov in 1806, and including a whole cohort of visitors in the 1810s, 1820s, and 1830s. See La Pérouse (1989), Langsdorff (1968), Menzies (1924), Rezanov (1989a), and Vancouver (1954). The later visitors' accounts are especially germane for this study because these visitors often compared their observations of Colony Ross with their observations of visits to the northern missions near San Francisco Bay and Monterey Bay. See, e.g., Duhaut-Cilly (1999), Golovnin (1979), Kotzebue (1830), Lazarev (1989), and Lütke (1989).

11. This point is very much appreciated by contemporary historians who are reinterpreting the classic histories of colonial California written by Hubert H. Bancroft (1886b), Herbert E. Bolton (1921), Zephyrin Engelhardt (1908–15), Charles Lummis (1936), and Irving Richman (1911). Since the 1970s, new life has been infused in the study of California's colonial past by an active cohort of historians and historical anthropologists who have built upon Sherburne

Cook's (1943a) pioneering work that focused on native and European interactions. Edward Castillo (1978, 1989a), Lisbeth Haas (1995), Albert Hurtado (1988), Robert Jackson (1994, 1995), John Johnson (1982, 1989, 2001), Randall Milliken (1995), Douglas Monroy (1990), George Phillips (1975, 1990, 1993), James Rawls (1984), and others have put the native back into California history. These "new" historians present a more balanced consideration of the past, by carefully deconstructing European texts that make observations of native peoples, and by incorporating California Indian "voices" through native writings, oral histories, or oral traditions.

12. See especially Vansina (1985). However, the current consensus among scholars is that oral traditions cannot be taken at face value. In reality, such traditions are often representations of the past as told in the present, and, as contemporary remembrances, are subject to processes (memory loss, social and political reorientations, reevaluations of the past, and the like) that can modify, update, or restructure oral accounts over time.

13. With the development of practice theory, a substantial literature now exists on how the study of daily practices provides insights into peoples' cultural meanings and social identities. See, e.g., Bourdieu (1977, 1990), Giddens (1979), and Ortner (1984).

14. For examples of practice-based archaeological studies of colonial California, see Lightfoot, Martinez, and Schiff (1998), Lightfoot, Schiff, and Wake (1997), Martinez (1998), Silliman (2001a, 2001b), and Voss (2002).

15. For examples of mercantile colonial relations with local native peoples, see Lightfoot (1991:11–28), Swagerty (1988), Wagner (1998:437–442), and Whelan (1993).

16. An extensive literature discusses the diverse relocation programs employed by missions. See Graham (1998), Jackson (1994:13–54). Milanich (1995: 178–190), Saunders (1998:405), Spicer (1962:570–571), and Weber (1992: 107–108).

17. The kinds of colonial settings that encouraged the establishment of interethnic unions are explored in Deagan (1995:452), Fedorova (1973:206–207), Hoffman (1997:28), Wade (1988:24), and White (1991:68–70).

18. A rich literature exists on the role of disease in native depopulation. See, for example, Crosby (1986), Dobyns (1983, 1991), Dunnell (1991), Hull (2002), Ramenofsky (1987), and Smith (1987).

2. VISIONS OF PRECOLONIAL NATIVE CALIFORNIA

1. By genetic relationships, they did not mean genetic in the biological sense. Rather, they were looking for similarities and differences in cultural traits, and defining those groups that were culturally related to one another.

2. Here, *gentile* is used to define a basic unit of social organization, on the order of a clan or lineage. In later chapters, I will follow the contemporary usage of *gentile* in colonial California history to denote non-Christian Indian groups, or native peoples not yet integrated into a mission program.

3. The late prehistoric settlement pattern of the Santa Barbara mainland, and some of the larger Channel Islands, consists of a coastal landscape brimming with a few large settlements and many smaller villages. Some of the larger sites are interpreted as political and religious centers for nearby smaller villages, based on their size, architectural features, and artifact distributions. See Arnold (1990), Gamble (1991), and Johnson (1988). However, many questions remain about these southern coast maritime societies. A healthy debate is now taking place about when these complex political organizations first arose and about the causal factors stimulating their development. See Arnold et al. (1997), Gamble et al. (2001), King (1990), and Raab and Larson (1997). It is still not clear how the coastal villages were organized into local polities, whether these polities were incorporated into broader political confederacies or chiefdoms, or how much power and authority was actually invested in political and religious leaders. See, e.g., Arnold (2001), Gamble et al. (2001), and Johnson (1988).

4. Recent archaeological fieldwork has documented some of the earliest coastal sites in the Americas, with more than eighty-five sites recorded for the period from twelve thousand to seven thousand years ago. See Erlandson (1994), Erlandson and Colten (1991), Jones (1991, 1992), and Moss and Erlandson (1995).

5. A number of recent studies have examined the potential effects that early European exploration had on coastal Native Californians. See Erlandson and Bartoy (1995, 1996), Johnson (1982), Lightfoot and Simmons (1998), Milliken (1995), Preston (1996, 1997), Walker and Hudson (1993), and Walker and Johnson (1992, 1994); see also Hull (2002) for a study of interior California.

3. FRANCISCAN MISSIONS IN ALTA CALIFORNIA

1. The majority of the mission complex was reconstructed between 1934 and 1937; the reconstruction was based on standing architecture, archaeological research, and historical documents. See Neuerburg (1987) and Whitehead (1991). The detailed archaeological research at La Purísima was an exception for its time, as most mission reconstructions tended to emphasize destructive building projects, with little regard for historical accuracy. See Thomas (1991:140–142).

2. Regrettably, the La Purísima experience differs from that of other reconstructed missions. Many of the old Franciscan estates have been literally swallowed by housing developments, streets, and noisy traffic, and only small portions of the mission complexes have been saved and/or restored for interpretive purposes. In these urban settings, it can be tough to appreciate fully the immense scale of the missions and their lands. A similar experience to that at La Purísima can be had by hiking the interpretive trail around Mission San Antonio, which contains an impressive number of intact archaeological features.

3. Excavations in 1998–99 suggest that this archaeological feature may be the foundations of a wind-powered post mill for the beating and washing of woolen textiles. This mill was possibly built by an American adventurer, or by Russian deserters from Colony Ross, in the early 1820s (Hoover 2002).

4. A number of excellent publications exist on the early European explorers and their voyages. See, for example, Bolton (1916), Engstrand (1997), Kelleher (1997), H. Kelsey (1979, 1998), Mathes (1968), Quinn (1979a, b, c, d, e, f, g), Von der Porten (1973), H. Wagner (1924), M. Wagner (1929, 1931, 1941), and Ziebarth (1974).

5. See Fray Andrés de Aguirre's 1584–85 letter to the Archbishop of Mexico, in Quinn (1979b).

6. Bill Simmons and I have analyzed these early encounters between European voyagers and Native Californians elsewhere (Lightfoot and Simmons 1998). European accounts of the voyages and archaeological research indicate that native peoples exhibited a keen interest in the material culture of the foreigners. For example, excavations of Coast Miwok villages north of San Francisco Bay unearthed ample evidence of sixteenth-century iron spikes, Asian ceramics, wax, and other objects. It appears that local natives went to considerable effort to salvage the cargo and hardware of Sebastian Rodríquez Cermeño's ship, the San Agustín, which sank during a storm in Drakes Bay in 1595. See Lightfoot and Simmons (1998:153–161).

7. During the late sixteenth and seventeenth centuries, native peoples along the Pacific Coast may have encountered stranded Manila galleons, Portuguese vessels, or even Chinese and Japanese vessels blown off course. Although Manila galleons tended to sail down the coast of California well beyond its rocky shores and reefs (Schurz 1917), there are several reported shipwrecks of Spanish merchant ships in Alta and Baja California waters (Johnson 1982:20, 30–32; Walker and Hudson 1993:20–21), including a native woman's account to Vizcaíno of a shipwreck near Santa Catalina Island (Bolton 1916:85). Erlandson and Bartoy (1996:305) report a 1630s Portuguese shipwreck on the Oregon coast. There is also the possibility that undocumented Asian vessels may have visited the California coast prior to European colonization, as suggested by several instances when storms brought fishing ships to the Golden State in the 1800s (as noted in, e.g., Heizer 1941:323).

8. Hutchinson (1969:1–42) presents an excellent account of Spain's growing apprehension of Russian expansion along the Pacific coast in his chapter "The Russian Lever."

9. For a more detailed discussion on the colonization of Sinaloa, Sonora, and Baja California, see Jackson (1994), Mason (1998:11–18), and Mathes (1989).

10. The Port of San Blas, with its small fleet of ships, shipyard for repairing and building new vessels, storage facilities, and naval center became an indispensable link in the successful exploration and settlement of Alta California. The San Blas fleet performed the yeoman's duty of transporting people, mail, food, and manufactured goods to the new colonies. Jean Francois de La Pérouse, a French naval officer who visited Alta California in 1786, described this fleet as consisting of four corvettes (three-masted ships with a single deck) of twelve guns, and a schooner (La Pérouse 1989:74–75). The diaries and letters of missionaries and civil administrators in Alta California are replete with references

to the critical importance of the supply ships, especially in the early years of the colonies before agricultural production was fully developed.

11. In retrospect, the isolated nature of the California frontier with respect to both Spain and New Spain proved a major obstacle in the colonization of California. The Gálvez/Croix plan would probably not have succeeded without the Franciscans. The sea route from San Blas was long and arduous, as ships sailing against the prevailing northern winds often took three to four months to travel only sixteen hundred kilometers to Alta California (Costello and Hornbeck 1989:310; Margolin 1989:14–16). Scurvy was a constant problem, unexpected storms blew ships off course, and the difficult voyages were exacerbated by crews that consisted primarily of petty criminals and Mexican fishermen, shanghaied to work on the vessels (Stanger and Brown 1969:31). These conditions were not conducive for convincing Hispanic settlers, self-identified as the *gente de razón,* to move to Alta California where they would have to live in an isolated backwater. David Weber succinctly makes this point in considering the difficulties of populating Alta California with Hispanics either from the motherland or from Spain's other American colonies.

> Even with vigorous recruiting, however, they attracted only a few artisans and their families, who stayed for several years to instruct Indians in crafts, and a token number of colonists from New Spain desperate to better their conditions. No single women responded to Gov. Diego de Borica's requests for "young healthy maids." Unable to find volunteers, officials sent married convicts, prostitutes, orphan boys and girls, and other unfortunates to New California, where they might be rehabilitated and increase the Hispanic population at the same time. The province developed an unsavory reputation as a Spanish Botany Bay, which diminished still further its appeal to potential immigrants. (Weber 1992:264–265)

12. During the period 1774 to 1834, the Dominicans founded an additional nine mission communities in Baja California. See Jackson (1994:36).

13. There is some confusion about the assignment of Mission Santa Cruz to the presidio district of either San Francisco or Monterey. It appears the mission fell within the jurisdiction of the Presidio of San Francisco, but Hubert Bancroft included it in the Monterey Presidio District when he calculated mission populations and other statistics in his pioneering historical analysis. See Bancroft (1886a:145, 154, 376).

14. As Costello and Hornbeck (1989:310–313) stress, much of our understanding of the physical configuration of mission complexes has come from archaeological excavations, as well as from contemporary visitors' descriptions. There is a wealth of information from archaeological excavations about the building materials, dimensions of rooms and structures, construction techniques, remodeling episodes, and spatial organization of residences, storage facilities, work areas, and religious space. See, for instance, Allen (1998:52–53),

Costello (1989a), Deetz (1963), Farnsworth (1987), Farris (1991), Farris and Wheeler (1998), Felton (1987), Greenwood (1975, 1976), Hoover and Costello (1985), and Skowronek and Wizorek (1997). It often took ten to thirty years to construct the full complement of buildings and facilities associated with a single mission complex. See Jackson and Castillo (1995:25). In their year-by-year inventory of the structures and facilities built at twenty of the missions, Jackson and Castillo (1995:145–168) show that much of the initial construction focused on the church and central quadrangle buildings, followed by work on outlying industrial workshops and on Indian housing.

15. Captain George Vancouver (1954:43) and Archibald Menzies (1924:279), in their visit to Mission Santa Clara in 1792, also reported two-room apartments that were being built for some neophyte families.

16. The agricultural program involved planting extensive fields of wheat and corn and smaller crops of barley, beans, and peas. After experimenting with agrarian practices and irrigation systems in a Mediterranean climate, the padres increased productivity immensely by multicropping in the winter, spring, and summer-fall. On the early, difficult years of mission agricultural production see Hornbeck (1985). Elaborate walled gardens, often containing reservoirs and *lavanderías*, were built for raising vegetables and for protecting orchards dotted with apple, cherry, almond, peach, olive, and pear trees. Archaeological investigations have recovered the ethnobotanical remains of a range of crops grown at the missions; these remains include wheat and barley grains, fava beans, peach pit fragments, olive pits, walnuts, pepper seeds, watermelon seeds, peas, almonds, cherry seeds, squash or pumpkin seeds, bottle gourds, beans, corn kernels, and carrot seeds. See Allen (1998:46), Farris (1991), Honeysett (1989), and Hoover (1980).

17. The missions would also serve as craft centers, especially after 1790, when the Spanish Crown supported a plan to transport artisans from Mexico to teach the mission Indians specialized skills that would increase the quality and diversity of goods produced in the mission shops. See Hackel (1997:120–121). Some colonists with blacksmith and carpentry skills had been recruited to the missions in the early 1770s (Serra 1955a:131), but the new recruits would greatly enhance the crafts program already in place. Schuetz-Miller (1994) presents an excellent and detailed discussion of the various artisans and craftsmen recruited to work in Alta California. About twenty stone-and-brick masons, carpenters, potters, shoemakers, millers, weavers, saddlers, blacksmiths, and leather workers arrived at the missions on four- or five-year contracts between 1791 and 1795, according to Bancroft (1888:615). With the infusion of these skilled workers and the rapid training of a few neophytes, the mission communities were soon producing soap, shoes, boots, saddles, beds, blankets, and even coffins, becoming "veritable general stores" that serviced Alta California colonists (Hackel 1997:116).

18. Hackel (1997:113–120) notes that by creating royal monopolies, restricting foreign access to the colonies, and allowing colonists to trade only with government-sanctioned merchants, a closed-door economic policy was implemented. This required that colonists produce raw materials and goods for the

mother country and purchase in return manufactured products (often made from the colony's raw materials) exclusively from her. Furthermore, the prices of food and goods in Alta California were strictly controlled by government agents (usually the provincial governors). See, for instance, Hackel (1997:118) and Monroy (1990:70). Consequently, there was no real market for surplus crops grown by pueblo producers. Without any profit motive, economic stagnation characterized the three pueblos until Mexican independence, when some of the restrictive trade policies were removed.

19. Spain's attention was diverted away from her American colonies by the Napoleonic Wars, which had disastrous consequences for King Carlos IV of Spain, forced to abdicate his throne to an invading French army in 1808. During this tumultuous time, a violent rebellion ignited in New Spain in 1810, ushering in an extended period of isolation for Alta California until Mexico gained its independence in 1821. The rebellion in New Spain and the geopolitical crisis in Spain cut off communication to Alta California; the supply ships from San Blas no longer sailed northward on a regular schedule with goods, government directives, and payrolls for soldiers and civil administrators. The colonists of Alta California were forced to conduct themselves as though they resided in an independent political entity, developing their own economic base through self-production and trade.

20. In 1823, most of the Franciscan padres signed three-year contracts with the British firm of McCulloch, Hartnell, and Company, contracts that guaranteed set prices for cattle products raised on the mission ranches (Costello 1992:68). However, the Mexican government imposed high customs duties on trade transactions, and smuggling continued to take place in secluded locations along the California coastline.

21. Hornbeck (1989:427–432) contends that, by the 1820s, the missions had made the transition from self-sufficient farms to commercial livestock enterprises. He argues that the missionaries became less focused on the acculturation of Indian people. Rather than employing surplus production to attract and support neophytes in the missions, the padres could now use this surplus to finance the acquisition of trade goods. See also Farnsworth (1987:618–620, 1992). Costello (1989b: 441–442), in undertaking an analysis of mission agricultural and livestock production, shows that there was a major drop in crop production after 1823, and that this trend was associated with a general reduction in numbers of livestock. She suggests that this was due, in part, to the liquidation of herds for the hide and tallow trade. Jackson and Castillo (1995: 15–26) argue that the decline in agricultural production was probably due to unfavorable climatic conditions and possibly to soil exhaustion, rather than to an overall reorientation of the missions to commercial livestock ranches; these authors further suggest that the decline in livestock herds might not have been due entirely to the hide and tallow trade, but also to factors such as Indian raiding. All these factors (participation in international trade, climatic variability, and raiding) probably contributed to the reduction of agricultural productivity and decrease in the size of livestock herds in the 1820s and early 1830s.

22. The enculturation program of the Fernandinos received a major boost from Viceroy Bucareli on May 6, 1773, when, at the urging of Father President Serra, a decree was issued that placed "the training, governance, punishment, and education of baptized Indians, and also Indians being prepared for baptism" under the exclusive control of the Franciscan missionaries (Guest 1989:28). The implication of this decree was that Native Californians who were baptized or preparing for baptism became the legal wards of the padres, and thus the padres could now protect them from abuse or mistreatment from Hispanic colonists or people of reason *(gente de razón)*. The decree also safeguarded the authoritative position of the padres, who interacted with the Indian converts in a very paternalistic manner, expecting native men and women to take on the subordinate relationship of "adult children." See Guest (1989:28–29).

23. Russian and French visitors to the missions were shocked by the padres' practice of separating young girls, and even boys, from their families. See Duhaut-Cilly (1999:114–115), Khlebnikov (1989:389), Kotzebue (1830:95), La Pérouse (1989:91), Lütke (1989:263–264), and Zavalishin (1973:380–381).

24. As Father Serra lamented to Viceroy Bucareli in a letter dated August 24, 1774, "if, for the said foundations, and for those as far as the Port of San Francisco, more soldiers are needed, as I suppose they are, let them not come from California, nor through it—that is, supposing they can come by way of the Colorado River Country. It would seem that with a lantern they pick out their very worst to send here" (Serra 1955a:143). See also Palóu 1926b:14–15 and 1955:119–120.

25. Colonial administrators attempted to modify the *reducción* program of the Fernandinos, but to no avail. Beginning in 1780, Teodoro de Croix, the first commandant general of the newly created Interior Provinces, initiated fundamental changes in the composition of the missions as he "deplored the coercive nature of traditional missions, and he regarded mission Indians as worse off than slaves" (Weber 1992:257). Two new missions were established on the California side of the Colorado River among the Yuman Indians, based on a new principle of missionization in which

> [t]here was to be no presidio; but eight soldiers and eight married
> colonists with their families were to be at each mission; a sergeant
> at one mission, and an ensign at another. These were to act as com-
> mandants. The missionary fathers were to take care only of spiritual
> matters, and the pagans who were baptized should continue to live
> in their villages and maintain themselves as in the days of their
> paganism. (Palóu 1955:216–217)

Unbeknown to the Fernandinos in Alta California, Commandant General de Croix and California Governor Neve had decided to establish three new missions on the Santa Barbara Channel using the same principle as employed on the Colorado River (Palóu 1955:231–232). However, in 1781, before this new plan could be implemented, the Yuman Indians revolted, burning down the new towns, clubbing the four missionaries to death, and killing many of the Spanish soldiers and colonists (Weber 1992:256–258). The Yuman rebellion not only closed the road that De Anza had opened from Sonora to Alta California in 1774 but also deflated the resolve of the key administrators to alter the reduction program of the Fernandinos. When the California padres found out about the plan, they refused to participate in the founding of the new missions. They argued

> that under the new method they would not be able to effect the conversion of the pagans living along the channel (which is the desire of His Majesty), for they were the same type of Indian as in other parts of New California. They are in the central part of the conquered land. They can be conquered first only by their interest in being fed and clothed, and afterwards they gradually acquire the knowledge of what is spiritually good and evil. If the missionaries had nothing to give them, they could not win them over. If the Indians did not live in a town within hearing of the mission bell, but rather in their villages after the fashion of their pagan days, naked and hungry, the missionaries would not be able to get them to leave off their vicious pagan practices. (Palóu 1955: 231–232)

The combination of the stiff resolve and protests lodged by the Fernandinos, and the disastrous outcome of the Colorado River experiment, provided the impetus to continue the old way of establishing missions in Alta California.

26. Margolin cites President Fermín Lasuén's statement about the difficulties of transforming "a savage race such as these into a society that is human, Christian, civil, and industrious": "This can be accomplished only by denaturalizing them. It is easy to see what an arduous task this is, for it requires them to act against nature. But it is being done successfully by means of patience and by unrelenting effort" (Father Fermín Lasuén, quoted in Margolin 1989:33).

27. A steady decline in the overall number of neophytes in the mission system took place during the 1820s and early 1830s. The total number of mission Indians in the 21 missions plummeted from 20,301 people ($\bar{x}$ = 968) in 1825, to 18,117 people ($\bar{x}$ = 863) in 1832, and to 15,225 people ($\bar{x}$ = 721) in 1834 (Jackson 1994:60).

28. Governor José María de Echeandía, dispatched by the Mexican government in 1825 to govern Alta California, began experimenting with the emancipation of neophytes in 1827 by granting freedom to those individuals with specialized skills who could be self-supporting (Haas 1995:34). In 1831, this program was modified to allow married couples who had been in the missions for ten or more years, or parents who had become widowed with children, to leave the missions.

29. For discussions and statistics on interethnic marriages in colonial California see Castaneda (1997:241), Hurtado (1988:23, 25, 170), Mason (1984:133–134; 1998:21, 63, 70), Meighan (1987:198), and Milliken (1995:102, see footnote 3). But see Kelsey (1985:510) for cautionary note.

30. The padres, as well as visitors to the missions, commented on the paucity

of medicines and the general lack of "physicians" or "surgeons." See Archibald (1978:179–180), Chamisso (1986:244–245), Geiger and Meighan (1976:64, 75–76), Jackson and Castillo (1995:42), and Langsdorff (1968:208–209).

31. For discussions of these two consequences, see Allen (1998:13), Archibald (1978:181), Farnsworth (1987:95), Heizer (1978c:126), Jackson (1994:37, 164), Jackson and Castillo (1995:52–53), Margolin (1989:33), and Phillips (1993:44–46).

32. A number of excellent demographic studies have shown this trend. See Cook (1976a:11–12), Jackson and Castillo (1995:56–58), Johnson (1989:372), and Walker and Johnson (1992:135–136; 1994:117–118).

4. NATIVE AGENCY IN THE FRANCISCAN MISSIONS

1. For recent perspectives on Franciscan recruitment and native involvement in the missions, see Archibald (1978:173), Haas (1995:19–22), Hoover (1989:397), Jackson and Castillo (1995:107–108), Johnson (1989:367), Margolin (1989:28,31), Monroy (1990:32–33), Phillips (1975:22–24), Sandos (1991:68), Shipek (1985: 489), and Weber (1992:106–108,115–116).

2. The following accounts provide some insights into this process of recruitment.

The natives did not show themselves during those days, since the many volleys of artillery and muskets fired by the soldiers had frightened them. But they began to approach after a little while, and the Venerable Father began to offer them gifts to bring about their entrance into the fold of Holy Church and gain their souls, which was the principal purpose of his presence. (Father Serra at the founding of Mission San Carlos de Monterey in 1770; in Palóu 1955:94)

As soon as Mass was over, he commenced to show friendliness and give presents to this pagan, with the purpose of attracting the others through him. He succeeded, for on that very day, attracted by curiosity, many approached. Lacking an interpreter, he let them know through signs that the Spaniards had come here to become their fellow citizens and to live in those lands. They gave signs of esteeming him greatly, proving this by the frequent visits they made and the gifts of pine-nuts and acorns they offered, which, together with other wild seeds (from which they make their flour for food), they gather in abundance. The Venerable Father and the others returned these amenities by giving them strings of shells or necklaces of varicolored glass, together with samples of our corn and beans, of which those Indians immediately become fond. (Father Serra at the founding of Mission San Antonio de Padua in July, 1771; in Palóu 1955:111)

[W]hen the Venerable Father found himself without the earlier difficulties, with an abundance of foodstuffs and clothing, he cast the net among the pagans, inviting them to the missions. So many of them came that every day he had a great circle of catechumens whom, with the aid of an interpreter, he instructed in the catechism and the required mysteries of the Faith. In this holy exercise he employed the greater part of his day. And as they became sufficiently instructed, he baptized them; and in a short time the number of Christians was greatly increased, so that while he was baptizing some, others were coming in search of instruction. (Father Serra involved in the recruitment program at Mission San Carlos de Monterey; May, 1774; in Palóu 1955:157)

3. Recent analyses of marine sediment cores from the Santa Barbara Basin (between the Santa Barbara coast and the Channel Islands) demonstrate the presence of the unique pollen grains of *Erodium cicutarium*, a Mediterranean annual, in deposits dating between 1755 and 1760 (Mensing and Byrne 1998). These findings indicate that when Mission San Diego was founded, in 1769, this old-world plant had already spread more than three hundred kilometers to the north. Scott Mensing and Roger Byrne (1998: 760–761) believe that *Erodium* invaded the California grasslands from the Baja California missions.

4. Archaeological studies of ethnobotanical and pollen remains indicate major changes in vegetation near some missions, with native oaks replaced by introduced grasslands (Costello 1989a:88).

5. Interestingly, Hispanic settlers also experienced problems with these ecological transformations. Auguste Duhaut-Cilly (1999:144) presents a vivid description of a "forest of mustard" (probably fennel) that had become a "terrible scourge" near the Pueblo of Los Angeles by 1827, and of how local settlers were unable to eradicate this pest from their pastures.

6. Unfortunately, the specific mortality rates of outlying gentile villages remain unknown, given the current status of archaeological and biological anthropological studies of these populations.

7. Hurtado (1988:23) suggests that, with increasing disease and death in gentile communities, some peoples may have begun to question the utility of their old ways of life, thereby enhancing the appeal of the missionaries.

8. One of the best-known resistance leaders was Estanislao, a former *alcalde* from Mission San José, who chose to become a fugitive when the furlough to his homeland ended in 1828. Attracting a large group of escaped neophytes and allied interior Indians to his cause, he built a fortified village near the Stanislaus River that withstood several attacks by Spanish soldiers and Indian auxiliary forces who tried to dislodge him. Estanislao was eventually forced to flee his fort when a well-armed attack led by Mariano G. Vallejo proved too much for his defenses, and he returned to Mission San José, where he was granted sanctuary by the padres (Holterman 1970a). Another well-known resistance leader was Yozcolo, an *alcalde* from Mission Santa Clara, who escaped into the interior after raiding the mission stores and releasing two hundred young women from the *monjerio*. He attracted a band of compatriots who harassed

the missions and ranchos, until Spanish soldiers eventually captured him in 1839 (Holterman 1970b).

9. Pablo Tac was one of two Indian boys from Mission San Luis Rey chosen to accompany Father Antonio Peyri to the Franciscan mission college of San Fernando in Mexico City in 1832–34 and to Rome in 1834. In Rome, Tac attended Urban College, taking courses in Latin, rhetoric, philosophy, and other subjects, but became ill with smallpox in 1840 and died in 1841. He wrote his account of Mission San Luis Rey sometime between 1834 and 1841. For a more detailed account of Tac's life, see Hewes and Hewes (1958).

10. Some of the stories recounted by Lorenzo Asisara, such as the assassination of Father Andrés Quintana in 1812, were told to him by his father Venancio Asar, a neophyte gardener at Mission Santa Cruz. I suspect that other stories, such as the cruelties of Father Ramon Olbés, also originated from Asisara's father or someone of that generation (see Castillo 1989a, b).

11. Julio César's account moves back and forth between events that happened at Mission San Luis Rey under the Fernandinos and those happening there under later Mexican administrators.

12. There is some question about the date and place of Librado's birth. Travis Hudson (1979:x) initially suggested that he was born in a native village on Santa Cruz Island sometime between 1804 and 1820. According to Hudson, Librado joined Mission San Buenaventura as a boy and many of his memories of the mission date to the 1830s. More recently, John Johnson (2001) pinpointed Librado's birth date to 1839, a date implying that Librado did not observe firsthand the neophyte community prior to secularization. Rather, his account describes Mission San Buenaventura in the immediate postsecularization period, but also incorporates stories of the Franciscans from before he was born, stories passed down by older mission Indians (Johnson 2001:58). In using Librado's narrative (Librado 1979), I recognize that he is largely describing the neophyte community of Mission San Buenaventura in the 1840s, when the mission community still existed but the Fernandinos had been replaced.

13. Costello's study focuses primarily on the *convento* of Mission Santa Inés, but it is useful for comparative purposes.

14. However, Allen (1998:60) finds little evidence of deep-water fish in the faunal remains recovered from Mission Santa Cruz, suggesting that most of the fishing involved shallow-water marine species.

15. In fact, Farnsworth's analysis indicates that neophytes at Mission San Antonio and Mission La Purísima retained "probably 50 percent or more" of their Indian material culture in the mission residences (Farnsworth 1987:620).

16. The much-feared Padre Ramon Olbés.

17. The period after 1810 was when Alta California became isolated from New Spain by civil war and the San Blas ships sailed to the northern frontier infrequently.

18. For example, Johnson (2001:58–59) describes several such neighborhoods established by Chumash Indians from the Channel Islands in missions in the Santa Barbara region.

5. RUSSIAN MERCHANTS IN CALIFORNIA

1. The Rotchev House is notable because it is the only structure in the park that was built by the Russian-American Company. Alexander Rotchev, the last Ross manager, refurbished an existing building in 1836 into a residence for his family. See Kalani et al. (1998:36). The other buildings in the stockade complex are reconstructions based on archival and archaeological research.

2. Russian entrepreneurs traded the sea mammal furs, along with sable, marten, and fox from Siberia, to Chinese merchants in Kiakhta, a small town on the Siberian-Chinese border, where the only legal trade between the two countries took place (Ogden 1941:1–14).

3. The directors were responsible for maintaining capital assets, for increasing profit margins, and for developing economic strategies for fur hunting and world trade (Dmytryshyn et al. 1989:xxxvii). They reported directly to the tsar and to certain government department heads on critical issues concerning the Company and Russia's American colonies.

4. During the first imperial charter of the Company (1799–1821), the board of directors and the chief manager were, primarily, civilian businessmen with considerable experience in the North Pacific fur trade. The board of directors selected, as their first chief manager, Aleksandr Baranov, a pragmatic and seasoned merchant with long service in commercial initiatives in Siberia and the North Pacific. However, with the increasing military interest in the Russian American colonies by the mid-1810s, the next two imperial charters for the Russian-American Company (in 1821 and 1841) stipulated that the tsar appoint chief managers from among senior Russian Imperial Navy officers (Dmytryshyn et al. 1989:xxxix). After the 1821 charter, a greater number of government officials and naval officers began serving terms on the board of directors (Gibson 1976:15).

5. The Russian-American Company, during its first two decades of operation (1799–1819), focused much of its attention on sea otter harvesting in Alaskan waters south of the Gulf of Alaska (that is, the waters of the Sitka coastline and southward), and in California (Fedorova 1973:107–109; Khlebnikov 1994:3–8).

6. The "fur rush" in the North Pacific exploded a year after Captain James Cook's well-publicized voyage to the Northwest Coast in 1778, when sea otter pelts obtained from natives in Nootka Sound were sold in Canton for phenomenal prices (Gibson 1988:379).

7. Furthermore, because they practiced highly diversified procurement practices, involving the exploitation of primarily coastal and terrestrial foods (rather than of pelagic resources), most coastal California groups placed less emphasis on the hunting of sea mammals than did North Pacific peoples. Even the maritime-oriented Chumash- and Gabrielino-speaking peoples focused little effort on the hunting of sea otters.

8. The first contract was initiated with Joseph O'Cain, who presented Baranov with an innovative plan for hunting sea otters on "a new island off the Cali-

fornia coast" (Khlebnikov 1994:8–9; Tikhmenev 1978:68). This contract plan provided the Americans with skilled hunters who could quickly harvest the California sea otter population, otherwise inaccessible to them. The plan also provided the Russian-American Company, which was very short on both ships and sailors in the early 1800s, with the means of transporting its hunters to California (Ogden 1941:45–47).

9. The initial "contract" hunting expedition was a great success: when Captain O'Cain returned the following year to Alaska, the crew had gathered eleven hundred pelts and purchased another seven hundred from the Fernandinos and local officials (Khlebnikov 1994:9). The total share for the Company from the "contract" hunts to 1813 was over eleven thousand pelts (Khlebnikov 1994:9–10).

10. While in Alta California, the charismatic Rezanov courted the beautiful Concepción Argüello (daughter of the Commandant of the Presidio of San Francisco), forged a friendship with Governor José Joaquin de Arrillaga, and skillfully negotiated the purchase of an entire cargo of foodstuffs grown at the missions in the San Francisco Presidio District. See Langsdorff (1968), Rezanov (1989a), Spencer Pritchard (1990:82–84), and Tikhmenev (1978:96–99). Specifically, Rezanov traded iron, iron utensils, work clothing, and other merchandise to the Spaniards for two thousand bushels of grain, five tons of flour, garden produce, salted meat, poultry, butter, tallow, and other goods (Russian-American Company 1989b:213; Spencer Pritchard 1990:83–84).

11. Rezanov recognized that regularized trade between the Russian-American Company and Spanish California would be beneficial for both. The Russians could obtain grains and beef from the missions at a relatively inexpensive price, and these could be readily transported to the Company's colonies in the North Pacific. The Franciscan fathers and Spanish officials, in turn, would obtain access to diverse merchandise not readily available in either Alta California or New Spain. Rezanov wrote the Viceroy of New Spain, José Iturrigaria, and Tsar Alexander I about the critical importance of forging trade relations between the Russian-American Company and Alta California (Rezanov 1989b, c).

12. Although the workers experienced some success in growing vegetables, primarily cabbage, turnips, radishes, and potatoes, grain production (wheat, rye, barley) proved frustrating and disappointing for most Russian colonies (Fedorova 1973:233,237; Gibson 1976:93–100; Khlebnikov 1994:178,181; Tikhmenev 1978:83–84). Similarly, although some cattle were raised on Kodiak Island, the difficulties of growing and preparing hay to feed cattle during the winter months made this enterprise extremely expensive (Fedorova 1973:239; Gibson 1976:101–106; Khlebnikov 1994:187; Tikhmenev 1978:84). Given that the higher northern latitudes were poorly suited for large-scale agricultural production and livestock raising, the Russian-American Company was forced to import most of its agrarian foods. As Gibson (1976:57–87) outlines in considerable detail, the Company attempted to import food from the agricultural belt of Russia, either over the precarious Siberian land route to the port of Okhotsk and from there on ships across the Sea of Okhotsk and the Bering Sea, or alternatively, through having merchants ferry goods around the world from the Baltic

port of Kronstadt. In either case, transporting food and goods from Russia proved extremely expensive and risky. Food typically spoiled en route; pack animals were lost on the long march across Siberia; and supply ships often sank in storms, especially in the unpredictable North Pacific waters.

13. Baranov instructed Kuskov, for the 1808 voyage, to hunt for sea mammals and "survey and describe the entire coast from the strait of Juan de Fuca to California, with complete accuracy placing on the charts plans of important sites such as harbors, bays and straits where there might be suitable anchorage, provided they have the means to carry out this assignment" (Baranov 1989:165). Baranov was especially interested in having Kuskov examine the coastal territory between San Francisco Bay and Bodega Bay, and he noted that the latter was supposed to be exceptionally rich in sea otters, according to the reports of Timofei Tarakanov, a Russian who had accompanied at least one earlier American "contract" hunting vessel to California (Baranov 1989:169–170).

14. In building the log structures, such as the Rotchev House, the carpenters cut and shaped each log individually so that each fit snugly with the ones below and above. The corners of the structures were formed by inserting the ends of the logs of one wall into the ends of the logs of another, forming a tight interlocking joint, which was sealed with clay and rope.

15. For example, Duhaut-Cilly, a French sea captain, made the following observation in 1828: "From where we had been lying to the settlement had quite a different look from that of the presidios of California, models of rude design and indifferent execution. Houses of elegant shape with roofs well constructed, fields well planted and surrounded by palisades gave this place an appearance that was quite European" (Duhaut-Cilly 1999:180).

16. In his 1828 visit to Ross, Duhaut-Cilly (1999:184) described the Russian Village: as "[o]utside the compound are lined up or scattered the pretty little houses of sixty Russian colonists." In 1833, Ferdinand Wrangell (1969:207) observed "two rows of small Company and private houses with gardens and orchards, occupied by employees of the Company."

17. Some accounts suggest they built Russian-style redwood log or plank houses, although other observations indicate that at least a few traditional semisubterranean *barabaras* (sod houses) or "flattened cabins" were also constructed (Blomkvist 1972:107; Duhaut-Cilly 1999:184; Fedorova 1973:359; Khlebnikov 1976:106b; Tikhmenev 1978:134).

18. Duhaut-Cilly (1999:184) contrasted the "conical huts of . . . many native Indians" to the "pretty little houses" of the Russian Village and the "flat huts of eighty Kodiaks" in the Native Alaskan Neighborhood.

19. The Coast Miwok are usually divided into two dialect groups: the Western or Bodega Miwok, centered around Bodega Bay, and the Southern or Marin Miwok, along the coast and valleys of what is now southern Marin County. See Kelly (1978:414). When the Russians built Port Rumiantsev on Bodega Bay, they became all too familiar to the local Bodega Miwok.

20. Nearby was a shed for protecting small boats and maritime equipment, as well as *baidarkas* not in use. The Company employed another shed to store

timber cut from the surrounding forests (Bancroft 1886a:630; Belcher 1843:315). Some of the wood might have been used in the shipyard, but much of it was earmarked for shipment to Alta California, Hawaii, and New Archangel. Cut planks, beams, and timbers were exported, as well as entire houses that were built and then disassembled for transportation (Duhaut-Cilly 1999:186). The Ross settlement was also a center for producing "oversized" fired bricks, and it is estimated that up to ten thousand were exported annually until the brickyard was moved to Bodega Harbor in 1832 (Gibson 1976:41; Khlebnikov 1990:135; Wrangell 1969:207). The exact location of the brickyards in either settlement is unknown. A wooden bathhouse was built into the side of the hill next to Fort Ross Cove; see Payeras (1995:332).

21. Watrous notes that the first known wind-powered flour mill in California was built north of the stockade complex in 1814, and that another windmill was added later and had the capacity to grind over thirty bushels of grain per day (Watrous 1998:15). The colonists installed a threshing machine in the 1830s that could clean one hundred bushels of grain per day (Belcher 1843:315).

22. By the early 1840s, the largest orchard supported 264 apple, pear, cherry, quince, and peach trees (Duflot de Mofras 1937:252).

23. By the 1840s, there were 1700 cattle, 940 mules and horses, and 900 sheep grazing in the hinterland of Colony Ross (Duflot de Mofras 1937:255).

24. By the 1830s and early 1840s, the merchants upgraded the port facilities to include: a large warehouse for storing grain, kegs of wine, hides, rigging, and other marine stores; three houses for accommodating the pilots and port captain, their wives and children, and visitors; a bathhouse; and at least two corrals for livestock (Belcher 1843:316–317; Duflot de Mofras 1937:7, 254; Vallejo 2000:1–2).

25. In the first six years, the hunters harvested twelve hundred to fifteen hundred fur seals each year, after which the yield decreased to two hundred to three hundred per year (Bancroft 1886a:633). About two hundred sea lions per year were garnered for use at the Ross Counter, and about five thousand to fifty thousand gulls were captured for meat, which was dried and shipped to Ross. The sea lion skins and sinews were essential for making *baidarkas*, while the sea lion and seal meat were salted or dried and, along with dried gull meat, transported to Ross as a principal dietary staple for the Company's workforce (Bancroft 1886a:633; Tikhmenev 1978:135). Sea lion bladders were used as watertight containers, sea lion guts for making waterproof outer garments *(kamleika)*, and seal and sea lion oil for lamps.

26. Company fur harvests yielded 877 prime/yearling otter pelts between 1812 and 1814, 153 in 1815, 97 in 1816, 55 in 1817, and only 13 in 1818 (Khlebnikov 1976:108). By 1817, some Company officials reported that sea otters had completely disappeared in the region from Trinidad Bay to San Antonio Bay, near the entrance to San Francisco Bay, while the number of fur seals on the Farallon Islands had been greatly reduced. See also Bancroft (1886a:634) and Tikhmenev (1978:135).

27. Earlier attempts at growing wheat and barley along the coastal strip had

met with only mediocre success. High winds and prevalent fogs reduced yields (Chernykh 1968:52–53). After the first few years of experimentation, the colonists established fields on nearby ridge slopes and ridge tops, above the fog belt of the coastal terrace, wherever they found pockets of tillable land. Eventually about thirty-three hectares of land were cultivated in the hinterland of the Ross settlement, with most of the small fields distributed within a three-kilometer radius (Gibson 1976:118; Khlebnikov 1976:117–119). By the mid-1820s and early 1830s, almost every plot of land within walking distance of the Ross settlement had been planted (Chernykh 1968:52; Gibson 1976:116; Kotzebue 1830:125).

28. The agricultural program in the Ross Counter was never very successful, and the colony never realized its full potential as the "granary to the colonies." A full discussion of the reasons underlying the failure of Ross agriculture is presented by Gibson (1976:113–140). Suffice it to say that poor yields resulted from outdated and labor-intensive agrarian methods, and from the combined effects of coastal fog, winds, and rodents. See, e.g., Khlebnikov (1976:121) and Tikhmenev (1978:135). Another significant problem in the Ross Counter was the inability to amass laborers to work in the fields and mills. The colony was chronically shorthanded. Until their secularization in 1834, Franciscan missions continually produced much higher yields than those reported for Colony Ross (Fedorova 1973:241; Gibson 1976:121). In some years, the wheat and barley crops in the Ross Counter were complete failures. Even in the best years, such as 1832, when the highest yields of wheat were produced, the Ross Counter still maintained a significant deficit (more than seventy-five hundred rubles) (Wrangell 1969:212).

29. The commander of the Presidio of San Francisco dispatched Ensign Gabriel Moraga to investigate in 1812, at which time he met with Kuskov and inspected the buildings and stockade of the Ross settlement. Upon returning home, Moraga met in person with Governor José Joaquin de Arrillaga about the situation. This meeting was followed by correspondence between Governor Arrillaga and Viceroy of New Spain Félix María Calleja del Rey, who in turn informed the Madrid government about the Russian problem. For details see Bancroft (1886a:300–303) and Hutchinson (1969:28–30). In early 1814, Governor Arrillaga sent Ensign Moraga and Gervasio Argüello to Colony Ross to make a formal request to the Russians to abandon their settlement immediately, before "the matter was brought to the attention of the national authorities." Kuskov responded, in a letter to the governor, that he did not understand the Spanish language sufficiently to justify an official action (Bancroft 1886a:303).

30. After Governor Arrillaga died in 1814, his successors, Acting Governor José de Argüello and Governor Pablo Vicente de Sola, made pointed requests, at the urging of the viceroy, for the Russians to withdraw from their California colony (Tikhmenev 1978:137–138). The Madrid government also sent official correspondence in 1817 to the Russian imperial government requesting that the tsar "indicate His supreme disapproval of such actions by ordering that measures be taken which in His wise judgement will result in their leaving this

place they have taken" (Bermudez 1989:248; Tatishchev 1989). The replacement of Viceroy Calleja with Juan Ruiz de Apodaca, in September 1816, resulted in a tougher Spanish policy in negotiating with the Russian-American Company. A plan was concocted between the new viceroy and Governor Sola in 1817 to force the Russians to leave Ross by launching a surprise attack with four ships and five hundred men. Since neither the governor nor the viceroy had the ships or men at their disposal, and Spain at this point confronted revolution in most of its American colonies, the fleet never sailed (Hutchinson 1969:37–39).

31. For example, working silently between dawn and noon so as to not alert the nearby Spaniards, four Unangans in two skin boats harvested either forty-two or seventy-two sea otters in a two-week period from the Russian ship, the *Kutuzov*, when it was anchored off Mission Santa Cruz in 1818 (Golovnin 1979:154; Lütke 1989:269). In another instance, Kuskov dispatched hunters in two *baidarkas* into the "rear" of San Francisco Bay while he and Otto Von Kotzebue met with Governor Sola about the status of Colony Ross and its infringement on Spanish territory (Chamisso 1986:109). Khlebnikov noted that Company ships sent to Alta California to purchase grain always carried two *baidarkas* for hunting purposes. "But eventually the Californians became suspicious, and this kind of hunting also came to a halt" (Khlebnikov 1976:110).

32. Some of the very finely crafted wooden benches and tables observed in the home of Luis Argüello, the commandant of the Presidio of San Francisco, were produced by a Russian captive (Spencer Pritchard 1990:86). A few of the prisoners, as well as deserters from Company ships or Colony Ross, were integrated into Spanish Californian communities. For example, a man from Kamchatka by the name of Bolcoff, who arrived on a Russian ship about 1815, was renamed José, had his Russian Orthodox baptism regularized by the Franciscans, married a Spanish Californian woman, and eventually became an *alcalde* in Santa Cruz (Farris 1989b:485).

33. The duties and fees charged in trade transactions could be used to pay the governor's and soldiers' salaries and to provide them with clothes, guns, ammunition, household equipment, and other necessary goods.

34. The missionaries' enthusiasm was not lost on the administrators of the Russian-American Company, who received communication in 1813 from a "California missionary who has influence on local authorities. The strong content is the same as that of the earlier response and carries a promise to supply our colonies with various necessities, without publicizing the matter, whenever our ship docks at the port of San Francisco" (Russian American Council 1989:206).

35. For example, in 1818 Fedor Lütke, a Russian naval officer on the sloop *Kamchatka*, observed how Governor Sola conducted transactions with Company agents.

All this while the Governor treated him [Hagemeister] very well and they parted friends, although he did reveal that he hoped this would be the last Russian ship [the *Kutuzov*] to come to Monterey

to trade; he said he permitted Hagemeister to trade this time only out
of personal respect for him. Of course this reply had a double meaning. Not only personal gain, but necessity forces the Spanish to want
foreign ships to visit; therefore one may hope that after this last ship,
permission will be given to one more and so on. Obviously, all of this
must be accomplished with skill and calculation. (Lütke 1989:263)

36. For example, when Otto Von Kotzebue visited the Ross settlement with
an honor guard of Spanish soldiers from the Presidio of San Francisco, the soldiers brought a number of old gun locks to be refurbished at the blacksmith shop
(Kotzebue 1830:123).

37. Furthermore, the new Mexican administration leveled a very hefty duty
fee of 25 percent for all goods sold in Alta California, 6 percent on goods purchased, in addition to an anchorage fee of 2½ piasters per ton (Khlebnikov
1990:119; 1994:115).

38. In 1835, Chief Manager Ferdinand Wrangell attempted to expand the
size of the Ross Counter by annexing much of the fertile land along the Russian River watershed. A tentative agreement was reached with Mexican officials
to allow the Russians to expand their agricultural production. But this agreement became null and void when Tsar Nicholas I refused to recognize the rev-
olutionary Mexican government (Gibson 1969:214).

39. The Russian Orthodox Church found it very difficult to recruit priests
to work as missionaries in Russian America. As Gibson (1992:20) cites one dea-
con, "[i]t is better to go into the army than to go to [Russian] America." The
sentiment is an indication of just how difficult and demanding life was in the
Russian colonies.

40. Father Sokolov was in charge of the spiritual affairs of the Sitka parish
until replaced in 1833 by Ivan Veniaminov. Father Sokolov apparently did not
invest much energy in missionary work. "Sokolov was described by Chief Manager of the Company Wrangell as 'a man of extreme negligence and remarkable unconcern' who for 15 years had 'done nothing' including teaching his own
children to read," notes Osborn (1997:189).

41. Mariano Payeras, the Father President of the Franciscan missions in Alta
California, interviewed Fedor Svin'in about church matters during Payeras's visit
to the Ross settlement in 1822.

I learned from him that in all the Russian domains baptisms are
legally performed and in confirmation he gave me proof of it: That
authorized by the Bishop who lives in Kodiak, he baptized in his
settlement as an emergency minister, and he marries people likewise
until a priest comes to do the rest. He notifies his commandant of
both actions, and in addition to noting it (Don Carlos confirms this)
he informs the governor at Sitka about it. (Payeras 1995:333)

42. I find it highly unlikely that the Indian convicts were baptized members
of the church, but possibly some of the women cohabiting with Native Alaskan,

Creole, or Russian men had become Christian converts. However, the only women listed in the Kuskov censuses (Istomin 1992) with Russian names—an excellent indicator of baptism and membership in the church, according to Fedorova (1975:12)—were those identified as Native Alaskan or Creole. Native Californian women, with few exceptions, were not listed by "Russified" or Christian names, but only by their Indian names, suggesting that they were not members of the local Russian Orthodox congregation.

43. James Gibson is even more conservative in estimating the number of Indian converts, suggesting that between the time the Ross chapel was built in 1824 and the abandonment of the settlement in 1841, "only some 40 Indians were converted to Russian Orthodoxy" (Gibson 1992:22, translator's note).

44. Father Mariano Payeras was told how this transaction took place by neophytes from Tomales Bay in 1822.

> The Christians of San Rafael, Vincente and Rufino of the Estero de San Juan Francisco Regis [Tomales Bay] opposite Bodega, say that it is true that the commander of a Russian ship named Talacani first came and stopped at Ross, and bought that place from its chief, Panac:úccux, giving him in payment three blankets, three pair of trousers, beads, two hatchets, and three hoes. Afterwards he went down to La Bodega and bought it from its chief, Iollo (he is already dead and his son Vali:ela is now chief) for an Italian-style cape, a coat, trousers, shirts, arms, three hatchets, five hoes, sugar, three files, and beads. This was not purchased, but rather it was like giving permission, and so the Indians would give them help. It is said that they did buy Ross, but only Ross, not the neighboring places. (Payeras 1995:335)

An analysis of the Payeras passage by Glenn Farris suggests that Talicani was really Timofei Tarakanov, the experienced Russian *promyshlennik* (Company fur trader) who had accompanied Native Alaskan hunters to California on American "contract" hunting vessels (probably the *Peacock* and *Isabella*) in 1806–1811. Farris believes that Tarakanov initiated transactions with local native leaders in 1810 or 1811 about the future Russian settlements at Bodega Harbor and Ross (Farris 1993b).

45. The 1817 treaty was shown to any foreign delegation, including the Spaniards, that questioned the legitimacy of the Ross Colony (see Golovnin 1979:161). Captain Vasilii M. Golovnin, commander of the *Kamchatka*, whose crew visited Colony Ross in September 1818, summarized the position of the Russians in his account of the voyage.

> According to established usage, the Russians had an absolute right to settle on this coast, whereas the Spanish want to drive them out on the basis of unfounded and trifling claims. The Russians established their settlement with the voluntary agreement and permission of the native inhabitants of this country, a people who do not

recognize the rule of the Spanish and are in constant warfare with them. These people gave permission to select a place and settle on their shores for a specific sum given to them in various goods. The friendly relations of these people with the Russians, which continue to this day, clearly prove that the Russians did not seize this land by force. (Golovnin 1979:163)

46. For an excellent discussion of Tikhanov's paintings and their insight into the ethnography of the Bodega Miwok, see Farris (1998).

47. For more information on these ceremonies, see Barrett (1917), Bean (1992), Loeb (1926, 1932), and Meighan and Riddell (1972). Bill Simmons and I have summarized previous discussions of the Kuksu and Old Ghost rituals recorded during the landfall of the Drake voyage in northern California in 1579 (Lightfoot and Simmons 1998:148–153).

48. Peter Kostromitinov served as manager of Colony Ross from 1830 to 1836.

49. By the late 1830s, the last manager of Ross, Alexander Rotchev, believed he had made considerable progress in developing a better rapport with Native Californian workers.

[T]hanks to a lot of perseverance and enticements, I have succeeded in diminishing a little this adverse sentiment to whites, among the natives of the tribes which frequent Bodega Bay; several chiefs and a good number of young people, encouraged by the bounty and generosity with which they were treated by the Russian agents, and finding, with reason, horribly miserable the life which they led during the winter in the woods where they had no other protection against the cold and snow than the caves or the shelter of trees, and no other means of subsistence than the unreliable products of the hunt, remain near the fort during the bad season, working with our colonists and are nourished like them. . . . Seeing their labors generously paid for, their freedom and religious beliefs, absurd as they are, respected; the most indulgent principle of justice to the point that deportation to one of our other establishments is the most severe punishments which I may inflict on those among them who have committed the worst derelictions against our properties. Seeing, I say, the interest that the public functionaries take in their well-being, they return each spring in larger number than the year before, to cultivate our fields, and attach themselves to us, to the degree that in their desire to remain always in good stead with the colonists, they are generally the first to denounce the trouble-makers who, for vengeance or by love of disorder, kill the beasts in the fields or even destroy our crops. (Rotchev, quoted in LaPlace 1986:68–69)

50. However, as pointed out to me by Glenn Farris, it appears that neophyte laborers from Mission San Rafael were working at Colony Ross as early as 1830. See Jackson (1983, 1984).

51. Farris (1998:7–9) provides detailed information from several European accounts of the chief, and various spellings of his name.

52. For example, as mentioned above, Murav'ev Ieromin and Zakharov Irodion, two Indians listed by the Company as employees, were transferred to Sitka when Colony Ross was sold to Johann Sutter in 1841 (Osborn 1997:409).

53. See, for example, the word *putilka* for broken glass and the word *kushka* for cat (Oswalt 1994:102).

6. NATIVE AGENCY IN THE ROSS COLONY

1. The Kashaya Pomo description of the "Undersea People" is detailed by Robert Oswalt (1994:104).

> The Kashaya called all those from the far north "people from under the water" or "Undersea People," perhaps because it seemed to them that, as the ships approached from beyond the horizon, they were rising up out of the water. Their term "Undersea People" includes without distinction the Russians and all the native people from the north that they brought with them.

2. The Kashaya refer to the land around the Ross settlement as Métini. The Métini region should not be confused with the historic village of Me?tini, located north of the Ross stockade in the Native California Neighborhood.

3. The Indians who lived near the presidio were probably neophyte auxiliaries.

4. For a discussion of the research agenda of the field program, and a summary of previous archaeological research in the area, see Lightfoot, Wake, and Schiff (1991:5–6) and Farris (1989b:490–492).

5. These designations (e.g., CA-SON-175) refer to individual archaeological sites that have been recorded and investigated in the Fort Ross State Historic Park.

6. For a similar perspective, see Farris (1997d).

7. The first archaeologists to record the site, in the 1930s, described a large central depression, which they interpreted as the remains of a "dance-house," surrounded by twelve to fifteen smaller "house pits" (Gifford 1967:9).

8. I have found Marshall Sahlin's (1981, 1985) theoretical approach on the "structure of the conjuncture" very useful in understanding Kashaya responses to foreigners in the Russian frontier. See Lightfoot et al. (1998).

9. Martinez conducted her investigation of Tomato Patch Village to provide us with a better understanding of a hinterland site. See Martinez (1997, 1998).

10. A diverse array of merchandise was imported by the Company into Alta California: iron, cast iron kettles, copper teapots, copper kettles, wax candles, white wax, sealing wax, lump and granulated sugar, sugar candy, Virginia tobacco, shot and lead, ropes, tea (Bohea and Sushon), coffee, pepper, thread, silk thread, broadcloth, calico (good, medium, and Bengal varieties), grey Flemish linen, raven duck, nankeen (white Kiakhta, blue Canton, and flesh-colored), baize, frieze, plush, flannel (ordinary and double), men's and women's cotton

stockings, beaver hats, axes, flat files, yellow plates, needles, Spanish socks, ticking, various kerchiefs, haberdashery goods, glass and crockery, carpenter's tools, shovels, anvils, adzes, saws, and so on. See also Khlebnikov (1990:62–63,178–179) and Khlebnikov (1994:112–113, 114). Some Company goods came from China, others from American skippers trading in Sitka, and still others were made in Russian factories. In addition, some inventory was specifically produced for the Alta California trade in workshops at New Archangel and Ross. Company blacksmiths, metal workers, and coppersmiths were geared up for the custom manufacture of plowshares, large bells (most likely for the missions), and new kitchen utensils of copper and tin, such as "kettles, drinking cups, teapots and coffeepots, siphons, funnels and other utensils" (Khlebnikov 1976:75).

11. That the Company provided little direct support for the women in interethnic households is highlighted in a letter to Kirill Khlebnikov from Karl Schmidt, Manager of the Ross Colony in June 1820.

> When the Aleut hunting party was sent to the port of San Francisco the second time, the men all asked me not to keep them for the hunt once the agreement had expired, because the last time that they had been separated from their families, their wives and children had received no assistance and had gone hungry; therefore they begged me to help them this time to feed their families. Notwithstanding the shortage of supplies at Ross, I tried to supply them with food as much as possible, but several of the women nevertheless ran away out of hunger, and the others endured the terrible privation. (Khlebnikov 1990:131–132)

Archaeological findings from the Native Alaskan Neighborhood suggest that Kashaya women supported themselves when their husbands were gone from Ross by gathering shellfish in the adjacent rocky intertidal habitats, by fishing for cabezon, ling cod, and rockfish with hook and line from the nearby shore, and by obtaining assistance from their outlying network of family and friends in the greater Ross region. See Lightfoot, Schiff, and Wake (1997:427–428).

12. LaPlace made the following observation in his 1839 visit to the Kashaya village near Ross:

> What has become of these often considerable quantities of varied merchandise which they had in their possession? We don't know yet. Were they sold, given to their compatriots who live in the forest all year? This is not likely. One is struck with the realization that giving in to the passion for play . . . they have seen their riches pass to the hands of players more clever or more lucky than they. . . . At every moment of the day, when they have something to lose, one sees them grouped four by four, squatting down on the ground, surrounded by numerous spectators awaiting, nearly always with impatience, the moment when it is their turn to take part. They play a sort of game which is hardly more complicated than *double or nothing,* so

common among our school-children; but to which they have come
to give a wholly greater importance by the singularly animated
pantomimes to which the action is accompanied among them. . . .

So that this description would have some interest for the reader,
it would be necessary for me to render all the vivid and lively (sudden) emotions which, on the mobile features of these children of
nature; the cries, the gesticulations, the laughter of those who won;
the cold impassive air of those who, losing often in a single stroke
the fruit of many months of work, became again poorer than they
had been before. In every case they suffer the bad fortune with a
philosophy, or to be more accurate, a dignified indifference like the
ancient stoics; and this savage who came to the game bedecked with
glass trinkets, or other ornaments, from head to foot, who had found
means in order to make himself more attractive to cover himself with
four or five shirts, as well as pants and vests superimposed one over
the other, returned to his hut as gay as a finch and naked as a worm.
(LaPlace 1986:69–71)

13. The Ross cemetery project was undertaken, in collaboration with the
Russian Orthodox Church, to restore and interpret the historic cemetery in the
Fort Ross State Historic Park.

7. MISSIONARY AND MERCANTILE
COLONIES IN CALIFORNIA: THE IMPLICATIONS

1. For a discussion of this issue, see Kirch and Green (2001:2–9), Nader (1994),
and Stein (1999:8–10).

2. And after mission secularization, there were probably ex-neophytes from
the greater San Francisco Bay Area living in the Native California Neighborhood at Ross, as well as at the three interior ranches.

3. Of course, the chronology of missionization among coastal hunter-gatherers varied markedly. A sizeable segment of the Island Gabrielino population
was not baptized until the establishment of the Plaza Church in Los Angeles in
1825, and some inhabitants of San Nicolas Island were not transported to mainland missions until 1835 (Johnson and McLendon 2000:647).

4. This is when Governor José María de Echeandía initiated the first of the
secularization decrees that allowed neophytes with special skills to leave the
missions.

5. Archaeologists commonly associate the presence of ceramic and glass artifacts with their use as tablewares, but this association needs to be carefully
reevaluated for native contexts in the missions and at Colony Ross. See Farris
(1997c: 131–132).

6. There are also some Franciscan accounts that describe the marriage of
newly baptized women with longtime neophyte men. For example, the padres
at Mission San Buenaventura wrote, "[a] neophyte twenty years a Christian

marries a woman but recently baptized. Such is the situation" (Geiger and Meighan 1976:61). However, it is not entirely clear if the women entering San Buenaventura at this time (about 1813) were from the local region or from the distant hinterland.

7. The comparative health of the population of Mission San Luis Rey is evident when the demographic trends of the neophyte community are compared to those of thirteen other Alta California missions analyzed by Robert Jackson (1994:83–107, 113–114).

8. THE AFTERMATH

1. To do this question justice would require another major project, one that traces the seven dimensions of colonial encounters into the late Mexican period (1834–46), when the ranchos became the dominant economic engine of coastal California. See Silliman 2000 for an excellent discussion of some of these dimensions. The dimensions of colonial encounters would then need to be explored in the American period, when in 1846 native peoples began to confront the waves of military envoys of the United States. This was followed by more than 150 years of confusing and often destructive Indian policies enacted by agents of federal and state governments.

2. The *Californios,* under the able leadership of Governor José Figueroa, moved swiftly in 1834 to insure that the mission lands would not be allocated to immigrants sent from Mexico, by issuing their *Manifiesto a la República Mejicana* (Haas 1995:35–36). The *Manifiesto* stipulated that the missions would be converted into pueblos for the neophytes.

3. It would be interesting to examine the dimension, in this social setting, of colonial encounters involving interethnic unions. Some scholars have argued that Indians who migrated to the pueblos eventually merged their identities into the Hispanic community, or found it prudent, in the face of white racial prejudice, to lose their Indian identities (Mason 1984:140; Meighan 1987:196–198; Phillips 1980:448–449).

4. A number of insightful analyses have been completed on the lethal perils that California Indians were exposed to during this traumatic period. See Castillo (1978), Cook (1943b), Farris (1997b), Heizer and Almquist (1971), Johnson (1995, 1997, 2001), Johnson and McLendon (2000), and Rawls (1984).

5. Jackson's writings and reform movement have had a long-term impact on our perspective of the Franciscan missions. As David Thomas (1991) eloquently writes, *Ramona* sparked a romantic vision of pastoral elegance for the old missions that fueled the public's interest in mission architecture, furniture, and history. The Mission Revival movement, however, turned out to be a mixed blessing for mission archaeology, as many sites were destroyed without proper investigation, in the rush to reconstruct mission buildings.

6. The ranch was eventually purchased by Edward F. Beale, who established the military reservation. While the number of Indian settlements declined to a single rancheria by 1877, a number of ex-neophytes from Mission San Fernando

continued to reside at Tejon Ranch through the twentieth century (Johnson 1997:265).

7. Helen Hunt Jackson wrote about her first glimpse of the San Carlos village:

> Whether it is that the Indians purposely always go ashore at dif-
> ferent points of the bank, so as to leave no trail; or whether they
> so seldom go out, except on foot, that the trail has faded away, I
> do not know. But certainly, if we had had no guide, we should have
> turned back, sure we were wrong. A few rods up from the river-
> bank, a stealthy narrow footpath appeared; through willow copses,
> sunk in meadow grasses, across shingly bits of alder-walled beach
> it creeps, till it comes out in a lovely spot,—half basin, half rocky
> knoll,—where tucked away in nooks and hollows, are the little Indian
> houses, eight or ten of them, some of adobe, some of the tule-reeds;
> small patches of corn, barley, potatoes, and hay; and each little front
> yard fenced in by palings, with roses, sweet-peas, poppies, and mi-
> gnonette growing inside. In the first house we reached, a woman was
> living alone. She was so alarmed at the sight of us that she shook. . . .
> In another house we found an old woman evidently past eighty,
> without glasses working button-holes in fine thread. Her daughter-
> in-law—a beautiful half-breed, with a still more beautiful baby
> in her arms—asked the old woman, for us, how old she was. She
> laughed merrily at the silly question, "She never thought about it,"
> she said; "it was written down once in a book at the Mission, but the
> book was lost."
>
> There was not a man in the village. They were all away at work,
> farming or fishing. This little handful of people are living on land
> to which they have no shadow of title, and from which they may
> be driven any day,—these Carmel Mission lands having been rented
> out, by their present owner, in great dairy farms. (Jackson 1902:154,
> 157)

8. I suspect this may be the Chumash-speaking Santa Ynez community mentioned above.

9. I am indebted to Ira Jacknis for this information.

10. For exceptions, see Kroeber (1904a, 1907, 1910) and Mason (1912, 1916).

11. It is interesting that many of the ethnolinguistic units originally outlined by Kroeber for the central and southern coasts are defined by the Indian communities associated with the Franciscan missions. See Kroeber (1922, 1925). For example, the Ohlone or Costanoan speakers were divided into ethnolinguistic units that included the San Francisco, Santa Clara, Santa Cruz, San Juan Bautista (Mutsun), Monterey (Rumsen), and Soledad peoples. See map 5.

12. This pattern of extensive intermarriage has also been documented for Indian settlements in the Santa Barbara region. Among the Chumash people, the number of marriages between ex-neophytes from different mission communities increased greatly after 1845, as did marriage to non-Indians. It is es-

timated that by 1870 more than 50 percent of the Chumash women were marrying non-Indians, primarily recent immigrants from Sonora and other Mexican states (Johnson 1995:7–8).

13. The tribal recognition process is quite rigorous and demanding, as native groups must demonstrate that they have existed as distinct and autonomous political and cultural entities from the time of first European contact to the present. Indian groups who purchased their own property in common or obtained federal or private land grants by the early twentieth century were well situated to become federally recognized. By maintaining a land base, they were able to retain a semblance of their tribal communities, and to withstand the detailed scrutiny and rigorous procedure employed by the Bureau of Indian Affairs, which ultimately makes recommendations about the legal status of Indian tribes.

14. An excellent case study, that of how this happened to the Muwekma Ohlone tribe, is presented in several recent publications (Field 1999; Field et al. 1992; Leventhal et al. 1994).

15. Land allotments were also made to some native peoples in Nevada, as well as to the Navajo Reservation in Arizona and New Mexico, the Turtle Mountain Reservation in North Dakota and Montana, and the Papago Reservation in Arizona (Parman 1994:20–21).

16. Also known as the Dawes Severalty Act, named after its chief proponent, Senator Henry L. Dawes of Massachusetts. See Hagan (1988:61).

References

Aginsky, B. W.
  1949. The Interaction of Ethnic Groups: A Case Study of Indians and Whites. *American Sociological Review* 14(2): 288–293.

Allan, J. M.
  2001. *Forge and Falseworks: An Archaeological Investigation of the Russian American Company's Industrial Complex at Colony Ross.* Ph.D. dissertation, Department of Anthropology, University of California, Berkeley.

Allen, R.
  1998. *Native Americans at Mission Santa Cruz, 1791–1834: Interpreting the Archaeological Record.* Perspectives in California Archaeology, vol. 5. Los Angeles: Institute of Archaeology, University of California.

Ames, J. G.
  1979. Report of Special Agent John G. Ames on the Condition of the Mission Indians, 1874. In *Federal Concern about Conditions of California Indians 1853 to 1913: Eight Documents,* edited by R. F. Heizer, pp. 51–73. Socorro, N.M.: Ballena Press.

Archibald, R.
  1978. Indian Labor at the California Missions: Slavery or Salvation? *The Journal of San Diego History* 24(2): 172–182.

Armstrong, D. V.
  1998. Cultural Transformation within Enslaved Laborer Communities in the Caribbean. In *Studies in Culture Contact: Interaction, Culture Change, and Archaeology,* edited by J. G. Cusick, pp. 378–401. Occasional Paper no. 25. Carbondale, Ill.: Center for Archaeological Investigations, Southern Illinois University.

Arnold, J. E.
  1990. An Archaeological Perspective on the Historic Settlement Pattern on

Santa Cruz Island. *Journal of California and Great Basin Anthropology* 12: 112–127.

1992. Complex Hunter-Gatherer-Fishers of Prehistoric California: Chiefs, Specialists, and Maritime Adaptations of the Channel Islands. *American Antiquity* 577(1): 60–84.

1995. Transportation Innovation and Social Complexity among Maritime Hunter-Gatherer Societies. *American Anthropologist* 97: 733–747.

2001. *The Origins of Pacific Coast Chiefdom: The Chumash of the Channel Islands.* Salt Lake City: University of Utah Press.

Arnold, J. E., R. Colten, and S. Pletka
1997. Contexts of Cultural Change in Insular California. *American Antiquity* 62(2): 300–318.

Asisara, L.
1892. Narrative of a Mission Indian, Etc. In *History of Santa Cruz County, California,* edited by E. S. Harrison, pp. 45–48. San Francisco: Pacific Press Publishing.

1989a. The Assassination of Padre Andrés Quintana by the Indians of Mission Santa Cruz in 1812: The Narrative of Lorenzo Asisara. *California History* 68(3): 117–125.

1989b. An Indian Account of the Decline and Collapse of Mexico's Hegemony over the Missionized Indians of California. *The American Indian Quarterly* 13(4): 391–408.

Axtell, J.
2001. *Natives and Newcomers: The Cultural Origins of North America.* New York: Oxford University Press.

Baker, B. J., and L. Kealhofer, eds.
1996. *Bioarchaeology of Native American Adaptation in the Spanish Borderlands.* Gainesville: University Press of Florida.

Ballard, H. S.
1995. *Searching for Metini: Synthesis and Analysis of Unreported Archaeological Collections from Fort Ross State Historic Park, California.* Senior Honors Thesis, Department of Anthropology, University of California, Berkeley.

1997. Ethnicity and Chronology at Metini, Fort Ross State Historic Park, California. In *The Archaeology of Russian Colonialism in the North and Tropical Pacific,* edited by P. R. Mills and A. Martinez, pp. 116–140. Kroeber Anthropological Society Papers, vol. 81. Berkeley, Calif.: Kroeber Anthropological Society.

Bancroft, H. H.
1886a. *The Works of Hubert Howe Bancroft, History of California,* vol. 19. *History of California,* vol. 2, *1801–1824.* San Francisco: The History Company.

1886b. *The Works of Hubert Howe Bancroft, History of California*, vol. 20. *History of California*, vol. 3, *1825–1840*. San Francisco: The History Company.

1888. *California Pastoral*. San Francisco: A.L. Bancroft and Company.

Baranov, A. A.
1989. October 14, 1808. Instructions from Aleksandr A. Baranov to His Assistant, Ivan A. Kuskov, Regarding the Dispatch of a Hunting Party to the Coast of Spanish California. In *The Russian American Colonies: Three Centuries of Russian Eastward Expansion, 1798–1867*: vol. 3, *A Documentary Record*, edited by B. Dmytryshyn, E.A.P. Crownhart-Vaughan, and T. Vaughan, pp. 165–174. Portland: Oregon Historical Society Press.

Barrett, S. A.
1908. The Ethno-Geography of the Pomo and Neighboring Indians. *University of California Publications in American Archaeology and Ethnology* 6.
1917. Ceremonies of the Pomo Indians. *University of California Publications in American Archaeology and Ethnology* 12(10): 397–441.

Basso, K. H.
1996. *Wisdom Sits in Places: Landscape and Language among the Western Apache*. Albuquerque: University of New Mexico Press.

Bean, L. J.
1976. Social Organization in Native California. In *Native Californians: A Theoretical Retrospective*, edited by L. J. Bean and T. C. Blackburn, pp. 99–123. Ramona, Calif.: Ballena Press.

1994. Introduction. In *The Ohlone Past and Present: Native Americans of the San Francisco Bay Region*, edited by L. J. Bean, pp. xxi–xxxii. Menlo Park, Calif: Ballena Press.

Bean, L. J., and T. C. Blackburn, eds.
1976. *Native Californians: A Theoretical Retrospective*. Ramona, Calif.: Ballena Press.

Bean, L. J., and T. F. King, eds.
1974. *?Antap: California Indian Political and Economic Organization*. Ramona, Calif.: Ballena Press.

Bean, L. J., and H. Lawton
1976. Some Explanations for the Rise of Cultural Complexity in Native California with Comments on Proto-Agriculture and Agriculture. In *Native Californians: A Theoretical Retrospective*, edited by L. J. Bean and T. C. Blackburn, pp. 19–48. Ramona, Calif: Ballena Press.

Bean, L. J., and F. C. Shipek
1978. Luiseño. In *Handbook of North American Indians:* vol. 8, *California*, edited by R. Heizer, pp. 550–563. Washington, D.C.: Smithsonian Institution.

Bean, L. J., and C. R. Smith
  1978. Cupeño. In *Handbook of North American Indians:* vol. 8, *California*, edited by R. Heizer, pp. 588–591. Washington, D.C.: Smithsonian Institution.

Bean, L. J., and S. B. Vane
  1992. California Religious Systems and Their Transformations. In *California Indian Shamanism*, edited by L. J. Bean, pp. 33–51. Menlo Park, Calif.: Ballena Press.

Beaver, R. P.
  1988. Protestant Churches and the Indians. In *Handbook of North American Indians:* vol. 4, *History of Indian-White Relations*, edited by W. E. Washburn, pp. 430–458. Washington, D.C.: Smithsonian Institution.

Belcher, C.S.E.
  1843. *Narrative of a Voyage Round the World, Performed in Her Majesty's Ship Sulphur, during the Years 1836–1842. Including Details of the Naval Operations in China, From Dec. 1840, to Nov. 1841.* London: Henry Colburn.

Bermudez, D. Z.
  1989. 15 April, 1817: A Statement from De Zea Bermudez, Spanish Ambassador at St. Petersburg, to Count Karl V. Nesselrode, Minister of Foreign Affairs, Protesting Russian Presence on the Coast of Upper California. In *The Russian American Colonies: Three Centuries of Russian Eastward Expansion, 1798–1867:* vol. 3, *A Documentary Record*, edited by B. Dmytryshyn, E.A.P. Crownhart-Vaughan, and T. Vaughan, pp. 246–248. Portland: Oregon Historical Society Press.

Berthrong, D. J.
  1988. Nineteenth-Century United States Government Agencies. In *Handbook of North American Indians:* vol. 4, *History of Indian-White Relations*, edited by W. E. Washburn, pp. 255–263. Smithsonian Institution.

Black, L.T.
  1990. Creoles in Russian America. *Pacifica* 2: 142–155.

  2001. Forgotten Literacy. In *Looking Both Ways: Heritage and Identity of the Alutiiq People*, edited by A. L. Crowell, A. F. Steffian, and G. L. Pullar, pp. 60–61. Fairbanks: University of Alaska Press.

Blomkvist, E. E.
  1972. A Russian Scientific Expedition to California and Alaska, 1839–1849. Translated by B. Dmytryshyn and E.A.P. Crownhart-Vaughan. *Oregon Historical Quarterly* 73 (2): 101–170.

Bolton, H. E.
  1916. *Spanish Exploration in the Southwest 1542–1706.* New York: Charles Scribner's Sons.

  1921. *The Spanish Borderlands: A Chronicle of Old Florida and the Southwest.* New Haven: Yale University Press.

Bourdieu, P.

1977. *Outline of a Theory of Practice.* Cambridge: Cambridge University Press.

1990. *The Logic of Practice.* Translated by R. Nice. Stanford, Calif.: Stanford University Press.

Breschini, G. S., and T. Haversat

2002. The Esselen Refuge Response to Spanish Intrusion. In *A Gathering of Voices: The Native Peoples of the Central California Coast,* edited by L. Yamane, pp. 37–47. *Santa Cruz County History Journal,* issue no. 5. Santa Cruz, Calif.: Museum of Art and History.

Brown, I. W.

1992. Certain Aspects of French-Indian Interaction in Lower Louisiane. In *Calumet and Fleur-De-Lys: Archaeology of Indian and French Contact in the Midcontinent,* edited by J. A. Walthall and T. E. Emerson, pp. 17–34. Washington, D.C.: Smithsonian Institution.

Bureau of Indian Affairs

2002. Indian Entities Recognized and Eligible to Receive Services from the United States Bureau of Indian Affairs; Notice. *Federal Register 67* (134): 46328–46333 (Friday, July 12, 2002).

Burley, D.

1985. Social Organization in Historic Societies: A Critical Commentary. In *Status, Structure and Stratification: Current Archaeological Reconstructions,* edited by M. Thompson, M. T. Garcia, and F. J. Kense, pp. 415–418. Calgary, Alberta: University of Calgary Archaeological Association.

Carrico, R. L., and F. C. Shipek

1996. Indian Labor in San Diego County, California, 1850–1900. In *Native Americans and Wage Labor: Ethnohistorical Perspectives,* edited by A. Littlefield and M. Knack, pp. 198–217. Norman: University of Oklahoma Press.

Castaneda, A. I.

1997. Engendering the History of Alta California, 1769–1848: Gender, Sexuality, and the Family. *California History* 76(2 and 3): 230–259.

Castillo, E. D.

1978. The Impact of Euro-American Exploration and Settlement. In *Handbook of North American Indians:* vol. 8, *California,* edited by R. F. Heizer, pp. 99–127. Washington, D.C.: Smithsonian Institution.

1989a. The Assassination of Padre Andrés Quintana by the Indians of Mission Santa Cruz in 1812: The Narrative of Lorenzo Asisara. *California History* 68(3): 116–125.

1989b. An Indian Account of the Decline and Collapse of Mexico's Hegemony over the Missionized Indians of California. *The American Indian Quarterly* 13(4): 391–408.

1989c. The Native Response to Colonization of Alta California. In *Columbian Consequences:* vol. 1, *Archaeological and Historical Perspectives on the Spanish Borderlands West,* edited by D. H. Thomas, pp. 377–394. Washington, D.C.: Smithsonian Institution.

1994. The Language of Race Hatred. In *The Ohlone Past and Present: Native Americans of the San Francisco Bay Region,* edited by L. J. Bean, pp. 271–295. Menlo Park, Calif: Ballena Press.

César, J.
1930. Recollections of My Youth at San Luis Rey Mission. *Touring Topics* 22: 42–43.

Chamisso, A. V.
1986. *A Voyage Around the World with the Romanzov Exploring Expedition in the Years 1815–1818.* Translated and edited by Henry Kratz. Honolulu: University of Hawaii Press.

Chernykh, Y.
1968. Two New Chernykh Letters: More Original Documentation on the Russian Post Relinquished in 1841 to General Sutter. Original 1836 Letters edited and translated by James Gibson. *The Pacific Historian* 12(3 and 4): 48–56, 54–60.

Coleman, D.C.
1969. Introduction. In *Revisions in Mercantilism,* edited by D.C. Coleman, pp. 1–18. London: Methuen and Company.

Collier, M. E. T., and S. B. Thalman
1996. *Interviews with Tom Smith and Maria Copa: Isabel Kelly's Ethnographic Notes on the Coast Miwok Indians of Marin and Southern Sonoma Counties, California.* MAPOM Occasional Papers no. 6. San Rafael, Calif.: Miwok Archaeological Preserve of Marin.

Cook, S. F.
1943a. *The Conflict between the California Indian and White Civilization:* vol. 1, *The Indian Versus the Spanish Mission.* Ibero-Americana 21. Berkeley: University of California Press.

1943b. *The Conflict between the California Indian and White Civilization:* vol. 3, *The American Invasion, 1848–1870.* Ibero-Americana 23. Berkeley: University of California Press.

1976a. *The Conflict Between the California Indian and White Civilization.* Berkeley and Los Angeles: University of California Press.

1976b. *The Indian Population of New England in the Seventeenth Century.* Berkeley and Los Angeles: University of California Press.

Costello, J. G.
1985. Brick and Tile Kiln. In *Excavations at Mission San Antonio, 1976–1978,*

edited by R. L. Hoover and J. G. Costello, pp. 122–151. Monograph 26. Los Angeles: Institute of Archaeology, University of California.

1989a. *Santa Inés Mission Excavations: 1986–1988.* Salinas, Calif: Coyote Press.

1989b. Variability among the Alta California Missions: The Economics of Agricultural Production. In *Columbian Consequences:* vol. 1, *Archaeological and Historical Perspectives on the Spanish Borderlands West,* edited by D. H. Thomas, pp. 435–449. Washington, D.C.: Smithsonian Institution.

1992. Not Peas in a Pod: Documenting Diversity among the California Missions. In *Text-Aided Archaeology,* edited by B. J. Little, pp. 67–81. Boca Raton, Fla.: CRC Press.

1997. Brick and Tile Making in Spanish California, with Related Old and New World Examples. In *Prehistory and History of Ceramic Kilns,* edited by P. M. Rice, pp. 195–217. Ceramics and Civilization, vol. 7. Westerville, Ohio: American Ceramic Society.

Costello, J. G., and D. Hornbeck
1989. Alta California: An Overview. In *Columbian Consequences:* vol. 1, *Archaeological and Historical Perspectives on the Spanish Borderlands West,* edited by D. H. Thomas, pp. 303–331. Washington, D.C.: Smithsonian Institution.

Costello, J. G., and P. L. Walker
1987. Burials from the Santa Barbara Presidio Chapel. *Historical Archaeology* 21(1): 3–17.

Costo, R., and J. H. Costo, eds.
1987. *The Missions of California: A Legacy of Genocide.* San Francisco: Indian Historian Press.

Crosby, A. W.
1986. *Ecological Imperialism: The Biological Expansion of Europe, 900–1900.* Cambridge: Cambridge University Press.

Crowell, A. L.
1997a. *Archaeology and the Capitalist World System: A Study from Russian America.* New York: Plenum Press.

1997b. Russians in Alaska, 1784: Foundations of Colonial Society at Three Saints Harbor, Kodiak Island. In *The Archaeology of Russian Colonialism in the North and Tropical Pacific,* edited by P. R. Mills and A. Martinez, pp. 10–41. Kroeber Anthropological Society Papers no. 81. Berkeley, Calif: Kroeber Anthropological Society.

Cusick, J. G.
1998. Introduction. In *Studies in Culture Contact: Interaction, Culture Change, and Archaeology,* edited by J. G. Cusick, pp. 1–20. Occasional Paper no. 25.

Carbondale: Center for Archaeological Investigations, Southern Illinois University.

Davydov, G. I.
1977. *Two Voyages to Russian America, 1802–1807.* Translated by C. Bearne. Materials for the Study of Alaska History 10. Kingston, Ontario: Limestone Press.

Deagan, K.
1990. Sixteenth-Century Spanish-American Colonization in the Southeastern United States and the Caribbean. In *Columbian Consequences:* vol. 2, *Archaeological and Historical Perspectives in the Spanish Borderlands East,* edited by D. H. Thomas, pp. 225–250. Washington, D.C.: Smithsonian Institution.

1991. Historical Archaeology's Contributions to Our Understanding of Early America. In *Historical Archaeology in Global Perspective,* edited by L. Falk, pp. 97–112. Washington, D.C.: Smithsonian Institution Press.

1995. After Columbus: The Sixteenth-Century Spanish-Caribbean Frontier. In *Puerto Real: The Archaeology of a Sixteenth-Century Spanish Town in Hispaniola,* edited by K. Deagan, pp. 419–456. Gainesville: University Press of Florida.

1998. Transculturation and Spanish American Ethnogenesis: The Archaeological Legacy of the Quincentenary. In *Studies in Culture Contact: Interaction, Culture Change, and Archaeology,* edited by J. G. Cusick, pp. 23–43. Occasional Paper no. 25. Carbondale: Center for Archaeological Investigations, Southern Illinois University.

Deetz, J.
1963. Archaeological Investigations at La Purisima Mission. *Archaeological Survey Annual Report* 5: 161–241.

1991. Archaeological Evidence of Sixteenth- and Seventeenth-Century Encounters. In *Historical Archaeology in Global Perspective,* edited by L. Falk, pp. 1–10. Washington, D.C.: Smithsonian Institution.

Dietler, M.
2000. The Archaeology of Colonization and the Colonization of Archaeology: Theoretical Reflections on an Ancient Colonial Encounter. Paper presented at the Archaeology of Colonies in Cross-Cultural Perspective, advanced seminar organized by Gil Stein, School of American Research, Santa Fe, New Mexico, March 19–23, 2000.

Dixon, R. B., and A. L. Kroeber
1913. New Linguistic Families in California. *American Anthropologist* 15(4): 647–655.

1919. Linguistic Families of California. *University of California Publications in American Archaeology and Ethnology* 16: 47–118.

Dmytryshyn, B., E.A.P. Crownhart-Vaughan, and T. Vaughan
1989. *The Russian American Colonies, 1798–1867: Three Centuries of Russian Eastward Expansion.* 3 vols. Portland: Oregon Historical Society.

Dobyns, H. F.
1983. *Their Number Become Thinned: Native American Populations Dynamics in Eastern North America.* Knoxville: University of Tennessee Press.

1991. New Native World: Links Between Demographic and Cultural Changes. In *Columbian Consequences:* vol. 3, *The Spanish Borderlands in Pan-American Perspective,* edited by D. H. Thomas, pp. 541–560. Washington, D.C.: Smithsonian Institution.

Drucker, P.
1937. Culture Element Distributions, 5: Southern California. *University of California Anthropological Records* 1(1): 1–52.

Du Bois, C.
1908. The Religion of the Luiseño and Diegueño Indians of Southern California. *University of California Publications in American Archaeology and Ethnology* 8(3): 228–236.

Duflot de Mofras, E.
1937. *Travels on the Pacific Coast.* Vols. 1 and 2. Translated and edited by Marguerite E. Wilbur. Santa Ana, Calif.: Fine Arts Press.

Duhaut-Cilly, A.
1999. *A Voyage to California, the Sandwich Islands, and Around the World in the Years 1826–1829.* Translated and edited by August Frugé and Neal Harlow. Berkeley and Los Angeles: University of California Press.

Dundes, A.
1980. *Interpreting Folklore.* Bloomington: Indiana University Press.

Dunnell, R. C.
1991. Methodological Impacts of Catastrophic Depopulation on American Archaeology and Ethnology. In *Columbian Consequences:* vol. 3, *The Spanish Borderlands in Pan-American Perspective,* edited by D. H. Thomas, pp. 561–580. Washington, D.C.: Smithsonian Institution.

Echo-Hawk, R. C.
2000. Ancient Histories in the New World: Integrating Oral Traditions and the Archaeological Record. *American Antiquity* 65(2): 267–290.

Edwards, T. C., and C. E. Kelsey
1979. Memorial of the Northern California Indian Association, Praying That Lands Will be Allotted to the Landless Indians of the Northern Part of the State of California. In *Federal Concern about Conditions of California Indians 1853 to 1913: Eight Documents,* edited by R. F. Heizer, pp. 95–121. Socorro, N.M.: Ballena Press.

Elkin, H.
1940. The Northern Arapaho of Wyoming. In *Acculturation in Seven American Indian Tribes,* edited by R. Linton, pp. 207–258. New York: D. Appleton Century.

Engelhardt, Z., O.F.M.
1908–1915. *The Missions and Missionaries of California.* 4 vols. San Francisco: James H. Barry.

Engstrand, I. H. W.
1997. Seekers of the "Northern Mystery": European Exploration of California and the Pacific. *California History* 76(2 and 3): 78–110.

Erdoes, R., and A. Ortiz, eds.
1984. *American Indian Myths and Legends.* New York: Pantheon Books.

Erlandson, J. M.
1994. *Early Hunter-Gatherers of the California Coast.* New York: Plenum Press.

Erlandson, J. M., and K. Bartoy
1995. Cabrillo, the Chumash, and Old World Disease. *Journal of California and Great Basin Anthropology* 17(2): 153–173.

1996. Protohistoric California: Paradise or Pandemic? *Proceedings of the Society for California Archaeology* 9: 304–309.

Erlandson, J. M., and R. Colten, eds.
1991. *Hunter-Gatherers of Early Holocene Coastal California.* Los Angeles: Institute of Archaeology, University of California.

Farnsworth, P.
1987. *The Economics of Acculturation in the California Missions: A Historical and Archaeological Study of Mission Nuestra Señora de la Soledad.* Ph.D. dissertation, Department of Anthropology, University of California, Los Angeles.

1989. The Economics of Acculturation in the Spanish Missions of Alta California. *Research in Economic Anthropology* 11: 217–249.

1992. Missions, Indians, and Cultural Continuity. *Historical Archaeology* 26(1): 22–36.

Farris, G. J.
1986. *Cultural Resource Survey at the Fort Ross Campground, Sonoma County, California.* Sacramento: Cultural Heritage Section, Archaeology Laboratory, California Department of Parks and Recreation.

1988. Recognizing Indian Folk History as Real History: A Fort Ross Example. *American Indian Quarterly* 13(4): 471–480.

1989a. A Peace Treaty Between Mariano Vallejo and Satiyomi Chief Succara.

Paper presented at the Fifth California Indian Conference, Humboldt State University, Arcata, California.

1989b. The Russian Imprint on the Colonization of California. In *Columbian Consequences:* vol. 1, *Archaeological and Historical Perspectives on the Spanish Borderlands West,* edited by D. H. Thomas, pp. 481–498. Washington, D.C.: Smithsonian Institution.

1990. Fort Ross, California: Archaeology of the Old *Magazin.* In *Russia in North America: Proceedings of the Second International Conference on Russian America,* edited by R. A. Pierce, pp. 475–505. Kingston, Ontario: Limestone Press.

1991. *Archaeological Testing in the Neophyte Housing Area at Mission San Juan Bautista, California.* Sacramento: Resource Protection Division, California Departments of Parks and Recreation.

1992. The Day of the Tall Strangers. *The Californians* 9(6): 13–19.

1993a. Life in the Sloboda: A View of the Village at Fort Ross, California. Paper presented at the Annual Meeting of the Society for Historical Archaeology, Kansas City, Missouri.

1993b. Talacani: The Man Who Purchased Fort Ross. *Fort Ross Interpretive Association Newsletter* (September-October): 7–9.

1997a. The Age of Russian Imperialism in the North Pacific. In *The Archaeology of Russian Colonialism in the North and Tropical Pacific,* edited by P. R. Mills and A. Martinez, pp. 187–194. Kroeber Anthropological Society Papers no. 81. Berkeley, Calif.: Kroeber Anthropological Society.

1997b. Captain José Panto and the San Pascual Indian Pueblo in San Diego County, 1835–1878. *Journal of San Diego History* 43(2): 116–131.

1997c. Historical Archaeology of the Native Alaskan Village Site. In *The Archaeology and Ethnohistory of Fort Ross, California:* vol. 2, *The Native Alaskan Neighborhood: A Multiethnic Community at Colony Ross,* edited by K. G. Lightfoot, A.M. Schiff, and T. A. Wake, pp. 129–135. Contributions of the University of California Archaeological Research Facility, no. 55. Berkeley, Calif.: Archaeological Research Facility.

1997d. Life at Fort Ross as the Indians Saw It: Stories from the Kashaya. In *The Archaeology and Ethnohistory of Fort Ross, California:* vol. 2, *The Native Alaskan Neighborhood: A Multiethnic Community at Colony Ross,* edited by K. G. Lightfoot, A.M. Schiff, and T. A. Wake, pp. 17–22. Contributions of the University of California Archaeological Research Facility, no. 55. Berkeley, Calif.: Archaeological Research Facility.

1998. The Bodega Miwok as seen by Mikhail Tikhonovich Tikhanov in 1818. *Journal of California and Great Basin Anthropology* 20(1): 2–12.

Farris, G. J., and R. M. Beebe

2000. Prologue. In *Report of a Visit to Fort Ross and Bodega Bay in April 1833 by Mariano G. Vallejo,* edited by G. J. Farris and R. M. Beebe, pp. iii–x. Occasional Paper no. 4. Bakersfield: California Mission Studies Association.

Farris, G. J., and J. R. Johnson

1999. *Prominent Indian Families at Mission La Purísima Concepción as Identified in Baptismal, Marriage, and Burial Records.* Occasional Paper no. 3. Bakersfield: California Mission Studies Association.

Farris, G. J., and E. Wheeler

1998. *The Neophyte and Infirmary at La Purísima Mission S[tate] H[istorical] P[ark]: A Review and Mapping of the Site.* Sacramento: California Department of Parks and Recreation.

Fedorova, S. G.

1973. *The Russian Population in Alaska and California, Late Eighteenth Century—1867.* Translated by R. A. Pierce and A. S. Donnelly. Kingston, Ontario: Limestone Press.

1975. *Ethnic Processes in Russian America.* Translated by A. Shalkop. Occasional Papers no. 1. Anchorage: Anchorage Historical and Fine Arts Museum.

Felton, D. L.

1987. *Santa Cruz Mission State Historic Park: Architectural and Archaeological Investigations, 1984–1985.* Sacramento: Cultural Heritage Section, California Department of Parks and Recreation.

Field, L. W.

1999. Complicities and Collaborations: Anthropologists and the "Unacknowledged Tribes" of California. *Current Anthropology* 40(2): 193–209.

Field, L. W., A. Leventhal, D. Sanchez, and R. Cambra

1992. A Contemporary Ohlone Tribal Revitalization Movement: A Perspective from the Muwekma Costanoan/Ohlone Indians of the San Francisco Bay Area. *California History* 71(3): 412–432.

Finnegan, R.

1996. Oral Tradition. In *Encyclopedia of Cultural Anthropology,* edited by D. Levinson and M. Ember, 3: 887–891. New York: Henry Holt and Company.

Font, P.

1931. *Font's Complete Diary: The Chronicle of the Founding of San Francisco.* Edited and translated by Herbert Eugene Bolton. Berkeley, Calif.: University of California Press.

Forbes, J. D.

1982. *Native Americans of California and Nevada.* Happy Camp, Calif.: Naturegraph Publishers.

1983. Hispano-Mexican Pioneers of the San Francisco Bay Region: An Analysis of Racial Origins. *Aztlan* 14: 175–189.

Galvan, P. M.
1968. The Ohlone Story. *The Indian Historian* 1(2): 9–13.

Gamble, L. H.
1991. *Organization of Activities at the Historic Settlement of Helo': A Chumash Political, Economic, and Religious Center.* Ph.D. dissertation, Department of Anthropology, University of California, Santa Barbara.

Gamble, L. H., P. L. Walker, and G. S. Russell
2001. An Integrative Approach to Mortuary Analysis: Social and Symbolic Dimensions of Chumash Burial Practices. *American Antiquity* 66(2): 185–212.

Garr, D.
1972. Planning, Politics, and Plunder: The Missions and Indian Pueblos of Hispanic California. *Southern California Quarterly* 54: 291–312.

Gates, G. R.
1976. The Ventura Foundations: No Stone Unturned. In *The Changing Faces of Main Street: Ventura Mission Plaza Archaeological Project*, edited by R. S. Greenwood, pp. 181–198. Ventura, Calif.: Redevelopment Agency, City of San Buenaventura.

Geiger, M., and C. W. Meighan, eds.
1976. *As the Padres Saw Them: California Indian Life and Customs as Reported by the Franciscan Missionaries, 1813–1815.* Santa Barbara, Calif.: Santa Barbara Mission Archive Library.

Gibson, J. R.
1969. Russians in California, 1833: Report of Governor Wrangel. *Pacific Northwest Quarterly* 60(4): 205–215.

1976. *Imperial Russia in Frontier America: The Changing Geography of Supply of Russian America, 1784–1867.* New York: Oxford University Press.

1988. The Maritime Trade of the North Pacific Coast. In *Handbook of North American Indians:* vol. 4, *History of Indian-White Relations*, edited by W. E. Washburn, pp. 375–390. Washington, D.C.: Smithsonian Institution.

1992. A Russian Orthodox Priest in Mexican California. *The Californians* 9(6): 20–27.

Giddens, A.
1979. *Central Problems in Social Theory: Action, Structure, and Contradiction in Social Analysis.* Berkeley and Los Angeles: University of California Press.

Gies, G. A.
2002. The Political Economy of Chumash Elites of Mission Santa Barbara,

1786–1824. Paper presented at the Thirty-fifth Conference on Historical and Underwater Archaeology, Mobile, Alabama, January 12, 2002.

Gies, L.

2002. Changing Roles of Elite Chumash Women in Mission Society. Paper presented at the Thirty-fifth Conference on Historical and Underwater Archaeology, Mobile, Alabama, January 12, 2002.

Gifford, E. W.

1918. Clans and Moieties in Southern California. *University of California Publications in American Archaeology and Ethnology* 14(2): 155–219.

1926. Miwok Lineages and the Political Unit in Aboriginal California. *American Anthropologist* 28(2): 389–401.

1932. The Northfork Mono. *University of California Publications in American Archaeology and Ethnology* 31(2): 15–65.

1967. Ethnographic Notes on the Southwestern Pomo. *Anthropological Records* 25: 1–48.

Gifford, E. W., and A. L. Kroeber

1937. Culture Element Distributions: 4, Pomo. *University of California Publications in American Archaeology and Ethnology* 37(4): 117–254.

Glassow, M. A.

1996. *Purisimeno Chumash Prehistory: Maritime Adaptations along the Southern California Coast.* Fort Worth, Tex.: Harcourt Brace College Publishers.

1997. Middle Holocene Cultural Development in the Central Santa Barbara Channel Region. In *Archaeology of the California Coast during the Middle Holocene,* edited by J. M. Erlandson and M. A. Glassow, pp. 73–90. Los Angeles: Institute of Archaeology, University of California.

Gobalet, K. W.

1997. Fish Remains from the Early Nineteenth-Century Native Alaskan Habitation at Fort Ross. In *The Archaeology and Ethnohistory of Fort Ross, California:* vol. 2, *The Native Alaskan Neighborhood: A Multiethnic Community at Colony Ross,* edited by K. G. Lightfoot, A.M. Schiff, and T. A. Wake, pp. 319–327. Contributions of the University of California Archaeological Research Facility, no. 55. Berkeley, Calif.: Archaeological Research Facility.

Goldstein, L.

1992. Spatial Organization and Frontier Cemeteries: An Example from a Russian Colonial Settlement. Paper presented at the Twenty-fifth Annual Meeting of the Society for Historical Archaeology, Kingston, Jamaica.

1995. Politics, Law, Pragmatics, and Human Burial Excavations: An Example from Northern California. In *Bodies of Evidence,* edited by A. L. Grauer, pp. 3–17. New York: John Wiley and Sons.

1996. Fort Ross Clothing: New Data from Old Sources. In *Clothing in Colonial Russian America: A New Look,* edited by J. Middleton, pp. 112–116. Kingston, Ontario: Limestone Press.

Golovnin, V. M.
1979. *Around the World on the Kamchatka, 1817–1819.* Translated by E. L. Wiswell. Honolulu: Hawaiian Historical Society and University Press of Hawaii.

Graham, E.
1998. Mission Archaeology. *Annual Review of Anthropology* 27: 25–62.

Grant, C.
1978. Chumash: Introduction. In *Handbook of North American Indians:* vol. 8, *California,* edited by R. Heizer, pp. 505–508. Washington, D.C.: Smithsonian Institution.

Greenwood, R. S.
1975. *3500 Years on One City Block: San Buenaventura Mission Plaza Project Archaeological Report, 1974.* Ventura, Calif.: Redevelopment Agency of the City of San Buenaventura.

1976. *The Changing Faces of Main Street: Ventura Mission Plaza Archaeological Project.* Ventura, Calif.: Redevelopment Agency of the City of San Buenaventura.

1989. The California Ranchero: Fact and Fancy. In *Columbian Consequences:* vol. 1, *Archaeological and Historical Perspectives on the Spanish Borderlands West,* edited by D. H. Thomas, pp. 451–465. Washington, D.C.: Smithsonian Institution.

Guest, F. F.
1966. The Indian Policy under Fermín Francisco de Lasuén, California's Second Father President. *California Historical Society Quarterly* (September): 195–224.

1978. Mission Colonization and Political Control in Spanish California. *The Journal of San Diego History* 24: 97–116.

1979. An Examination of the Thesis of S. F. Cook on the Forced Conversions of Indians in the California Missions. *Southern California Quarterly* 61(1): 1–77.

1983. Cultural Perspectives on California Mission Life. *Southern California Quarterly* 65(1): 1–65.

1989. An Inquiry into the Role of the Discipline in California Mission Life. *Southern California Quarterly* 71(1): 1–68.

1994. The California Missions Were Far from Faultless. *Southern California Quarterly* 76(3): 255–307.

Haas, L.

1995. *Conquests and Historical Identities in California, 1769–1936.* Berkeley and Los Angeles: University of California Press.

Hackel, S. W.

1997. Land, Labor, and Production: The Colonial Economy of Spanish and Mexican California. *California History* 76(2 and 3): 111–146.

Hagan, W. T.

1988. United States Indian Policies, 1860–1900. In *Handbook of North American Indians:* vol. 4, *History of Indian-White Relations,* edited by W. E. Washburn, pp. 51–65. Washington, D.C.: Smithsonian Institution.

Hagemeister, L. A.

1989. April 18, 1817. A Report from Leontii A. Hagemeister, Commanding Officer of the Russian American Company Ship *Kutuzov,* to the Main Administration of the Company. In *The Russian American Colonies: Three Centuries of Russian Eastward Expansion, 1798–1867:* vol. 3, *A Documentary Record,* edited by B. Dmytryshyn, E.A.P. Crownhart-Vaughan, and T. Vaughan, pp. 249–254. Portland: Oregon Historical Society Press.

Hanson, C. A.

1995. The Hispanic Horizon in Yucatan: A Model of Franciscan Missionization. *Ancient Mesoamerica* 6: 15–28.

Hantman, J. L.

1983. *Social Networks and Stylistic Distributions in the Prehistoric Plateau Southwest.* Ph.D. dissertation, Department of Anthropology, Arizona State University.

Harper, L.

1969. Mercantilism and the Colonies. In *Mercantilism: System or Expediency?* edited by W. E. Minchinton, pp. 64–70. Lexington, Mass.: D.C. Heath and Company.

Harris, J. S.

1940. The White Knife Shoshoni of Nevada. In *Acculturation in Seven American Indian Tribes,* edited by R. Linton, pp. 39–118. New York: D. Appleton Century.

Hastings, R. B.

1975. San Buenaventura Mission, an Architectural View. In *3500 Years on One City Block: San Buenaventura Mission Plaza Project Archaeological Report,* edited by R. S. Greenwood, pp. 97–140. Ventura, Calif.: Redevelopment Agency, City of San Buenaventura.

Heckscher, E. F.

1955. *Mercantilism.* Vols. 1 and 2. London: Allen and Unwin.

1969. Mercantilism. In *Revisions in Mercantilism,* edited by D.C. Coleman, pp. 19–34. London: Methuen and Company.

Heizer, R., and M. A. Whipple, eds.
1971. *The California Indians: A Source Book.* 2nd ed. Berkeley and Los Angeles: University of California Press.

Heizer, R. F.
1941. Archeological Evidence of Sebastian Rodríguez Cermeño's California Visit in 1595. *California Historical Society Quarterly* 20(4): 315–328.

1972. *The Eighteen Unratified Treaties of 1851–1852 between the California Indians and the United States Government.* Berkeley, Calif.: University of California Archaeological Research Facility.

1975. A Note on Harrington and Kroeber. *Journal of California Anthropology* 2(2): 233–234.

1978a. *Handbook of North American Indians:* vol. 8, *California.* Washington, D.C.: Smithsonian Institution.

1978b. History of Research. In *Handbook of North American Indians:* vol. 8, *California,* edited by R. Heizer, pp. 6–15. Washington, D.C.: Smithsonian Institution.

1978c. Impact of Colonization on the Native California Societies. *The Journal of San Diego History* 24: 121–139.

1978d. Natural Forces and Native World View. In *Handbook of North American Indians:* vol. 8, *California,* edited by R. Heizer, pp. 649–653. Washington, D.C.: Smithsonian Institution.

Heizer, R. F., and A. F. Almquist
1971. *The Other Californians: Prejudice and Discrimination under Spain, Mexico, and the United States to 1920.* Berkeley and Los Angeles: University of California Press.

Heizer, R. F., and A. B. Elsasser
1980. *The Natural World of the California Indians.* California Natural History Guides, no. 46. Berkeley and Los Angeles: University of California Press.

Heizer, R. F., and A. E. Treganza
1971. Mines and Quarries of the Indians of California. In *The California Indians: A Source Book,* edited by R. F. Heizer and M. A. Whipple, pp. 346–359. Berkeley and Los Angeles: University of California Press.

Hendry, G. W.
1931. The Adobe Brick as a Historical Source. *Agricultural History* 5: 110–127.

Hester, T. R.
1978a. Esselen. In *Handbook of North American Indians:* vol. 8, *California,* edited by R. Heizer, pp. 496–499. Washington, D.C.: Smithsonian Institution.

1978b. Salinan. In *Handbook of North American Indians:* vol. 8, *California,* edited by R. Heizer, pp. 500–504. Washington, D.C.: Smithsonian Institution.

Hewes, M., and G. Hewes

1958. Preface: Introduction by the Editors. In *Indian Life and Customs at Mission San Luis Rey: A Record of California Mission Life by Pablo Tac, An Indian Neophyte. Written about 1835*, edited and translated by M. Hewes and G. Hewes, pp. 3–9. San Luis Rey, Calif.: Old Mission.

Hill, J. D.

1998. Violent Encounters: Ethnogenesis and Ethnocide in Long-Term Contact Situations. In *Studies in Culture Contact: Interaction, Culture Change, and Archaeology*, edited by J. G. Cusick, pp. 146–171. Occasional Paper no. 25. Carbondale: Center for Archaeological Investigations, Southern Illinois University.

Hinton, L.

1994. *Flutes of Fire: Essays on California Indian Languages*. Berkeley, Calif.: Heyday Books.

Hoffman, K.

1997. Cultural Development in La Florida. *Historical Archaeology* 31(1): 24–35.

Hollimon, S. E.

1989. Groundstone Artifacts from Santa Inés Mission. In *Santa Inés Mission Excavations: 1986–1988*, edited by J. G. Costello, pp. 137–141. Salinas, Calif.: Coyote Press.

Holterman, J.

1970a. The Revolt of Estanislao. *Wassaja, the Indian Historian* 3(1): 43–54.

1970b. The Revolt of Yozcolo: Indian Warrior in the Fight for Freedom. *Wassaja, the Indian Historian* 3(2): 19–23.

Honeysett, E. A.

1989. Seed Remains from Santa Inés Mission. In *Santa Inés Mission Excavations: 1986–1988*, edited by J. G. Costello, pp. 177–179. Salinas, Calif.: Coyote Press.

Hoover, R. L.

1977. Ethnohistoric Salinan Acculturation. *Ethnohistory* 24(3): 261–268.

1979. The Mission San Antonio de Padua in California. *Archaeology* 32(6): 56–58.

1980. Agricultural Acculturation at Mission San Antonio. *The Masterkey* 54(4): 142–145.

1985. The Archaeology of Spanish Colonial Sites in California. In *Comparative Studies in the Archaeology of Colonialism*, edited by S. L. Dyson, pp. 93–114. BAR International Series 233. Oxford: British Archaeological Reports.

1989. Spanish-Native Interaction and Acculturation in the Alta California Missions. In *Columbian Consequences: vol. 1, Archaeological and Histor-*

ical Perspectives on the Spanish Borderlands West, edited by D. H. Thomas, pp. 395–406. Washington, D.C.: Smithsonian Institution.

2002. *Excavations at the Mystery Column: A Wind-Powered Wool Fulling Post Mill in Mission La Purísima State Historic Park*. Ms. on file with author.

Hoover, R. L., and J. G. Costello
1985. *Excavations at Mission San Antonio, 1976–1978*. Monograph 26. Los Angeles: Institute of Archaeology, University of California.

Hornbeck, D.
1978. Land Tenure and Rancho Expansion in Alta California, 1784–1846. *Journal of Historical Geography* 4(4): 371–390.

1985. Early Mission Settlement. In *Some Reminiscences about Fray Junípero Serra*, edited by F. F. Weber, pp. 55–66. Santa Barbara, Calif.: Kimberly Press.

1989. Economic Growth and Change at the Missions of Alta California, 1769–1846. In *Columbian Consequences:* vol. 1, *Archaeological and Historical Perspectives on the Spanish Borderlands West*, edited by D. H. Thomas, pp. 423–434. Washington, D.C.: Smithsonian Institution.

Hudson, T.
1979. Editor's Introduction. In *Breath of the Sun: Life in Early California as told by a Chumash Indian, Fernando Librado to John P. Harrington*, edited by T. Hudson, pp. ix–xiii. Banning, Calif.: Malki Museum Press, Morongo Indian Reservation.

Hughes, R. E.
1992. California Archaeology and Linguistic Prehistory. *Journal of Anthropological Research* 48: 317–338.

Hull, K. L.
2002. *Culture Contact in Context: A Multiscalar View of Catastrophic Depopulation and Culture Change in Yosemite Valley, California*. Ph.D. dissertation, Department of Anthropology, University of California, Berkeley.

Humphrey, R.
1965. The La Purísima Mission Cemetery. *Annual Reports of the University of California Archaeological Survey* 7: 179–192.

Hurtado, A. L.
1988. *Indian Survival on the California Frontier*. New Haven, Conn.: Yale University Press.

1992. Sexuality in California's Franciscan Missions: Cultural Perceptions and Sad Realities. *California History* 71(3): 370–385.

Hutchinson, C. A.
1969. *Frontier Settlement in Mexican California: The Hijar-Padres Colony and Its Origins, 1769–1835*. New Haven, Conn.: Yale University Press.

Hylkema, M.
1995. *Archaeological Investigations at Mission Santa Clara (CA-SCL-30) for the Re-Alignment of Route 82.* Oakland: California Department of Transportation, District 4.

Istomin, A. A.
1992. *The Indians at the Ross Settlement According to the Censuses by Kuskov, 1820–1821.* Fort Ross, Calif.: Fort Ross Interpretive Association.

Jackson, H. H.
1885. *A Century of Dishonor: A Sketch of the United States Government's Dealings with Some of the Indian Tribes.* Boston: Roberts Brothers.

1902. *Glimpses of California and the Missions.* Boston: Little, Brown and Company.

Jackson, H. H., and A. Kinney
1979. Report on the Condition and Needs of the Mission Indians of California, Made by Special Agents Helen Jackson and Abbot Kinney to the Commissioner of Indian Affairs. In *Federal Concern about Conditions of California Indians, 1853 to 1913: Eight Documents,* edited by R. F. Heizer, pp. 75–93. Socorro, N.M.: Ballena Press.

Jackson, R. H.
1983. Intermarriage at Fort Ross: Evidence from the San Rafael Mission Baptismal Register. *Journal of California and Great Basin Anthropology* 5(1 and 2): 240–241.

1984. Gentile Recruitment and Population Movements in the San Francisco Bay Missions. *Journal of California and Great Basin Anthropology* 6(2): 225–239.

1994. *Indian Population Decline: The Missions of Northwestern New Spain, 1687–1840.* Albuquerque: University of New Mexico Press.

Jackson, R. H., and E. Castillo
1995. *Indians, Franciscans, and Spanish Colonization: The Impact of the Mission System on California Indians.* Albuquerque: University of New Mexico Press.

John, E. A. H.
1996. *Storms Brewed in Other Men's Worlds: The Confrontation of Indians, Spanish, and French in the Southwest, 1540–1795.* 2nd ed. Norman: University of Oklahoma Press.

Johnson, J. R.
1982. *An Ethnohistoric Study of the Island Chumash.* M.A. thesis, Department of Anthropology, University of California, Santa Barbara.

1988. *Chumash Social Organization: An Ethnohistoric Perspective.* Ph.D. dissertation, Department of Anthropology, University of California, Santa Barbara.

1989. The Chumash and the Missions. In *Columbian Consequences:* vol. 1, *Archaeological and Historical Perspectives on the Spanish Borderlands West,* edited by D. H. Thomas, pp. 365–376. Washington, D.C.: Smithsonian Institution.

1995. *The Chumash Indians after Secularization.* Bakersfield: California Mission Studies Association.

1997. The Indians of Mission San Fernando. *Southern California Quarterly* 79(3): 249–290.

2001. Ethnohistoric Reflections of Cruzeño Chumash Society. In *The Origins of a Pacific Coast Chiefdom: The Chumash of the Channel Islands,* edited by J. R. Arnold, pp. 53–70. Salt Lake City: University of Utah Press.

Johnson, J. R., and D. Crawford
1999. Contributions to Luiseño Ethnohistory Based on Mission Register Research. *Pacific Coast Archaeological Society Quarterly* 35(4): 79–102.

Johnson, J. R., and S. McLendon
2000. The Social History of Native Islanders Following Missionization. In *Proceedings of the Fifth California Islands Symposium, March 29 to April 1, 1989,* edited by D. R. Browne, K. L. Mitchell, and H. W. Chaney, pp. 646–653. Costa Mesa, Calif.: MBC Applied Environmental Sciences.

Jones, T. L.
1991. Marine-Resource Value and the Priority of Coastal Settlement: A California Perspective. *American Antiquity* 56: 419–443.

1992. *Essays on the Prehistory of Maritime California,* no. 10. Davis, Calif.: Center for Archaeological Research at Davis, Department of Anthropology, University of California.

Judge, A. V.
1969. The Idea of a Mercantile State. In *Revisions in Mercantilism,* edited by D.C. Coleman, pp. 35–60. London: Methuen and Company.

Kalani, L., L. Rudy, and J. Sperry
1998. *Fort Ross.* Jenner, Calif.: Fort Ross Interpretive Association.

Kammeyer, D., G. Emberson, and G. D. Singleton
2002. *2002 Field Directory of the California Indian Community.* Sacramento: California Indian Assistance Program, Department of Housing and Community Development, State of California.

Kan, S.
1988. The Russian Orthodox Church in Alaska. In *Handbook of North American Indians:* vol. 4, *History of Indian-White Relations,* edited by W. E. Washburn, pp. 506–521. Washington, D.C.: Smithsonian Institution.

Kardulias, P. N.
1990. Fur Production as a Specialized Activity in a World System: Indians in

the North American Fur Trade. *American Indian Culture and Research Journal* 14(1): 25–60.

Kari, J.
1983. Kalifornsky, the Californian from Cook Inlet. *Alaska in Perspective* 5: 1–11.

Kealhofer, L.
1996. The Evidence for Demographic Collapse in California. In *Bioarchaeology of Native American Adaptation in the Spanish Borderlands*, edited by B. J. Baker and L. Kealhofer, pp. 56–92. Gainesville: University Press of Florida.

Kelleher, B. T.
1997. *Drake's Bay: Unraveling California's Great Maritime Mystery*. Cupertino, Calif.: Kelleher and Associates.

Kelly, I.
1978. Coast Miwok. In *Handbook of North American Indians:* vol. 8, *California*, edited by R. F. Heizer, pp. 414–425. Washington, D.C.: Smithsonian Institution.

Kelly, L. C.
1988. United States Indian Policies, 1900–1980. In *Handbook of North American Indians:* vol. 4, *History of Indian-White Relations*, edited by W. E. Washburn, pp. 66–80. Washington, D.C.: Smithsonian Institution.

Kelsey, C. E.
1979. Report of Special Agent for California Indians, C.E. Kelsey. In *Federal Concern about Conditions of California Indians, 1853 to 1913: Eight Documents*, edited by R. F. Heizer, pp. 123–150. Socorro, N.M.: Ballena Press.

Kelsey, H.
1979. The California Armada of Juan Rodríguez Cabrillo. *Southern California Quarterly* 61: 313–337.

1985. European Impact on the California Indians, 1530–1830. *The Americas* 41(4): 494–511.

1998. *Juan Rodríquez Cabrillo*. San Marino, Calif.: Huntington Library.

Kennedy, M. J.
1955. *Culture Contact and Acculturation of the Southwestern Pomo*. Ph.D. dissertation, Department of Anthropology, University of California, Berkeley.

Khlebnikov, K.
1976. *Colonial Russian America: Kyrill T. Khlebnikov's Reports, 1817–1832*. Translated by B. Dmytryshyn and E.A.P. Crownhart-Vaughan. Portland: Oregon Historical Society.

1989. From Notes on California by Kyrill T. Khlebnikov, 1829, Manager of the

New Arkhangel Office of the Russian American Company. In *The Russian American Colonies: Three Centuries of Russian Eastward Expansion, 1798–1867*: vol. 3, *A Documentary Record*, edited by B. Dmytryshyn, E.A.P. Crownhart-Vaughan, and T. Vaughan, pp. 386–398. Portland: Oregon Historical Society Press.

1990. *The Khlebnikov Archive: Unpublished Journal (1800–1837) and Travel Notes (1820, 1822, and 1824)*. Edited by L. Shur, translated by J. Bisk. Fairbanks: University of Alaska Press.

1994. *Notes on Russian America, Part I: Novo-Arkhangel'sk*. Translated by S. LeComte and R. Pierce. Kingston, Ontario: Limestone Press.

Kicza, J.
1997. Native American, African, and Hispanic Communities during the Middle Period in the Colonial Americas. *Historical Archaeology* 31(1): 9–17.

King, C. D.
1990. *Evolution of Chumash Society: A Comparative Study of Artifacts Used for Social System Maintenance in the Santa Barbara Channel Region before A.D. 1804*. New York: Garland Publishing.

Kirch, P. V., and R. C. Green
2001. *Hawaiki, Ancestral Polynesia: An Essay in Historical Anthropology*. Cambridge: Cambridge University Press.

Klimek, S.
1935. Culture Element Distributions: 1, The Structure of California Indian Culture. *University of California Publications in American Archaeology and Ethnology* 37(1): 1–70.

Kniffen, F.
1939. Pomo Geography. *University of California Publications in American Archaeology and Ethnology* 36(6): 353–400.

Kostromitinov, P.
1974. Notes on the Indians in Upper California. In *Ethnographic Observations on the Coast Miwok and Pomo by Contre-Admiral F. P. Von Wrangell and P. Kostromitinov of the Russian Colony Ross, 1839*, edited by F. Stross and R. Heizer, pp. 7–18. Berkeley: Archaeological Research Facility, University of California.

Kotzebue, O. V.
1830. *A New Voyage Round the World, in the Years 1823, 24, 25, and 26*. Vols. 1 and 2. London: Henry Colburn and Richard Bentley.

Kroeber, A. L.
1904a. The Languages of the Coast of California South of San Francisco. *University of California Publications in American Archaeology and Ethnology* 2(2): 29–80.

1904b. Types of Indian Culture in California. *University of California Publications in American Archaeology and Ethnology* 2(3): 81–103.

1907. Indian Myths of South Central California. *University of California Publications in American Archaeology and Ethnology* 4(4): 167–250.

1908. Notes on the Luiseño. *University of California Publications in American Archaeology and Ethnology* 8(3): 174–186.

1910. The Chumash and Costanoan Languages. *University of California Publications in American Archaeology and Ethnology* 9(2): 237–271.

1917. California Kinship Systems. *University of California Publications in American Archaeology and Ethnology* 12(9): 339–396.

1920. California Culture Provinces. *University of California Publications in American Archaeology and Ethnology* 17(2): 151–169.

1922. Elements of Culture in Native California. *University of California Publications in American Archaeology and Ethnology* 13(8): 259–328.

1923. The History of Native Culture in California. *University of California Publications in American Archaeology and Ethnology* 20: 125–142.

1925. *Handbook of the Indians of California.* Bulletin 78, Bureau of American Ethnology, Smithsonian Institution. Washington, D.C.: Smithsonian Institution.

1932. The Patwin and Their Neighbors. *University of California Publications in American Archaeology and Ethnology* 29(4): 253–423.

1935. Preface: Culture Element Distributions: 1, The Structure of California Indian Culture. *University of California Publications in American Archaeology and Ethnology* 37(1): 1–11.

1936. Culture Element Distributions: 3, Area and Climax. *University of California Publications in American Archaeology and Ethnology* 37(3): 101–116.

1939. Cultural and Natural Areas of Native North America. *University of California Publications in American Archaeology and Ethnology* 38(2): 1–242.

1966. The Nature of Land-Holding Groups in Aboriginal California. In *Aboriginal California: Three Studies in Culture History,* edited by R. F. Hiezer, pp. 82–120. Berkeley: Archaeological Research Facility, University of California.

Kroeber, A. L., and R. F. Heizer
1970. Continuity of Indian Population in California from 1770/1848 to 1955. *Contributions of the University of California Archaeological Research Facility* 9: 1–22.

Kunkel, P. H.
1974. The Pomo Kin Group and the Political Unit in Aboriginal California. *The Journal of California Anthropology* 1(1): 7–18.

La Pérouse, J. F. de
1989. The Journals of Jean Francois de La Pérouse. In *Monterey in 1786: Life in a California Mission*, edited by M. Margolin, pp. 51–111. Berkeley, Calif.: Heyday Books.

LaPlace, C.
1986. Description of a Visit to an Indian Village Adjacent to Fort Ross by Cyrille LaPlace, 1839. Translation and Editing of 1854 Original French Publication by Glenn Farris. Appendix B of *Cultural Resource Survey at the Fort Ross Campground, Sonoma County, California*, by Glenn Farris, pp. 65–80. Sacramento: Cultural Heritage Section, Archaeology Laboratory, California Department of Parks and Recreation.

Langellier, J. P., and D. B. Rosen
1996. *El Presidio de San Francisco: A History under Spain and Mexico, 1776–1846*. Spokane, Wash.: The Arthur H. Clark Company.

Langenwalter, P. E., and L. W. McKee
1985. Vertebrate Faunal Remains from the Neophyte Dormitory. In *Excavations at Mission San Antonio, 1976–1978*, edited by R. L. Hoover and J. G. Costello, pp. 94–121. Monograph 26. Los Angeles: Institute of Archaeology, University of California.

Langsdorff, G. H. V.
1968. *Voyages and Travels in Various Parts of the World*. Vol. 2. Bibliotheca Australiana no. 41. New York: Da Capo Press.

Larsen, C. S.
1994. In the Wake of Columbus: Native Population Biology in the Postcontact Americas. *Yearbook of Physical Anthropology* 37: 109–154.

Larsen, C. S., and G. Milner, eds.
1994. *In the Wake of Contact: Biological Responses to Conquest*. New York: John Wiley and Sons.

Larson, D. O., J. R. Johnson, and J. C. Michaelson
1994. Missionization among the Coastal Chumash of Central California: A Study of Risk Minimization Strategies. *American Anthropologist* 96(2): 263–299.

Lazarev, A. P.
1989. November 30, 1823–January 12, 1824. From the Journal of Andrei P. Lazarev, Captain-Lieutenant of the Sloop, *Ladoga*, Describing Conditions in California in the Region of the Presidio of San Francisco. In *The Russian American Colonies: Three Centuries of Russian Eastward Expansion, 1798–1867*: vol. 3, *A Documentary Record*, edited by B. Dmytryshyn, E.A.P. Crownhart-Vaughan, and T. Vaughan, pp. 370–382. Portland: Oregon Historical Society Press.

Leventhal, A., L. Field, H. Alvarez, and R. Cambra
1994. The Ohlone: Back from Extinction. In *The Ohlone Past and Present: Native Americans of the San Francisco Bay Region*, edited by L. J. Bean, pp. 297–336. Menlo Park, Calif.: Ballena Press.

Levy, R.
1978. Costanoan. In *Handbook of North American Indians:* vol. 8, *California*, edited by R. Heizer, pp. 485–495. Washington, D.C.: Smithsonian Institution.

Lewis, H. T.
1973. *Patterns of Indian Burning in California: Ecology and Ethnohistory.* Ramona, Calif.: Ballena Press.

Librado, F.
1979. *Breath of the Sun: Life in Early California as told by a Chumash Indian, Fernando Librado to John P. Harrington.* Edited with notes by T. Hudson. Banning, Calif.: Malki Museum Press, Morongo Indian Reservation.

Lightfoot, K. G.
1992. Coastal Hunter-Gatherer Settlement Systems in the Southern North Coast Ranges. In *Essays on the Prehistory of Maritime California*, edited by T. L. Jones, 10: 39–53. Davis, Calif.: Center for Archaeological Research at Davis, Department of Anthropology, University of California.

1995. Culture Contact Studies: Redefining the Relationship between Prehistoric and Historical Archaeology. *American Antiquity* 60(2): 199–217.

1997a. Cultural Construction of Coastal Landscapes: A Middle Holocene Perspective from San Francisco Bay. In *Archaeology of the California Coast during the Middle Holocene*, edited by J. Erlandson and M. Glassow, pp. 129–141. Los Angeles: Institute of Archaeology, University of California.

1997b. Russian Colonialism in the North and Tropical Pacific: An Introduction. In *The Archaeology of Russian Colonialism in the North and Tropical Pacific*, edited by P. R. Mills and A. Martinez, pp. 1–9. Kroeber Anthropological Society Papers, no. 81. Berkeley, Calif.: Kroeber Anthropological Society Papers.

Lightfoot, K. G., and A. Martinez
1995. Frontiers and Boundaries in Archaeological Perspective. *Annual Review of Anthropology* 24: 471–492.

1997. Interethnic Relationships in the Native Alaskan Neighborhood: Consumption Practices, Cultural Innovations, and the Construction of Household Identities. In *The Archaeology and Ethnohistory of Fort Ross, California:* vol. 2, *The Native Alaskan Neighborhood: A Multiethnic Community at Colony Ross*, edited by K. G. Lightfoot, A.M. Schiff, and T. A. Wake, pp. 1–16. Contributions of the University of California Archaeological Research Facility, no. 55. Berkeley: Archaeological Research Facility.

Lightfoot, K. G., A. Martinez, and A. Schiff
1998. Daily Practice and Material Culture in Pluralistic Social Settings: An Archaeological Study of Culture Change and Persistence from Fort Ross, California. *American Antiquity* 63(2): 199–222.

Lightfoot, K. G., and A.M. Schiff
1997. Archaeological Field Investigations at the Fort Ross Beach Site. In *The Archaeology and Ethnohistory of Fort Ross, California: vol. 2: The Native Alaskan Neighborhood: A Multiethnic Community at Colony Ross*, edited by K. G. Lightfoot, A.M. Schiff, and T. A. Wake, pp. 23–41. Contributions of the University of California Archaeological Research Facility, no. 55. Berkeley: Archaeological Research Facility.

Lightfoot, K. G., A.M. Schiff, and L. Holm
1997. Archaeological Field Investigations at the Native Alaskan Village Site. In *The Archaeology and Ethnohistory of Fort Ross, California:* vol. 2, *The Native Alaskan Neighborhood: A Multiethnic Community at Colony Ross*, edited by K. G. Lightfoot, A.M. Schiff, and T. A. Wake, pp. 42–95. Contributions of the University of California Archaeological Research Facility, no. 55. Berkeley: Archaeological Research Facility.

Lightfoot, K. G., A.M. Schiff, A. Martinez, T. A. Wake, S. Silliman, P. Mills, and L. Holm
1997. Culture Change and Persistence in the Daily Lifeways of Interethnic Households. In *The Archaeology and Ethnohistory of Fort Ross, California:* vol. 2, *The Native Alaskan Neighborhood: A Multiethnic Community at Colony Ross*, edited by K. G. Lightfoot, A.M. Schiff, and T. A. Wake, pp. 355–419. Contributions of the University of California Archaeological Research Facility, no. 55. Berkeley: Archaeological Research Facility.

Lightfoot, K. G., A.M. Schiff, and T. A. Wake, eds.
1997. *The Archaeology and Ethnohistory of Fort Ross, California:* vol. 2, *The Native Alaskan Neighborhood: A Multiethnic Community at Colony Ross*. Contributions of the University of California Archaeological Facility, no. 55. Berkeley: Archaeological Research Facility.

Lightfoot, K. G., and W. S. Simmons
1998. Culture Contact in Protohistoric California: Social Contexts of Native and European Encounters. *Journal of California and Great Basin Anthropology* 20(2): 138–170.

Lightfoot, K. G., T. A. Wake, and A.M. Schiff
1991. *The Archaeology and Ethnohistory of Fort Ross, California:* vol. 1, *Introduction*. Contributions of the University of California Archaeological Research Facility, no. 49. Berkeley: Archaeological Research Facility.

Linton, R.
1940a. Acculturation and the Processes of Culture Change. In *Acculturation*

in *Seven American Indian Tribes,* edited by R. Linton, pp. 463–482. New York: D. Appleton Century.

1940b. *Acculturation in Seven American Indian Tribes.* New York: D. Appleton Century.

1940c. The Distinctive Aspects of Acculturation. In *Acculturation in Seven American Indian Tribes,* edited by R. Linton, pp. 501–519. New York: D. Appleton Century.

Loeb, E. M.
1926. Pomo Folkways. *University of California Publications in American Archaeology and Ethnology* 19(2): 149–405.

1932. The Western Kuksu Cult. *University of California Publications in American Archaeology and Ethnology* 33(1): 1–137.

Lummis, C. F.
1936. *The Spanish Pioneers and the California Missions.* Chicago: A.C. McClurg and Company.

Lummis, T.
1992. Oral History. In *Folklore, Cultural Performances, and Popular Entertainments,* edited by R. Bauman, pp. 92–97. New York: Oxford University Press.

Luomala, K.
1978. Tipai and Ipai. In *Handbook of North American Indians:* vol. 8, *California,* edited by R. Heizer, pp. 592–609. Washington, D.C.: Smithsonian Institution.

Lütke, F. P.
1989. September 4–28, 1818. From the Diary of Fedor P. Lütke during his Circumnavigation aboard the Sloop Kamchatka, 1817–1819: Observations on California. In *The Russian American Colonies: Three Centuries of Russian Eastward Expansion, 1798–1867:* vol. 3, *A Documentary Record,* edited by B. Dmytryshyn, E.A.P. Crownhart-Vaughan, and T. Vaughan, pp. 257–285. Portland: Oregon Historical Society Press.

Magnusson, L.
1994. *Mercantilism: The Shaping of an Economic Language.* London: Routledge.

Margolin, M.
1989. Introduction. In *Monterey in 1776: Life in a California Mission,* edited by M. Margolin, pp. 3–50. Berkeley, Calif.: Heyday Books.

Martinez, A.
1997. View from the Ridge: The Kashaya Pomo in a Russian-American Company Context. In *The Archaeology of Russian Colonialism in the North and Tropical Pacific,* edited by P. R. Mills and A. Martinez, pp. 141–156. Kroeber Anthropological Society Papers, vol. 81. Berkeley, Calif.: Kroeber Anthropological Association.

1998. *An Archaeological Study of Change and Continuity in the Material Remains, Practices and Cultural Identities of Native California Women in a Nineteenth-Century Pluralistic Context.* Ph.D. dissertation, Department of Anthropology, University of California, Berkeley.

Mason, J. A.
1912. The Ethnology of the Salinan Indians. *University of California Publications in American Archaeology and Ethnology* 10(4): 97–240.

1916. The Mutsun Dialect of Costanoan Based on the Vocabulary of De La Cuesta. *University of California Publications in American Archaeology and Ethnology* 11(7): 399–472.

Mason, R. J.
2000. Archaeology and Native American Oral Traditions. *American Antiquity* 65(2): 239–266.

Mason, W. M.
1984. Indian-Mexican Cultural Exchange in the Los Angeles Area, 1781–1834. *Aztlan* 15(1): 123–144.

1998. *The Census of 1790: A Demographic History of Colonial California.* Menlo Park, Calif.: Ballena Press.

Mathes, W. M.
1968. *Vizcaino and Spanish Expansion in the Pacific Ocean, 1580–1630.* San Francisco: California Historical Society.

1989. Baja California: A Special Area of Contact and Colonization, 1535–1697. In *Columbian Consequences:* vol. 1, *Archaeological and Historical Perspectives on the Spanish Borderlands West,* edited by D. H. Thomas, pp. 407–422. Washington, D.C.: Smithsonian Institution.

Matiushkin, F. F.
1996. From "A Journal of a Round-the-World Voyage on the Sloop Kamchatka, under the Command of Captain Golovnin." Translated from the Russian by Stephen Watrous. *Fort Ross Interpretive Association Newsletter* (September–October): 5–6.

McEwan, B. G.
1993. *Spanish Missions of La Florida.* Gainesville: University Press of Florida.

1995. Spanish Precedents and Domestic Life at Puerto Real: The Archaeology of Two Spanish Homesites. In *Puerto Real: The Archaeology of a Sixteenth-Century Spanish Town in Hispaniola,* edited by K. Deagan, pp. 197–230. Gainesville: University Press of Florida.

McGuire, R.
1982. The Study of Ethnicity in Historical Archaeology. *Journal of Anthropological Archaeology* 1: 159–178.

McIntyre, M. J.

1976. Analysis of a Mission-Era Trash Pit. In *The Changing Faces of Main Street: Ventura Mission Plaza Archaeological Project*, edited by R. S. Greenwood, pp. 257–284. Ventura, California: Redevelopment Agency, City of San Buenaventura.

McKenzie, J. C.

1996. Another "First" by the Russians in California: Early Attempts to Control Smallpox Epidemics. *Fort Ross Interpretive Association Newsletter* (March–April): 3.

McLendon, S., and R. L. Oswalt

1978. Pomo: Introduction. In *Handbook of North American Indians:* vol. 8, *California*, edited by R. F. Heizer, pp. 274–288. Washington, D.C.: Smithsonian Institution.

Meighan, C. W.

1976a. An Anthropological Commentary on the Mission Questionnaires. In *As the Padres Saw Them: California Indian Life and Customs as Reported by the Franciscan Missionaries, 1813–1815*, edited by M. Geiger and C. W. Meighan, pp. 3–9. Santa Barbara, Calif.: Santa Barbara Mission Archive Library.

1976b. The Eagle Ceremony. In *As the Padres Saw Them: California Indian Life and Customs as Reported by the Franciscan Missionaries, 1813–1815*, edited by M. Geiger and C. W. Meighan, pp. 160–161. Santa Barbara, Calif.: Santa Barbara Mission Archive Library.

1987. Indians and California Missions. *Southern California Quarterly* 69(3): 187–201.

Meighan, C. W., and F. A. Riddell

1972. *The Maru Cult of the Pomo Indians: A California Ghost Dance Survival*. Southwest Museum Paper no. 23. Los Angeles: Southwest Museum.

Mendoza, R. G.

2001. On the Question of Ohlone Mutsun Acculturation at Mission San Juan Bautista: Recent Findings from the Lost Convento. Paper presented at the the Gran Quivira 30 Conference, Mission San Juan Capistrano, California.

2002. This Old Mission: San Juan Bautista Archaeology and the Hispanic Tradition. *California Mission Studies Association Boletín* 19(2): 35–40.

Mensing, S., and R. Byrne

1998. Pre-mission Invasion of *Erodium cicutarium* in California. *Journal of Biogeography* 25: 757–762.

Menzies, A.

1924. Menzies' California Journal. *California Historical Society Quarterly* 2(4): 265–340.

Merck, C. H.

1980. *Siberian and Northwestern America, 1788–1792: The Journal of Carl Heinrich Merck, Naturalist with the Russian Scientific Expedition Led by Captains Joseph Billings and Gavriil Sarychev.* Translated by F. Jaensch. Kingston, Ontario: Limestone Press.

Merrill, W. L.

1994. Cultural Creativity and Raiding Bands in Eighteenth-Century Northern New Spain. In *Violence, Resistance, and Survival in the Americas: Native Americans and the Legacy of Conquest,* edited by W. B. Taylor and F. Pease G. Y., pp. 124–152. Washington, D.C.: Smithsonian Institution.

Milanich, J. T.

1995. *Florida Indians and the Invasion from Europe.* Gainesville: University Press of Florida.

Milliken, R.

1994. The Costanoan-Yokuts Language Boundary in the Contact Period. In *The Ohlone Past and Present: Native Americans of the San Francisco Bay Region,* edited by L. J. Bean, pp. 165–181. Menlo Park, Calif.: Ballena Press.

1995. *A Time of Little Choice: The Disintegration of Tribal Culture in the San Francisco Bay Area 1769–1810.* Menlo Park, Calif.: Ballena Press.

Mills, P. R.

2002. *Hawai'i's Russian Adventure: A New Look at Old History.* Honolulu: University of Hawai'i Press.

Minchinton, W. E.

1969. Introduction. In *Mercantilism: System or Expediency?,* edited by W. E. Minchinton, pp. vii–xiii. Lexington, Mass.: D.C. Heath and Company.

Miranda, G. E.

1981. *Gente de Razón* Marriage Patterns in Spanish and Mexican California: A Case Study of Santa Barbara and Los Angeles. *Southern California Quarterly* 63(1): 1–21.

Momaday, N. S.

1974. Native American Attitudes to the Environment. In *Seeing with a Native Eye: Essays on Native American Religion,* edited by W. Capps, pp. 79–85. New York: Harper and Row.

Monks, G.

1985. Status and Fur Trade in the Northern Department, 1821–1870. In *Status, Structure, and Stratification: Current Archaeological Reconstructions,* edited by M. Thompson, M. T. Garcia, and F. J. Kense, pp. 407–411. Calgary, Alberta: University of Calgary Archaeological Association.

Monroy, D.

1990. *Thrown Among Strangers: The Making of Mexican Culture in Frontier California.* Berkeley and Los Angeles: University of California Press.

Moratto, M. J.
1984. *California Archaeology.* Orlando, Fla.: Academic Press.

Moss, M. L., and J. M. Erlandson
1995. Reflections on the Prehistory of the Pacific Coast of North America. *Journal of World Prehistory* 9(1): 1–45.

Murley, D. F.
1994. The Travels of Native Alaskan Marine Mammal Hunters in the Service of the Russian-American Company. Paper presented at the Twenty-Seventh Annual Chacmool Conference, University of Calgary, Calgary, Alberta.

1998. Native Alaskans. In *Fort Ross,* edited by L. Kalani, L. Rudy, and J. Sperry, pp. 8–10. Jenner, Calif: Fort Ross Interpretive Association.

Nader, L.
1994. Comparative Consciousness. In *Assessing Cultural Anthropology,* edited by R. Borofsky, pp. 84–96. New York: McGraw-Hill.

Nash, P.
1988. Twentieth-Century United States Government Agencies. In *Handbook of North American Indians:* vol. 4, *History of Indian-White Relations,* edited by W. E. Washburn, pp. 264–275. Washington, D.C.: Smithsonian Institution.

Neri, M. C.
1976. Narcisco Duran and the Secularization of the California Missions. *Americas* 33(3): 411–429.

Neuerburg, N.
1987. *The Architecture of Mission La Purísima.* Santa Barbara, Calif.: Bellerophon Books.

Noller, J. S., and K. G. Lightfoot
1997. An Archaeoseismic Approach and Method for the Study of Active Strike-Slip Faults. *Geoarchaeology* 12(2): 117–135.

Ogden, A.
1941. *The California Sea Otter Trade, 1784–1848.* Berkeley: University of California Press.

Oleksa, M. J.
1990. The Creoles and Their Contributions to the Development of Alaska. In *Russian America: The Forgotten Frontier,* edited by B. S. Smith and R. J. Barnett, pp. 185–196. Tacoma: Washington State Historical Society.

Ortiz, B. O.
1994. Chocheño and Rumsen Narratives: A Comparison. In *The Ohlone Past and Present,* edited by L. J. Bean, pp. 99–163. Menlo Park, Calif.: Ballena Press.

Ortner, S. B.
1984. Theory in Anthropology since the Sixties. *Comparative Studies in Society and History* 26: 126–166.

Osborn, S. K.

1997. *Death in the Daily Life of the Ross Colony: Mortuary Behavior in Frontier Russian America*. Ph.D. dissertation, Department of Anthropology, University of Wisconsin, Milwaukee.

Osio, A.M.

1996. *The History of Alta California: A Memoir of Mexican California*. Translated by R. M. Beebe and R. M. Senkewicz. Madison: University of Wisconsin Press.

Oswalt, R. L.

1957. Russian Loanwords in Southwestern Pomo. *International Journal of American Linguistics* 23: 123–131.

1966. *Kashaya Texts*. University of California Publications in Linguistics 36. Berkeley: University of California Press.

1971. The Case of the Broken Bottle. *International Journal of American Linguistics* 37(1): 48–49.

1988. History through the Words Brought to California by the Fort Ross Colony. *News from Native California* 2(3): 20–22.

1994. History through the Words Brought to California by the Fort Ross Colony. In *Flutes of Fire: Essays on California Indian Languages,* edited by L. Hinton, pp. 100–105. Berkeley, Calif.: Heyday Books.

Palóu, F. F.

1926a. *Historical Memoirs of New California:* vol. 2., edited and translated by Herbert Eugene Bolton. Berkeley: University of California Press.

1926b. *Historical Memoirs of New California:* vol. 3, edited and translated by Herbert Eugene Bolton. Berkeley: University of California Press.

1955. *Palóu's Life of Fray Junípero Serra*. Translated and annotated by Maynard J. Geiger. Washington, D.C.: Academy of American Franciscan History.

1966. *Historical Memoirs of New California*. Translated by Herbert Eugene Bolton. 4 vols. New York: Russell and Russell.

Parkman, E. B.

1990. *Excavation of CA-SON-1446H (also designated as CA-SON-1896)*. Report on file, Silverado District, California Department of Parks and Recreation, Sonoma, California.

1996/1997. Fort and Settlement: Interpreting the Past at Fort Ross State Historic Park. *California History* 75(4): 354–369.

Parman, D. L.

1994. *Indians and the American West in the Twentieth Century*. Bloomington: Indiana University Press.

Parrish, O., D. Murley, R. Jewett, and K. Lightfoot
2000. The Science of Archaeology and the Response from within Native California: The Archaeology and Ethnohistory of Meˀtini Village in the Fort Ross State Historic Park. *Proceedings of the Society for California Archaeology* 13: 84–87.

Payeras, M.
1995. *Writings of Mariano Payeras.* Translated and edited by Donald Cutter. Santa Barbara, Calif.: Bellerophon Books.

Pérez, E.
1988. An Old Woman and Her Recollections. In *Three Memoirs of Mexican California,* edited by V. Fisher, pp. 73–82. Berkeley: The Friends of the Bancroft Library, University of California, Berkeley.

Phillips, G. H.
1975. *Chiefs and Challengers: Indian Resistance and Cooperation in Southern California.* Berkeley and Los Angeles: University of California Press,.

1980. Indians in Los Angeles, 1781–1875: Economic Integration, Social Disintegration. *Pacific Historical Review* 49: 427–451.

1989. The Alcaldes: Indian Leadership in the Spanish Missions of California. In *The Struggle for Political Autonomy,* edited by F. E. Hoxie, pp. 83–87. Occasional Papers in Curriculum Series, no. 11. Chicago: D'Arcy McNickle Center for the History of the American Indian, The Newberry Library.

1990. *The Enduring Struggle: Indians in California History.* Sparks, Nev.: Materials for Today's Learning.

1993. *Indians and Intruders in Central California, 1769–1849.* Norman: University of Oklahoma Press.

1997. *Indians and Indian Agents: The Origins of the Reservation System in California, 1849–1852.* Norman: University of Oklahoma Press.

Powers, S.
1976. *Tribes of California.* Berkeley and Los Angeles: University of California Press.

Prager, G.
1985. A Comparison of the Social Structure in the Northwest Company and the Hudson's Bay Company. In *Status, Structure, and Stratification: Current Archaeological Reconstructions,* edited by M. Thompson, M. T. Garcia, and F. J. Kense, pp. 387–391. Calgary, Alberta: University of Calgary Archaeological Association.

Preston, W.
1996. Serpent in Eden: Dispersal of Foreign Diseases into Pre-Mission California. *Journal of California and Great Basin Anthropology* 18(1): 2–37.

1997. Serpent in the Garden: Environmental Change in Colonial California. *California History* 76(2 and 3): 260–298.

Pyszczyk, H.

1985. The Role of Material Culture in the Structure of Fur Trade Society. In *Status, Structure and Stratification: Current Archaeological Reconstructions*, edited by M. Thompson, M. T. Garcia and F. J. Kense, pp. 399–406. Calgary, Alberta: University of Calgary Archaeological Association.

Quinn, D. B.

1979a. 1542–1543. The Voyage of Juan Rodríguez Cabrillo (João Rodrigues Cabrilho) up the Pacific Coast. In *New American World: A Documentary History of North America to 1612:* vol. 1, *America from Conception to Discovery. Early Exploration of North America*, edited by D. B. Quinn, pp. 450–461. New York: Arno Press and Hector Bye, Inc.

1979b. [1584–1585]. Fray Andrés de Aguirre to the Archbishop of Mexico, Proposing the Continuation of the California Voyages. In *New American World: A Documentary History of North America to 1612:* vol. 5, *The Extension of Settlement in Florida, Virginia, and the Spanish Southwest*, edited by D. B. Quinn, pp. 399–401. New York: Arno Press and Hector Bye, Inc.

1979c. The "Famous Voyage" Account of Drake's California Visit. In *New American World: A Documentary History of North America to 1612:* vol. 1, *America from Concept to Discovery. Early Exploration of North America*, edited by D. B. Quinn, pp. 463–467. New York: Arno Press and Hector Bye, Inc.

1979d. May 5, 1602 to March 21, 1603. Fray Antonio de la Ascensión's "Brief Report" of the Voyage of Sebastian Vizcaíno up the California Coast. In *New American World: A Documentary History of North America to 1612:* vol. 5, *The Extension of Settlement in Florida, Virginia, and the Spanish Southwest*, edited by D. B. Quinn, pp. 413–426. New York: Arno Press and Hector Bye, Inc.

1979e. Recollections of Drake's Voyage to California. In *New American World: A Documentary History of North America to 1612:* vol. 1, *America from Concept to Discovery. Early Exploration of North America*, edited by D. B. Quinn, pp. 476–477. New York: Arno Press and Hector Bye, Inc.

1979f. Spain in the Southwest, 1580–1612. In *New American World: A Documentary History of North America to 1612:* vol. 5, *The Extension of Settlement in Florida, Virginia, and the Spanish Southwest*, edited by D. B. Quinn, pp. 359–363. New York: Arno Press and Hector Bye, Inc.

1979g. The "World Encompassed" Account of Drake's California Visit. In *New American World: A Documentary History of North America to 1612:* vol. 1, *America from Concept to Discovery. Early Exploration of North America*, edited by D. B. Quinn, pp. 467–476. New York: Arno Press and Hector Bye, Inc.

Raab, L. M.

1996. Debating Prehistory in Coastal Southern California: Resource Intensification versus Political Economy. *Journal of California and Great Basin Anthropology* 18(1): 64–80.

Raab, L. M., K. Bradford, and A. Yatsko

1994. Advances in Southern Channel Islands Archaeology: 1983–1993. *Journal of California and Great Basin Anthropology* 16(2): 243–270.

Raab, L. M., and D. O. Larson

1997. Medieval Climatic Anomaly and Punctuated Cultural Evolution in Coastal Southern California. *American Antiquity* 62(2): 319–336.

Ramenofsky, A. F.

1987. *Vectors of Death: The Archaeology of European Contact.* Albuquerque: University of New Mexico Press.

Rathburn, R. R.

1981. The Russian Orthodox Church as a Native Institution among the Koniag Eskimo of Kodiak Island, Alaska. *Arctic Anthropology* 18(1): 12–22.

Rawls, J. J.

1984. *Indians of California: The Changing Image.* Norman: University of Oklahoma Press.

Rawls, J. J., and W. Bean

1998. *California: An Interpretive History.* 7th ed. Boston: McGraw Hill.

Ray, A. J.

1988. The Hudson's Bay Company and Native People. In *Handbook of North American Indians:* vol. 4, *History of Indian-White Relations,* edited by W. E. Washburn, pp. 335–350. Washington, D.C.: Smithsonian Institution.

Rezanov, N. P.

1989a. June 17, 1806. A Confidential Report from Nikolai P. Rezanov to Minister of Commerce Nikolai P. Rumiantsev, Concerning Trade and Other Relations between Russian America, Spanish California, and Hawaii. In *The Russian American Colonies: Three Centuries of Russian Eastward Expansion, 1798–1867:* vol. 3, *A Documentary Record,* edited by B. Dmytryshyn, E.A.P. Crownhart-Vaughan, and T. Vaughan, pp. 112–148. Portland: Oregon Historical Society Press.

1989b. June 17, 1806. Dispatch from Nikolai P. Rezanov to Emperor Alexander I Regarding Trade with New Spain and the Investigation of the Kurile Islands. In *The Russian American Colonies: Three Centuries of Russian Eastward Expansion, 1798–1867:* vol. 3, *A Documentary Record,* edited by B. Dmytryshyn, E.A.P. Crownhart-Vaughan, and T. Vaughan, pp. 111. Portland: Oregon Historical Society Press.

1989c. May 5, 1806. A Letter Concerning Trade from Nikolai P. Rezanov to the Viceroy of New Spain, José Iturrigaria. In *The Russian American Colonies:*

Three Centuries of Russian Eastward Expansion, 1798–1867: vol. 3, *A Documentary Record,* edited by B. Dmytryshyn, E.A.P. Crownhart-Vaughan, and T. Vaughan, pp. 109–110. Portland: Oregon Historical Society Press.

1989d. November 6, 1805. A Letter from Nikolai P. Rezanov to the Directors of the Russian American Company Regarding Russian Orthodox Missionaries in Alaska. In *The Russian American Colonies: Three Centuries of Russian Eastward Expansion, 1798–1867:* vol. 3, *A Documentary Record,* edited by B. Dmytryshyn, E.A.P. Crownhart–Vaughan, and T. Vaughan, pp. 102–104. Portland: Oregon Historical Society Press.

Richman, I. B.
1911. *California Under Spain and Mexico: 1535–1847.* Boston: Houghton Mifflin Company.

Rogers, J. D.
1990. *Objects of Change: The Archaeology and History of Arikara Contact with Europeans.* Washington, D.C.: Smithsonian Institution.

Ronda, J. P.
1984. *Lewis and Clark among the Indians.* Lincoln: University of Nebraska Press.

Ross, L. A.
1997. Glass and Ceramic Trade Beads from the Native Alaskan Neighborhood. In *The Archaeology and Ethnohistory of Fort Ross, California:* vol. 2, *The Native Alaskan Neighborhood: A Multiethnic Community at Colony Ross,* edited by K. G. Lightfoot, A.M. Schiff, and T. A. Wake, pp. 179–212. Contributions of the University of California Archaeological Research Facility, no. 55. Berkeley: Archaeological Research Facility.

Rozaire, C. E.
1976. Analysis of Basketry Impressions in Asphaltum from Site Ven-87. In *The Changing Faces of Main Street: Ventura Mission Plaza Archaeological Project,* edited by R. S. Greenwood, pp. 211–213. Ventura, Calif.: Redevelopment Agency, City of San Buenaventura.

Ruhl, D. L., and K. Hoffman
1997. Diversity and Social Identity in Colonial Spanish America: Native American, African, and Hispanic Communities during the Middle Period. *Historical Archaeology* 31(1): 1–3.

Russian American Council
1989. After December 16, 1813. A Report to Emperor Alexander I from the Russian American Council, Concerning Trade with California and the Establishment of Fort Ross. In *The Russian American Colonies: Three Centuries of Russian Eastward Expansion, 1798–1867:* vol. 3, *A Documentary Record,* edited by B. Dmytryshyn, E.A.P. Crownhart-Vaughan, and T. Vaughan, pp. 204–208. Portland: Oregon Historical Society Press.

Russian-American Company

1989a. March 22, 1817. A Dispatch from the Main Administration of the Russian American Company to Aleksandr A. Baranov Instructing Him to Discharge Dr. Georg Schaffer, and Not to Build Schools in California. In *The Russian American Colonies: Three Centuries of Russian Eastward Expansion, 1798–1867*: vol. 3, *A Documentary Record*, edited by B. Dmytryshyn, E.A.P. Crownhart-Vaughan, and T. Vaughan, pp. 239–240. Portland: Oregon Historical Society Press.

1989b. May 15, 1814. A Report from the Main Administration of the Russian American Company to Nikolai P. Rumiantsev, Minister of Commerce and Foreign Affairs, Concerning Trade with California. In *The Russian American Colonies: Three Centuries of Russian Eastward Expansion, 1798–1867*: vol. 3, *A Documentary Record*, edited by B. Dmytryshyn, E.A.P. Crownhart-Vaughan, and T. Vaughan, pp. 212–215. Portland: Oregon Historical Society Press.

1989c. Not after December 20, 1820. An Official Report from the Main Administration of the Russian American Company to Emperor Alexander I. In *The Russian American Colonies: Three Centuries of Russian Eastward Expansion, 1798–1867*: vol. 3, *A Documentary Record*, edited by B. Dmytryshyn, E.A.P. Crownhart-Vaughan, and T. Vaughan, pp. 331–336. Portland: Oregon Historical Society Press.

1989d. November 3, 1818. A Report from the Main Administration of the Russian American Company to Emperor Alexander I Concerning Conditions in the Russian Colonies in Alaska and California. In *The Russian American Colonies: Three Centuries of Russian Eastward Expansion, 1798–1867*: vol. 3, *A Documentary Record*, edited by B. Dmytryshyn, E.A.P. Crownhart-Vaughan, and T. Vaughan, pp. 305–309. Portland: Oregon Historical Society Press.

Sahlins, M.

1981. *Historical Metaphors and Mythical Realities: Structure in the Early History of the Sandwich Islands Kingdom*. Association for the Study of Anthropology in Oceania, Special Publication no. 1. Ann Arbor: University of Michigan Press.

1985. *Islands of History*. Chicago: University of Chicago Press.

1992. *Anahulu: The Anthropology of History in the Kingdom of Hawaii. Historical Ethnography*. Vol. 1. Chicago: University of Chicago Press.

Salisbury, N.

1982. *Manitou and Providence*. Oxford: Oxford University Press.

Salls, R.

1989. The Fishes of Mission Nuestra Señora de la Soledad, Monterey County, California. *Research in Economic Anthropology* 11: 251–284.

Sanchez, R.
1995. *Telling Identities: The Californio Testimonios.* Minneapolis: University of Minnesota Press.

Sandos, J. A.
1991. Christianization among the Chumash: An Ethnohistoric Perspective. *American Indian Quarterly* 40(1): 65–90.

1997. Between Crucifix and Lance: Indian-White Relations in California, 1769–1848. *California History* 76(2 and 3): 196–229.

Saunders, R.
1998. Forced Relocation, Power Relations, and Culture Contact in the Missions of La Florida. In *Studies in Culture Contact: Interaction, Culture Change, and Archaeology,* edited by J. G. Cusick, pp. 402–429. Occasional Paper no. 25. Carbondale: Center for Archaeological Investigations, Southern Illinois University.

Sayers, A.M.
1994. Noso-N "In Breath So It Is In Spirit"—The Story of Indian Canyon. In *The Ohlone Past and Present: Native Americans of the San Francisco Bay Region,* edited by L. J. Bean, pp. 337–356. Menlo Park, Calif.: Ballena Press.

Schabelski, A.
1993. Visit of the Russian Warship Apollo to California in 1822–1823. Translated and edited by Glenn Farris. *Southern California Quarterly* 75(1): 1–13.

Schiff, A.M.
1997a. Lithic Assemblage at the Fort Ross Beach and Native Alaskan Village Sites. In *The Archaeology and Ethnohistory of Fort Ross, California:* vol. 2, *The Native Alaskan Neighborhood: A Multiethnic Community at Colony Ross,* edited by K. G. Lightfoot, A.M. Schiff, and T. A. Wake, pp. 213–237. Contributions of the University of California Archaeological Research Facility, no. 55. Berkeley: Archaeological Research Facility.

1997b. Shellfish Remains at the Fort Ross Beach and Native Alaskan Village Sites. In *The Archaeology and Ethnohistory of Fort Ross, California:* vol. 2, *The Native Alaskan Neighborhood: A Multiethnic Community at Colony Ross,* edited by K. G. Lightfoot, A.M. Schiff, and T. A. Wake, pp. 328–336. Contributions of the University of California Archaeological Research Facility, no. 55. Berkeley: Archaeological Research Facility.

Schuetz-Miller, M. K.
1994. *Building and Builders in Hispanic California, 1769–1850.* Tucson, Ariz.: Southwestern Mission Research Center and Santa Barbara, Calif.: A Santa Barbara Trust for Historic Preservation, Presidio Research Publication.

Schurz, W. L.
1917. The Manila Galleon and California. *The Southwestern Historical Quarterly* 21(2): 107–126.

Selverston, M. D.
1999. An Introduction to the Vasili Khlebnikov Ranch. Paper presented at the Thirty-third Annual Meeting of the Society for California Archaeology, Sacramento, California.

Serra, J.
1955a. *Writings of Junípero Serra.* Vol. 2. Edited and translated by Antonine Tibesar. Washington, D.C.: Academy of American Franciscan History.

1955b. *Writings of Junípero Serra.* Vol. 3. Edited by Antonine Tibesar. Washington, D.C.: Academy of American Franciscan History.

Servin, M. P.
1965. The Secularization of the California Missions: A Reappraisal. *Southern California Quarterly* 47(2): 133–149.

Settipane, G. A.
1995. Introduction: Columbus: Medical Implications. In *Columbus and the New World: Medical Implications,* edited by G. A. Settipane, pp. 1–10. Providence, R.I.: Oceanside Publications.

Shipek, F. C.
1977. *A Strategy for Change: The Luiseño of Southern California.* Ph.D. dissertation, Department of Anthropology, University of Hawaii.

1978. History of Southern California Mission Indians. In *Handbook of North American Indians:* vol. 8, *California,* edited by R. Heizer, pp. 610–618. Washington, D.C.: Smithsonian Institution.

1985. California Indian Reactions to the Franciscans. *The Americas* 41(4): 480–493.

Shur, L.
1990. Glossary. In *The Khlebnikov Archive: Unpublished Journal (1800–1837) and Travel Notes (1820, 1822, and 1824),* edited by L. Shur, translated by J. Bisk, pp. 203–204. Fairbanks: University of Alaska Press.

Silliman, S. W.
1997. European Origins and Native Destinations: Historical Artifacts from the Native Alaskan Village and Fort Ross Beach Sites. In *The Archaeology and Ethnohistory of Fort Ross, California:* vol. 2, *The Native Alaskan Neighborhood: A Multiethnic Community at Colony Ross,* edited by K. G. Lightfoot, A.M. Schiff, and T. A. Wake, pp. 136–178. Contributions of the University of California Archaeological Research Facility, no. 55. Berkeley: Archaeological Research Facility.

2000. *Colonial Worlds, Indigenous Practices: The Archaeology of Labor on a Nineteenth-Century California Rancho.* Ph.D. dissertation, Department of Anthropology, University of California, Berkeley.

2001a. Agency, Practical Politics, and the Archaeology of Culture Contact. *Journal of Social Archaeology* 1(2): 190–209.

2001b. Theoretical Perspectives on Labor and Colonialism: Reconsidering the California Missions. *Journal of Anthropological Archaeology* 20: 379–407.

Simmons, W. S.
1997. Indian Peoples of California. *California History* 76(2 and 3): 48–77.

Simons, D. D.
1997. Bird Remains at the Fort Ross Beach and Native Alaskan Village Sites. In *The Archaeology and Ethnohistory of Fort Ross, California:* vol. 2, *The Native Alaskan Neighborhood: A Multiethnic Community at Colony Ross,* edited by K. G. Lightfoot, A.M. Schiff, and T. A. Wake, pp. 310–318. Contributions of the University of California Archaeological Research Facility, no. 55. Berkeley: Archaeological Research Facility.

Singleton, T. A.
1998. Cultural Interaction and African American Identity in Plantation Archaeology. In *Studies in Culture Contact: Interaction, Culture Change, and Archaeology,* edited by J. G. Cusick, pp. 172–188. Occasional Paper no. 25. Carbondale: Center for Archaeological Investigations, Southern Illinois University.

Skowronek, R. K.
1998. Shifting the Evidence: Perceptions of Life at the Ohlone (Costanoan) Missions of Alta California. *Ethnohistory* 45(4): 675–708.

Skowronek, R. K., and J. C. Wizorek
1997. Archaeology at Santa Clara de Asis: The Slow Rediscovery of a Moveable Mission. *Pacific Coast Archaeological Society Quarterly* 33(3): 54–92.

Smith, M. T.
1987. *Archaeology of Aboriginal Culture Change in the Interior Southeast: Depopulation during the Early Historic Period.* The Ripley P. Bullen Series. Gainesville: University Press of Florida.

Smith, M. W.
1940. The Puyallup of Washington. In *Acculturation in Seven American Indian Tribes,* edited by R. Linton, pp. 3–38. New York: D. Appleton Century.

Soto, A.
1961. Mission San Luis Rey, California—Excavations in Sunken Gardens. *The Kiva* 26(4): 34–43.

Sparkman, P. S.
1908. The Culture of the Luiseño Indians. *University of California Publications in American Archaeology and Ethnology* 8(4): 187–234.

Spencer Pritchard, D.
1990. Joint Tenants of the Frontier: Russian-Hispanic Relationships in Alta California. In *Russian America: The Forgotten Frontier,* edited by B. Sweetland Smith and R. J. Barnett, pp. 81–93. Tacoma: Washington State Historical Society.

1991. The Good, the Bad, and the Ugly: Russian-American Company Employees of Fort Ross. *The Californians* 8(6): 42–49.

Spencer-Hancock, D., and W. E. Pritchard
1980/1981. Notes to the 1817 Treaty between the Russian American Company and Kashaya Pomo Indians. *California History* 59(4): 306–313.

Spicer, E. H.
1962. *Cycles of Conquest: The Impact of Spain, Mexico, and the United States on the Indians of the Southwest, 1533–1960.* Tucson: University of Arizona Press.

Spier, L.
1923. The Culture of the Luiseño Indians. *University of California Publications in American Archaeology and Ethnology* 20(16): 295–358.

Stanger, F. M., and A. K. Brown
1969. *Who Discovered the Golden Gate? The Explorers' Own Accounts.* San Mateo, Calif.: San Mateo County Historical Association.

Stein, G. J.
1999. *Rethinking World-Systems: Diasporas, Colonies, and Interaction in Uruk Mesopotamia.* Tucson: University of Arizona Press.

Stevenson, R. L.
1892. *Across the Plains.* London: Chatto and Windus.

Stewart, O. C.
1943. Notes on Pomo Ethnogeography. *University of California Publications in American Archaeology and Ethnology* 40(2): 29–62.

Stewart, O. C., and R. F. Heizer
1978. Litigation and Its Effects. In *Handbook of North American Indians:* vol. 8, *California*, edited by R. Heizer, pp. 705–712. Washington, D.C.: Smithsonian Institution.

Stillinger, R.
1975. *A Preliminary Analysis of Sonoma S.D.A.-1 (CA-SON-670).* On file, Manuscript No. S-6295, Northwest Information Center, Sonoma State University, Rohnert Park, California.

Stoler, A. L., and F. Cooper
1997. Between Metropole and Colony: Rethinking a Research Agenda. In *Tensions of Empire: Colonial Cultures in a Bourgeois World*, edited by F. Cooper and A. L. Stoler, pp. 1–56. Berkeley and Los Angeles: University of California Press.

Strong, W. D.
1929. Aboriginal Society in Southern California. *University of California Publications in American Archaeology and Ethnology* 26: 1–358.

Swagerty, W. R.

1988. Indian Trade in the Trans-Mississippi West to 1870. In *Handbook of North American Indians:* vol. 4, *History of Indian-White Relations,* edited by W. E. Washburn, pp. 351–374. Washington, D.C.: Smithsonian Institution.

Tac, P.

1958. *Indian Life and Customs at Mission San Luis Rey: A Record of California Mission Life by Pablo Tac, an Indian Neophyte. Written about 1835.* Edited and translated by M. Hewes and G. Hewes. San Luis Rey, Calif.: Old Mission.

Tatishchev, D. P.

1989. March 14, 1817: A Report from Dmitrii P. Tatishchev, Russian Ambassador to Madrid, to Count Karl Nesselrode, Minister of Foreign Affairs, Detailing Spanish Reaction to Russian Activity in Establishment of a Russian Colony in California. In *The Russian American Colonies: Three Centuries of Russian Eastward Expansion, 1798–1867:* vol. 3, *A Documentary Record,* edited by B. Dmytryshyn, E.A.P. Crownhart–Vaughan, and T. Vaughan, pp. 236–237. Portland: Oregon Historical Society Press.

Taylor, A.

2001. *American Colonies.* New York: Viking Penguin.

Thomas, B. W.

1998. Power and Community: The Archaeology of Slavery at the Hermitage Plantation. *American Antiquity* 63(4): 531–551.

Thomas, D. H.

1991. Harvesting Ramona's Garden: Life in California's Mythical Mission Past. In *Columbian Consequences:* vol. 3, *The Spanish Borderlands in Pan-American Perspective,* edited by D. H. Thomas, pp. 119–157. Washington D.C.: Smithsonian Institution.

Tikhmenev, P. A.

1978. *A History of the Russian-American Company.* Translated by R. A. Pierce and A. S. Donnelly. Seattle: University of Washington Press.

Tiller, V.E.V.

1996. *Guide to Indian Country: Economic Profiles of American Indian Reservations.* Albuquerque, N.M.: BowArrow Publishing Company.

Tomlin, K., and S. Watrous

1990. *Outpost of an Empire, Fort Ross: The Russian Colony in California.* Fort Ross, Calif.: Fort Ross Interpretive Association.

Upton, D.

1996. Ethnicity, Authenticity, and Invented Tradition. *Historical Archaeology* 30(2): 1–7.

Vallejo, M. G.
2000. *Report of a Visit to Fort Ross and Bodega Bay in April 1833 by Mariano G. Vallejo.* Translated by Glenn Farris and Rose-Marie Beebe and annotated by Glenn Farris. Occasional Paper no. 4. Bakersfield: California Mission Studies Association.

Vancouver, G.
1954. *Vancouver in California, 1792–1794: The Original Account of George Vancouver.* Edited and annotated by Marguerite Eyer Wilbur. Los Angeles: Glen Dawson.

Vansina, J.
1985. *Oral Tradition as History.* Madison: University of Wisconsin Press.

Veltre, D. W.
1990. Perspectives on Aleut Culture Change during the Russian Period. In *Russian America: The Forgotten Frontier,* edited by B. S. Smith and R. J. Barnett, pp. 175–183. Tacoma: Washington State Historical Society.

Veniaminov, I.
1992. A Russian Orthodox Priest in Mexican California. Travel Journal of Father Ioann Veniaminov Kept during his Trip to California and Back from July 1st to October 13th, 1836. Edited by James Gibson. *The Californians* 9(6): 22–25.

Verano, J. W., and D. H. Ubelaker, eds.
1992. *Disease and Demography in the Americas.* Washington, D.C.: Smithsonian Institution Press.

Von der Porten, E. P.
1973. *Drake and Cermeno in California: Sixteenth-Century Chinese Ceramics.* Point Reyes, Calif.: Drake Navigators Guild.

Voss, B. L.
2000. Colonial Sex: Archaeology, Structured Space, and Sexuality in Alta California's Spanish-Colonial Missions. In *Archaeologies of Sexuality,* edited by R. A. Schmidt and B. L. Voss, pp. 35–61. London: Routledge.

2002. *The Archaeology of El Presidio de San Francisco: Culture Contact, Gender, and Ethnicity in a Spanish-Colonial Military Community.* Ph.D. dissertation, Department of Anthropology, University of California, Berkeley.

Wade, M.
1988. French Indian Policies. In *Handbook of North American Indians:* vol. 4, *History of Indian-White Relations,* edited by W. E. Washburn, pp. 20–28. Washington, D.C.: Smithsonian Institution.

Wagner, H. R.
1924. The Voyage to California of Sebastan Rodríguez Cermeño in 1595. *California Historical Society Quarterly* 3(1): 3–24.

1929. *Spanish Voyages to the Northwest Coast of America in the Sixteenth Century.* San Francisco: California Historical Society.

1931. The Last Spanish Exploration of the Northwest Coast and the Attempt to Colonize Bodega Bay. *Quarterly of the California Historical Society* 10(4): 313–345.

1941. *Juan Rodríguez Cabrillo: Discoverer of the Coast of California.* San Francisco: California Historical Society.

Wagner, M. J.
1998. Some Think It Impossible to Civilize Them at All: Cultural Change and Continuity among the Early Nineteenth-Century Potawatomi. In *Studies in Culture Contact: Interaction, Culture Change, and Archaeology,* edited by J. G. Cusick, pp. 430–456. Occasional Paper no. 25. Carbondale: Center for Archaeological Investigations, Southern Illinois University.

Wake, T. A.
1995. *Mammal Remains from Fort Ross: A Study in Ethnicity and Culture Change.* Ph.D. dissertation, Department of Anthropology, University of California, Berkeley.

1997a. Bone Artifacts and Tool Production in the Native Alaskan Neighborhood. In *The Archaeology and Ethnohistory of Fort Ross, California:* vol. 2, *The Native Alaskan Neighborhood: A Multiethnic Community at Colony Ross,* edited by K. G. Lightfoot, A.M. Schiff, and T. A. Wake, pp. 248–278. Contributions of the University of California Archaeological Research Facility, no. 55. Berkeley: Archaeological Research Facility.

1997b. Mammal Remains from the Native Alaskan Neighborhood. In *The Archaeology and Ethnohistory of Fort Ross, California:* vol. 2, *The Native Alaskan Neighborhood: A Multiethnic Community at Colony Ross,* edited by K. G. Lightfoot, A.M. Schiff, and T. A. Wake, pp. 279–309. Contributions of the University of California Archaeological Research Facility, no. 55. Berkeley: Archaeological Research Facility.

1997c. Subsistence, Ethnicity, and Vertebrate Exploitation at the Ross Colony. In *The Archaeology of Russian Colonialism in the North and Tropical Pacific,* edited by P. R. Mills and A. Martinez, pp. 84–115. Kroeber Anthropological Society Papers, vol. 81. Berkeley, Calif.: Kroeber Anthropological Association.

Walker, P. L., and K. D. Davidson
1989. Analysis of Faunal Remains from Santa Inés Mission. In *Santa Inés Mission Excavations: 1986–1988,* edited by J. G. Costello, pp. 162–176. Salinas, Calif.: Coyote Press.

Walker, P. L., and T. Hudson
1993. *Chumash Healing: Changing Health and Medical Practices in an American Indian Society.* Banning, Calif.: Malki Museum Press.

Walker, P. L., and J. R. Johnson

1992. Effects of Contact on the Chumash Indians. In *Disease and Demography in the Americas*, edited by J. W. Verano and D. H. Ubelaker, pp. 127–139. Washington, D.C.: Smithsonian Institution.

1994. The Decline of the Chumash Indian Population. In *In the Wake of Contact: Biological Responses to Conquest*, edited by C. S. Larsen and G. Milner, pp. 109–120. New York: John Wiley and Sons.

Walker, P. L., P. Lambert, and M. J. DeNiro

1989. The Effects of European Contact on the Health of Alta California Indians. In *Columbian Consequences:* vol. 1, *Archaeological and Historical Perspectives on the Spanish Borderlands West*, edited by D. H. Thomas, pp. 349–364. Washington, D.C.: Smithsonian Institution.

Wallerstein, I.

1980. *The Modern World-System 2: Mercantilism and the Consolidation of the European World-Economy, 1650–1750.* New York: Academic Press.

Waterman, T. T.

1910. The Religious Practices of the Diegueño Indians. *University of California Publications in American Archaeology and Ethnology* 8(6): 271–358.

Watrous, S.

1998. Fort Ross: The Russian Colony in California. In *Fort Ross*, edited by L. Kalani, L. Rudy, and J. Sperry, pp. 11–20. Fort Ross, Calif.: Fort Ross Interpretive Association.

Weber, D. J.

1992. *The Spanish Frontier in North America.* New Haven, Conn.: Yale University Press.

West, G. J.

1989. Early Historic Vegetation Change in Alta California: The Fossil Evidence. In *Columbian Consequences:* vol. 1, *Archaeological and Historical Perspectives on the Spanish Borderlands West*, edited by D. H. Thomas, pp. 333–348. Washington, D.C.: Smithsonian Institution.

Whelan, M. K.

1993. Dakota Indian Economics and the Nineteenth-Century Fur Trade. *Ethnohistory* 40: 246–276.

White, R.

1991. *The Middle Ground: Indians, Empires, and Republics in the Great Lakes Region, 1650–1815.* Cambridge: Cambridge University Press.

Whitehead, R. S., ed.

1991. *An Archaeological and Restoration Study of Mission La Purísima Concepción. Reports Written for the National Park Service by Fred C. Hageman and Russell C. Ewing.* Santa Barbara, Calif.: Santa Barbara Trust for Historic Preservation.

Wilkie, L. A.

2000a. *Creating Freedom: Material Culture and African-American Culture and African-American Identity at Oakley Plantation, Louisiana, 1845–1950.* Baton Rouge: Louisiana State University Press.

2000b. Culture Bought: Evidence of Creolization in the Consumer Goods of an Enslaved Bahamian Family. *Historical Archaeology* 34(3): 10–26.

Wilkie, L. A., and P. Farnsworth

1999. Trade and the Construction of Bahamian Identity: A Multi-Scalar Exploration. *International Journal of Historical Archaeology* 3(4): 283–320.

Wlodarski, R. J., and D. Larson

1975. Soapstone and Indian Missionization. In *3500 Years on One City Block: San Buenaventura Mission Plaza Project Archaeological Report*, edited by R. S. Greenwood, pp. 149–168. Ventura, Calif.: Redevelopment Agency, City of San Buenaventura.

1976. Soapstone and Indian Missionization: Part 2. In *The Changing Faces of Main Street: Ventura Mission Plaza Archaeological Project*, edited by R. S. Greenwood, pp. 39–62. Ventura, Calif.: Redevelopment Agency, City of San Buenaventura.

Wobst, M. H.

1974. Boundary Conditions for Paleolithic Social Systems: A Simulation Approach. *American Antiquity* 39: 147–178.

1976. Locational Relationships in Paleolithic Society. In *The Demographic Evolution of Human Populations*, edited by R. H. Ward and K. M. Weiss, pp. 49–58. New York: Academic Press.

Wolf, E.

1982. *Europe and the People without History*. Berkeley and Los Angeles: University of California Press.

Wrangell, F.P.V.

1969. Russia in California, 1833, Report of Governor Wrangel. Translated and edited by James R. Gibson. *Pacific Northwest Quarterly* 60: 205–215.

1974. Some Remarks on the Savages on the Northwest Coast of America. The Indians in Upper California. In *Ethnographic Observations on the Coast Miwok and Pomo by Contre-Admiral F. P. Von Wrangell and P. Kostromitinov of the Russian Colony Ross, 1839*, edited by F. Stross and R. Heizer, pp. 1–6. Berkeley: Archaeological Research Facility, University of California.

Yamane, L., ed.

2002. *A Gathering of Voices: The Native Peoples of the Central California Coast. Santa Cruz County History Journal*, no. 5. Santa Cruz, Calif.: Museum of Art and History.

Zavalishin, D.

1973. California in 1824. Translated and annotated by James R. Gibson. *Southern California Quarterly* 55(4): 369–412.

Ziebarth, M.

1974. The Francis Drake Controversy: His California Anchorage, June 17–July 23, 1579. *California Historical Quarterly* 53(3): 197–292.

Index

Italicized page numbers refer to figures, maps, and tables.

Text: 10/13 Aldus
Display: Aldus
Compositor: Integrated Composition Systems

CPSIA information can be obtained
at www.ICGtesting.com
Printed in the USA
FSOW03n1533120816
23677FS